# ISRAELITE WISDOM

Photo by Cécile J. Terrien/San Francisco

Samuel Terrien

# ISRAELITE WISDOM

Theological and Literary Essays
in Honor of Samuel Terrien

Edited by
**JOHN G. GAMMIE**
**WALTER A. BRUEGGEMANN**
**W. LEE HUMPHREYS**
**JAMES M. WARD**

SCHOLARS PRESS

For
Union Theological Seminary
New York

Distributed by
SCHOLARS PRESS
University of Montana
Missoula, Montana 59806

# ISRAELITE WISDOM
Theological and Literary Essays
In Honor of Samuel Terrien

Edited by
JOHN G. GAMMIE
WALTER A. BRUEGGEMANN
W. LEE HUMPHREYS
JAMES M. WARD

Library of Congress Cataloging in Publication Data

Israelite wisdom.

   Bibliography: p.
   Includes index.
   1. Wisdom literature—Criticism, interpretation, etc.—
Addresses, essays, lectures. 2. Bible. O.T. Prophets—
Criticism, interpretation, etc.—Addresses, essays,
lectures. 3. Terrien, Samuel L., 1911-    —Addresses,
essays, lectures. I. Terrien, Samuel L., 1911-
   II. Gammie, John G.
BS 1455.I84                223                77–17862
ISBN 0–89130–208–5 pbk.

PRINTED IN THE UNITED STATES OF AMERICA
1 2 3 4 5
Edwards Brothers, Inc.
Ann Arbor, Michigan 48104

# CONTENTS

# ABBREVIATIONS

## SERIALS, REFERENCE WORKS, PERIODICALS

| | | | |
|---|---|---|---|
| AB | Anchor Bible | FRLANT | Forschungen zur Religion und Literatur des Alten und Neuen Testaments |
| AJSL | American Journal of Semitic Languages and Literature | GKC | Gesenius' Hebrew Grammar, ed. E. Kautzsch, tr. E. Cowley |
| AnBib | Analecta biblica | | |
| ANET | J. B. Pritchard (ed.) Ancient Near Eastern Texts | HAT | Handbuch zum Alten Testament |
| AnOr | Analecta orientalia | HKAT | Handkommentar zum Alten Testament |
| ATD | Das Alte Testament Deutsch | | |
| ATR | Anglican Theological Review | HSM | Harvard Semitic Monographs |
| | | HTR | Harvard Theological Review |
| BA | Biblical Archaeologist | | |
| BASOR | Bulletin of the American Schools of Oriental Research | HUCA | Hebrew Union College Annual |
| | | IB | The Interpreter's Bible |
| BBB | Bonner biblische Beiträge | ICC | International Critical Commentary |
| BDB | F. Brown, S. R. Driver, and C. A. Briggs, Hebrew and English Lexicon of the Old Testament | IDB | The Interpreter's Dictionary of the Bible |
| | | IDBSup | Supplementary volume to IDB |
| BETL | Bibliotheca ephemeridum theologicarum lovaniensium | Int | Interpretation—A Journal of Bible and Theology |
| BHK | R. Kittel, Biblia hebraica | | |
| Bib | Biblica | JAAR | Journal of the American Academy of Religion |
| BJRL | Bulletin of the John Rylands University Library of Manchester | JB | A. Jones (ed.), Jerusalem Bible |
| BKAT | Biblischer Kommentar: Altes Testament | JBL | Journal of Biblical Literature |
| BZ | Biblische Zeitschrift | JBR | Journal of Bible and Religion |
| BZAW | Beihefte zur ZAW | | |
| CAT | Commentaire de l'Ancien Testament | JPSV | Jewish Publication Society Version |
| CBQ | Catholic Biblical Quarterly | JSS | Journal of Semitic Studies |
| CBQMS | Catholic Biblical Quarterly —Monograph Series | JTC | Journal for Theology and the Church |
| CSEL | Corpus scriptorum ecclesiasticorum latinorum | JTS | Journal of Theological Studies |
| CTA | A. Herdner, Corpus des tablettes en cunéiformes alphabétiques | KAI | H. Donner and W. Röllig, Kanaanäische und aramäischen Inschriften |
| DJD | Discoveries in the Judaean Desert | KAT | E. Sellin (ed.), Kommentar zum A. T. |
| EBib | Etudes bibliques | KB | L. Koehler and W. Baumgartner, Lexicon in Veteris Testamenti libros |
| EvTh | Evangelische Theologie | | |
| ExpTim | Expository Times | | |

| | | | | |
|---|---|---|---|---|
| LCL | Loeb Classical Library | | SJT | Scottish Journal of Theology |
| LD | Lectio divina | | | |
| NAB | New American Bible | | ThB | Theologische Blätter |
| NEB | New English Bible | | TBü | Theologische Bücherei |
| NICOT | New International Commentary on the Old Testament | | TDOT | G. J. Botterweck and H. Ringgren (eds.), Theological Dictionary of the Old Testament |
| NKZ | Neue kirchliche Zeitschrift | | | |
| NovT | Novum Testamentum | | TLZ | Theologische Literaturzeitung |
| OLZ | Orientalische Literaturzeitung | | TWAT | G. J. Botterweck and H. Ringgren (eds.), Theologisches Wörterbuch zum Alten Testament |
| OTS | Oudtestamentische Studiën | | | |
| OTL | The Old Testament Library | | | |
| OTS | Oudtestamentische Studiën | | | |
| PEQ | Palestine Exploration Quarterly | | USQR | Union Seminary Quarterly Review |
| PJB | Palästina-Jahrbuch | | UT | C. H. Gordon, Ugaritic Textbook |
| RB | Revue biblique | | | |
| RevExp | Review and Expositor | | VT | Vetus Testamentum |
| RGG | Religion in Geschichte und Gegenwart | | VTSup | Vetus Testamentum, Supplements |
| RHPR | Revue d'histoire et de philosophie religieuses | | WMANT | Wissenschaftliche Monographien zum Alten und Neuen Testament |
| RQ | Revue de Qumran | | | |
| RSO | Rivista degli studi orientali | | WUNT | Wissenschaftliche Untersuchungen zum Neuen Testament |
| RSV | Revised Standard Version | | | |
| SAT | Die Schriften des Alten Testaments | | ZAW | Zeitschrift für die alttestamentliche Wissenschaft |
| SBL | Society of Biblical Literature | | | |
| SBT | Studies in Biblical Theology | | ZTK | Zeitschrift für Theologie und Kirche |
| Sem | Semitica | | | |

## BIBLICAL, RABBINIC, DEAD SEA SCROLLS, PSEUDEPIGRAPHICAL

| | | | | |
|---|---|---|---|---|
| CD | Cairo (Genizah text of the) Damascus (Document) | | 1QapGen | Genesis Apocryphon from Qumran Cave 1 |
| DSD | = 1QS | | 1QH | Hôdāyôt (Thanksgiving Hymns) from Qumran Cave 1 |
| Dtr | Deuteronomist or Deuteronomistic historian | | | |
| E | Elohist or Elohistic source | | 1QIsa^a | First copy of Isaiah from Qumran Cave 1 |
| Ep. Arist. | Epistle of Aristeas | | | |
| J | Yahwist or Yahwistic source | | 1QpHab | Pesher on Habakkuk from Qumran Cave 1 |
| LXX | Septuagint | | | |
| MT | Massoretic text | | 1QM | Milḥāmâ (War Scroll) |
| p | Pesher (commentary) | | 1QS | Serek hayyaḥad (Rule of the Community, Manual of Discipline) |
| P | Priestly source | | | |
| Q | Qumran | | | |
| 1Q, 2Q, 3Q, etc. | Numbered caves of Qumran, yielding written material; followed by abbreviation of biblical or apocryphal book | | 4QMess ar | Aramaic "Messianic" text from Qumran Cave 4 |

| | | | |
|---|---|---|---|
| 11QtgJob | *Targum of Job* from Qumran Cave 11 | *Rab.* | *Rabbah* (following abbreviation for biblical book = Midrash on that book) |
| 11QPs<sup>a</sup> | First copy of the Psalm Scroll from Qumran Cave 11 | T. Jud. | Testament of Judah |
| | | T. Levi | Testament of Levi |

Blessed is a man when he has found wisdom
    and the man who has acquired understanding.

Length of days is in her right hand,
    and in her left hand wealth and honor.

She is a tree of life to those who have taken hold of her,
    and the ones who have grasped her may be accounted blessed.

                        (Proverbs 3:13, 16, 18)

Blessed is a man when he has found wisdom
    and the man who has acquired understanding.

Length of days is in her right hand,
    and in her left hand wealth and honor.

She is a tree of life to those who have taken hold of her,
    and the ones who have grasped her may be accounted blessed.

                        (Proverbs 3:13, 16, 18)

# DEDICATORY PREFACE

THIS volume came into being because of the desire of friends and colleagues of Samuel Terrien to express to him the affection and esteem in which he is held. The contributors consist of former students and colleagues at Union Theological Seminary and other scholars working in the field of Israelite wisdom who responded to an invitation to join in the project. The volume is addressed to all those persons interested in observing what a portion of the community of contemporary scholars is discovering and questioning in the wisdom traditions of ancient Israel.

i

Samuel Terrien is a citizen of two continents and the impact of his work and witness have been felt on both. In this country countless persons are in his debt for his self-sacrificing labors as Associate Editor for Old Testament Introduction and Exegesis of *The Interpreter's Bible* and as Associate Editor for Old Testament Articles of *The Interpreter's Dictionary of the Bible*. In the opening essay of this volume his former colleague at Union Theological Seminary, James A. Sanders, assesses further this and other aspects of Professor Terrien's work on both sides of the Atlantic. Some contributors to the volume—expecially those from Europe—have indicated their appreciation of Professor Terrien in the words which precede their essays. Many others, former colleagues at Union and former students, have expressed to us their desire to extend to Professor Terrien and his wife Sara their greetings and warm good wishes on the occasion of the publication of this Festschrift.

ii

Professor Terrien's students remember with gratitude the model he presents in blending theological with scholarly commitment, his aesthetic sensibilities and sensitivity to literary nuance, his high regard for the Masoretic text which allows for emendation only under the most compelling of circumstances, the historical surveys with which he introduced his lectures on central theological issues, and not least his opening of every class session— and sometimes closing them—with simple, yet often moving and profound prayers. His colleagues remember with gratitude his wit and elegance of expression, the breadth of his learning, the fidelity with which he represented to them the insights of the French and Swiss Reformed tradition, the care and exactitude with which he dispatched his duties as Secretary of the Faculty for so many years, and his willingness critically to review any work submitted to him for his judgments. Former students and former colleagues alike remember with gratitude the extent to which he takes delight in liturgy, music, poetry, and the rich literary tradition of the Western world. The circle of his theological concern has never been narrow or provincial. We are all grateful for the way in which he demonstrates that depth of theological commitment does not necessitate disparagement of human creations. He shows himself indeed to be a spiritual heir of John Calvin by his repeated willingness to write for, and communicate to, the laity of the church. He was and is not content to speak to scholars alone. In sum, at Union Theological Seminary from 1935 to 1976 he demonstrated through his scholarship, and the direction it took, the meaning of theological wisdom. In his labors and in the manner of his presence he exemplified for us the ideal *vivere et studere ad maiorem Dei gloriam.*

iii

The plan of the volume may be discerned by a glance at the table of contents. In most instances Hebrew and Greek have been transliterated. The 1976 *Journal of Biblical Literature* "Instructions for Contributors" has been followed. Two essays originally written in German, two in French and one in Spanish have been translated. Each translation has been reviewed by, and received the approval of, the author. To the translators we owe our deep thanks. Citations of Professor Terrien's French in the first essay of the volume and elsewhere have been allowed to stand.

Our special appreciation is expressed to the financial sponsor of this volume: The University of Tulsa; the Women's Committee of Union Theological Seminary; Perkins School of Theology, Southern Methodist University; and, the Mary Ellenberger Camp Fund for the Study of Religions at the University of Tennessee. We are grateful also to Cécile J. Terrien, Professor Terrien's daughter, for the photograph she took and presented to her father for use here. Finally we wish to acknowledge our appreciation for the personal support and encouragement, counsel and labors of Donald W. Shriver, Jr., John G. L. Dowgray, Jr., James A. Sanders, Fr. Joseph A. Fitzmyer, and especially the staff of Scholars Press and its director, Robert W. Funk.

# I
# THE WORKS OF SAMUEL TERRIEN

# COMPARATIVE WISDOM: L'OEUVRE TERRIEN

JAMES A. SANDERS

SCHOOL OF THEOLOGY AT CLAREMONT, CLAREMONT, CALIFORNIA 91711

SAMUEL Lucien Terrien received his early theological and philological education in Paris between 1927 and 1933. During those years he studied and lived at the Faculté Libre de Théologie Protestante de Paris, boulevard Arragot. During the last three of those years he attended lectures also at the École des Hautes Études, the Louvre, and in 1932-33 at the Institut d'Archéologie. It was in those formative and impressionable years that the course of his life's work was set. Then it was that he perceived the mind and thinking of such scholars as Charles Virolleaud, Adolphe Lods and René Dussaud in Akkadian and Ugaritic at the Hautes Études, Étienne Drioton in Egyptian at the Louvre, and Eduard Dhorme at the Institut. In 1933-34 he spent a year at the École Biblique in Jerusalem continuing Egyptian with Courroyer and reading Hammurabi with Barrois. He then came to Union Seminary as French Fellow taking the S.T.M. in 1936 and the Th.D. in 1941. His dissertation for the latter was written while teaching at Wooster College 1936-40, his first position and the only one outside Union Seminary where he taught for 35 years until retirement in 1976.

Which of the French giants had the greatest influence on Terrien? They were all important in the formation of his thinking; but it was perhaps Drioton's course in "le théatre égyptien," in which the dramatic element in ancient ritual was stressed, combined with Dhorme's comprehensive and engrossing lectures on Job, that posed the leading questions Terrien was to pursue the next four decades. Already as a student in his last year in Paris he began the quest for divine presence-in-absence in a series of causeries or conversations at the Association d'étudiants chrétiens. It was in study of the Book of Job that these central interests took focus and became the mark of originality of Terrien's contribution to scholarship on Job—the ritual setting for the dialogues and the theological import of the whirlwind speeches.

What is the shape of the Terrien corpus to date?[1] It is best described, perhaps, as a tension between two forces, that of a history-of-religions perspective on the Bible, and that of a search for a theological unity to it. The resolution of the tension (if such indeed there be) has centered in Terrien's appreciation of the contribution of international Ancient Near East Wisdom to biblical thought and literature.

3

I

Neither the S.T.M. thesis (1936) nor the Th.D. dissertation (1941) was published, and that is regrettable for two reasons: they are very revealing in terms of the direction Terrien's mind was to take in later years; and they were at the time fresh and valuable contributions to Ancient Near Eastern Studies. The thesis on "La valeur des Tablettes de Ras Shamra pour l'étude de l'Ancien Testament" judiciously explored the rich contributions of Canaanite faith and theology to the OT, anticipating some of the later ideas of Marvin Pope, Mitchell Dahood and Ephraim Speiser. The dissertation, "The Sceptics in the Old Testament and in the Literature of the Ancient Near East," was a study of heterodoxy in the OT. Those in the OT who questioned orthodox beliefs did so in the same terms generally as other sceptics of the Ancient Near East: they all confronted the problem of existence experientially and they shared a respect for an ancient international Wisdom which knew no boundaries and seemed to be part of many cults and cultures. Such Wisdom entered the OT in two principal ways, through laws adapted in the Pentateuch and reflected throughout the Bible, and through popular thought such as one finds in Proverbs and in numerous OT stories and legenda.

Terrien came to biblical studies with a love of classics. From lycée he brought to Paris more interest in reading Sophocles than in reading the Bible. His appreciation of a wide range of literature from the Ancient Near Eastern and the classical through modern existentialism, and how one can illumine the other, shows up in numerous writings. As one reads the Terrien corpus one gains an impression of a scholar engaging in a discipline as yet unnamed: Comparative Wisdom. For Terrien not only has a vivid appreciation of the commonality of human experience in Near Eastern antiquity, but he also has demonstrated, perhaps more than any other modern scholar, how ancient and modern wisdom may illumine each other. The riches of Western poetry contained in his thematic books on Psalms[2] and on Job[3] betray not only an enviable file compiled by an ordered mind, they reveal a basic conviction discernible already in the S.T.M. and doctoral theses—the importance of reading the Bible in as broad a literary and experiential *Sitz* as possible, both ancient and modern.

For Terrien the history of religions is not a narrowly conceived method. It hardly knew bounds, and in his hands Comparative Literature became Comparative Wisdom. Whether he is attempting to determine the abiding contribution of Canaanite religion to Israel's faith,[4] or exploring Christianity's debt to a modern pagan,[5] Terrien is treading one and the same route, that which brought him to love Sophocles, explore ancient Egyptian drama and discover Ugarit. It was a conviction that *J. B.* should, despite objections, be compared to Job,[6] Albee's theological message be underscored,[7] painters be viewed as theologians,[8] and contemporary theatre be exposed where polytheism lurked.[9]

In other words, Terrien, quietly but persistently, raised a voice for God as

Creator of All in an era when God's redemptive Mighty Acts were being celebrated by most others, theologians and biblical scholars, as a canon within the canon and the unity of the Bible. His interest in history of religions was manifest also in his contributions on the history of Israel's religion to the revised Hastings[10] and to *The Interpreter's One-Volume Commentary*,[11] as well as in the little *Golden Bible Atlas*.[12] Such comparative studies formed a part of Terrien's vision of the place of the Bible in the literary heritage of the world.

His greatest contributions stemming from that vision are in his studies on Job[13] and in his article on Wisdom in Amos.[14] In Joban studies Terrien has been a worthy successor of Dhorme whose influence was considerable. His first work on Job, beyond the incidental treatment in the dissertation, was the fully developed commentary in the *IB*.[15] His mastery of the literature and the weighty arguments advanced on the major issues brought him immediate recognition as an authority on Job. The fresh perspective he brought to the problem of the date of Job lent new credence to what had theretofore been a minority opinion: Job antedated Deutero-Isaiah for the simple reason that the Joban poet who had so skillfully shown intimate knowledge of Israel's literature up to his time betrays no knowledge whatever of crucial contributions of Deutero-Isaiah, especially that of vicarious suffering. The latter, on the contrary, drew skillfully on some points in Job. The perspective was not entirely new, but it was daring. Since Terrien's work it is the regnant position.

The basic results of his work on the *IB* commentary show up in *Job: Poet of Existence* (1957) three years later. *Job: Poet of Existence*, however, is a work of an entirely different order. As noted above, Terrien here literally surrounded Job with hundreds of quotations from the world's poetry, especially English, not so much to show the influence of the biblical book on later authors, but to engage in Comparative Wisdom, letting modern poetry illumine the ancient and vice versa.

The best of Terrien on Job, however, is the volume in the French commentary series,[16] followed by what is perhaps his most brilliant single article, exploring a valid literary and historical relation between Job and Deutero-Isaiah.[17] In fact, it is in this article that Terrien betrays the clearest self-awareness of his own personal pilgrimage from the history-of-religion studies in thesis and dissertation to his appreciation of international Ancient Near Eastern Wisdom in the OT generally. A truly valid issue of the old history-of-religion approach to the OT is Comparative Wisdom. Here he cites the early work of Jirku, Causse, Humbert and Gressmann, and concludes: "C'est grace à ces enquêtes de littérature comparée que l'étude de la sagesse d'Israël est entrée dans une phase véritablement révolutionnaire."[18] It is in this study that he makes most clear his argument for the priority of Job over Deutero-Isaiah, the force of which centers in parallel observations in each work. The problematic passage in Isa 53:9 where it is stated that the Servant had committed no violence or deceit is solved if it is viewed as dependent on Job 6:30, 16:17 and other passages which claim that Job had no falsehood or violence on his hands. On the other hand, says Terrien, Job's suffering had no significance in itself whereas that of the servant was claimed to be an offering for sin (Isa 53:10). The reason that the Joban poet does not broach the question of vicarious suffering, neither accepting it nor rejecting it, is that he simply did not know Deutero-Isaiah. The most likely reason for that, concludes Terrien, is that, as only a few scholars had suggested (Cheyne, Dillmann, Naish, Pfeiffer), Job antedated Deutero-Isaiah.[19] In this paper he anticipated his next major study: ". . . C'est le poème de Job qui a introduit le motif de la création transcendentale au sein des combats existentiels de la foi. Le Deutéro-Esaïe a transposé ce thème et l'a appliqué à son interprétation de la mission d'Israël dans l'histoire."[20]

Three years later Terrien published his work on Job as a pararitual drama for celebration of the New Year.[21] Here as in perhaps no other single study the several aspects of his interest in history-of-religions were woven together. The dialogue form of the Joban poem suggests a cultic celebration. Both Job and the great Greek tragedies were influenced by a common source in the ceremonial past of the Mediterranean East, especially Egyptian.

In this view Job might be seen as the incarnation of a collective personality in royal terms, the primordial first-person. Young and virile he had a personal deity in the heavenly council which met on the New Year Day. In view of the destruction of the temple the poet would have composed his poem for a para-cultic celebration of the autumn feast. There is evidence for such experimentation. "Chassés de l'espace sacré, ils se regroupèrent autour des temps sacrés."[22] The poet himself would not have thought consciously of an allegory of the elect people, but discovering the story we know in the prose prologue about a hero tortured by dialogue and theophany, wrote a dramatic poem for an autumn New Year feast. He thought of the royal servant of Yahweh baffled, naked, emasculated and symbolically put to death. "La théophanie cultuelle lui permit de proclamer l'inanité de la justification de soi (40:8), la foi sans calcul, le service sans récompense, un sens théologique du péché, et la participation de l'homme en tant qu'homme—l'homme universel—à l'acte gratuit."[23]

Such a thesis, attractive as it is in accounting for so many troublesome elements in Job, nonetheless raised the question for Terrien of why Job was preserved not in the priestly cult for Rosh ha-shanah but in didactic circles. The answer lay in the Zion myth which Terrien views as perhaps the strongest element in the character and birth of Judaism in the sixth century B.C.

In the following year, then, "The Omphalos Myth and Hebrew Religion"[24] was published. The historian of religion asks what from the legacy of old Canaanite faith and religion of ancient Jebus persisted into the new Judaism of the exilic era. It was the old omphalos myth in which Jerusalem was viewed as the navel of the earth. It was then called upon in postexilic Zionism for spatialization of the presence of God and the dehistoricization of the covenant. Belief in the Zion-space myth permitted surviving Judaism after 587 B.C. to maintain sociological identity and create Judaism.[25] Zion viewed as a sort of cosmic umbilical gave shape to the eschatological hope of nascent Judaism. The eternal mission of Judaism may be traced to the old Jebusite omphalos myth and not to Mosaic Yahwism. "The importance of the omphalos myth for Judaism cannot be underestimated."[26]

The logical progression of thought in these studies on Job and its origins testifies to the ordered mind of Samuel Terrien. They symbolize in intensity the history-of-religion approach in his method.

But it is not only on Job that Terrien has brought this method to bear. Of great influence in the field of study of the prophets is Terrien's single study on the prophet Amos, in the Muilenburg Festschrift.[27] Hans Walter Wolff has credited him with the discovery of the importance of Wisdom influence on Amos.[28] He found in Amos' rhetorical and stylistic features language common in Ancient Near Eastern Wisdom; he also related some of Amos' ideas to Wisdom thought: such as the designation of Israel by the name Isaac with the association there to Beer-Sheba and the connections with Edom, a center of Wisdom thinking; and Amos' knowledge of astronomy as well as geography, history and social customs outside Israel. The focal observation, however, was on ethics in Amos. Amos made ethical behavior the prerequisite of divine favor; but Terrien found it to be an ethic common to many peoples and independent of revealed legislative traditions of Israel.[29]

It cannot be surprising to find, therefore, in the writings of such a scholar, interest in the "Wisdom" of our own time and essays which extend such Comparative Wisdom to consideration of modern and contemporary literature and art.[30]

## II

But concurrent with Terrien's interest in what was common to Israel and her ancient neighbors is an equally keen desire to locate the theological unity of the Bible, and to demonstrate its relevance to contemporary issues. His inaugural address, given on the occasion of his promotion to full professorship at Union Seminary in the fall of 1953, was on what he termed an aspect neglected at that time in biblical theology, the importance of the individual in Israelite and Jewish faith.[31] It was published in the same year (1954) as his commentary on Job in the *IB* 3, and dealt with Job as an individual of great faith: Job and Paul, he found, viewed righteousness as a gift of God. The same theme found expression again some twenty years later in an unpublished paper by Terrien:

> The disproportionate interest of the theology of salvation in the problems of history seems to have been replaced by an equally disproportionate interest in the political scene, and this trend (from covenant theology to the theology of liberation) is concomitant with a neglect of the reality of individual faith and the disregard of the sacrality of the solitary life. . . . The

theological ministry of the church will not serve the ethics of the gospel without at the same time facing the void of the inner self in search of the ultimate, witness either the flashy comeback of all forms of fundamentalism or the secular inroads within church membership.[32]

But Terrien's quest for theological unity has not ended in some form of biblical individualism. Far from it, that unity is discernible only in a theocentric view of the Bible as a whole; and such a view leads one directly to a theology of the presence of God.

"The Hebraic theology of presence may provide the principle of canonical growth which Wright, Childs and Sanders (to mention only those on these shores) have been calling for."[33] The fascination of the biblical concept of the Deus Absconditus, or the presence of God in his absence, was evident already in Paris in the causeries he conducted there with fellow students. It was also the concept of presence-in-absence in the ritual drama of ancient Egyptian theatre which captured the young man's attention in Drioton's lectures. In speaking of irony in the theophany of Job[34] he shows that Job had tried to limit God by conceiving justice not in theocentric macrocosm but in anthropocentric microcosm; Job had ignored the theocentricity of life in living in his egocentricity: evil is a symbol of the freedom of God. About the psalmists Terrien says, "While poets they were profound theologians. And that is the reason for which their hymnal remains a living book for today."[35]

Is this the same searcher who in his inaugural address spoke up in the high neo-orthodox days for the importance of the individual of faith, and who, soon after the publication of Karl Barth's *Menschlichkeit Gottes* and Abraham Heschel's *God in Search of Man*, wrote movingly of "The Anthropology of God"?[36] Can the historian of religion be a biblical theologian? Samuel Terrien is both.

In his contribution to *The Interpreter's One-Volume Commentary* on "The Religion of Israel" the approach and method are clearly that of Comparative Religion. And the sum of his search he states thus: the distinctiveness of Israel's religion was a "determined and even obstinate will to live in the presence of the Holy God."[37] Once more it is Job which provides the focus for understanding. Terrien refers to the failure of the sublime theism of the friends as a "failure of monotheism."[38] That was written in the fifties when one suspects Terrien, as in the inaugural and other writings, felt the need to challenge the regnant neo-orthodoxy of the time. In the sixties in speaking of the same problem in Job he wrote of the failure of religion to assure anthropocentric happiness.[39] In the latter he makes clear that Job's "confession" in 42:6 was not repentence of moral error but abandonment of egocentricity.[40] Why was it Job could sacrifice his egocentricity? Because, as Terrien movingly put it, God had transcended his transcendence and manifested himself to suffering man.[41] The goal of the poet was to show the triumph of faith in the complete "dénuement du moi."[42] The problem of theodicy arises only in anthropocentrism. Because God transcended his transcendence, as the creator God in the theophany, Job could and did transcend his anthropocentrism. The God who thus offers himself to man is not yet, Terrien insists, the God who empties or despoils himself in the Philippian hymn. True monotheism for Terrien (not the theism of the friends) leads to a trinitarian understanding of God. The communion with the God who offers himself permits humanity to triumph over the scandals of existence and to persevere in being. Like Paul Job knew that justice is the work not of humanity but of God; it is a gift of God so that humanity can practise *imitatio dei* and participate with the creator in creative work.[43]

Having reached such stages of thinking in focusing on the problems presented by the Book of Job, Terrien turned once more to weave such insights into his developing theology of the presence of God in absence. The time was ripe in January 1969 to do so when he prepared his lecture for the traditional Monday Morning Lectures of the Women's Committee of Union Seminary.[44] The committee asked each of the four speakers for the series to speak generally on new directions in faith and life-style; Terrien's topic was "Toward a New Theology of Presence." The time was ripe indeed; for Terrien directed his remarks not only to sceptics in whom he had long been interested[45] but also to the then popular Death-of-God theologies as well as to "activists." Union Seminary had been hit by the gale of protest both in the spring of 1967 and, along with Columbia University, in the spring of 1968. Terrien claimed that a theology of presence would ". . . prevent Protestants from separating their spirituality or their moral activism from a life of ritual and prevent Catholics . . . from separating their sacramentalism from the insecurity and risks of faith."[46] But a theology-of-presence-in-absence would also challenge the new secular and political theologians.

Terrien could thus address himself to those contemporaries who, like himself, identified with sceptics and humanists, yet speak out of the Bible about a God who hides himself to good purpose and for human benefit. His work on Job brought him to realize that the sheer honesty and candor of the Bible exceeded his own; and he wanted to share that with fellow Christians, especially the secularists who in his day were expressing an appreciation for international modern wisdom similar to that of the Joban poet, and other biblical thinkers, for international Ancient Near Eastern Wisdom in their day. Job, Qoheleth, Proverbs and other wisdom literature in biblical antiquity were able to present God as creator without any reference whatever to God as redeemer and sustainer. Terrien has found that the absent presence of the creator God of the Job theophany was the Joban poet's answer to the problems raised by the old *heilsgeschichtlich* doctrines of redemption and providence; and he found it immediately relevant to the newly developing secular and political theologies of the sixties.

God as creator of all the world was the source of even the world's very humanistic-sounding wisdom; and that wisdom found its place in the Bible precisely or especially where the doctrine of God the creator was stressed so that the doctrines of redemption and providence were set aside or bracketted.[47] What Terrien had in the fifties seen as relevant to Christian existentialism[48] he now knew to be a direct challenge to Christian secularism and particularism. Terrien had entered into the world of the Bible through probing ancient secularism; he now found in its theocentrism, and its persistent quest for the presence of God in his absence, a voice for the new age. The voice was, however, not one that gave support willy-nilly to the new secularism; far more often it challenged its shallowness and immaturity.

## III

Terrien's calm assurance in the relevance and pertinence of the Bible to the problems arising out of modern wisdom can be traced at several junctures. In fact he has been not infrequently ahead of his time on some issues.

A full ten years before Gerhard von Rad wrote his commentary on Genesis Terrien wrote a paper on the theological significance of Genesis[49] in which he anticipated redaction-critical treatments of the book as a whole.

> In many ways Genesis resembles a mediaeval church which was built on the foundations of a Gallo-Roman temple dedicated to the goddess Isis: the stones of its crypt reveal the signs of Byzantine art, the columns of its apse are in pure Romanesque, the vaulting of its transept and nave show the grace of middle Gothic, its Western rose window displays the wealth of the Flamboyant; and one of its portals, which fell during the VIIIth century, has been rebuilt in the Baroque style. In spite of its composite origin . . . it offers an esthetic message which is wholly its own, and it must be interpreted and understood as a single work of art. *Mutatis mutandis*, the book of Genesis as it exists today may represent several schools of widely different or conflicting conceptions of ethics and religion. Nevertheless, its final editor has succeeded in presenting a relatively homogeneous document, with a singleness of purpose, and a dominant message which overshadows the discrepancies of details.[50]

Distinctly Terrien in style and imagery, drawing as he would on the arts,[51] such a description of the final textual state of Genesis, though made up of numerous sources, is as apt today as it was thirty years ago. But it was ahead of its time.

His concern for the faith (and doubt) of the individual expressed as a distinctly minority view when he gave his inaugural address[52] was a forerunner of those theologians today whose interest is in private journeys and pilgrimmages.

His quest for the anthropology of God[53] was well in advance of current secular theology.

His pioneering work in these regards has not always been fully recognized. His work on Wisdom in the book of Amos, by contrast, has received international attention.

And in his paper on a biblical theology of womanhood[54] Terrien shows himself to be in the forefront of those who are rethinking the question of Bible as canon and are attempting to recover the dynamics of the hermeneutics employed in and back of biblical literature itself.

Canonical hermeneutics will not attempt to harmonize the conflicting points of view which appear in the sixty-six books, as if the canon had to be statically conceived. . . . It will seek to discover, beyond atomistic scholarship, the motivating principle of continuity which leads from the faith of the early Hebrews to the proclamation of the loving Lord in the early church. The function of canonical hermeneutics is no longer to look at the question of law versus gospel . . . the faith of Israel began with gospel. . . . The faith of Israel and of Christendom alike began with a gospel of liberation, at the Exodus, and at Easter, the New Exodus. . . . It is from the perspective of their destiny that man and woman discover not only their equality and their complementariness but also the paradox of their freedom. Biblical faith . . . lays the basis of a theology of womanhood which goes counter to the traditional attitudes and practices of Christendom and challenges the church of today to rethink critically and creatively the respective functions of man and woman.[55]

The following excerpts from an unpublished paper by Samuel Terrien on the long relation between biblical theology and dogmatic theology are typical of the vigor and timeliness of his thinking. With his long experience in quest of the presence of God in absence Terrien stands ready to be of service when the field comes to realize once more that biblical theology is not only a viable but a necessary pursuit in biblical studies.

If a Biblical Theology is to emerge from the present hermeneutical questioning stage, with its consequent fragmentariness and analytical parochialism, it will have to respect the Hebraic theology of presence. The entire literature of the Bible portrays the Deity as coming to man. . . . [Earlier attempts to center biblical theology in the idea of covenant] ignored the diversity of its meaning in Israel and its relative absence from the crucial expressions of biblical faith from the patriarchal times to the end of the first century B.C. It is in effect to impose an unimportant and fluid motif on all periods and on all aspects of biblical religion. It is also to confuse the means with the end, for the idea of covenant was in any case subservient to the prior reality of presence. . . . The sapiential literature assigned no role whatever to the motif, ritual or ideology of covenant. . . . It was not the covenant theology but the Hebraic theology of presence which constituted the most potent impulse in the field of forces that linked Hebraism, over against Zion-centered Judaism, with the church, and the canonical growth from Hebrew Bible to New Testament must be viewed in a new light. . . . The Hebraic theology of presence may provide the principle of canonical growth [which students in the field are calling for.][56]

The apparent tension in the work of Samuel Terrien between a history-of-religion method of study of the Bible and an abiding quest for a valid biblical theology and theological unity to the Bible is caught up in his appreciation of the contribution of international Ancient Near Eastern wisdom to biblical thought and literature. Fully to appreciate that considerable element in the biblical make-up is to seek the presence of God not only where he may be found, but even in the absent places; for the unity of the Bible is in God's presence, the presence not only of Israel's covenant God of redemption and providence, but also in the presence of the creator God of all the world, the source of all wisdom. Resolution of such an apparent tension may well be called Comparative Wisdom.

## IV

Fortunately l'oeuvre Terrien is by no means complete. The retirement in Connecticut is a well-planned sabbatic jubilee. The long-awaited book, *The Elusive Presence: Toward an Ecumenical Theology of the Bible*, is due soon from Harper & Row. The much-needed commentary on the Psalms is in purview. The public lectures "Toward a Biblical Theology of Womanhood" will be edited for publication; and we can expect a history of interpretation of the Magnificat. A history of interpretation of Job in literature and in art is in progress: the iconography of Job will have a prominent place. There are already 783 representations of Job in hand and the word is that throughout history the two types of interpretation complement each other and form parallel commentaries.

Clearly the shape of the corpus will be the one we already know from the work in hand; happily it is to be greatly expanded and enriched. May the God of the Eternal Presence, "the only Wise God, our Savior," give Sam and Sara long life and strength that the rest of us may be blessed by what remains to be done. Those who know l'oeuvre Terrien know the truth of the Terrien family motto (since 1476): *firmus in terra, ad coelum securus.*

[1] There are to date eight published books of single authorship, beyond the S.T.M. and Th.D. dissertations; five more on which he has collaborated; and seven composite works to which he has contributed, including two Festschriften. He worked some eighteen years total as associate editor and contributor to the *IB* and *IDB*. There have been twenty-three articles in thirteen journals and fifty-seven reviews in twelve.

[2] *The Psalms and Their Meaning for Today* (New York and Indianapolis: Bobbs-Merrill, 1952).

[3] *Job: Poet of Existence* (New York and Indianapolis: Bobbs-Merrill, 1957).

[4] "The Omphalos Myth and Hebrew Religion," *VT* 20 (1970) 315-38.

[5] "Christianity's Debt to a Modern Pagan: Albert Camus (1913-60)," *USQR* 15 (1960) 185-94.

[6] "J. B. and Job," *The Christian Century* 76 (Jan. 7, 1959) 9-11; cf. Letter to the Editor, *The Christian Century* 76 (Feb. 4, 1959) 138.

[7] "Albee's Alice: A Warning on Our Tiny Gods," *Christianity and Crisis* 25/11 (June 28, 1965) 140-43.

[8] "Modern Painting and Theology," *Religion in Life* 38 (1969) 170-82.

[9] "Demons also Believe: The Parody of the Eucharist in Contemporary Theatre," *The Christian Century* 87 (Dec. 9, 1970) 1481-86.

[10] "Israel," *Dictionary of the Bible*, J. Hastings (ed.) rev. ed; eds. F. C. Grant and H. H. Rowley; New York: Scribners, 1963) 429-49.

[11] "The Religion of Israel," *The Interpreter's One Volume Commentary on the Bible* (ed. C. M. Laymon; New York and Nashville: Abingdon, 1971) 1150-58.

[12] *Golden Bible Atlas* (New York: Simon and Shuster, 1963). This illustrated atlas was first published under the title *Lands of the Bible* (New York: Simon and Shuster, 1957).

[13] "The Book of Job: Introduction and Exegesis," *IB* 3 (ed. G. Buttrick et al.; New York and Nashville: Abingdon, 1954) 875-1198; *Job: Poet of Existence; Job* (CAT 13; Neuchâtel: Delachaux et Niestlé, 1963; "The Book of Job," *Oxford Annotated Bible with the Apocrypha* (eds. H. G. May and B. M. Metzger; New York: Oxford University, 1965) 613-55; "Quelques remarques sur les affinités de Job avec le Deutéro-Esaïe," *Volume du Congrès, Genève 1965* (VT

Sup 15; Leiden: Brill, 1966) 295-310; "Le poème de Job: drame para-rituel du Nouvel-An?" *Congress Volume, Rome 1968* (VT Sup 17; Leiden: Brill, 1969) 220-35; (with D. Barthélemy) *Le Livre de Job, Traduction oecumenique de la Bible* (Paris: Les Bergers et les Mages, Editions du Cerf, 1971); "The Yahweh Speeches and Job's Responses," *RevExp* 68 (1971) 497-509.

14 "Amos and Wisdom," *Israel's Prophetic Heritage: Essays in Honor of James Muilenburg* (eds. B. W. Anderson and W. Harrelson; New York: Harper & Bros. 1962) 108-15.

15 "The Book of Job: Introduction and Exegesis," *IB* 3, 875-1198.

16 *Job* (CAT 13).

17 "Quelques remarques," VTSup 15 (1966) 295-310.

18 Ibid., 296.

19 Ibid., 298-310.

20 Ibid., 310.

21 "Le poème de Job," VTSup 17 (1969) 220-35.

22 Ibid., 233.

23 Ibid., 234.

24 *VT* 20 (1970) 315-38.

25 Ibid., 333-34.

26 Ibid., 338.

27 "Amos and Wisdom," *Israel's Prophetic Heritage*, 108-15.

28 See. H. W. Wolff, *Amos the Prophet* (Philadelphia: Fortress, 1973) 14 n. 40, 89 n. 203 and also Wolff's remarks at the outset of his essay in this volume.

29 "Amos and Wisdom," *Israel's Prophetic Heritage*, 115.

30 *Job: Poet of Existence*; "J. B. and Job," *The Christian Century* 76 (1959) 9-11, 138; "Christianity's Debt," *USQR* 15 (1960) 185-94; "Am I Alone?" *International Journal of Religious Education* 39 (1962-63) 16-18; "Albee's Alice: A Warning on our Tiny Gods," *Christianity and Crisis* 25/11 (1965) 140-43; "Modern Painting and Theology," *Religion in Life* 38 (1969) 170-82; "Demons also Believe: The Parody of the Eucharist in Contemporary Theatre," *The Christian Century* 87 (1970) 1481-86 et al.

31 "A Currently Neglected Aspect of Biblical Theology," *USQR*, Special Issue (1954) 3-13.

32 The paper was written for a small professional discussion group during the days of campus unrest. It is to appear in a revised form in Professor Terrien's new book.

33 Ibid.

34 *Job* (CAT 13) 46.

35 *The Psalms and Their Meaning for Today*, 270.

36 *USQR* 13 (1957) 13-17; cf. K. Barth, *Die Menschlichkeit Gottes* (Theologische Studien 48; Zürich: Evangelischer Verlag AF Zollikon, 1956) and A. J. Heschel, *God in Search of Man; A Philosophy of Judaism* (New York: Harper & Row, 1955).

37 *Interpreter's One Volume Commentary*, 1158.

38 *Job: Poet of Existence*, 66-100.

39 *Job* (CAT 13) 6.

40 Ibid., 47.

41 Ibid.

42 Ibid., 48.

43 Ibid., 47.

44 "Toward A New Theology of Presence," (Union Theological Seminary, Monday Morning Lectures; Mimeographed, 1969); "Toward A New Theology of Presence," *USQR* 24 (1969) 227-37; reprinted in *New Theology, No. 7: The Recovery of Transcendence* (eds. M. E. Marty and D. G. Peerman; New York: Macmillan, 1970) 132-51.

45 Cf. "The Sceptics in the Old Testament and in the Literature of the Ancient Near East" (Th.D. Diss., Union Theological Seminary, 1941).

46 "Toward a New Theology of Presence," *USQR* 24 (1969) 235; reprinted in *New Theology, No. 7*, 148.

47 Cf. "Creation, Cultus and Faith in the Psalter," *Theological Education* 2/4 (1966) 116-28.

[48] *Job: Poet of Existence*; "J. B. and Job," *The Christian Century* 76 (1959) 9-11; "Christianity's Debt," *USQR* (1960) 185-94; "Am I Alone?" *International Journal of Religious Education* 39 (1962-63) 16-18.

[49] "The Theological Significance of Genesis," *JBR* 14 (1946) 29-32.

[50] Ibid., 29.

[51] "Modern Painting and Theology," *Religion in Life* 38 (1969) 170-82.

[52] "A Currently Neglected Aspect of Biblical Theology," *USQR*, Special Issue (1954) 3-13; cf. "Am I Alone?" *International Journal of Religious Education* 39 (1962-63) 16-18.

[53] "The Anthropology of God," *USQR* 13 (1957) 13-17.

[54] "Toward a Biblical Theology of Womanhood," *Religion in Life* 42 (1973) 322-33; reprinted in *Male and Female: Christian Approaches to Sexuality* (eds. R. T. Barnhouse and U. T. Holmes, III; New York: Seabury, 1976) 17-27.

[55] *Religion in Life* 42 (1973) 322, 333; *Male and Female*, 17, 27.

[56] For the occasion of this unpublished paper, see n. 32 above.

# A BIBLIOGRAPHY
# OF THE BOOKS, ARTICLES AND REVIEWS
# OF SAMUEL TERRIEN

COMPILED BY BRUCE E. NIELSEN, NEW YORK, NEW YORK 10027

## 1936

"La valeur des Tablettes de Ras Shamra pour l'étude de l'Ancien Testament." S.T.M. Thesis, Union Theological Seminary, 1936.

## 1939

Review of *La Clé de l'Apocalypse, étude sur la composition et l'interprétation de la grande prophétie de St. Jean* by André Olivier in *The Review of Religion* 3 (March 1939) 317-21.

## 1940

a. Review of *La personnalité divine: comment faut-il l'envisager?* by Edmond Rochedieu in *The Review of Religion* 4 (January 1940) 223-28.
b. Review of *La strophe sacreé en St. Jean* by André Olivier in *The Review of Religion* 4 (March 1940) 370-71.
c. Review of *La religion d'Israël* by Adolphe Lods in *The Review of Religion* 4 (May 1940) 452-55.

## 1941

"The Sceptics in the Old Testament and in the Literatures of the Ancient Near East." Th.D. Dissertation, Union Theological Seminary, 1941.

## 1945

a. Review of *The Challenge of Israel's Faith* by G. Ernest Wright in *The Review of Religion* 9 (March 1945) 322-23.
b. Review of *Plea for Liberty: Letters to the English, the Americans, the Europeans* by Georges Bernanos in *The Review of Religion* 9 (May 1945) 432-33.

## 1946

a. "The Old Testament and the Christian Preacher Today" in *Religion in Life* 15 (1946) 262-71.
b. "El Antiquo Testamento y el Predicador Cristiano" [in *El Predicador Evangelico* (?), 1946] 127-34. Translation of 1946a.
c. "The Theological Significance of Genesis" in *JBR* 14 (1946) 29-32.

## 1947

a. Review of *Revelation in Jewish Wisdom Literature* by J. Coert Rylaarsdam in *JBL* 66 (1947) 245-47.
b. Review of *Light from the Ancient Past. The Archeological Background of the Hebrew-Christian Religion* by Jack Finegan in *The Review of Religion* 11 (March 1947) 316-17.
c. Review of *Pilgrim of the Absolute* by Léon Bloy in *USQR* 3/1 (1947-48) 43-47.

## 1949

a. "Bible Digest," edited by Samuel Terrien. In *Thesaurus of Book Digests*, edited by Hiram Haydn and Edmund Fuller. New York: Crown Publishers, 1949.
b. Review of *The Modern Message of the Minor Prophets* by Raymond Colkins in *The Review of Religion* 13 (January 1949) 172-74.

## 1950

"A Survey of Recent Theological Literature: Old Testament" in *USQR* 5/2 (1949-50) 29-34.

## 1951

a. "Biblical Interpretation in Recent Periodicals" in *Interpretation* 5 (1951) 92-102.
b. Review of *History of New Testament Times, with an Introduction to the Apocrypha* by Robert H. Pfeiffer in *The Review of Religion* 16 (November 1951) 40-42.

## 1952

a. *The Psalms and Their Meaning for Today.* New York and Indianapolis: Bobbs-Merrill, 1952.
b. Associate Editor for Old Testament Introduction and Exegesis, *IB.* 12 vols., edited by George Arthur Buttrick et al. New York and Nashville; Abingdon [-Cokesbury], 1952-57.

c. "History of the Interpretation of the Bible: III. Modern Period" in *IB* 1, pp. 127-41. New York and Nashville: Abingdon-Cokesbury, 1952.

## 1954

a. *The Hebraic Roots of Christian Worship.* Washington: Henderson Services, 1954.
b. "The Book of Job: Introduction and Exegesis" in *IB* 3, pp. 875-1198. New York and Nashville: Abingdon, 1954.
c. "A Currently Neglected Aspect of Biblical Theology" in *USQR*, Special Issue (1954) 3-13. Inaugural Address.
d. Review of *Das hebräische Denken im Vergleich mit den Griechischen* by Thorlief Boman in *ATR* 36/1 (1954) 70.

## 1956

"Prophets and Prophetism" in *Encyclopedia Americana*, Vol. 22, pp. 664-65. New York: Americana, 1956.

## 1957

a. *Job: Poet of Existence.* New York and Indianapolis: Bobbs-Merrill, 1957.
b. *Lands of the Bible.* New York: Simon and Schuster, 1957.
c. "The Anthropology of God" in *USQR* 13/1 (1957-58) 13-17.

## 1959

a. "J. B. and Job" in *The Christian Century* 76/1 (January 7, 1959) 9-11; cf. Letter to the Editor, *The Christian Century* 76/5 (February 4, 1959) 138.
b. Review of *Samaria: The Capital of the Kingdom of Israel* by André Parrot in *USQR* 14/2 (1958-59) 69-70.
c. Review of *Babylon and the Old Testament* by André Parrot in *USQR* 14/2 (1958-59) 69-70.
d. Review of *The Geography of the Bible* by Denis Baly in *USQR* 14/2 (1958-59) 69-70.
e. Review of *Jeremiah, Prophet of Courage and Hope* by J. Philip Hyatt in *USQR* 15 (1959-60) 63-66.
f. Review of *Prophetic Faith in Isaiah* by Sheldon H. Blank in *USQR* 15 (1959-60) 63-66.

## 1960

a. Preface to *The Old Testament*, arranged and illustrated by Marguerite de Angeli. New York: Doubleday, 1960.
b. "Christianity's Debt to a Modern Pagan: Albert Camus (1913-60)" in *USQR* 15 (1959-60) 185-94.

c. Review of *A Christian Theology of the Old Testament* by George A. F. Knight in *USQR* 15 (1959-60) 329-30.
d. Review of *The Cruel God: Job's Search for the Meaning of Suffering* by Margaret B. Crook in *USQR* 15 (1959-60) 330-32.

## 1962

a. *The Bible and the Church; an Approach to Scripture.* Philadelphia: Westminster, 1962.
b. "Amos and Wisdom," *Israel's Prophetic Heritage: Essays in Honor of James Muilenburg*, edited by Bernhard W. Anderson and Walter Harrelson, pp. 108-15. New York: Harper & Brothers, 1962.
c. "Am I Alone?" in *International Journal of Religious Education* 39 (1962-63) 16-18.
d. Associate Editor for Old Testament Articles, *IDB.* 4 vols., edited by George Arthur Buttrick et al. New York and Nashville: Abingdon, 1962.
e. Review of *Maqqél Shâqédh, la branche d'amandier: Hommage à Wilhelm Vischer*, edited by Jean Cadier in *Interpretation* 16 (1962) 326-29.

## 1963

a. *Job.* Commentaire de l'Ancien Testament 13. Neuchâtel: Delachaux & Niestlé, 1963.
b. "Faith and Ritual in the Old Testament" in *Alumni Bulletin of Bangor Theological Seminary* 38/2 (1963) 13-23.
c. "Israel" in *Dictionary of the Bible*, edited by James Hastings, revised edition by Frederick C. Grant and H. H. Rowley, pp. 429-49. New York: Scribners, 1963.
d. Review of *The Prophets* by Abraham J. Heschel in *Interpretation* 17 (1963) 482-88.
e. Review of *The Psalms* by Artur Weiser in *USQR* 18 (1962-63) 406-08.
f. Review of *The Psalms* by Artur Weiser in *JBR* 31 (1963) 334-36.
g. Review of *The Psalms in Israel's Worship* by Sigmund Mowinckel in *Religion in Life* 33 (1963) 144-46.
h. *The Golden Bible Atlas.* New York: Simon and Shuster, 1963. Republication of 1957b.

## 1964

Review of *The Old Testament and Christian Faith: A Theological Discussion* by Bernhard W. Anderson in *USQR* 19 (1963-64) 238-41.

## 1965

a. *The Children's Bible: The Old Testament, the New Testament*, edited by Joseph E. Krause, Samuel Terrien, David H. Wice. New York: Golden, 1965.

b. "Albee's Alice: A Warning on Our Tiny Gods" in *Christianity and Crisis* 25/11 (June 28, 1965) 140-43.
c. "The Book of Job" in *The Oxford Annotated Bible with the Apocrypha*, edited by Herbert G. May and Bruce M. Metzger, pp. 613-55. New York: Oxford University, 1965.
d. Review of *The Epistles of James, Peter and Jude* by Bo Reicke in *USQR* 20 (1964-65) 289-93.
e. Review of *Genesis* by E. A. Speiser in *USQR* 20 (1964-65) 289-93.

### 1966

a. "The Bible: Obsolete and Timely." New York: Union Theological Seminary, 1966. Monday Morning Lectures. Mimeographed.
b. "Creation, Cultus and Faith in the Psalter" in *Theological Education* 2, no. 4 (1966) 116-28.
c. "Quelques remarques sur les affinités de Job avec le Deutéro-Ésaïe" in *Volume du Congrès, Genève 1965*. VTSup 15 (1966) 295-310.
d. Review of *Job: Introduction, Translation and Notes* by Marvin H. Pope in *USQR* 21 (1965-66) 253-55.
e. Review of *Job: Introduction, Translation and Notes* by Marvin H. Pope in *JBL* 85 (1966) 94-96.
f. Review of *The Book of God and Man: A Study of Job* by Robert Gordis in *USQR* 22 (1966-67) 65-69.

### 1967

a. Review of *The Book of God and Man: A Study of Job* by Robert Gordis in *JAAR* 35 (1967) 67-70.
b. Review of *The Book of God and Man: A Study of Job* by Robert Gordis in *JSS* 12 (1967) 285-90.
c. Review of *Introduction to the Psalms* by Christoph F. Barth in *Religion in Life* 36 (1967) 479-80.
d. Review of *Worship in Israel: A Cultic History of the Old Testament* by H.-J. Kraus in *Interpretation* 21 (1967) 460-65.

### 1968

a. *The Power to Bring Forth; Daily Meditations for Lent* (Philadelphia: Fortress, 1968).
b. Review of *Psalms, Part II (51-100)* by Mitchell Dahood in *USQR* 23 (1967-68) 389-92.
c. Review of *Worship in Ancient Israel: Its Form and Meaning* by H. H. Rowley in *USQR* 23 (1967-68) 203-04.

### 1969

a. "Le Poéme de Job: drame para-rituel du Nouvel-An?" in *Congress*

*Volume, Rome 1968.* VTSup 17 (1969) 220-35.

b. "Modern Painting and Theology" in *Religion in Life* 38 (1969) 170-82.

c. "Toward a New Theology of Presence" New York: Union Theological Seminary, 1969. Monday Morning Lectures. Mimeographed. See 1969d and 1970b.

d. "Toward a New Theology of Presence" in *USQR* 24 (1968-69) 227-37.

e. Review of *The Covenants in Faith and History* by Stephen Szikszai in *Alumni Bulletin of Bangor Theological Seminary* 44 (1969) 39-40.

f. Review of *In Memoriam Paul Kahle*, edited by Matthew Black and Georg Fohrer in *CBQ* 31 (1969) 549-50.

g. Review of *Introduction to the Old Testament* by Georg Fohrer in *USQR* 24 (1968-69) 204-07.

h. Review of *Theocracy and Eschatology* by Otto Plöger in *USQR* 24 (1968-69) 222.

## 1970

a. *The New Testament in Shorter Form. In Modern Translation* by J. B. Phillips. Selected and introduced by Samuel Terrien. New York: Macmillan, 1970.

b. "Toward a New Theology of Presence," *New Theology, No. 7: The Recovery of Transcendence*, edited by Martin E. Marty and Dean G. Peerman, pp. 132-51. New York: Macmillan, 1970. Republication of 1969d.

c. "The Omphalos Myth and Hebrew Religion" in *VT* 20 (1970) 315-38.

d. "Demons also Believe: The Parody of the Eucharist in Contemporary Theater" in *The Christian Century* 87/49 (December 9, 1970) 1481-86.

e. Review of *Christian Art in Africa and Asia* by Arno Lehmann in *Religion in Life* 39 (1970) 464-66.

f. Review of *The New English Bible with the Apocrypha* in *USQR* 25 (1969-70) 549-55.

g. Review of *Theology of the Old Testament*, Vol. 2 by Walther Eichrodt in *JAAR* 38 (1970) 87-90.

h. Review of *The Book of Job: Its Origins and Purpose* by Norman Snaith in *USQR* 25 (1969-70) 239-42.

i. Review of *The Dimensions of Job: A Study and Selected Readings* by Nahum N. Glatzer in *USQR* 25 (1969-70) 239-42.

## 1971

a. *Le livre de Job, Traduction oecuménique de la Bible.* Introduction Traduction et Notes, by Samuel Terrien and Denis Barthélemy. Paris: Les Bergers et les Mages, Editions du Cerf, 1971.

b. "The Religion of Israel" in *The Interpreter's One-Volume Commentary on The Bible*, edited by Charles M. Laymon, pp. 1150-58. New York and Nashville: Abingdon, 1971.

c. "Setting the House on Fire, A Sermon for the Burning of a Mortgage" in *Pulpit Digest* 52 (November 1971) 35-38.
d. "The Yahweh Speeches and Job's Responses" in *Review and Expositor* 68 (1971) 497-509.
e. Review of *Gilgal et les récits de la traversée du Jourdain (Jos., III-IV)* by F. Langlamet, O.P. in *CBQ* 33 (1971) 121-23.
f. Review of *Proclamation and Presence: Old Testament Essays in Honor of Gwynne Henton Davies*, edited by John I. Durham and J. R. Porter in *CBQ* 33 (1971) 567-68.
g. Review of *Proverbs: A New Approach* by William McKane in *USQR* 26 (1970-71) 444-46.
h. Review of *Psalms, Part III (101-150)* by Mitchell Dahood, S.J. in *USQR* 26 (1970-71) 431-34.

### 1972

a. Review of *Isaiah and Wisdom* by J. William Whedbee in *Religion in Life* 41 (1972) 120-21.
b. Review of *No Graven Images: Studies in Art and the Hebrew Bible* by J. Gutmann in *CBQ* 34 (1972) 502-03.
c. "Psalms, Book of" in *Encyclopædia Britannica*, Vol. 18, pp. 704A-06. Chicago: Benton, 1972.

### 1973

a. "A Time to Speak" in *To God Be the Glory: Sermons in Honor of George Arthur Buttrick*, edited by Theodore A. Gill, pp. 92-97. New York and Nashville: Abingdon, 1973.
b. "Toward a Biblical Theology of Womanhood" in *Religion in Life* 42 (1973) 322-33.
c. Review of *History of Israelite Religion* by Georg Fohrer in *Religion in Life* 42 (1973) 413-14.
d. Review of *Isaiah 1-12: A Commentary* by Otto Kaiser in *USQR* 28 (1972-73) 259-60.
e. Review of *The Remnant* by Gerhard F. Hasel in *USQR* 28 (1972-73) 259-60.

### 1974

a. Review of *The Cosmic Mountain in Canaan and in the Old Testament* by Richard J. Clifford in *Bib* 55 (1974) 443-46.
b. Review of *Wisdom in Israel* by Gerhard von Rad in *USQR* 29 (1973-74) 131-34.

### 1975

a. Review of *La symbolique du livre d'Esaïe: essai sur l'image littéraire comme élément de structuration* by Rémi Lack in *JBL* 94 (1975) 290-92.

b. Foreword to *Yesterday, Today and Tomorrow: Time and History in the Old Testament* by Simon J. De Vries. Grand Rapids and London: Eerdmans and SPCK, 1975.

## 1976

"Toward a Biblical Theology of Womanhood" in *Male and Female: Christian Approaches to Sexuality*, edited by Ruth T. Barnhouse and Urban T. Holmes, III, pp. 17-27. New York: Seabury, 1976. Republication of 1973b.

## 1977

a. " 'Equus': Human Conflicts and the Trinity" in *The Christian Century* 94/18 (May 18, 1977) 472-76.
b. Review of *Paul Tillich: His Life and Thought*, Vol. 1 by Wilhelm and Marion Pauck in *Religion in Life* 46 (1977) 249-50.

# II

# ON THE MEANING AND STUDY
# OF ISRAELITE WISDOM

# ISRAELITE PERCEPTIONS OF WISDOM AND STRENGTH IN THE LIGHT OF THE RAS SHAMRA TEXTS

ANDRÉ CAQUOT
COLLÈGE DE FRANCE, 75005 PARIS, FRANCE
Translated by Kathryn Nowell, Knoxville, Tennessee 37916

SAMUEL Terrien is among those who have most contributed rightfully to restoring Israelite wisdom to the front rank of theological research. He has shown that prophets such as Amos and Deutero-Isaiah were permeated with ways of thinking and speaking that are characteristic of cultured men with humanist as well as religious concerns, whom we usually call wise men. He has pointed out that the culture which the Bible reflects is a continuation of that found in more ancient literatures, and he has made space in his studies and in his comments for these "oriental sources" of the thought of Israel. Among them, the texts from Ugarit, which are the most direct, the most coherent, and, for the time being, the most ancient testimony available to us, allow us to glimpse the intellectual and spiritual attitudes of the "predecessors of Israel." (Would it not be better to speak of "ancestors" and/or "teachers"?) Israelite reflections on ḥokmâ ("wisdom"), understood as a human and divine capacity and not as a current of thought or a literary genre, are clarified in part, it seems to me, through what we learn from the alphabetic texts found in Ras Shamra.

I

The shortest definition given of wisdom is also the most fitting. From the practical craftsmanship of Bezalel (Exod 31:2-3), of the makers of holy vestments (Exod 28:3), of the weavers of tents (Exod 35:36), of the bronzesmith Hiram (1 Kgs 7:14), up to the supreme art of living in which space must be made for the "fear of God" (Prov 9:10, Ps 111:10), including the tricks of the various trades: the intuitive technique of the sailor, the cleverness of the merchant, the finesse of the diplomat, the keen eye of the strategist, the perspicacity of the judge, the craft of the investigator, even the Machiavellism of the man in power, every ḥokmâ is an "ability to cope."[1] Every man skilled in his trade is a ḥākām, whether he be a magician (Isa 3:3) or King Solomon.[2] Israelite wisdom closely resembles the virtue that the ancient Greeks called μῆτις and which has been described as "a type of intelligence, a way of thinking, a mode of knowing; it implies a complex but very coherent whole of

25

mental attitudes, of intellectual behaviors which combine flair, wisdom, foresight, flexibility of the mind, dissimulation, watchful attention, a sense of opportunity, varied skills, an experience acquired over time; it applies to transient, mobile, disconcerting and ambiguous realities which do not lend themselves to precise measurement, nor to exact calculations, nor to rigorous reasoning."[3] Almost identical by nature to the μῆτις of the Greeks, the *hokmâ* of the Israelites enjoyed a higher appreciation. The Greek philosophers, specialists in discursive knowledge and armed with logic and mathematics, cast back into the shadows the "cunning intelligence," the exercise of intuition born of experience. The thinkers of Israel only had one reservation as to *hokmâ*: they warned their followers not to rely excessively on it. Though it is important, the reservation itself pertains to the highest wisdom because the supreme skill for a man is to live in his place, without the excesses which generate illusion and corruption. It is especially in this sense that *hokmâ* is a "fountain of life" (Prov 13:14), a factor in the success and prosperity of the individual. As to the communities, their prestige and their success is measured by the number of their "wise men," of people skilled in their art, except when God obstructs their plans.

One of the commonplaces in the prophets' polemic is the denunciation of the error of men who trust too much in human wisdom when they defy Israel and its God. But the Gentiles take not only an inopportune pride in their technical, commercial or political achievements, their armed forces are also sources of pride for them, and a peril for Israel. They are also fragile before God. Jer 51:57 announces that YHWH will make drunk the *ḥăkāmîm* of Babylon and also its *gibbôrîm*, its valiant soldiers, in order to defeat them. One and a half centuries earlier, Isa 10:13 ridicules the King of Assur who attributes his success to his *hokmâ* and his strength *(kōaḥ)*. The King of Assur speaks here as a collective person, representing a people which includes many "wise" men (diplomats or strategists) and "strong" men, i.e., soldiers, uniting the physical vigor and moral virtues required of a good fighter: endurance, courage, and the spirit of sacrifice. These two prophetic references show that strength comes against the same stumbling block as wisdom: one risks placing too much trust in it. No one has said it more clearly than Jeremiah (9:22): "Let not the wise man glory in his wisdom, let not the mighty man glory in his might."[4]

The union of wisdom and strength in one person seems to represent for the Israelite the equivalent of what καλοκἀγαθόν is for the Greek, the very image of a human ideal. Biblical portrayals of the accomplished man are not numerous, but they are explicit and consistent. According to 1 Sam 16:18, the young David unites the spiritual and corporal qualities; hence, his aptitude for combat. In the same way, Daniel possesses both wisdom and strength, *hokmĕtā°* and *gĕbûrtā°* (Dan 2:23), and he has as companions young men "skillful in all wisdom" "endowed with vigor" (Dan 1:4). The perfect woman, described in Proverbs 31, and who is rather virile, unites *hokmâ* (vs. 26) and strength (ᶜ*ōz*, vs. 17).[5]

The reflections of the thinkers of Israel on the relationship between wisdom and strength, on the usefulness and the difficulty which their union would present, on the respective value of these two qualities, shows through in some parts. Perhaps people argued in the town square or in the schools on the superiority of one over the other. Ecclesiastes (9:16) seems to have come up with the ritual conclusion to the debate *tôbâ ḥokmâ miggĕbûrâ*, "Wisdom is better than strength." But I see the trace of a more pragmatic answer in Prov 24:5: *geber ḥakām baʿ ôz wĕʾîš daʿat mĕʾammeṣ kôaḥ*, "The brave are capable thanks to strength, but a man of wisdom reinforces (his) power."[6] This maxim emphasizes the advantages of a cooperation between wisdom and strength, both useful to the success of the individual and of the group, but which are often not found together.

There is a most natural reason for this. Whatever its field of application may be, wisdom is improvable; it is the fruit of experience; thus it ripens with age, and it is common to identify "wise" with "old" (*zāqēn*) and wisdom with white hair (*śêbâ*).[7] On the other hand, corporal strength and ardor in combat are the domain of youth. Each age has its virtue, as noted in Prov 20:29, in a sentence which would be lame if one did not immediately identify *śêbâ* and wisdom: *tipʾeret baḥûrîm kōḥām waḥădar zĕqēnîm śêbâ*, "The glory of young men is their strength, the dignity of old men their grey hair." Thus, a man of flesh and bone cannot fulfill this ideal of the conjunction of wisdom and strength. The portraits of David, of Daniel and of his companions are clichés created by idealizing history or by edifying legend. The royal phraseology must have resorted to this literary device;[8] thus, Isa 11:2, promises that the Messiah will have the "spirit of wisdom" and the "spirit of counsel and strength." Moralists are not the only ones to have noted the polarity of wisdom and strength and how they complement each other. Historians also confirm that these dialectics were deeply rooted in Israelite thought. It is difficult not to see a deliberate purpose in the manner in which deuteronomistic history has arranged the traditions relative to David and Solomon: it sought to contrast Solomon the *ḥakām* with David the *gibbôr*, a little like the legendary history of the origin of Rome which portrayed Romulus and Numa as two contrasting and complementary aspects of sovereignty.

## II

Other cultures have imagined a perfect man who would harmonize the opposites in exemplifying the virtues of two ages of life. Classical Antiquity conceived the model of the *puer senilis* and bequeathed it to the Latin Middle Ages.[9] Ovid explains in this way that the union of maturity and youth in one person is a gift from above which is only granted to Caesars and demigods.[10] Much closer to the Bible, and preceding it, the Ugaritic literature suggests a comparable reflection on the relationship between wisdom and strength, without seeking to reconcile them into an ideal figure. A classic of this literature, the poem of Danel and Aqhat, of which only fragments remain, attempted to incarnate strength into the person of the young prince Aqhat, victim of his passion for hunting and of the goddess ᶜAnat's jealousy; and to personify wisdom in the old king Danel who is remembered in a well-known verse by Ezekiel (28:3) and in the biblical legend of the wise man Daniel. But it is the Ugaritic myth of Baᶜal which reveals in the most vivid manner how the search for the indispensable balance between the virtues of strength and wisdom inspired the poets of Ugarit.

Wisdom belongs to El and strength to Baᶜal. In four instances,[11] El is referred to as *ḥkm*. He has the beard and white hair of an old man, and in all likelihood, his title of *ʾab šnm* must be translated as "the father of years," which indicates his advanced age. He is the father of the gods, although it seems hard to imagine him procreating, so much is his image bound to that of old age.[12] He is the "creator of creatures," who has fashioned man from clay.[13] The Ras Shamra tablets have not revealed any cosmogonic myth, but it is probable that El was held to be the demiurge if one considers that more recent Semitic inscriptions make mention of a *ʾl qn ʾrṣ*, "El creator of the earth." He certainly is the keeper of the cosmic order, for it is he who ensures the permanence of the world by maintaining a balance between antagonistic powers. Against the noxious aggressiveness which threatens to overtake the universe, El sides with life. But he himself does not take up arms. Contrary to what has been maintained by F. M. Cross[14] and P. D. Miller,[15] the Ugaritic god called El was not a warrior in any way. One cannot argue from the title *ʾel gibbôr*, for it is given only by an Israelite document.[16] Neither can one take into consideration anthroponyms composed of the name *ʾl* and of another name denoting bravery (like the Sabaean *ḏmrʾl*), for in formations of this type, *ʾl* is a generic name referring to any god. The testimony of Sanchunyaton - Philo of Byblos on the fight between Kronos-El and his father Uranus is not acceptable, since this euhemeristic mythology is "Phoenician" only in the names of most of its heroes. The stories in which they play a role, and in particular the account of the theomachy, have models alien to the Semitic world.[17] Finally, an etymology explaining the divine name by a root *ʾwl* which would denote strength, is extremely doubtful.

Strength is the attribute of Baᶜal and of his companion, the goddess ᶜAnat. Just as Athirat, consort of the God El, is more wily than wise, ᶜAnat is more violent than brave, and the beneficial aspect of Baᶜal's strength is highlighted even better by this contrast. Baᶜal's strength serves Man. His initial triumph over the god of the Sea reassures men that their gardens near the coast will not be ravaged by the waves and it gives the sailors of Ugarit the courage to face the seas. Baᶜal is the guardian of the gate and the walls of Ugarit.[18] Baᶜal is the heroic god who voluntarily abandons the palace he has just erected and delivers himself unto death in order to ensure subsistence for the human beings. Baᶜal's physical strength, implied by his title of *ʾalʾiyn*, "very powerful," which is illustrated in the myth by the sexual power which enables him to mount the heifer "seventy seven and eighty eight times,"[19] and which is represented by a famous relief showing the god armed with a spear and brandishing the sledge hammer, is therefore accompanied by undeniable moral traits: intrepidity, abnegation, generosity.

The contrasting roles which the Ugaritic poems confer on Baᶜal and El translate into mythological terms the result of reflection upon the different and complementary functions of wisdom and of strength in the life of men and societies. Wisdom and strength are both necessary, but they risk opposing each other, and a balance is reached only when strength serves wisdom. In Ugarit, Baᶜal is the true god of men; it is he who arouses admiration, pathetic enthusiasm, religious fervor; but it is El who has the last word and who, by his mere word, decides the outcome of conflicts. The pre-eminence of wisdom is thus established. In Ugarit, reflection on wisdom and strength can be expressed dramatically because polytheism allows the attribution of each virtue to a god who is in some way its incarnation.

III

Some of the passages of the Bible cited above show that the thinkers of Israel continued regarding wisdom and strength as two of the cardinal virtues of human behavior. But monotheism forbids the transposition of two moral functions into a myth of conflict and collaboration. The two poles can no longer be occupied by two different divinities, El and Baᶜal. The one true God must simultaneously assume the role of the wise and of the strong.

The God of Israel appears more often as a strong God than as a wise one. The references to the strength of YHWH, by *gĕbûrâ*, *kōaḥ* or *ᶜōz* are more numerous than the affirmations of his *ḥokmâ*. Could this circumspection on God's wisdom be due to the discredit that the prophets seem to have cast upon *ḥokmâ*? It is certain that the attestations cited below do not belong to the most ancient sources of the Bible. But rather than see in the presumed reserve of these writings on wisdom the effect of the prophets' polemics against the wise, should we not consider that the fundamental myth of the religion of Israel expresses the appreciation and trust of a nation proud and assured of the *gĕbûrôt* of its god, that is, in the first place, of its military successes? God's wisdom thus finds itself overshadowed by his strength, at least in our eyes. God's strength could not, however, be exercised without a certain *ḥokmâ*, without the skills indispensable to conduct a war. Perhaps the most ancient witness to God's wisdom is Isa 31:2: in saying that YHWH is *ḥākām*, the prophet wants to show that he is wily and capable of playing tricks on the enemy. A word which is characteristic of the "sapiential" vocabulary, *ᶜēṣâ*, "counsel," denotes most often a stratagem or a devastating plan when it refers to God.[20] Wisdom and strength are attributed to YHWH fighting the sea monsters, according to Job 26:12: "By his power he stilled the sea; by his understanding he smote Rahab." Does the "understanding" (*tĕbûnâ*) mentioned here designate the maneuvering skill of the warrior? This verse of Job uses again the well-known theme of YHWH triumphant over the dragons, but it uses it in a hymn celebrating the omnipotence of the creator of the universe, so that this reference to the union of wisdom and strength in God can be classified with those that follow and which verify the cooperation between the two virtues in the primordial work of YHWH.

In three instances, the Hebrew Bible refers to the creation of the world through the wisdom (ḥokmâ) or through the understanding (tĕbûnâ) of God: Pss 104:24; 136:5; Prov 3:19. The poets who have praised the creator's wisdom probably imagined the demiurge as an architect or an artist, the perfect master of his art. The ḥokmâ of God the creator is comparable to that of Bezalel or of Hiram the bronzesmith, i.e., what the Wisdom of Solomon calls the σοφία τεχνῖτις, a virtue ascribed to God (7:21) as well as to a ship builder (14:2). Why is the strength of God mentioned elsewhere even in instances where reference is made to creation?

Little importance is ascribed to the joint mention of God's wisdom and his power in Ps 147:5 and Dan 2:20. These verses belong to two doxologies— where God is celebrated for the exploits that he has accomplished in nature and in history. Praise of God's strength seems to focus on God's interventions in history, praise of wisdom on cosmic motifs. It is more surprising to encounter the association of wisdom and strength in the texts which speak only of the initial work of YHWH, such as Isa 40:28: He is "the creator of the ends of the earth, he does not faint or grow weary, his understanding is unsearchable," and especially the hymnic formula of unknown date, but which is very explicit and can be read twice in Jeremiah (10:12 and 51:15): "It is he who made the earth by his power (kōaḥ), who established the world by his wisdom (ḥokmâ) and by his understanding (tĕbûnâ) stretched out the heavens." Job 9:4 also associates the two virtues before stating the omnipotence of the demiurge,[21] as does Job 12:13 in a recollection of God's power over all creation.

It is even more astonishing to see the creation of the universe reduced, at least superficially, to a work of strength. Thus in a formula quoted twice in Jeremiah: at the beginning of the oracle which the prophet has transmitted to the nations surrendered to Nebuchadnezzar, God declares: "It is I who by my great power and by my outstretched arm, have made the earth" (27:5); the prophet reiterates the same expression at the beginning of a prayer filled with reminiscences of the gesta Dei in the history of Israel (32:17). As the two texts insist upon the victories of YHWH, one understands that the principle of these victories, the divine power, must be recalled as much as possible, and that the prophet resorts for that purpose to a cliché (the "great power and outstretched arm") which the deuteronomic and deuteronomistic literature uses to present Israel's saving God. Psalm 65:7 is explained in the same way: "By thy strength thou hast established the mountains, being girded with might." God's power is highlighted, not to suggest that displacing mountains requires great physical vigor, for God's strength is not that of a weightlifter, but in order to adapt the praise to the dominant thought of a poem which celebrates the God of Zion as the conqueror of the Sea and of peoples, the dispenser of fertility; in brief, as a god closely resembling what Baᶜal was for the people of Ugarit.

The attribution of strength to God the creator is, however, not entirely justified because it is a part of doxologies addressed to a victorious God. It is often said that the religion of Israel, which has as a myth a national history marked by liberations manifesting the military power of YHWH, has made God the creator a sort of extension of God the savior. In this way, the strength of God would have overtaken God's wisdom. The answer seems unsatisfactory to me unless it takes into account the cultural and religious background upon which Israelite monotheism developed. In Ugarit, Ba°al, the strong god, bears no resemblance to a demiurge, but "in the beginning" he conquered the sea and the dragons. The Israelites attributed this mythical exploit to YHWH who had also replaced the god El as a demiurge. The two feats of the origins: the creation of the earth, the work of El, the work of wisdom, and the victory over the sea, the work of power, in which Israel has seen the prototype of its God's wars, have tended to merge into one primordial act accomplished by the one true God, strong and wise at the same time. Therefore, it was not improper for an Israelite to speak of the power of God when evoking the creation of the world.

The God of Israel is at the same time strong and wise: he is the true El and the true Ba°al, and even though one of those two aspects may be emphasized in certain circumstances, the second one is never completely forgotten. By uniting in YHWH the power of Ba°al and the wisdom of El, the monotheist revolution gave its God the complexity of a human being, while the gods of polytheism remained much more the representatives of a function than persons. While El represented the plenitude of wisdom and Ba°al the fullness of power, YHWH possesses both completely, and thus achieves anthropological perfection. As a consequence, however, he can no longer be given a face. The people of Ugarit did not hesitate to conceive the image of their gods: El was an old man, seated, with a long white beard; Ba°al, a young warrior, armed to the hilt, moving forward decisively. The God of Israel could not be represented one way or the other: to paint him as El would have meant to deny his strength, and the image of Ba°al would have been incapable of signifying the wisdom of YHWH. The Bible did not deviate significantly from its hesitance to describe the physical appearance of the divinity. The most notable exception is Dan 7:9: the "Ancient of Days" with white hair, sitting on his throne, is not a newcomer, but the God of Israel with the features of El. Perhaps during the three relatively peaceful centuries which followed the return from Babylon, this image of a propitiated divinity was able to displace gradually that of the warrior god heir to the fiery Ba°al. Yet, the latter must have returned fairly quickly into the collective consciousness, revived by the Maccabean wars. This is proven by the Qumran texts which abound with references to divine strength.

<sup>1</sup> The definition is Alexander Kenworthy's; it is quoted by J. Crenshaw (ed. J. Crenshaw, *Studies in Ancient Israelite Wisdom* [New York: Ktav, 1976] 4).

<sup>2</sup> An always improvable ability to deal directly with a concrete situation, there is nothing in *ḥokmâ* that we could call book knowledge. It is regrettable that these last decades have hardened an hypothesis that A. Alt announced in 1951 with some reservation ("Die Weisheit Salomos," *Kleine Schriften* [3 vols.; Munich: Beck, 1953] 2. 90-99), and which now appears to be considered certain: that "Solomon's wisdom" resulted in a science of nomenclature. More exact, I believe, is a judgment that Edouard Reuss made a century ago on 1 Kings 5:13 (*Histoire des Israélites depuis la conquête de la Palestine jusqu'à l' Exil* [Paris: Sandoz and Fischbacher, 1877] 420): "We venture here the idea that Solomon could be the author of numerous fables in which animals and plants play roles or could pass for the author of those which popular tradition liked to repeat."

<sup>3</sup> M. Detienne and J. P. Vernant, *Les ruses de l'intelligence; la mētis des Grecs* (Paris: Flammarion, 1974) 9-10.

<sup>4</sup> The oracle goes on: "Let not the rich man glory in his riches." The mention of the wise, the strong and the rich causes this verse to be regarded by G. Dumézil as possible evidence of the "functional tripartition" which is characteristic of the Indo-European ideology (*Mythes et épopée* 3 [Paris: Gallimard, 1973] 359-60). As Dumézil rightly denies that the Israelites have shared this ideology, he thinks that Jeremiah is addressing foreigners here, perhaps Egyptians imbued with Aryan ideas. It is more likely that the prophet's polemic is directed at his compatriots, and that it may not entail any reference to the "functional tripartition." If riches are put here on the same plane with wisdom, it is solely to denounce the presumption which it also risks generating. (The same motive is found in Prov 11:28). The founders of the Indo-European ideology reflected as students of society mindful of the division of social work; the authors of the Bible are moralists, observers of human behavior, who understood that corporal strength and strength of character on one hand, understanding and know-how on the other, are the two ways to success of which riches are but a sign. For a further discussion on Jer 9:22-23, see the essay by W. Brueggemann in this volume. [Ed.]

<sup>5</sup> The portrayal of David and that of Daniel's companions add a physical detail—beauty. That of the "strong woman" does not take this trait into consideration (Prov 31:30). That is a deliberate bias, for beauty is a characteristic of the ideal woman as proven by the portrait of Abigail (1 Sam 25:3) where beauty seems to be substituted for strength. An Aramaic inscription of the 2d century B.C. pays a compliment to a woman for her wisdom and beauty (*KAI* [3 vols.; Wiesbaden: Harrassowitz, 1962-64] 1. 51; 2. 311 [Nr. 264]).

<sup>6</sup> Modern commentaries generally correct this verse as did the Septuagint, the Peshitta and the Targum. Let us quote the *NEB*: "Wisdom prevails over strength, knowledge over brute force." The interpretation of the Vulgate and of Rashi respected the text, but, making out of *ḥākām* an epithet of *geber*, it did not take into account the synthetic parallelism of two hemistichs (thus *RSV*: "A wise man is strong; a man of knowledge increases strength"). It is preferable to give *geber* the meaning of "strong man" and to make *ḥākām* the predicate of the nominal sentence: it is in this way that the first hemistich has been understood by the Midrash (*Lev. Rab.* 23:11, *Ruth Rab.* 6:4) and by the commentary of Gersonides who have understood: "Man becomes wise through fortitude."

<sup>7</sup> Thus, Ezek 27:9. In Ps 105:22: *zĕqēnāyw yĕḥakkēm*, "He made wise the elders (of Egypt)," does not mean that the Egyptian elders had not been wise, but that Joseph was wiser than they were. When David counsels Solomon to use his *ḥokmâ* in order to get rid of Joab's "white hair" (*śêbâ*) (1 Kgs 2:9), he warned him by this simple word that he would have to deal with an "old fox." Job 32:9, and Qoh 4:13 contest this commonplace, while at the same time, acknowledging its existence.

<sup>8</sup> A good example is given by a long-misunderstood passage of the Phoenician inscription of Karatepe (*KAI* 1. 6; 2. 37, 42[Nr. 26:111 5-6]). The king Azitawadda beseeches Baʿal to bless him, giving him *longevity* (literally, "length of days and multitude of years," *wrš°t nᶜmt* and "a powerful vigor." The word *rš°t* has been convincingly explained by F. Bron (*RSO* 35 [1975] 345-46), as a Phoenician correspondant to the Ethiopian *rĕšĕ°at*, "old age." F. Bron translates "a happy old age" which doubles, in my opinion, the request for longevity. I think that "old age" is a

metaphor here for "wisdom" as in Prov 20:29, and that Azitawadda solicited from the god, before strength, "a beneficial wisdom." Prov 3:17 makes out of $n\bar{o}^c am$ one of the consequences of ḥokmâ.

9 "The old child" was pointed out by E. R. Curtius (*Europäische Literatur und lateinisches Mittelalter* [Berne: A. Francke, 1948] 106), who defines him as a projection of the collective unconscious.

10 See the praise of Caïus, Agrippa's son, in P. Ovidius Naso, *Ars amatoria* (ex Rudolph Merkelii recognitione; ed. R. Ehwald; Leipzig: Teubner, 1940) 1. 181-94 (cf. esp. 1. 188).

11 *UT* (An Or 38; Rome, Pontifical Biblical Institute, 1965) 51: IV 41, V 65; 126:IV 3; $^c nt$: V 38 (pp. 171, 193, 225).

12 The poem on the "Birth of the gods" (*UT* 52; pp. 174-75) tells of El's impotence and how he remedies it.

13 We do not know directly the anthopogonic myth of Ugarit, but it is certainly reflected in the tale of the fabrication of Sha$^c$taqat, the winged healer of King Keret (*UT* 126: V 26-30; p. 194).

14 *Canaanite Myth and Hebrew Epic* (Cambridge, MA.: Harvard University, 1973) 40.

15 *The Divine Warrior* (Cambridge, MA.: Harvard University, 1973) 48-62.

16 In Isa 10:21 an epigone repeated the expression $^{\jmath}el\ gibb\hat{o}r$ of Isa 9:5, applying it to God. In the original messianic epithet, $^{\jmath}el$ does not refer to God, but to a god, an extraordinary being.

17 J. Barr ("Philo of Byblos and his Phoenician History," *BJRL* 57 [1974-75] 17-68), was the last to caution Semitists to go to this source only with circumspection.

18 The complaint of El against Ba$^c$al in UT 67:VI 23-24 (p. 180) speaks of human beings as the people of Ba$^c$al. Tablet RS 24.266 contains a "prayer to Ba$^c$al of the Ugaritans in danger," published by A. Herdner (*Comptes-rendus des séances de l'année 1972* [Académie des Inscriptions et Belles lettres; Paris: C. Klincksieck, 1972] 693-97), which confirms that Ba$^c$al is the protector god of Ugarit. When the people of Ugarit speak of "our gates, our walls" they use the possessive ending of the first person dual (*tgr-ny, ḥmyt-ny*) which here is the equivalent of an inclusive: "our gates/our walls, to us, the people of Ugarit and to you, Ba$^c$al."

19 UT 67:V 18-21 (p. 180).

20 Military connotations are no longer perceivable in Isa 40:13, 46:10-11; Job 42:3; Prov 19:21.

21 There is disagreement over whether Job 9:4a refers to God or to the man who might grow bold enough to defy him. Those who hold to the former position are: the midrash *Exod. Rab.* 9:7; L. Hirzel and J. Olshausen, *Hiob*[2] (Kurzegefasstes exegetisches Handbuch zum A. T. 2; Leipzig: S. Hirzel, 1852) 56; S. R. Driver (and G. B. Gray), *The Book of Job* (ICC; Edinburgh: Clark, 1921) 84; P. Dhorme, *A Commentary on the Book of Job* (Leiden: Nelson, 1967) 127; A. Weiser, *Das Buch Hiob*[2] (ATD 13; Göttingen: Vandenhoeck & Ruprecht, 1951) 72; G. Hölscher, *Das Buch Hiob*[2] (HAT 1/17; Tübingen: Mohr, 1952) 29; and, F. Horst, *Hiob* (BKAT 16/1; Neukirchen-Vluyn, Neukirchener Verlag, 1968) 145. Those who hold that Job 9:4a refers to man are: A. B. Ehrlich, *Randglossen zur hebräischen Bibel* (7 vols.; Leipzig: Hinrichs, 1908-14) 6 (1913). 214; N. H. Tur-Sinai (H. Torczyner), *The Book of Job: A New Commentary* (Jerusalem: Kiryath Sepher, 1975) 155; S. Terrien, *Job* (CAT 13; Neuchâtel: Delachaux & Niestlé, 1963) 93; "The Book of Job: Introduction and Exegesis," *IB* 3 (New York and Nashville: Abingdon, 1954) 975-78; *Job: Poet of Existence* (New York and Indianapolis: Bobbs-Merrill, 1957) 108-09 and M. Pope, *Job* (AB 15; Garden City, NY: Doubleday, 1965) 67. The passage emphasizes, in any case, that God is both wiser and stronger than man.

# WISDOM—THESES AND HYPOTHESES

ROLAND E. MURPHY, O. CARM.

THE DIVINITY SCHOOL, DUKE UNIVERSITY, DURHAM, NORTH CAROLINA 27706

OVER the past thirty years there has been a remarkable development in the area of research into biblical wisdom literature. One need only advert to the modest twenty-seven page entry of W. Baumgartner in H. H. Rowley's *The Old Testament and Modern Study* (1951).[1] That article represented the current understanding of the topic; basically it is a treatment of "wisdom books," without much discussion of theological issues or any recognition of the complexity of wisdom. In retrospect this approach strikes one as myopic, but there must have been many factors (emphasis on Pentateuchal criticism, etc.) which created the situation. This is not the place to survey the efflorescence of studies in biblical wisdom.[2] Several years ago I tried to formulate wisdom theses, firm statements of assured results. By the time the theses were published,[3] old uncertainties reappeared. This is another effort in the same direction, more modest perhaps, and dedicated to a man who has both emulated and written well of the biblical sages in his teaching career.

*Theses*

1. *Biblical wisdom issues from the effort to discover order in human life.*

This thesis is held by so many scholars that it seems to be one of the "assured results." It describes what is presumably a philosophical stance or presupposition of the ancient Israelite. A phrase often used to describe the search for order is "mastery of life" (not merely, "coping with life," or "steering"). Humans seek to sift out the hidden orders in the confusion of varied experiences to which they are subject. Thus, the saying is analyzed as a literary expression of a quest for the order that makes the task of living easier and more profitable. The orders that govern human intercourse are deduced from experience: a soothing word, control of the tongue, honesty, diligence, humility, friendliness, avoidance of a quarrel, discipline—this kind of conduct leads to more or less guaranteed good results. The contravention of this order is folly, and the contrasts between wisdom and folly abound in the proverb literature. The stylistic means may vary ("better" sayings, admonitions, paradoxes), but the end result is the same: order. While the writer has

35

already expressed his misgivings about this approach to Israelite wisdom,[4] the fact remains that it is a widely accepted conclusion.

Flowing from this conclusion is the understanding of the "fate-working deed," the idea that deed and result are aspects of the one reality. This view is associated particularly with the study of K. Koch,[5] although it had been asserted on psychological grounds by J. Pedersen. Several examples from wisdom literature can be quoted in support of this view:

> Ill-gotten treasures profit nothing,
>> but virtue saves from death. (Prov 10:2)
> The just man will never be disturbed,
>> but the wicked will not abide in the land. (Prov 10:30)

The order that underlies these sayings is simple: good deeds/attitudes bring reward intrinsically as part of the action; similarly, evil deeds/attitudes bring evil results for the one who performs them.

The basic difficulty I have with this view is that it fails to take into account the fundamental Israelite attitude that the Lord is the primary cause of everything; this does not leave any room for him as "mid-wife" (Koch's term) in the functioning of an order. This association between deed and consequence may be a valid logical construction of the mentality behind Prov 10:2, 30 and many other passages. But did it ever exist in reality? Would it have prevailed against Israel's understanding of the Lord as one who reacts favorably to good, and unfavorably to evil? When the alleged order breaks down with the development of wisdom literature (Job and Ecclesiastes), it is the Lord, not an order, who must bear the brunt of the attack. Despite von Rad's adoption and persuasive presentation of this point of view, more discussion seems necessary lest it become one of the "assured results."[6]

## 2. Wisdom theology is creation theology.

This thesis was clearly articulated for the first time by W. Zimmerli,[7] although it was implicit in the observable fact that wisdom literature was strangely silent about God's interventions in Israel's history (Exodus, covenant, cult, etc.).

But now the issue is: where does creation theology fit into the OT? The antithesis between the creation belief and the kerygmatic proclamation of Yahweh's involvement with his people has complicated biblical theology. As is well known, G. von Rad sought to integrate creation theology with salvation history, after the model of "soteriological creation" provided in Deutero-Isaiah and in the structuring of Genesis 1-12.[8] That is perhaps one way of reading the situation, but it hardly does justice to the antiquity of the notion of creation in the ancient Near East, including Israel. Is the idea of Yahweh as creator secondary to Yahweh as savior? Even Zimmerli's basic study seems to betray a concern to justify the creation theology of wisdom out of the Torah; it is an extension of Gen 1:28. But recently he has asked about the question which Israel's wisdom puts to OT theology: must one always have an historical axis as the center of theology?[9]

An entirely different approach to the question has been taken by H. H. Schmid.[10] He goes far beyond the claims he made for order as a wisdom category in his first publication.[11] He now proposes world order as the basic category of thought in the ancient Near East. This idea is the dominant background of OT thought and faith, within which Israel had her experiences, even the particular experiences of her history. Schmid claims that understanding in terms of world order is the total horizon of the thought involved in biblical theology ("Gesamthorizont biblisch-theologischen Denkens"). It follows from this claim that it is a false problem to ask how creation fits with history. The horizon of world order subsumes both areas into itself. In this view, faith is not limited to the area of God's history with his people, but to the total experience of the world. The Lord is known and experienced in the context of world order, which is the basic structure of thought.

### 3. The origins of the wisdom movement are to be sought both in the ethos of the people and in the royal court.

This thesis combines the new with the old. The older view sought to explain the origins of the wisdom literature in terms of the activities of the wise men at the Jerusalem court. This was reasonable, especially in view of the following arguments: The biblical references to Solomon's wisdom (1 Kgs 4, 10) and to the activity of the men of Hezekiah (Prov 25:1), the similarity to the Egyptian "teachings" which clearly had their origin in a court atmosphere, the training of a responsible courtier could be seen as part of the wisdom ideal (e.g., Prov 16:10-15; 25:1-5), and finally, the probability that a court school existed in Jerusalem.[12] But the studies of Audet and Gerstenberger pushed the question of origins further back, and into a period when law and wisdom were still undifferentiated.[13] Early on, O. Eissfeldt had surveyed the wisdom sayings and other genres which had circulated early in Israel's experience, and had even argued that some folk wisdom had been incorporated into Proverbs itself.[14] Obviously, Israel did not wait until Solomon to have its share of experiential wisdom. The wisdom cultivated by Solomon and the men of Hezekiah must necessarily reflect the ethos of the people for whom it was destined. It is reasonable therefore to correlate the court activity with the experiential wisdom of the people. This would imply a recognition of the impulse given to a literary cultivation of wisdom in the court. Wisdom is well on its way to becoming a literature, thus gaining a certain prestige that will preserve it. The literary association between royalty and wisdom is continued in Qoheleth and in the Wisdom of Solomon. But it is obvious that the sages responsible for Job, Qoheleth, Sirach and Wisdom have nothing to do with the court; these are all certainly postexilic, with the possible exception of Job. And our knowledge of the Sitz im Leben of postexilic sages is not better than that for the preexilic. The details in Qoh 12:9-11 and Sir 51:23 ("my house of learning," —but this could be metaphorical) are too sparse.

## Hypotheses

*1. Personified wisdom is immanent to creation, while distinct from the "works" of God; she speaks in the name of Yahweh.*

One of the most difficult areas of research has been the personification of wisdom (Job 28; Proverbs 8; Sirach 24; Wisdom of Solomon 7-9; Baruch 3-4). This figure stands at such a distance from the didactic sentences that go under the name of wisdom. Interpreters usually fall into one of two camps: (1) personified wisdom is an attribute of God; (2) it is an hypostasis, and often understood as a figure of a primitive gnostic myth. R. Marcus has given convincing reasons why wisdom is to be seen as a personification, and not as a person, and this is not the place to try to evaluate the huge amount of literature that has gathered around this topic.[15] But if wisdom is personified, what is it? As an attribute of God, the wisdom of Proverbs 8 and even of Sirach 1 (apart from Sirach 24, where wisdom is identified with Torah), seems pale and inert. Why is there no hymn to other personified attributes of God, such as his justice, etc.? Perhaps it was the easiest solution in view of the apparent meaning of Prov 3:19, "The Lord by wisdom founded the earth, established the heavens by understanding."

G. von Rad has made a daring move in this area.[16] He takes a firm stand against a reconstructed gnostic myth, and he styles wisdom as a "personified entity immanent in creation." This idea is developed in a chapter entitled, "The Self-revelation of Creation." There is perhaps just enough evidence in the text to support his contention, but it remains an hypothesis.

Job 28 argues that in contradistinction to precious metals that are found in the earth, the most precious entity, wisdom, is *not* to be found by humans; it is known only to God. When God created, performing the most mysterious things, such as "giving the wind its weight," and making a way "for the lightning of the thunder,"

> Then he saw wisdom and declared it;
> he established it, and searched it out. (Job 28:27)

The key verbs in this passage (*spr, kwn, ḥqr*) are tantalizingly vague. They can include the idea that God created wisdom, but where is it? The preceding verses made much of the fact that it could not be found, that it was only with God. But von Rad concludes that it must be somewhere in the world, while being distinct from the works of creation. It is immanent in the world; whether it is called "mysterious order" or the "meaning" created in the world, it turns towards men and appeals to them with the authority, the voice, of the Lord himself. Several commentators have pointed to Sir 1:9 as a kind of expansion of Job 28:27. The context of both is similar. Man is unable to number or explore the outstanding works of creation (heaven's height, earth's breadth, etc., Sir 1:1-4). There is one alone who knows wisdom: the Lord who "created her, has seen her and taken note of her. He has poured her forth upon all his works, upon every living thing according to his bounty; he has lavished her upon his friends" (vss. 9-10). Thus, wisdom is something God has numbered (vs. 9, *exērithmēsen*; cf. *spr* in Job 28:27), and then poured out (*execheen*) on the works of creation, from which wisdom itself is distinct.

The eighth chapter of Proverbs fairly bristles with problems, such as the meaning of *ʾāmôn* ("craftsman"? "nursling"? "darling"? vs. 30), or the significance of *qānānî* ("created me"? "begot me"? vs. 22). It is clear that wisdom describes her origins from God before creation. But what is her relationship to creation?

Her role in the creative activity itself is debatable, and hence can be left aside. She herself lays claim to being a delight, first to the Lord (?), and secondly and surely she found delight in human beings. Presumably the latter is reflected in the constant appeals she has made to them to love her (8:17), to acquire her (4:5). She is somehow happy to be present to human beings. In the context of the chapter and of general wisdom teaching, this seems to mean that she is present in their experience of the created world, in the world of experiential wisdom in its broadest sense. However *ʾāmôn* is translated, wisdom is not a casual bystander. She proclaims her orientation to human beings. In the perspective of Ben Sira the delight of wisdom to be with humankind is made more graphic. She receives the command from the Lord to dwell in Israel, and Ben Sira is able to identify her with the Torah.[17]

*2. The problem of the relationship between wisdom literature and other portions of the Old Testament needs to be reformulated in terms of a shared approach to reality.*

This hypothesis follows upon J. Crenshaw's critique of the efforts of several scholars to associate the Joseph narrative (von Rad), or the Succession Narrative (Whybray), or other parts of the OT with wisdom. On the basis of the way in which the question was put, Crenshaw succeeded in denying such an association, especially when the conclusion is as sharply put as in the case of the Joseph narrative by von Rad: "a didactic wisdom-story."[18] But if one puts the question in terms of wisdom thinking (what von Rad called *Wirklichkeitsverständnis*), a better judgment of the relationship seems possible.

It is not a question of the direct influence of the sages or of the wisdom literature, but rather of an approach to reality which was shared by all Israelites in varying degrees. The teachers were of course the experts, particularly sensitive to the insights that experience offered, and upon which conduct was to be based. But the existence of experts even presupposes that the average Israelite shared to some extent in the sapiential understanding of reality (which was, without doubt, not alien to Yahwism for them). Such an understanding was not a mode of thinking cultivated exclusively by one class; it was shared at all levels of society that interpreted daily experience. It came to be crystallized in a recognizable body of "wisdom literature," but the mentality itself was much broader than the literary remains that have come down to us. I think this approach is what Whybray was struggling for in his study on Israel's intellectual tradition.[19] But instead of settling for a more modest perspective of wisdom understanding, he went on to deny the existence of a class of sages, and concluded with a doubtful argument for wisdom influence based upon wisdom vocabulary.

This hypothesis will open up the research of wisdom influence upon various parts of the OT without the false problems raised by the mixing of genres, or the extent of wisdom vocabulary, or the existence of wisdom motifs. Thus it should come as no surprise (and hence provide no basis for classifying Isaiah among the wise) that Isaiah should use a parable, any more than the author of the Book of Job utilized a legend concerning Job the patriarch for the framework of his sapiential discussion of a wisdom problem. Similarly, a broader basis for judging "wisdom psalms" can be reached by going beyond the arguments of form-criticism. This has been done successfully by B. Vawter for Psalm 90, although he does not refer explicitly to wisdom mentality or understanding of reality.[20]

### 3. A distinction between religious and secular is not applicable to Old Testament wisdom teaching.

This hypothesis may hinge upon definitions. But since the terminology of religious/secular and sacred/profane is widely used in wisdom research, there is no escape from attempting to set limits on these words and upon what is implied in their usage. First, sacred (= sacral) and profane are best reserved to the cultic sphere; we shall deal only with religious/secular. Secondly, we may define the terms broadly as relating to the divine and relating to the world. Here the issue is joined: is the modern conceptual disjunction between divine and worldly really applicable to OT thought? I believe not. One cannot deny that the Israelite distinguished between the two but they are not separated as independent areas. The world, as the creation of God, is the arena of his activity and of human life. Here are manifested various aspects of the divine—even in the most "worldly" things (Psalm 19; Job 28:24-27; Wis 13:1-9). While the modern can distinguish between degrees of religious and worldly, there is no evidence that Israel did so. Hence there is a profound truth in von Rad's statement, "The experiences of the world were for her always divine experiences as well, and the experiences of God were for her experiences of the world."[21]

This hypothesis is in keeping with the view that wisdom theology is creation theology. It runs counter to the views of McKane that some proverbs are a Yahwistic interpretation (because of the introduction of "God-language," etc.) of an older "mundane" wisdom.[22] It undercuts as well the attempt of H. D. Preuss to exclude from older wisdom any rootage in Yahwism.[23]

The problems that remain, about which more hypotheses could be offered, are legion. The greatest difficulty lies in our ignorance of the sociological background of the sages. In the preexilic period how did the *ḥakam* function? If a school existed, what was its nature? Although we know Ecclesiastes and Ben Sira were established "wise men" in the postexilic period, we know hardly more than those bare facts. Moreover, not enough attention has been given to the fact that, as literature, the wisdom books are primarily postexilic. This does not deny the existence of wisdom literature (and more than Proverbs 10–29) in the preexilic period. But the literary phenomenon should be a topic of investigation in itself. What provoked it? Did it function within a scholastic frame of reference? What connection should be made between the wise men and other parts of the Hebrew Bible that were being redacted or even composed? With the renewal of interest in Israel's wisdom, one may hope that insights into these and other questions will be forthcoming.

[1] H. H. Rowley (ed.), *The Old Testament and Modern Study* (London: Oxford University, 1951) 210-37.

[2] The most recent treatment is the prolegomenon, with a full bibliography, which J. Crenshaw contributed to *Studies in Ancient Israelite Wisdom* (ed. J. Crenshaw; New York: Ktav, 1976) 1-60.

[3] See "Wisdom Theses," in the Papin Festschrift: *Wisdom and Knowledge* (ed. J. Armenti; 2 vols.; Philadelphia: Villanova University, 1976) 2. 187-200.

[4] "Wisdom and Yahwism," *No Famine in the Land: Studies in honor of John L. McKenzie.* (eds. J. W. Flanagan, A. W. Robinson; Claremont: Institute for Antiquity and Christianity, 1975) 117-26. As I see it, wisdom's alleged search for order is our modern reconstruction. It asks a question never raised by Israel: On what conviction is your wisdom based? Answer: on the order of the universe. Such an answer seems logical and probably correct; but Israel never asked it, nor consciously assumed the answer that we give to it. Secondly, the emphasis on order seems to me to be induced by an overreliance upon the parallelism between Egyptian *Maat* and Hebrew *ḥokmâ*. Finally, the thesis describes a presupposition, an aspect of the Israelite understanding of reality; it does not bear upon the didactic emphasis of wisdom teaching.

[5] Cf. K. Koch, "Gibt es ein Vergeltungsdogma im Alten Testament?" *Um das Prinzip der Vergeltung in Religion und Recht des Alten Testaments* (ed. K. Koch; Wege der Forschung 125; Darmstadt: Wissenschaftliche Buchgesellschaft, 1972) 130-80. This volume contains his 1955 article and other studies pertinent to the topic.

[6] The existence of this mechanical order of deed and consequence is made the basic reason behind H. D. Preuss' rejection of any role for Old Testament wisdom in Christian theology. His most recent study summarizes previous articles: "Alttestamentliche Weisheit in christlicher Theologie," *Questions Disputées d'Ancien Testament,* ed. C. Brekelmans (BETL 23; Leuven University, 1974) 165-81.

[7] "The Place and Limit of the Wisdom in the Framework of Old Testament Theology," *SJT* 17 (1964) 146-58.

[8] *Old Testament Theology* (2 vols.; New York: Harper & Row, 1965) 1. 136-40; 2. 240-41.

[9] Cf. "Erwägungen zur Gestalt einer alttestamentlichen Theologie," *Studien zur alttestament-*

*lichen Theologie und Prophetie: Gesammelte Aufsätze* II (Theologische Bücherei 51; Munich: Kaiser, 1974) 27-54, esp. p. 50.

[10] H. H. Schmid, *Altorientalische* Welt in der *alttestamentlichen* Theologie [sic] (Zürich: Theologischer Verlag, 1974), esp. pp. 33-35, 61-63.

[11] *Wesen und Geschichte der Weisheit* (BZAW 101; Berlin: Töpelmann, 1966).

[12] A classical exposition of the court background of wisdom is contained in H. Duesberg-I. Fransen, *Les Scribes Inspirés* (Maredsous, 1966) 99-176. More recently, H.-J. Hermisson has argued sharply for the existence of a court school; cf. *Studien zur israelitischen Spruchweisheit* (WMANT 28; Neukirchen-Vluyn: Neukirchener Verlag, 1968) 97-136.

[13] J. P. Audet, "Origines comparées de la double tradition de la loi et de la sagesse dans la proche-orient ancien," *International Congress of Orientalists (25th)* (Moscow, 1960) I. 352-57. E. Gerstenberger, *Wesen und Herkunft des "apodiktischen Rechts"* (WMANT 20; Neukirchen-Vluyn: Neukirchener Verlag, 1965).

[14] O. Eissfeldt, *Der Maschal im Alten Testament* (BZAW 24; Giessen: Töpelmann, 1913).

[15] R. Marcus, "On Biblical Hypostases of Wisdom," *HUCA* 23 (1950-51) 157-71. Among more recent literature, see M. Hengel, *Hellenism and Judaism* (2 vols.; London: SCM, 1974) 1. 155-62 and, on other personifications, J. M. Reese, *Hellenistic Influence on the Book of Wisdom and Its Consequences* (AnBib 41; Rome: Biblical Institute, 1970) 127-28, 138.

[16] *Wisdom in Israel* (Nashville and New York: Abingdon, 1972) 144-76. His hypothesis was put forward rather obscurely in *Old Testament Theology*, 1. 446, 451-52.

[17] The identity of the referent of Torah is not immediately obvious. Von Rad has pointed out the wisdom hue which attaches to Torah in Sirach (*Wisdom in Israel*, 245-47).

[18] See the volume cited in n. 2 edited by Crenshaw, pp. 439-47 and 481-94.

[19] R. N. Whybray, *The Intellectual Tradition in the Old Testament* (BZAW 115; Berlin: de Gruyter, 1974).

[20] Cf. "Postexilic Prayer and Hope," *CBQ* 37 (1975) 460-70.

[21] *Wisdom in Israel*, 62. Similarly on p. 61: "The conclusion has, for example, been drawn that this old proverbial wisdom was still scarcely touched by Yahwism and that it was still only at the very beginning of a process of interpretation by Yahwism. Against this, it can be categorically stated that for Israel there was only one world of experience and that this was apperceived by means of a perceptive apparatus in which rational perceptions and religious perceptions were not differentiated. Nor was this any different in the case of the prophets." These words are not to be seen as inconsistent with von Rad's view of the transition in Hebrew mentality from the old "pan-sacralism" to the "worldly" sphere; as von Rad says, "all the events lay in Yahweh's hands" (p. 59). However, the validity of von Rad's sweeping claims about the effect of the Solomonic "Enlightenment" upon the pan-sacralism can be questioned.

[22] *Proverbs* (Philadelphia: Westminster, 1970) 17.

[23] See n. 6 above and also R. E. Murphy, "Wisdom and Yahwism," cited in n. 4.

# OBSERVATIONS ON THE CREATION THEOLOGY
# IN WISDOM

HANS-JÜRGEN HERMISSON

THE UNIVERSITY OF BONN, 53 BONN, GERMANY

Translated by Barbara Howard, Dallas, Texas 75080

My greeting honors Samuel Terrien, Old Testament scholar and teacher, whose commentary on Job has especially impressed me, through its theological reflection, its richness of ideas, and its careful treatment of the text—which is especially required in wisdom texts!

T HE wisdom of the Old Testament stays quite determinedly within the horizon of creation. Its theology is creation theology."[1] These two sentences by Walther Zimmerli formulate in an almost classical way a generally accepted conviction. However, anyone who sets out consequently to look for the theology of creation in the "proper" wisdom writings will arrive at a result which is disappointing at first. Among the numerous proverbs of the older proverbial wisdom he will find a small number in which Yahweh is named as creator of the poor and the rich, of eye and ear, and even of the culprit.[2] He will find a few remarks by Ecclesiastes about the work of God, which is opaque to man;[3] and even the great poem on wisdom in Proverbs 8, the central section of which (8:22-31) lists the events of creation somewhat broadly, does not want to speak in the first place about the creation of the world, but about the creation of wisdom *before* the world and about wisdom's resulting superiority (so, too, Sirach 24). Prov 3:19-20 also has been formulated in the interest of wisdom: it was through wisdom that Yahweh founded the earth, and thus the significance of wisdom is stressed again. Things look different in the Book of Job, particularly in the hymnic passages, which are probably secondary,[4] and above all in the concluding speeches of God (Job 38-41); but of this, more later. Lastly, the hymnic praise of the God of creation takes up ample space in Jesus ben Sira,[5] and beyond that the subject of creation is a basic theme of his theology.[6] However, Jesus ben Sira's book is a late fruit of OT wisdom, and one with which someone wanting to speak about Israel's wisdom will hardly begin.

Someone glancing thus at the evidence might further gain the impression that here one is dealing only with the much discussed phenomenon of a supposedly late theologizing of an originally quite secular wisdom. But as Gerhard von Rad has already shown,[7] this is not so; rather that which becomes the explicit theme only in late texts has long been implicitly presupposed in the older wisdom. Therefore the two sentences by Zimmerli quoted in the beginning are indeed right. But it is not unimportant to see that Zimmerli gives a negative rather than a positive reason for this statement: the God of *Israel* is nowhere mentioned in the older wisdom literature, and this gap is then filled "occasionally" by predication of the creator.[8] This presents an important problem of wisdom theology which will have to be discussed again briefly at the end. But before we can ask about wisdom in OT theology, we first have to ask about the place of creation theology in wisdom. If the topic of creation has been at least presupposed from the beginning, and later made explicit, then one must be able to say what significance it has for wisdom and whether in functioning thus it also has to take a special form. The main part of this study is devoted to the second question, the question about significance may be briefly presented first.

I

As is well known, wisdom searches for the knowledge of order, or, for those to whom this seems too rigid, for a certain regularity within the diversity of the phenomena of the world. This world, however, is *unitary*. Although for us it may customarily divide into nature, regulated by (seemingly firm) natural laws, and history, which is more or less contingent, ancient wisdom starts from the conviction that the regularities within the human and the historical-social realm are not in principle different from the ones within the realm of nonhuman phenomena.[9] Therefore "nature wisdom" and "culture wisdom" are not as far apart as it may seem at first. Knowledge of the world and the education of man belong together. The endeavor to recognize the regularities in this unitary world is the appropriate context for wisdom to ask about creation,[10] for it involves the actual correspondence between the created world and the knowledge of it, and, therefore, the necessary conditions for proper knowing *and* for proper conduct (inasmuch as *knowing* [e.g. the good] and the *doing* of it are not already identical!). What God created "in wisdom"[11] can also be comprehended and stated in the sentences of wisdom. There must be correspondence here or there will be no true knowledge. If, for instance, it were at all thinkable that God created the world as chaos—which however is a *contradictio in adjecto!*—any question about regularity would be senseless. "In wisdom" then means more than "not chaotic." It also says something about the intelligibility of the world,[12] and, indeed, for this, the perfect expression was found in Proverbs 8. Here wisdom was personified for the purpose of being able to address man; however, it is the same wisdom which is present in the created world as regularity, purposiveness, and therefore also as beauty. Thus Proverbs 8 talks about creation when it talks about wisdom: about creation with respect to its intelligible orders, to which man is to adapt himself.[13]

II

If the creation theology of wisdom has its place and its special function in the close relationship between an effective knowledge and human education, it has to be expected that it also takes a special form. Now, "theology" is hardly presentable in the form of individual (and originally quite independent) proverbs; therefore, if only on the ground of their conformity to the literary type, one must not expect too much of the older collections of proverbs, and must look for other texts. Still we may begin with a brief glance at the sporadic mention of the creator in Proverbs 10–29.

Four of the seven proverbs in question should be taken in one group. All of them speak about Yahweh's having created the poor as well as the rich, and even the oppressor:

> He who mocks the poor insults his Maker. . . . (17:5)

> He who oppresses a poor man insults his Maker,
> but he who is kind to the needy honors him. (14:31)

> The rich and the poor meet together;
> the Lord is the maker of them all. (22:2)

> The poor man and the oppressor meet together;
> the Lord gives light to the eyes of both. (29:13)[14]

As one can easily see, these proverbs form two pairs, the second member of which varies a previously formulated insight; thus, 17:5 is probably the original version over against 14:31 (correspondence of verbs!). But what do such proverbs say? Taken by themselves, they are ambiguous; but in the context of wisdom this wide scope of usage and meaning can be discerned more precisely. One should not understand them as the expression of a social order stabilized by a creation ideology, for it is a misinterpretation of wisdom if it is credited with the stabilizing of an unchangeably rigid order.[15] Wisdom is much more reserved: it does not even try to *understand* the phenomenon of poverty, but it says that the poor are to be respected. One could apply wisdom sentences and ask: Is it not his own fault—through lack of wisdom, through laziness, etc.? No, says wisdom, even with his poverty the poor man is God's creature; therefore, whoever mocks the poor man insults his creator. The variant text (14:31) goes a step further by implicitly warning not to oppress the poor man but to have mercy upon the needy. The sentence about the poor man and the oppressor seems to be the most scandalous: is this said out of cynicism or resignation in the face of reality? Perhaps it is indicative that creation is not explicitly mentioned here. "The Lord gives light to their eyes" does mean the granting of existence, to be sure, but it also signifies the dependence and limitation of the oppressor—certainly not his justification.

The "ethical world order" has been portrayed much more satisfactorily in the following proverb:

> The Lord has made everything for its purpose,
> even the wicked for the day of trouble. (16:4)

This may already be an apologetic in view of the question why in a meaningfully arranged world there is also evil, there is the wicked. However in the world of the old wisdom it certainly is a satisfying answer, not an expedient one. The boundaries are only starting to become visible: the Lord has made *everything* for its purpose. This is the principle, the rule, and the proverb goes only one step further: not even an element as disturbing as the oppressor is an exception. Creation is the basis not only of regularity, but of a meaningful and satisfactory order of events in the world, a purposefulness of created beings and things.

It would seem that the following proverb was also conceived from the idea of right fulfillment of purposes, of ordered functions:

> A just balance and scales are the Lord's
> all the weights in the bag are his work. (16:11)

The sentence also has an ethical implication (the implicit admonition to commercial honesty) and thus corresponds to Prov 11:1 ("False balance— abomination to the Lord . . ."). But here again the proof of a meaningfully functioning individual order in Yahweh's (creation-) work has priority. Therefore one could have formulated it: Who falsifies the balance offends against an order of corporate human life which was established and guaranteed by the creator. This formulation has not been made, at least not in the tradition passed on to us, because it was naturally presupposed and, certainly specified in a proverb like this one—*sapienti sat.*

The final saying once again deals with the aboriginal business of wisdom, with knowledge:

> The hearing ear and the seeing eye,
> the Lord has made them both. (20:12)

Applied to the individual and his participation in knowing, this means something like predestination:[16] only those can hear and see to whom it is granted by Yahweh. Principally it means—and this will be placed in the foreground here—the ability to know is not an autonomous quality of man, but it is just as much Yahweh's creation as the world which he made in its regularities. For this very reason, however, knowing is possible at all; for the same creator created the "world" and the organs of cognition adequate to it.

The texts which we have viewed so far thus confirm at first only the image of Yahweh's creative activity as the foundation of the orders of the world: meaningful and rational orders, and also at the borderline of cognition, a knowing which itself was created by Yahweh and thus properly associates with the orders and "functions." One can add that such activity of the creator

obviously persists. Creation did not only happen at the beginning of the
world, but takes place continuously; therefore, the orders have not become
rigid, but necessarily remain flexible. If "activity of the creator" is understood
in this broad sense (or if Yahweh is principally understood as the creator), one
can probably refer to further sayings; however, this does not alter the fact of
the relative scarcity of such statements. Certainly the wise were far from
explicitly seasoning their moral teachings each time by referring to the orders
of creation.[17] Finally it can be observed that the sentences pointing to the
creator in the older part of the Book of Proverbs generally deal with the
creation of man, with human situations, or matters within man's sphere of
activity. This, however, is not to be evaluated in the sense of a fundamental
differentiation between man and nature (and correspondingly of natural
wisdom and cultural wisdom), but it simply serves a purpose, since knowledge
of the conditions of the world has to guide human behavior directly. For this
there are, of course, more immediate and more remote objects of knowledge.
But if we are searching for statements in which the broader connection
between moral teaching and creation stands out more clearly, we will be
forced to leave the area of short proverbs and look for wisdom texts which
speak directly and pointedly about creation.

### III

Apart from that late and mature product of Israelite creation theology,
which appears in Genesis 1 as a didactic, historical tale, Israel spoke about
Yahweh's creation activity above all in hymnic praise. There is at least one
hymn which was definitely composed in the handwriting of wisdom: Psalm
104.[18] As is well known, the psalm begins with the heavenly activities of the
creator God (vss. 1-4), moves from there to the foundation of the earth
through the expulsion of the original floods (vss. 5-9), continues with the life-
giving irrigation of the earth through brooks and rain (vss. 10-12 + 13-18) and
links with this the placement of plants and animals within their environment
(esp. vss. 11-12 + 16-18). Vss. 19-23 then deal with the coordination of the
creatures with their times—night and day. Vss. 24-26—after an exclamation
of astonishment at the multitude of Yahweh's works—occupy themselves
once again with the sea and its inhabitants, and vss. 27-30 finally describe the
permanent dependence of all life upon Yahweh's creative activity, until the
hymnic coda (*Abgesang*) concludes the entire psalm (vss. 31-35).[19]

What reminds one of wisdom in this psalm? Whoever is only looking for
the vocabulary, may be comforted by *ḥokmâ* in the central and all-
encompassing vs. 24. But actually there is much more. If one first examines
the middle section of the psalm in that regard, it seems to offer a perfect
example of that "nature wisdom" which is described in 1 Kgs 5:13 (Engl. 4:33)
as Solomon's special skill,[20] although here not in a style of sober statement,
but of hymnic usage. If "Solomon" made proverbs "from the cedar that is in
Lebanon to the hyssop that grows out of the wall" (1 Kgs 5:13), one may find

in the psalm the same assignment of beings to their local and temporal realms: the badger to the rocks, the stork to the cedar trees, the lion to the night, and man and his work to the day. Naturally, then, there is more here than the mere compilation of creatures and environments. The meaningfulness of such coordination becomes evident, too: in this world and its manifold spaces everything is well arranged ecologically. There is even more: everything fulfils its purpose in this world, as is shown especially by the statements about the beneficial effects of water from springs and from Yahweh's heavenly chambers. Ps 104:13-15 may be read as a perfect example of a whole chain of consecutive purposes. This points to man again, just as vs. 23 also is directed to the time of man. It corresponds indeed with the often noted "anthropocentric" character of wisdom, however in such a way that man is introduced without strain into a wonderfully ordered world—a world which moreover does not only exist for the sake of man, but in which everything has a meaning—even such a bizarre creature as Leviathan out there in the distant ocean whom God created as his toy.[21] A world thus meaningfully ordered in all its parts is beautiful in the eyes of the Hebrews—beautiful in its intelligible functioning. Thus the form of the creation statement corresponds thoroughly with the declaration by Ecclesiastes: "He has made everything beautiful in its time (*yāpeh bĕ'ittô*)" (Qoh 3:11), although not with his following statement about the works of God being indiscernible; for to the poet of Psalm 104, as well as to the old wisdom, the world as creation is intelligible enough.

Only in passing let me point to the well-known relationship between Psalm 104 and the Egyptian solar hymnody (especially from the Amarna Age).[22] Here too "wisdom" recommends itself as the place of tradition and as the place for taking over features of foreign culture.[23] Now and again the relationship between the psalm and the "catalogue science" of the onomostica (passed on in Egypt and Mesopotamia and probably to be presupposed in Israel) has been pointed out.[24] In this also a relation to wisdom would come into play. However, some reserve is advisable here: in any case the psalm is not interested in a *successive* order of things, and, with the exception of the widespaced movement from heaven to earth, the phenomena seem to be listed more by random association than with a side-glance at a catalogue of things. (For instance, the poet goes from mentioning the rain, to the cedars of Lebanon, and from there, on the one hand, to the birds nesting in them, and, on the other hand, to the mountain animals, etc.)

The poet of Proverbs had formulated, "The Lord has made everything for its purpose. . . ." (16:4). Is not Psalm 104 the comprehensive presentation of such a wisdom concept of creation? The meaningful, purposeful ordering of things and spaces and creatures first reaches its goal indeed in the hymnic form of presentation, for in it the ordered world appears as the result of a continuous devotion of the creator to his creation. Here, too, then we find the continuation of Yahweh's creative activity which we encountered already in Proverbs.

But this does not apply to all parts of the psalm. In two places the style shows obvious deviations from this psalm's mode of expression, which uses mostly participial and imperfect constructions. We are referring to the two verbs in the perfect in vs. 5 and vs. 19, each of which introduces a new paragraph: "He has founded the earth. . ."and "He has made the moon. . . ." Although it is customary to adapt the two verbs to the style of the context and read them as participles,[25] this is hardly right. For obviously the poet wants to speak here about the basic data of the past: the environment of earth, like the changing of festival times and the times of the day, has been created by Yahweh once, and once and for all, and this work continues in existence even where Yahweh "hides his face" (vs. 29): He renews the face of the ground (vs. 30), but he does not have to found it anew.

This becomes especially clear through the example of the earth. The poet uses here the old mythical motive of the chaos struggle—a noticeably adapted, tamed version, but that is not the point here. Yahweh rebuked and let his voice of thunder sound: then the waters fled and mountains and valleys appeared.[26] What is decisive, however, is the continuation in vs. 9. The original chaotic sea can never return, for Yahweh excluded it from the world once and for all. He has set a boundary which the chaotic original waters can never again transgress. This corresponds with the statement that Yahweh gave the earth such a firm foundation that it can never be shaken again (vs. 5). And this way of talking about a basic datum of the creator's activity that is altogether past, so that the "chaos" (in the form of those original floods) remains completely outside the world, seems to be a creation-concept typical of wisdom. In order to make this clear, it is necessary for us to cast a side glance at creation statements of a different kind, for in this respect one must not measure Psalm 104 against the very well known model of Genesis 1, but must compare it with texts which start from the confrontation of creation and chaos.

## IV

These texts are first of all separate passages within larger complexes. A nice example may be found in the hymnic part of the royal lamentation, Psalm 89:

> Thou dost rule the raging of the sea;
>> when its waves rise, thou stillest them.
> Thou didst crush Rahab like a carcass,
>> thou didst scatter thy enemies with thy mighty arm.
> The heavens are thine, the earth also is thine;
>> the world and all that is in it, thou hast founded them.
> The north and the south, thou hast created them;
>> Tabor and Hermon joyously praise thy name.
> Thou hast a mighty arm;
>> strong is thy hand, high thy right hand.
>> (Ps 89:10-14; Engl. 9-13)

This form of the creation statement is already significant. Here, too, the chaos struggle is mentioned in connection with creation—in fact *also* as an event of the past—and here for good reason the stronger mythological image of the chaos dragon, "Rahab" (vs. 11) is used. But the matter does not rest with this event of the past. It certainly is the *fundamental* happening in the strict sense of the word—at that time Yahweh made the foundation of the earth. But there remains the sea, and the necessity that the creator display his power against the raging of the sea (vs. 9). Not without reason does the poet also praise Yahweh's mighty arm (vs. 13): the created world needs it because of the resistance of the chaotic. This is still clearer in Psalm 93, as a few sentences from it may show:

> The Lord has become king; he has put on majesty;
> . . . he has girded himself with strength.
> The world also is established;
> so it cannot be moved;
> Thy throne is established from of old;
> thou art from everlasting.
> The floods have lifted up, O Lord,
> the floods have lifted up their voice,
> (again) the floods lift up their roaring.
> Mightier than the thunders of many waters . . .
> the Lord on high is mighty!

We find here traits already known. That deed of the past, the conquering of the chaotic original flood, is mentioned again. But in this psalm something else stands in the foreground, namely, Yahweh's present creative activity as experienced at the festival. Therefore, creation is perceived here not primarily as a distant past, but as an event which is presently repeating itself. For *now* the earth would be threatened, would be in danger of sinking back into chaos—if Yahweh had not become king, that is, if he had not proven himself as the one he has been since primeval time, as the one he proved to be then, in the beginning, the sovereign king.[27]

Now someone may say that the chaos struggle in these texts is "nothing but" poetic imagery, and, besides, has lost its vividness more or less. That there is this tendency is certainly correct; only, what is gained by it? Hardly a particular superiority for Israel, for spiritualization and the use of myth as image were found also in the surrounding religions. Israel's peculiarity, Yahweh's superiority, consisted in the fact that Yahweh was *mēᶜôlām*, eternal—he had not come into existence—and through this Israel was confronted with its own theological problems, which cannot be discussed here. However, one has to recognize the metaphorical importance of the sea insofar as it concerns not only the chaotic waters around the world but also the powers of chaos within the world. For the community assembled at Zion and singing this psalm is indeed threatened in different ways by the chaotic.

This ever present evidence of the creative power, the *creatio continua* (or rather, *continuata*) through which the world has to become the world again and again, could be documented by a number of further texts.[28] Instead, we shall look at the other comparable motif. Ps 104:5 reads:

> He has set the earth on its foundations,[29]
> so that it should never be shaken.

It is not shaken (*bal-timmôṭ*). The same thing seems to be said in Ps 93:1, as well as in 96:10. But it is not the same, for there the certainty over the unshakable earth stands in the immediate context of the renewed proof of Yahweh's sovereign power; according to Psalm 104, however, the stabilizing occurred once for all time. Psalm 93 then can speak at best indirectly about the earth's being unshakable "forever," that is, only with regard to the unshakable throne of Yahweh, whose kingship guarantees the duration of the earth even now, as in the future. But this certainty by no means excludes for this community the experience—at a different time—of the earth's shaking. In distress from an enemy (Ps 60:4), or when law and justice are lacking on earth, then the foundations of the earth shake (Ps 82:5).

These remarks must suffice here. The difference between these creation statements and those in Psalm 104 should have become sufficiently clear, for the differences are especially visible in portions which are otherwise similar. These psalms of the Jerusalem cult reflect the experience of a world which time and again is kept away from chaos by Yahweh's superior creative power. In the creation hymn conceived by wisdom, on the other hand, there is the conviction that chaos was eliminated fundamentally from this world at one time. Chaos is located temporally at a great distance, before the beginning of the world, or, spatially, outside the boundaries of the world. As one can easily see, this is presupposed in the statements in Ps 104:10-26, just as it is presupposed in wisdom's cognition of the world. One might argue the point whether this view of creation belongs specifically to wisdom, but this question may be left open until further texts have been studied.

## V

Such a radiant view of the created world as is presented in Psalm 104 is certainly not without problems in the face of reality. But one must not scold the poet for being a dreamer, a hopeless advocate of a world intact. With all of ancient Israel he knew how to distinguish between a time to praise and a time to weep. And he composed his hymn with the modesty of a wisdom which, being well aware of its limits, knows how to enjoy within these limits the beauty of the world in its rationally transparent functioning. It is only at the edges of this world that the enigmas of existence, that which is unintelligible, appears. Among these enigmas is not that Yahweh hides his face, or that he makes all life return to dust (vs. 29); for the rhythm of becoming and passing away belongs to the order of the created world. But it is different in vs. 32, when Yahweh makes the earth tremble and the mountains smoke. And finally, the concluding pleas of the psalm reveals that in this well ordered world there is still the disturbing element of the wicked, the sinner (Ps 104:35). This is a dark tone in the otherwise bright picture. One can find here the first traces of a later quite evident fact: that wisdom found itself confronted by the problem of theodicy by having excluded chaos once and for all from creation. But, as has been said, this problem appears at the very periphery here; the boundaries of knowledge and existence are insignificant in comparison with the intelligibility of the world.

The picture becomes different already in our second major text, the speeches of God in the Book of Job (Job 38–41). To be sure, they, too, presuppose and describe a world well ordered in all of its parts; only here a basically different note is to be heard. A human being, Job, the suffering one, is unable to discern such a world. In the context of the Book of Job, this is not yet the utterly devastating insight it became later for Ecclesiastes, for the suffering person is taken up by a primal trust which is prior to all rational understanding.[30] For the good order which the creator gave to the world is not limited by man's not understanding it. What is hidden from him are the origins, the inter-relations, the background; but there remains his amazement at that which lies before him as the result of the wise creator's activity.

That these speeches of God in the Book of Job are also a piece of wisdom literature is hardly to be disputed. Obviously, they stand in the vicinity of "catalogue science."[31] Moreover, the form of speech may be related to the standard questions of Egyptian wisdom teachers,[32] or it may be compared to the "disputation of the wise."[33] In composing these speeches the poet seems to have made use largely of the wisdom tradition. This tradition is functionally adapted to the present context, through the questioning, imperative address to Job, but it is conspicuous that Job's own problems appear only in the outer frame of God's speeches. This may be intentional, so we do not mean to imply that the author of Job did not compose God's speeches himself. However, he was not free in his composition, but was bound by tradition.

In this context of mostly wisdom thought, again we come across the motif of the sea, and here again—let us state our conclusion at the outset—in the beginning and once and for all the sea is confined to its limits by Yahweh's commanding word—he does not need to rebuke any more!

> Thus far shall you come, and no farther,
> and here shall your proud waves be stayed. (38:11)

Or, again, bars and doors have been set for the sea (38:8, 10).[34] There is no question any more of a struggle,[35] and the previously described foundation of the earth seems to be something independent of the limitation of the sea.[36] Giving precedence to the earth certainly accords with its importance within the whole of creation; but it is striking that the primeval ocean does not need to be removed first. The sea is "born" (vs. 8), and it still has some traits of that primeval sea—above all the "pride" (gāʾôn) of its waves—but it no longer comes into play; it is shut out from birth on. Now apparently the description here is consciously kept ambiguous: as the chaotic sea it is locked out by gates and bars; but at the same time it appears as the infant for whom Yahweh provides swaddling clothes, and under this metaphor it is even less conceivable as an adversary.[37] On the other hand the sea appears visibly as part of the earth, and is again limited concretely by the coastlines. But in such a context there is no longer anything threatening about the sea; therefore, it is not suitable as a metaphor of the chaotic powers of the world, as they were expressed in those very different creation texts referring to the primordial floods.

From this point we shall glance briefly at a third testimony to a strict limitation of the sea, namely Jer 5:22. This text is found not in a Jeremian context, but in a context of wisdom (vss. 20-25), as is shown by the didactic introduction of the speech (certainly adapted to prophetic forms of speech), the address to the audience (readers) as "stubborn people" ($^{c}am\ s\bar{a}k\bar{a}l$), and the comparison between the order of nature and the order of man. It is stated in a speech of Yahweh:

> Do you not fear me? says the Lord;
>   Do you not tremble before me?
> I placed the sand as the bound for the sea,
>   a perpetual barrier which it cannot pass;
> though the waves toss, they cannot prevail,
>   though they roar, they cannot pass over it. (Jer 5:22)

This at first looks very much like a comparison in which the earthly sea is used as a motif of contrast. This is undoubtedly the case, but in the allusion to the fury of the waves and to the "eternal order" one can hear something of a double meaning in the barring of the chaotic sea from the world once and for all. What actually disturbs the order of the world is not an evil power, but rather human beings and their wicked actions. These are the addressees in Jer 5:22. Similarly, in Job 38:13, 15, and in Ps 104:35 the addressees are the wicked and sinners.

## VI

The world well-ordered, chaos excluded, the world therefore comprehensible within limits: this fits very well with the concepts of wisdom. We had raised the question whether the motif of the final limitation of the chaotic flood is a notion peculiar to wisdom. We may state now that in the OT at least it occurs only in wisdom contexts,[38] and that it fits them excellently. We are not dealing with a *quisquiliae* concerning the origin of the world, but with a basic statement which determines how man is to understand himself in his world. This became clear in connection with the hymnic statements of the festival cult, where the presence of the creator God is experienced in quite a different way, namely, as the creator's impulsive-dynamic penetration in his world, thus suppressing chaos in a constantly renewed proof of his sovereign power, and stabilizing the shaking earth. There Yahweh must be present to his world in the highest degree as the creator, while in the creation texts of wisdom the creator's activity is directed more toward continuation, toward perseverance, the maintenance of order and regularity. In this way, however, the creator God remained at a greater distance. Certainly this difference between cult and wisdom involved the difference between times of festivity and those of everyday life. Therefore, the two concepts do not have to be completely separated. Yet they lead to very different views of the world, each with its own theological problems. As far as the problems in wisdom's concept of the world are concerned, they have already been mentioned in reference to the wicked and to the real suffering in the world. Actually there is no room for either in this concept. Let us return to the Book of Job: Is the distant and unintelligible activity of the divine creator—beneficial as it is for the whole— an answer to Job's question? It is only part of the answer. The supplementary part, however, appears in a motif alien to wisdom and yet interestingly enough adopted by it, namely, the theophany of Yahweh, the unmediated turning of the distant creator God to the suffering person, who through this turning regains trust and finds healing in his suffering. But as Ecclesiastes, for example, might indicate, not all wisdom managed to resolve the perplexity over the good order and the incomprehensibility of the world and the aloofness of the creator God.

## VII

We have attempted to comprehend something of the creation theology in selected wisdom texts and its fundamental significance for wisdom's perspective and its understanding of man and the world. The texts we have treated represent a small sample, which should be followed by a treatment of the comprehensive concepts of Proverbs 8 or Jesus ben Sira. What has been described here, of course, was never anything like a dogma of wisdom, which each sage had to recite when asked about creation. It was an attempt by wisdom to orient itself to the world, to give an explanation for that which one experienced in the world as wholesome order, and which could be recognized and named. In this the motif of the chaotic floods and their limitation was naturally not compulsory—it appears much too seldom and in too varied a form—but it was suitable, especially in a world which was able to understand itself in very different ways with the aid of mythical metaphors. For the important question is not whether Israel took over mythical material, but rather how in each case such adopted mythical elements were employed. On the basis of its traditions, wisdom incorporated the myth of the chaos struggle in thorough accordance with Yahwistic faith, that is, in such a way that every dualistic overtone was excluded.[39] But it then found itself confronted by problems which in the long run it could not solve by itself. This was connected finally with its universalism—the reverse side of that characteristic noted with W. Zimmerli at the outset, namely, that wisdom was unable to say anything about Israel and the "covenant," nothing that is about the particular, unique relationship of God to his people. It is in such particularity—and still the particularity of the celebrating community gathered at Zion—that God's relationship to the world and to humanity could become concrete and be immediately experienced. The author of Job still knew this when he told of the creator God, who was present to the creation but scarcely to the individual, encountering the individual sufferer in a theophany. If on the other hand, in the scepticism of wisdom, the aloofness of the universal creator God became an unbearable problem, the identification of wisdom and Torah—most clearly in Jesus ben Sira—was one possible answer to the problem. The other answer—if in conclusion, with a great leap, the comprehensive theological context should at least be indicated—was the foolishness of the cross, as God's wisdom (1 Cor 1:17-18), whereby God came to man. Not that the ancient creation theology of wisdom became invalid and obsolete; rather it was only in this way that it could be maintained.

[1] W. Zimmerli, "Ort und Grenze der Weisheit im Rahmen der alttestamentlichen Theologie," *Gottes Offenbarung. Gesammelte Aufsätze zum Alten Testament* (TBü 19; Munich: Kaiser, 1963) 302.

[2] Prov 14:31; 17:5; 22:2; 29:13; 20:12; 16:4; 16:11.

[3] E.g., Qoh 3:11, 14; 7:14-15; 30; 8:17; 11:5.

[4] Job 9:5-10; 26:5-14.

[5] Sir 16:26-30 + 17:1-13; 39:12-35; 42:15-43:33; cf. 18:1-6.

[6] Cf., E.g., Sir 36:7-15.

[7] G. von Rad, *Wisdom in Israel* (New York and Nashville: Abingdon, 1972) 153-55.

[8] W. Zimmerli, "Ort und Grenze . . .," 302.

[9] Cf. H.-J. Hermisson, *Studien zur israelitischen Spruchweisheit* (WMANT 28; Neukirchen-Vluyn: Neukirchener Verlag, 1968) 140-41, 149-51.

[10] When J. Crenshaw, in his useful discussion of creation theology of wisdom, begins with the problem of retribution and divine righteousness (*Studies in Ancient Israelite Wisdom* [New York: Ktav, 1976] 26), then this is rather a special case of the general question concerning the establishment of the orders of the world. Indeed, this special case seems rather to be an accident with respect to the fundamental concept of wisdom, the exception by which wisdom pushes against its boundaries, boundaries which it can accept because the space within them is wide enough. Nevertheless, Crenshaw is right to stress that where the problems emerge, creation faith is also expounded explicitly (p. 34). It is questionable to me whether this happens there *only* and *first*, if, as Crenshaw rightly concludes, "the orderliness of creation" is "the fundamental premise" of wisdom's striving toward understanding (p. 33). On this question, see below.

[11] Prov 3:19; Ps 104:24.

[12] Cf. also Crenshaw, *Studies*, p. 34: "Creation . . . assures . . . that the universe is comprehensible."

[13] For particulars, see, G. von Rad, *Wisdom*, 144-76.

[14] The RSV is used for biblical quotations except for Ps 104:5 (see note 29) and Ps 93:1, 3. [Ed.].

[15] That this had already been done in old Israel is not inconceivable, but it remained in that case a misuse. To be sure, this proverbial wisdom developed no revolutionary pathos.

[16] Cf. Ptahhotep 545-46 (pap. Prisse 16, 6-7) in Zbyněk Žába, *Les Maximes de Ptahhotep* (Prag: Editions de l'Académie Tchécoslovaque des Science, 1956).

[17] Cf. Zimmerli's scepticism of 1933 concerning such a grounding of wisdom instructions, and further concerning the relation of the standard of human conduct to Yahweh's work as creator ("Zur Struktur der alttestamentlichen Weisheit," *ZAW* 51 [1933] 177-204). However, in his recent article (see note 1, above), Zimmerli has revoked in part the more far-reaching conclusions.

[18] The question may be answered briefly as to why this psalm appears to be an example of wisdom, even though R. Murphy, in his important and illuminating essay on the subject ("A Consideration of the Classification 'Wisdom Psalms,'" *Congress Volume, Bonn 1962*; VTSup 9 [1963] 156-67) does not place it among the wisdom psalms. Murphy is concerned with the *Gattung* wisdom psalm, and Psalm 104 cannot be spoken of in this category, since it is clearly a hymn (of an individual). But it will be shown in what follows how far this hymn exhibits characteristics of wisdom. In this connection there is a fundamental observation to be made concerning the demarcation of "wisdom." It is advisable to proceed from a central core as it is encountered literarily in Proverbs, and then move to further wisdom books like Ecclesiastes, Jesus ben Sira, and also Job (in part). The literary deposit is then to be related to its historic circle of transmission, most probably in my opinion a circle of the wise which was associated with the formation of an educated class (I see no reason to abandon my previous model). However, no historical phenomenon is to be understood simplistically. Even such a thing as a "central core" is only a historical abstraction. This means on the one hand that the "Wise" were more than merely "wise," and on the other that a narrow restriction to such a "core" would be unhistorical, since this core does not exist in splendid isolation. In sum, the question of terminology is, in the last analysis, only a vexing one. Therefore I think it a historically correct proceeding to look carefully for the conceptions of wisdom mentality (and their linguistic expression, but indeed not only in proverbs nor alone in a fixed vocabulary)—certainly, starting with this abstracted core, as well as with its non-Israelite context, and then proceeding to further texts in which these conceptions are also found, perhaps even in their finished form. Then one may speak of an "intellectual tradition." Still, this phrase of Whybray's seems to me too wide-ranging, while the concept of wisdom/*ḥokmâ* is sufficiently flexible on the one hand and more specific on the other.

[19] On the structure and some details, see H.-J. Kraus, *Die Psalmen* (BKAT 15/2; Neukirchen-Vluyn: Neukirchener Verlag, 1960) 708-15.

[20] On this, see, A. Alt, "Die Weisheit Salomos" (1951), in *Kleine Schriften* (3 vols.; Munich: Beck, 1953) 2. 90-99.

[21] Surely the mythical prehistory of Leviathan stands in the background, but it is essentially superceded here, significant only insofar as the "giant's toy" indicates the superior greatness of its creator (!).

[22] On this, see especially J. Assmann, *Ägyptische Hymnen und Gebete* (Die Bibliothek der alten Welt/Der alte Orient; Zurich and Munich: Artemis, 1975) esp. 209-25.

[23] See also G. von Rad, "The Theological Problem of the Old Testament Doctrine of Creation" (1936), in *The Problem of the Hexateuch and Other Essays* (New York: McGraw-Hill, 1966) 131-43.

[24] Cf. H.-J. Kraus, *Psalmen*, 712, and G. Fohrer, *Das Buch Hiob* (KAT 16; Gütersloh: Mohn, 1963) 497.

[25] See, e.g., Kraus, *Psalmen*, 708.

[26] I prefer this interpretation of vs. 8 to the one defended mostly today (in which the water is taken as subject to the verbs in vs. 8a), because the verb *ysd* could hardly be construed as applying to the waters or to their "place" (*maqôm*). *Ysd* means "to found, to ground"; it is a technical term of building, which suits the earth and the mountains (with their valleys) very well. Hab 1:12 does not provide contrary evidence. The meaning conveyed by *ysd* there is suggested by the metaphorical use of *ṣûr* (rock). ("Rock" is to join with *ysd*—"as a rock . . ."; see, J. Jeremias, *Kultprophetie und Gerichtsverkündigung in der späten Königszeit* (WMANT 35; Neukirchen-Vluyn: Neukirchener Verlag, 1970) 101, n. Contrast W. Rudolph (*Micha – Nahum – Habakuk – Zephanja* [KAT 13/3; Gütersloh, Mohn, 1975]) who, however, must opt for the translation "*my* Rock." The disturbance of the context is only an apparent problem: an interjected idea of this kind is quite inappropriate. The work of E. F. Sutcliffe ("A Note on Psalm CIV 8," *VT* 2 [1952] 177-79), according to which the poet refers to springs in the mountains, would also result in an

interjected idea. Finally, one must not be disturbed with the seemingly twisted logic (the mountains already exist in vs. 6 but are just taking shape here). The verse is conceived with respect to the vivid picture of the waters which are flowing away: then mountains and valleys first "become" real (in the observer's view), and this indeed comes to pass *at* the place (ʾ*el* as a "pregnant construction" may mean here "(coming into existence) *towards* . . ."; cf. *KB²*, ʾ*el* no. 9, pp. 48-49) which Yahweh had founded for them.

[27] I shall not enter here into the debate over festival theories because it is irrelevant to our present question. It is thus a matter of indifference as to when this psalm was sung in the cult, whether annually in the harvest festival, etc. Also the debate over the translation of *mlk*, whether "be king" or "become king," does not lead one step further. If *mlk* means "be king," one must translate: Yahweh is *now* king, displays his royal power now, shows himself to be who he is: the point is the actual experience of the kingship of Yahweh.

[28] See Ps 65:6-8, esp. vs. 8; also Hab 3:8-11, or Nah 1:4, in connection with depictions of theophany.

[29] "He," following MT.

[30] The questions to Job concern only partly his ability to imitate the divine work, but much more his insight into the coherences, the whence and whither of things.

[31] Cf. G. von Rad, "Job XXXVIII and Ancient Egyptian Wisdom" (1955), in *The Problem of the Hexateuch and Other Essays*, 281-91.

[32] Cf. ibid.

[33] Cf. Fohrer, *Hiob*, pp. 496-98, and the further account of the characteristics of wisdom given there, e.g. in vocabulary.

[34] On this, see S. Terrien, *Job* (CAT 13; Neuchâtel: Delachaux et Niestlé, 1963) 249, n. 2 (and p. 86 with n. 2). He indicates that the bounding of the sea is a motif borrowed from the creation epic, *enuma eliš*; "but it has been adapted to a theology of omnipotence"!

[35] See Terrien, *Job*, 249.

[36] On this, see the important conclusions of Terrien (*Job*, 248-49). He emphasizes among other things that these expressions of creation, whose objective is the human environment, permit no allusion to the myth of a chaos battle. "The description of the creation of the world does not permit one's thinking that the forces of evil have escaped from the creator's reach" (p. 248). Where borrowing from the myth is found, the original dualism is eliminated (p. 249). This holds true, in my judgment, especially for the wisdom view of things, and then naturally for the Priestly source of the Pentateuch, whose characteristic conception has possibly, though not necessarily, adopted elements of wisdom.

[37] One should not press these shifting expressions so as to ask, for example, why a bar was necessary for a helpless infant.

[38] Genesis 1, with its especially complex conception is being disregarded here. On this, see O. H. Steck, *Der Schöpfungsbericht der Priesterschrift* (FRLANT 115; Göttingen: Vandenhoeck & Ruprecht, 1975). For the Priestly writing creation concludes with the seven days, and one cannot speak at all of a continuing creation by Yahweh. Cf. also W. H. Schmidt, *Die Schöpfungsgeschichte der Priesterschrift* (WMANT 17; 3d ed.; Neukirchen-Vluyn: Neukirchener Verlag, 1974).

[39] See, S. Terrien, *Job*, 249.

# THE UNFILLED SEA: STYLE AND MEANING IN ECCLESIASTES 1:2-11

EDWIN M. GOOD
STANFORD UNIVERSITY, STANFORD, CALIFORNIA 94305

THERE are fundamentally two ways of interpreting a text. One is to see it whole, finding the unifying structure, theme, image, or idea that lights up the entirety and gives place and perspective to the parts. The other is to follow the text through its own process, to pursue its linearity in order to uncover the meaning progressively as the text itself presents it. The former way is analogous to viewing a painting, in which the point is to stand back and see the whole. The latter is analogous to listening to a piece of music, which is followed through time, the musical process itself disclosing the meaning. To be sure, a temporal process in viewing a painting leads the eye and the mind from this place to that across the canvas until the whole is seen and comprehended. And in hearing music a concluding reflection may, for some listeners, provide a kind of map of the whole. But the main mode of communication in a painting is non-temporal, for one may receive a sense of it entire on first glance. A musical work *must* be heard through before any sense of its whole is possible. Its relations are relations in time, necessarily non-simultaneous and successive, while those in a painting are best when comprehended simultaneously.

On the whole, I believe, biblical interpreters have operated on the first way of interpreting, seeking out that which unifies a passage or book, looking for structures, unitary messages or ideas. That is not surprising, given the philosophical and theological bias of the cultural context within which we all stand. But I suggest that a linear or temporal (I am tempted to say, musical) mode of approach may elicit from a text something that the unitary or structural one misses. The process of presentation, the methods of discourse, the stylistic devices that carry a poem, a story, an argument along are not mere embellishments, dispensable by a clever interpreter, but are themselves integral elements of meaning.

Take the pithy curse of Gen 9:6, in which a central element of meaning is the sound repetitions and chiasmic word order:

*šōpēk dam hāʾādām | bāʾādām dāmô yiššāpēk*

"Who spills the blood of man, by man his blood will be spilled." One could epitomize this sentence as a statement of the talionic law, remark about the balance of retributive justice involved in it, and point out how the very retribution upon the guilty party is presumably a moral (or at least legal) advance on the more primitive system of family justice, whereby any member of the murderer's tribe might be sacrificed by any member of the murdered person's tribe for satisfaction. Nothing in that interpretation is wrong; it simply misses the point. To begin with, *dam hāʾādām* is spilled, and the very repetition of the syllable *dam* suggests the identity of person and blood. Again, the consequent phrase, by its subtle changes (*bā* for *hā*, but retaining the same vowel pattern, the closer repetition of the syllable *dam* with its attendant changed rhythm, and the eloquent pronominal suffix in *dāmô*), suggests that the retribution is not the identical act to that for which it is justice but involves another *ʾādām* in the act of vengeance, and the spilling of other *dām*, the suffix on that second *dām* harking back to the main vowel of the initial participle, *šōpēk*. Likewise, the intensification of the *šin* in the second verbal member at once connects the act of vengeance with the act of aggression in kind but distinguishes them in tone, the very hissing of *yiššāpēk* proposing something other than mere rational exchange. Thus, the exactly reversed word order of the consequent phrase indicates the correlation of vengeance with aggression, while the slight changes in the consequent indicate the difference between legitimate retribution and illegitimate aggression. Notice, moreover, that the chiasmus delays the completion of the thought until the last possible moment. Until *yiššāpēk* we do not know what the form of retribution may be, although the two reversed repetitions, *bāʾādām* and *dāmô* lead us progressively to think that it will have something to do with *špk* (it is perhaps redundant to remark that the interpreter of any text must at the outset expunge from her mind the assumption that she knows what the text means, on pain of finding nothing new in it).

I want to argue that, however irrefutable, correct, and relevant may be the first interpretation I gave of that couplet, it is drastically incomplete and unsatisfying. The incompleteness stems from its not taking seriously the *way* the sentence goes, not asking why the statement is made in just this way and not in another. One could play with the statement, revise it, change its wording, or word order. For example, one could imagine:

*šōpēk dam hāʾādām | yiššāpēk dāmô bāʾādām.*

The correlation is equally complete, the consequent now being in the same order. Here, however, the meaning emphasizes the correlation of vengeance and aggression, and the question to which the word order gives rise is, "By whom will the blood be spilled?" The element of suspense is the concluding *bāʾādām*, and this arrangement of the sentence emphasizes human, perhaps in distinction from divine, retribution. Or think of another revision:

*šōpēk dam hāʾādām | yišpōk ʾādām dāmô*

In one respect only is this revision preferable to the other revision: that the repetitions of the syllable *dām* in the consequent are closer together and the more significant because of it. But *ʾādām* in the consequent is ambiguous; does it mean any human being, some particular human being, the very human being whose blood was spilled in the antecedent? No sure way of deciding can be found.

The point of this little exercise—not a bad kind of exercise to practise, by the way, if only to remind one of inexorable fallibility—is two-fold. First it suggests that even different word orders propose different meanings. The sense of a sentence is not merely the compilation of lexical equivalents gleaned from Koehler-Baumgartner into some sort of overall thought. Second, it suggests, in this case at least, that the text has it right, that the chiastic word-order with its changes in the consequent is more satisfying as a presentation of the thought than alternative, hypothetical possibilities. By such revisions, one may, in fact, sharpen the perception of what the text actually says, by seeing that other ways of saying what seems to be the same thing are not really the same.

I should like to take such a linear tour through Qoh 1:2-11. Before doing so, however, I should preface the interpretive account with an account of the interpretive method, making clear what sorts of questions I am asking in the interpretation. And if Professor Terrien is irresistibly reminded of young Elihu, whose long introductions make one wish exasperatedly that he would get on to say what he keeps assuring us he is going to say, why, he can take it as any kind of joke he likes.

I take my departure from the theory of affect of Gestalt psychology. That theory, put over-simply, says that affect, or emotion felt, is aroused when a tendency to respond becomes inhibited. A stimulus leads one to expect a particular consequent, hence arouses a tendency to respond. If the expected consequent does not occur, the tendency to respond is inhibited, and affect arises. Subsequently the expected consequent may occur, and the inhibition of the tendency to respond is relieved. One feels satisfied, the affect subsides, and the meaning of the process is perceptible.

I may illustrate this process with an autobiographical example. In response to some stimulus, into which I need not go, I reach into my pocket for a cigarette. No cigarette is there. That arouses affect. If there had been a cigarette, the tendency to respond, namely the expectation of lighting and puffing a cigarette, would not have been inhibited. Finding no cigarettes in my pocket, I go to the drawer where I keep them. They are all gone. The affect not only persists but is heightened. If there had been cigarettes there, the affect aroused by the first absence would have been relieved, the expected consequent would have followed. Now I think, "I shall go to the store and buy some cigarettes." The affect does not immediately subside, for I have not yet achieved the expected consequent, and the delay in its arrival will continue, may even worsen, the affect until I am actually able to light up. Now I think, "it is late on Sunday evening, and all the stores are closed." If you think that realization does not make for affect, then you have never been a smoker.

Notice, in this tragic little vignette, that each step in the series of inhibitions to the tendency to respond raises the level of affect. If the inhibition is never removed, the subject may fall into neurosis, psychosis, or a nicotine fit, for emotion felt is a stage in a process, not a constant state. When I finally get the cigarette, the emotion aroused by the series of inhibitions will at last be removed, and the sense of pleasure will itself be heightened by the level of affect reached, although there may well be a point of diminishing returns, when I have taken all that I can take and in frustration vent rage on any person or object in sight.

I must pause briefly to acknowledge my indebtedness for the basic matter of the two foregoing paragraphs to a remarkable book by Leonard B. Meyer, *Emotion and Meaning in Music.*[1] Meyer uses the theory for analysis of musical works, and, having followed him several times through that enterprise, I realized that it might apply *mutatis mutandis* to the analysis of the literary work as well. The illustration of the smoker is Meyer's too, but, since I am a smoker, it came home to me with existential clarity, and I have felt free to make it autobiographical. In anticipation of the discussion below, I should also say that the three levels of meaning, "hypothetical," "evident," and "determinate," are derived from Meyer.

To apply such a model to the literary work, we hypothesize that something in the work first sets up in the reader a tendency to respond, arouses the expectation of a consequent, then inhibits the tendency, and finally brings the (or an) expected consequent. As we shall see, statements are often ambiguous, patent of more than one possible meaning; questions may imply more than one possible answer. Ambiguity itself is a stimulus to expect a consequent, though one may be split among several possible expectations. Or the stimulus may be the beginning of a pattern or series of statements, which we expect to continue or, conversely, to close. The possibilities of the kinds of tendency to respond or of expectation are many, and their illustration in Qoh 1:2-11 will show several. If the hypothesis works, if the meaning of the passage (or meanings, if there are several) is to be found not simply in its unified "message" but in the very process by which the passage makes its linear way, then the style *is* the meaning, and perceiving the process as it unfolds is the interpretation.

In this respect, "meaning" and "affect" are synonymous terms. In dealing with verbal material, "affect" is the realization that one's mental expectations are being frustrated, that the consequent of the stimulus is different from what one had expected. In itself, that is a process of seeing what the mental consequent actually is, or recognizing the relation between antecedent and consequent and, therefore, the meaning in the text. It is important to read, on this interpretational model, not merely by thumbing through the text to see casually what is there but with the closest attention to what is being said. One must think through one statement and its possibilities, becoming aware of the expected consequences, before moving on to see what the actual consequents are. And one must continue to bear in mind what has been said, how its stimuli

have operated, what the order of things and the trend of the argument have
been. Sometimes, indeed, one must pause before a statement is completed to
notice where it appears to be headed. It is as if the reader were composing the
passage anew, as if part of the business of interpretation were to say, "If I were
writing this text, the next thing I would say is _____." Then one proceeds
to see what the author actually said next. To repeat, the interpreter must, as
far as possible, empty the mind of suppositions of prior knowledge, must try
to forget what comes next in the interests of a rigorous pursuit not of what one
thinks is there but of what really is there.

I turn, at last, to Qoh 1:2-11 in illustration.

> *hăbēl hăbālîm ʾāmar qōhelet*
> *hăbēl hăbālîm hakkōl hābel*     (Qoh 1:2)

"*Hebel* of *hebels*, says Qoheleth, *hebel of hebels*—everything is *hebel*." For
purposes of this interpretation, it is not necessary to refuse to go on until we
have cracked the code of *hebel* and can say exactly what *hăbēl hăbālîm* means
lexicographically. For the time being, we may content ourselves with thinking
that *hebel* at least contains the metaphor of vapor or of a little puff of wind.
The shape of the phrase tells us that, whatever *hebel* means, it is being adduced
in its superlative degree. The sententious "says Qoheleth," followed by the
repetition of *hăbēl hăbālîm* not only underscores the phrase's importance but
also makes us wonder what is going to be said about it and to what it will be
attributed. The repetition of the phrase both intensifies the expectation that it
will be applied to something and delays the arrival of the application: *hakkōl
hābel*, "everything is *hebel*," is somehow vaporous or a mere breeze. But
"everything" is not self-evident in meaning, and it needs further specification.
Two questions arise as stimuli out of this opening motto: first, what does the
vapor or breeze metaphor in *hebel* signify, and, second, what might
attributing *hebel* to "everything" mean specifically?

> *mah-yitrôn lāʾādām bĕkol-ʿămālô šeyyaʿămōl taḥat haššemeš*   (vs. 3)

"What is left over for man in all the toil at which he toils under the sun?" The
form of the question does not allow us to be sure of its answer. The answer
might be positive, that something is left over for man, and the range of
theoretical specifics is very wide. Money might be left over from toil, or goods,
or weariness, or pleasure, in amounts ranging from very little to a great deal.
The answer to the question might, however, be negative, that nothing is left to
man from his toil. Is that the sense, then, of the *hebel* metaphor, that the
greatest degree of *hebel* is the most ephemeral, the character of *hebel* is to
vanish? Then is *ʿāmāl*, "toil," the counterpart here of *hakkōl*, "everything," in
vs. 2? If so, then toil disappears into nothing as vapor or wind does. But it is
not self-evidently clear that "toil" is equivalent to "everything," especially

since it is modified by the very adjective, *kol*, "all," that previously was used as a noun, *hakkōl*.

The stimulus of vs. 2 would doubtless have led us to expect some answer to the questions arising out of it. Instead, we have another question, and that question has no clearly implied answer, or rather it has two possible answers. The consequent that the reader might have expected and would certainly wish has not followed. The question of the relation of these two sentences must be answered in order to arrive at their meaning. But we cannot yet answer it.

$$dôr\ hōlēk\ wĕdôr\ bā^{\circ}\ /\ wĕhā^{\circ}āreṣ\ lĕ^{c}ôlām\ ^{c}ōmedet\quad (vs.\ 4)$$

"A generation goes and a generation comes, and the earth stands there forever." *Dôr* seems in some way to continue *°ādām*, since the word has to do with human generations. Yet it is a new idea, which we would not have predicted from the foregoing. There it was not clear whether *°ādām* signified humankind in general or an individual human being. Nor does the consequent *dôr* clarify that question, since it might be either an extension of the individual to the generation or the narrowing of the generic "humankind" to its form in a particular time span. But *hōlēk* and *bā°* appear to take us back to that vapor metaphor in *hebel* with its possible connotation of the ephemeral. The theme of the constant going and coming of generations is contrasted with the permanence of *°ereṣ*. Does that contrast illustrate an answer to the question before it? A generation goes, a generation comes, and that one goes and another comes, and so on in endless series, while the *°ereṣ* always stands still. What is left over for *°ādām*? If anything is left, it is not the permanence of a generation, for the generations are impermanent. There is the permanent earth, but its permanence seems not to be a *yitrôn* for humankind. Moreover, that very constancy of the earth puts a question back to the beginning: does the earth fall outside of the definition of *hakkōl* in vs. 2? There it seemed that everything was defined as evanescent, yet here something is defined in a very strong contrast as stable. Perhaps the point of the metaphor in *hebel* is not impermanence. Or perhaps we discover only here that *hakkōl*, "everything," is not an inclusive "everything" but refers to everything within some boundary. What boundary? The only one we see is that around *°ādām*, his toil, his generations, the way *°ādām* occupies life and the time of life so occupied.

*°Ereṣ*, however, might mean "underworld." In that case, its very permanence is a reminder of inexorable death. Then the comings and goings of generations come out to nothing, and nothing is left over, no *yitrôn*, for humanity. Thus the question of vs. 3 would be answered decisively in the negative, and the factor allowing the perception that "everything is *hebel*" is death. But we cannot be sure that *°ereṣ* here means "underworld"; it may mean simply "earth," the human habitat. There stands earth, permanent, and its contrast may serve to emphasize the ephemeral quality of all that is human, or it may serve to set a boundary to the ephemeral.

A brief pause for a remark: I have so far sought to avoid firm conclusions, for the good reason that every expression appears to have more than one possible meaning. The linear mode of interpretation works best if one resists haste in making decisions but, reading with care, ponders possibilities and remains in suspense of conviction. Such possibilities may be tagged "hypothetical meanings." A word, phrase, or sentence may mean this, or it may mean that. What it means in the context is still hypothetical. We persist in thinking that sooner or later we shall be able to have more conviction, and that thought is an expected consequent. If, indeed, we never find out, then we may have some critical things to say about the style of the work. Meanwhile we proceed in search of meanings more than hypothetical.

A surprise comes with the first words of vs. 5: *wĕzārah haššemeš*, "And the sun rises." Nothing in what preceded could have prepared us for a remark about the sun's rising, unless it was the reference to humanity's toil "under the sun" in vs. 3, or unless the earth in vs. 4 really meant the entire universe, of which the sun is a part. That thought had not occurred to us there, but it may now be another hypothetical meaning. In vs. 3, the sun seemed to stand for the impersonal context in which humanity does its toil. Might the sun's rising here allude back to the generations that "come," presumably to pursue the toil of the time until they go? Or have we entered on a new train of thought? We must read on: *wĕzārah haššemeš ûbā' haššemeš*. Now there is a connection: the sun "comes" (*bā'*) as a generation "comes" (vs. 4). But *bā'* said of the sun means "to set," to enter into the western sea: "The sun rises and the sun sets." It did not occur to us in vs. 4 that the remark about the generations meant anything but "A generation goes (out of life) and a generation comes (into life)." In the light of vs. 5, however, it now seems possible to read vs. 4 as "A generation walks (its way of life) and a generation enters (like the sun into death)." The expression, therefore, would refer not to two different generations and by implication to a whole series of them but to only one, would epitomize a single generation's career. This verbal connection between *bā'* in vs. 4 and *bā'* in vs. 5 adds another hypothetical meaning to vs. 4. At least vs. 5 has to do with two actions of the one body, rising and setting, and its similarity to that of vs. 4 (although the nouns in vs. 5 follow the verbs rather than precede them) suggests some parallel to the earlier statement. Of what sort we cannot yet be sure.

We are not yet finished with the sun: *wĕ'el-mĕqômô šô'ēp / zôrēah hū' šām*. The second clause is puzzling; I translate: "It goes panting back to its place, there where it rises." We have the idea of repeated action, where the sun's rising and setting issue in the same activity again. The idea tends to legitimize one of the hypothetical meanings we saw in *dôr hōlēk wĕdôr bā'*, that it presents an endless series of generations, but it does not remove the other hypothetical meaning in the parallelism between *bā'* said of the generation and *bā'* said of the sun. We have moved from the generation, which comes and goes and is not seen again, to the sun, which rises and sets and appears again. The sun's recurrent rising suggests that when a generation goes, another comes in its place. We can now say something about the juxtaposition of the two ideas. Phenomena come to ends, which are succeeded by new appearances either repetitive of the first, as with the sun, or (we must be tentative about this inference) in effect identical with the first, as with the generations. But the relation between this image of the circle to the *hebel* metaphor in vs. 2, which seems to suggest a disappearance without reappearance, remains unclear. The idea of repetition, or of the effective identity of the new with the old, takes us back to the rhetorical question about profit (*yitrôn*) from toil. If the image of repetition controls the remark about the sun, which hurries around to start its round again, we seem to have support for a negative answer to that question. *ʾĀdām* has no profit, nothing left over, from toil, for the generations come and go, just as the sun comes and goes with no change.

We can conclude, though with some residual tentativeness, about what was happening in vss. 2-4. Some of the hypothetical meanings attached to those verses have been borne out by vs. 5, even though they are not necessarily conclusive to the exclusion of others. But we have a new level of meaning, because expectations aroused by statements in vss. 2-4 have to some extent been fulfilled. Such meanings may be tagged "evident meaning." There is now something besides merely internal logic or hypothesis to support them, and some—but not all—puzzlement as to what to expect has been removed.

What do we expect next? A continuation of that hypothetical repetition image contained in the sun's dashing back to its place would not be surprising. In fact that is what comes next, so the continuation of the image does not inhibit our tendency to respond, is not therefore affective, seems not to add to the points of meaning. Or does it? *Hôlēk ʾel-dārôm wĕsôbēb ʾel-ṣāpôn.* "Goes to the south and circles to the north." *Hôlēk*, of course, reverberates with *dôr hōlēk* in vs. 4. Is it the same "going" as there? Hypothetically it is, though we have yet to see the subject. With the parallel *sôbēb* we come for the first time to the explicit image of circling, which was implied by the sun's running back to its place to rise again. Are we continuing the discussion of the sun? Hypothetically again, we are. Perhaps the analogy between the sun's movement and the series of generations will be more clearly specified. *Hôlēk ʾel-dārôm* does not undercut that connection. At the right time of year in Palestine the sun is in the south. But when we read *wĕsôbēb ʾel-ṣāpôn* we know that the subject of vs. 6 cannot be the sun. In the northern hemisphere, one never looks north for the sun, except in Arctic latitudes—which can hardly be at issue here. But notice how the crucial word, *ṣāpôn*, is delayed until the end of the statement, and only there do we clearly know that the text is no longer speaking about the sun. The image of circling takes us in a direction we might have expected and thus is not affective, but the tendency to respond becomes inhibited when at *ṣāpôn* we realize that we do not know the subject of these actions.

To what phenomenon does the author refer with this circling to south and to north? The method of operation is changed. Earlier the author has given the subject first, or so close to first that it doesn't matter. *Mah-yitrôn lāʾādām* leaves us with no difficulties in knowing the subject; certainly *dôr hōlēk* tells us immediately, and *hāʾāreṣ lěʿôlām ʿōmedet* delays only the verb briefly. *Wězāraḥ haššemeš* gives both subject and verb first thing. In vs. 6 we hear only verbs, first a verb that has previously occurred (*hôlēk*), then a new one (*sôbēb*) making explicit an implicit image. In the next line *sôbēb* is repeated, not once but twice, and *hôlēk* recurs before at last, with a kind of gasp of relief, we come to the noun. Notice how the poet fends us off, forces us to hold our breath in suspense:

> *hôlēk ʾel-dārôm wěsôbēb ʾel-ṣāpôn | sôbēb sôbēb hôlēk — hārûaḥ*

"Goes to the south, circles to the north, circles, circles, goes—the wind." Then, as if to go through it all again, the following clause plays with a cognate to *sôbēb* and an assonance with it, the same subject again coming at the end: *wěʿal-sěbîbōtāyw šāb hārûaḥ*. "And on its circles turns the wind." That is style! To delay certainty of meaning as shrewdly and as long as these lines do is remarkably effective. We could quickly perceive the connection of the statement to the earlier ones, but we could not divine its actual meaning until the last moment. The delay is of the essence. And it is affective.

The technique at once makes clear a continuity of image, that of circling, and shrewdly masks a discontinuity of subject, from sun to wind. It thus first fulfills the expectation that vs. 6 has a place in the series of repetitions begun with the generations, then frustrates a hypothetical meaning that the sun continues to be the subject, and finally delays identification of the subject to remarkable lengths. In the end, the description of the wind underlines the image of repetition and establishes the sense of a series of phenomena so identified. The question that is raised is, will the series continue? Sooner or later it must end, and the longer the end is delayed, the more the affect will be.

At vs. 7, the poet gives the subject first:

> *kol-hanněḥālîm hōlěkîm ʾel-hayyām | wěhayyām ʾênennû mālēʾ*

"All the streams go to the sea, and the sea is never full." The subject is another natural phenomenon, the streams, which in one respect continues the series of natural forces from the sun and the wind. With the repetition of *hōlěkîm*, moreover, the first line is interlocked with those about the wind and the generations. And the initial *kol* reminds us of vss. 2 and 3. Hypothetically, at the beginning of the line the series begun with generations is continued, and we must wonder whether that series will ever end. But after *ʾel-hayyām* we might expect some continuation of the circling or repetition image. We do not find it. "The sea is never full." The image of circling seems to be replaced by that of a container. The first thought, that the series is being continued when we might have expected it to be ended, is then succeeded by the second thought that, having supposed the series was being continued, we find it is not, but a new image raises a new idea. Hypothetically we must now suppose that we have come into a new direction of thought.

The second half of vs. 7, however, seems to belie the hypothesis:

᾽el-mĕqôm šehannĕḥālîm hôlēkîm / šām hēm šābîm lāleket

"To the place where the rivers go, there they continually turn." The verbal reiterations from earlier in the poem give a very strong impression of continuity. *Māqôm* links this line to the sun, vs. 5; *hōlĕkîm* ties it to the preceding couplet, and *hôlēk* said about generations in vs. 4, and the wind in vs. 6; *šām* was connected with *māqôm* and the sun in vs. 5; and *šābîm* repeats what was said of the wind in vs. 6 (*wĕᶜal-sĕbîbōtāyw šāb hārûaḥ*). These connectives urge almost irresistibly that the streams continue the images of repetition and circling that we had thought had been concluded by the new image of the container in *wĕhayyām ᾽ênennû mālē᾽*. Indeed, the very profusion of the connections might lead us to think that the repetition motif is being summarized and thus brought to an end.

But a closer look makes that also unclear. The first line is verbally almost identical with the first line of the preceding couplet, *kol-hannĕḥālîm hôlĕkîm ᾽el-hayyām*, except that the synonym of *hayyām* has been moved to the first position. This line, then, no more than the preceding couplet proposes circling. It is the second line that seems to do so. But *šām* is another way of saying "the sea," *hēm* another way of saying "the streams," and *lāleket* is another form of the verb "to go." Only *šābîm* might suggest repetition, and that only if *šûb* is to be translated "return." But *šûb* has as much to do with "turning," changing direction, as with "returning," coming back to the same place. In the earlier statement about the wind, it was the *sĕbîbôt* that carried the image of circling, not *šāb*. In this line, there seems to be no necessary idea that the streams go back to a beginning place; rather the image seems to be of their moving forward to an ending place. That ending place, the sea, was described before in an image that suggests incompleteness. It is "never full." Indeed, if the second couplet of vs. 7 resumes the image of circling, we have no clear connection from the container image in the first couplet, which stands out anomalously in the context. But if the whole of vs. 7 has departed from the circling-repetition images, its continuity with what precedes is problematic. Recall that one of the hypothetical meanings of vs. 4, about the generations, as it was illuminated by the repetition of *bā᾽* in vs. 5, was that each single generation lives and then dies, thus moving from a beginning to an end. The continuation of the description of the sun in vs. 5 as hurrying back to start its course again left us with two hypothetical meanings about the generations, namely, that their "going and coming" might signify either their successions in series or the career of one generation, which comes to an end. Now from the streams in vs. 7, we have support, as it seems, for the latter hypothetical meaning, and that may suggest the second level of meaning, namely "evident meaning." Just as the streams constantly empty into the never-full sea, so each generation lives and comes to its end, each enters into death.

That evident meaning takes us back to the problem of the answer to vs. 3: "What is left over for man in all his toil?" As the streams run down into the sea, which is never filled, and as the generations go down to death, which is never ended, so humanity toils down to the end with nothing left over, no profit. With a definitively negative answer to vs. 3, the intervening images of circling have about them an air of oppressiveness of which we could not earlier be sure. From vs. 7 and its connections to what goes before it, I think we can now know that the question about the *yitrôn* proposed a negative answer: no *yitrôn* for humankind can be found. The hypothetically positive answer to the question cannot be upheld by anything in the passage so far, but we have had to undergo a considerable process to be sure of that. A third level of meaning has been achieved, beyond the hypothetical and the evident, and it may be called "determinate meaning."

The first word of vs. 8, *kol*, gives a construction parallel to the foregoing verse. The consequent is, however, very confusing, for it seems to have no other connection:

*kol-haddĕbārîm yĕgēᶜîm / lōᵓ-yûkal ᵓîš lĕdabbēr*

"All the words (or things) are wearisome, a man is not able to speak." The earlier series of natural phenomena, beginning with the earth in vs. 4 and continuing with sun, wind, and streams, established a sequence that we might expect to continue. It does not, but, with a parallel construction that slightly delays our realization that the sequence has been broken off, it moves into new territory. What have "words" to do with sun, wind, and streams? What, moreover, has the "weariness" of words to do with anything? It may remind us of that "toil" at which man "toils" profitlessly back in vs. 3. "A man is unable to speak." Now there is something quite new. Before, repetitions or continuations of actions have been emphasized, comings and goings, standings, hurryings, risings, settings, circlings. Here an action cannot happen, and an implicit "therefore" is between the two clauses. It is quite unexpected and raises the question of meaning. Have we left the old thought behind? Hypothetically we have, and we do not yet know what the new one is. Another hypothetical meaning suggests itself. Perhaps *kol-haddĕbārîm* is the implicit accusative of *lĕdabbēr*: "All the words are wearisome, a man is unable to speak (them)." The words are wearisome because, just as the streams run into the sea but never fill it, one never comes to the end of the words. Is that the point? I think we do not know. We still have two hypothetical meanings.

*lōᵓ tiśbaᶜ ᶜayin lirᵓôt*

"The eye is not sated with seeing." The new metaphor of eating ("not sated") is compatible with the notion that a man is weary because he cannot come to the end of the words; likewise the eye doesn't come to the end of seeing.

*wĕlōᵓ-timmālēᵓ ᵓōzen miššĕmōaᶜ*

"And the ear is not filled by hearing." The image reverberates with that of the sea that is never filled by the streams, vs. 7, a line that, because it broke continuity of images, was itself a point of uncertainty. Only here where its verb recurs is vs. 7 clarified. It is a subtle point, since to "fill" the ear with "hearing" is a metaphor. The ear is not a container for hearing as the sea is for water. But through the metaphor about the ear, the unfilled sea can now be understood as a metaphor for unfulfillment in the distinctively human operations of speaking, seeing, and hearing (and the poet has sneaked in the sense of taste by the metaphor of satiation).

A new thought seems to have obtruded itself. Where the earlier phenomena achieved an oppressive pessimism by the repetitiveness of their actions, returning to the same place, circling about through the same points of the compass, constantly going to the same place, this one proposes that weariness consists not in repetition of the old but in its opposite, the never-ending arrival of the new. New things to say, to see, to hear are always coming, and it is wearisome. If that is the idea, perhaps the first hypothetical meaning we attached to "A man cannot speak" is right: that we have departed the image of circling and have come to something else. We are left with two hypothetical meanings for this passage, one that it continues the image of the foregoing, especially of vs. 7, and the other that it does not.

The poet hits us again: *mah-šehāyâ*. That is a question: "What is it that has been?" If that question had preceded vs. 8, we would have had a clear answer already. "What has been is what will be again," for the entire circling imagery in vss. 4-7 suggested just that. But vs. 8 puts a question mark against the implication, and we have no answer. But the poet does: *hûʾ šeyyihyeh*. "That is what will be." We would have been right, as it turns out, but vs. 8 has been interposed in such a way as to make it uncertain whether the answer to the question, *mah-šehāyâ*, would be in line with vss. 4-7. As if to insist on the matter, the question and its answer are rephrased: *ûmah-šennaʿăśâ? Hûʾ šeyyēʿāśeh*. "And what has been done? That is what will be done." We now recognize that vs. 8 was a bit of a smokescreen thrown up before us, in such a way that the evident meaning of vss. 4-7 became unclear for a moment. Now, however, we seem to have a determinate meaning for all that. The circling image really does signify repetition, and the weariness of words, seeing, and hearing in vs. 8 seems (can we yet be really sure?) to be that of constant sameness. The next line at last puts the cap on it:

*wěʾên kol-ḥādāš taḥat haššemeš*

"And there is nothing at all new under the sun." The last phrase takes us all the way back to vs. 3, and man's profitless toil "under the sun." The determinate meaning of that statement is underscored here. Does this one take care of vs. 8? We can call it an evident meaning, but the question somehow nigglingly remains: in what does the wearisomeness of words consist?

As if to answer that question, the poet comes back to words:

*yēš dābār šeyōʾmar rĕʾēh-zeh, ḥādāš hûʾ*

"There's a word (or thing) of which someone says, 'Look at this, it's new.'"
*Dābār* takes us back to the "words" in vs. 8, and thus to all that it signified, and the poet underscores the connection with *rĕʾēh*, recalling *lirʾôt*. But the very indication that the question about vs. 8 will be answered delays the answer to it. Someone alleges newness about a word. Can it be done? No:

*kĕbār hāyâ lĕʿōlāmîm ʾăšer hāyâ millĕpānēnû*

"Already it belonged to ages that were ahead of us." And so we have a determinate meaning for vs. 8. The wearisomeness of all the words that a man can't speak is that finally they are not new, and even though a man never comes across all of them, he can be quite sure that he has not uttered any never before said, has not seen a new sight or heard a new sound.

Vs. 11 seems to give back part of what vs. 10 has taken away. The syntax of the concluding quatrain is confusing:

*ʾên zikrôn lārîʾšōnîm | wĕgam lāʾaḥārōnîm šeyyihyû*
*lōʾ-yihyeh lāhem zikkārôn | ʿim šeyyihyû lāʾaḥārônâ*

Perhaps *zikrôn* should be read *zikkārôn*, the absolute state of the word. Often *zikkārôn lĕ* means a memorial or a monument to somebody, which is a very odd thought here. Moreover, the denotations of *rîʾšōnîm* and *ʾaḥărōnîm* are quite uncertain. Is it "earlier" and "later" generations of people, or simply first and later phenomena? I'm not sure we can say. If we take *zikkārôn* to mean "remembrance" rather than a memorial, then we can take *rîʾšōnîm* and *ʾaḥărōnîm* as simply generalizations about earlier and later things, including people. "There is no remembrance of earlier things, and even of later things that will be, they have no remembrance with those that are still later." What does that mean? It is perhaps typical of this thinker to leave us with a statement patent only of a hypothetical meaning. It seems to say that we know there is nothing new, but since there is no remembrance of anything, or ever will be any, we simply cannot say of anything either that it is or that it is not new. We begin with the hypothesis that it is not new, but we can't remember. Does that suggest that it doesn't matter, that we have no alternative to being wearied by it all? Or might it mean that, since we can't remember, then what seems new is for us new? I don't know. And since vs. 12 goes on to something different, I think we have to read on through the book to find out. This poem, at least, ends, for all the determinate meanings that it has already given, with a question in the mind of the reader, and perhaps that was the whole point. It is, to say the least, unlike Qoheleth to wrap everything into a tidy package.

Even the motto with which the poem began is left in the poem without determinate meaning. The notion of the evanescent seems denied by the images of repetition, but supported by the implication of death in vs. 4. It is

difficult to square with the image of the container in vs. 7 but consonant with
the lack of memory in vs. 11. The meaning of *hebel*, then, must be discovered
progressively by following it through the rest of Qoheleth's essay. We might
think hypothetically of it as portending the unsatisfactory, the uncertain,
maybe even (as I have suggested elsewhere)[2] the incongruous. But we must
rest content with hypothesis about *hebel* from this poem.

There are some perceptible stylistic techniques in the passage, and I have
already argued for their high correlation with meaning. One of them is the
delay of an expected consequent. That can be done in various ways. Qoheleth
does it in part with the use of the interrogative. *Mah-yitrôn lāʾādām* is a
question that cries out for an answer, but no answer comes for some time, and
then it is only by implication. *Mah-šehāyâ* is another (both questions use the
same interrogative particle), and, as we saw, the reader could have supplied
the answer a verse earlier but, with the interposition of vs. 8, the answer is not
immediately in mind. The poet gives it right away. Another way to delay an
expected consequent is to hold off a key word for some time. An example of
the technique is *hārûaḥ* in vs. 6, and in the same verse we could not be sure
until the fourth word that the subject had changed. Recall, moreover, how the
line "The sea is never full" hung over for some time until completed by "The
ear is not filled with hearing." Thus, still another way to delay an expected
consequent is to interpose something else, or what seems like something else,
between the expectation and its completion, to give a consequent that is not
expected.

To be sure, in order for an expectation to be aroused, you must have
enough preceding so that the expectation can be present. The opening line,
*hăbēl hăbālîm*, etc., is not enough. All we know from that verse is the
importance through repetition of that phrase. What it signifies is not clear. It
is through the series of subjects—generations, sun, wind, streams—with its
tight verbal interlocking that the expectations begin to fly thick and fast.
Notice, moreover, that the longer the series goes, the more we must expect it to
end, and the longer the end is delayed, the more affective is the continuation of
the series. Thus when we come to the verse about words, we think all the more
strongly that we are in a new subject. When it turns out, with vss. 9-10, that we
really are not in a new subject, the affect of the continuation is all the greater.

In this reading I have neither depended on nor argued with other
interpreters of the passage. That has been deliberate. In one sense, I suspect
that this method of reading is one that ought to precede rather than
accompany or follow any consultation of one's colleagues. Having done it,
one is in a position of strength to compare what one sees in the text with what
other interpreters see, to recognize alternative meanings that had not occurred
before, to spot errors of judgment or omissions on the part of the others, or on
one's own part. On the other hand, other interpretations of this passage
present the unitary kind of reading, looking for the structure and "the"
meaning and omitting mention of possibilities that have had to be discarded
along the way. They are concerned to purvey the truth. I have been concerned

rather to purvey the process through which the poem goes and, with it, the process through which the interpreter may go to perceive and follow the poem's process.

Self-evidently, the same sorts of procedures may be followed in dealing with narrative and other kinds of prose. Narrative in particular is a literary mode in which the linear is essential, where the relations of antecedents and consequents carry the load of the presentation. Three quarters of the fun in reading any story is in wondering what will come next.

But that same pleasure can be a part of reading other kinds of material as well. To read the wisdom thinkers as thinkers, to follow their thoughts through the processes by which they present them, may be a means not to dismiss the search for unitary truth but to widen the parameters of truth, to be less worried about the kind of consistency that leads people to emend texts in its favor and to be more satisfied to let texts have their own way. In the end of the day, interpretation that does anything else is not interpretation.

[1] L. B. Meyer, *Emotion and Meaning in Music* (Chicago: University of Chicago, 1956).
[2] E. M. Good, *Irony in the Old Testament* (Philadelphia: Westminster, 1965) 176-83.

# III
# ON THE PROPHETIC INTERACTION
# WITH, AND ALTERNATIVES TO,
# ISRAELITE WISDOM

# MICAH THE MORESHITE — THE PROPHET
# AND HIS BACKGROUND

HANS WALTER WOLFF

THE UNIVERSITY OF HEIDELBERG, 69 HEIDELBERG, GERMANY

Translated by Charles E. Weber, The University of Tulsa, Tulsa, Oklahoma 74104

I am indebted to Professor Samuel Terrien for his essay, "Amos and Wisdom"; it was his contribution to the Muilenburg Festschrift (1962) which turned out to be a decisive stimulus on my observations in "Amos' geistige Heimat." My work was published under that title in 1964 and was translated as *Amos the Prophet — The Man and His Background* (1973). Similarly Professor Terrien became my teacher for some important perceptions set forth in my commentary on Amos which is now also available in English in the Hermeneia series (1977). For this also I herewith send respectful greetings. My contribution to this Festschrift dedicated to him shall seek to make further observations on Micah of Moresheth as I did in my earlier studies of Amos.*

THE interpretation of the Book of Micah still involves numerous unsolved problems. In this regard, the question of the context in which Micah learned to observe, think and speak is of pivotal importance. The question is difficult to answer because the extent of the secondary material in the Book of Micah is as controversial as ever. However, precisely because of this uncertainty, it is important to clarify from the outset where the forms and themes of Micah's language had their actual origins. As far as method is concerned, it is imperative to proceed from a critically secured minimum of sayings. From this point of departure criteria have to be established which would permit a judgment as to which other passages in the book could have originated from the prophet himself and which ones would be better explained from a different origin.

Present-day research unanimously ascribes to Micah the sayings in Micah 1:8-16; 2:1-11 and 3:1-12; only small passages of the text in this area are problematic as possible editorial additions. Moreover, there are in my opinion good reasons for asking if utterances originally from Micah are not present especially in the case of Micah 1:6-7, in the difficult-to-determine case of Micah 4:9-5:3 and in Micah 6:9-16. The criteria for a decision here are not uniform, however. For this reason it appears advisable to me to consider only Micah 1:8-16; 2:1-11 and 3:1-12 relevant to the question of Micah's intellectual and cultural background.

Beyond this, only one passage is now indispensible, namely the information in the title of the book (Mic 1:1) that Micah originated from Moresheth. This information is confirmed in Jer 26:17-18: "certain of the elders of the land" cite "Micah of Moresheth." In this instance his threat against Jerusalem is referred to, apparently independently of the literary tradition of Micah 3:12. This is the case because the threat is proclaimed in the Jeremiah passage "to the whole nation of Judah," while in the Micah passage it is "to the heads of the house of Jacob and to the rulers of the house of Israel" (Mic 3:9); in the former passage it is introduced with the messenger's formula כה אמר יהוה, in the latter passage it is lacking; in the former passage on the other hand the admonishment is lacking that Zion's demise will occur because of the guilt of the leading classes ("therefore for your sake"). The analyst of the report in Jeremiah 26 will correctly observe that "the elders of the land" have alive in their memory those words of Micah spoken a century ago. The priests and prophets of the Jerusalem Temple as well as the court officials, however, have to be reminded of them.

The reference to Micah in Jeremiah 26 now makes clear three certainties of fact: first, an epithet like "the Moreshite" is bestowed only on a person outside of his homeland. In just the same manner, Amos, who appeared in the northern kingdom far from his homeland, is called the man "from Tekoa." It is probable that Micah was called the Moreshite in Jerusalem on the basis of his appearance there. He can be known as the "Micah of Moresheth" particularly amongst certain "elders of the land," who convened from various cities of Judah.[1] Second, Jer 26:17-18 makes possible the conjecture that Micah's words were first handed down amongst certain "elders of the land." If this is the case we would then have to seek the primary transmitters of the sayings of Micah amongst circles similar to those of the old Amos school.[2]

Third, Jer 26:17-18 permits us to conclude that Micah himself may have originally belonged to the circle of the "elders of the land." The appearance then of a man from Moresheth in Jerusalem would be comprehensible on the grounds of his institutional membership, so to speak. The fact that Micah preached as a prophet in Jerusalem is established without doubt by Mic 3:9-12 in addition to Jer 26:17-18. The "elders of the land" are identical with the "elders of Judah" (1 Sam 30:36). They convene in Jerusalem not only on the occasion of the great festivals but also at the special directive of the king (1 Kgs 23:1). The possibility is not to be discounted that they visit the capital on their own initiative, particularly at the prophetic command. Each one of them represents his own city and the tribe residing in it (cf. Ruth 4:1-12; Deut 19:12; 21:2-3, 6, 19-20). We thus arrive at the working hypothesis that the prophet Micah should be regarded as having been from the outset one of the elders of Moresheth. This hypothesis explains many characteristics of his language and appearance.

(1) The term of address of the leaders in Jerusalem as "heads of the house of Jacob and rulers of the house of Israel" (Mic 3:1, 9). ראש and קצין are to be found as a word pair in only one other instance in the OT, and specifically as a designation of the function of Jephthah in Judg 11:11; ראש and קצין have

synonymous meanings in this connection, as Judg 11:6 and 8 show. Jephthah is installed as a ruler by the elders of Gilead, and specifically as a military leader; cf. also Josh 10:24. Micah addresses neither the king nor the royal officials as such, as they are presented, for example, in Jer 26:10 as שרי יהודה. Also, the area of work of the leaders is not designated "Judah" or "Jerusalem" in accordance with the current political usage, but rather "Jacob" and "Israel" in keeping with ancient Israelite thinking. Micah, however, can probably not mean persons other than those officials charged with judicial functions, who were responsible not only for Jerusalem, but also for the Judaean country towns, especially the ones fortified.[3] The judicial proceedings presided over by these officials easily came into conflict with the old local jurisprudence at the gates of the clan settlements,[4] especially inasmuch as even family elders could be employed as royal officials by the king.[5] Accordingly, Micah in his address to the Jerusalem officials, addresses the leading circles in Jerusalem which are in competition with the office of an elder from Moresheth.

(2) The situation becomes even clearer if consideration is taken of Micah's own role: when he describes his commission it is with precisely the designation, משפט (Mic 3:8), about which the judicial officials in Jerusalem would have to be informed by the virtue of their office (Mic 3:1). They, however, shy away from משפט and pervert all that is righteous (כל-הישרה, 3:9). The officials in Jerusalem and the clan elder from Moresheth are bound to the same body of law. The elder from Moresheth, however, proves to be the prophet of Yahweh by virtue of the fact that he "declares to Jacob his transgression and to Israel his sin" far beyond the boundaries of his clan (Mic 3:8b), and by virtue of the fact that he is provided with "power, [a consciousness of] justice, and valor" (Mic 3:8a). According to 2 Chr 19:6, the דבר משפט is entrusted to the judges in the land installed by the king. According to 2 Chr 19:8 the משפט יהוה is entrusted to the heads of families (together with Levites and priests) in Jerusalem (cf. Mic 3:11a). Micah becomes the accuser of those who betray and pervert this law. In the person of Micah the law of Yahweh encounters the falsifiers of law in the form of accusation and pronouncement of sentence. The accusation points to the mistreatment of workers (3:2-3; 10; cf. Jer 22:13-14) and bribery (Mic 3:11; cf. Amos 5:12; Isa 1:23; 5:23). As a punishment the fall of Jerusalem is proclaimed. The prophet Micah transcends by far the office of a judge in Israel not only in the daring of the accusation, but at the same time in the totality of the threatened fall of Jerusalem. The fact that Yahweh himself is the judge is explained by him with notable infrequency (Mic 2:3; 3:4).[6] Almost in the manner of a boast (cf. 1 Sam 17:43-44) he puts himself into a prominent position as the representative of justice.

(3) At the same time he views himself as the representative of his compatriots. No less than four times does he say "my people" (1:9; 2:9; 3:3, 5).[7] What does he mean when he says עמי? It is not easy to explain the lament of 1:9, where there is mention of the incurable blow (of an advancing hostile army), which "reaches to Judah, indeed, which extends to the gate of my

people, to Jerusalem." Why is Jerusalem called here "the gate of my people"? Is Jerusalem meant as the seat of government, where the decisions are made for Micah's people, just as decisions are sought in litigations at the gates of small cities?[8] Or does "the gate of my people" mean here the access route of the enemy (from the North) into the region of Judah,[9] the cities and towns of which are named in the subsequent text, amongst which is mentioned expressly also Micah's home Moresheth-gath? In any case, עמי means the country population and does not include that of the residential city of Jerusalem. Perhaps the term only refers to Micah's compatriots from the rather close proximity of Moresheth.

The matter comes into even clearer focus in Mic 2:9. Here he accuses those "who drive out the women of my people from their cherished houses." The context of Mic 2:6-11 constitutes a discussion with those whom the prophet has reproached and threatened in Mic 2:1-5. In Mic 2:2 it was said:

> They covet fields, and seize them;
>     and houses, and take them away;
> they oppress a man and his house,
>     a man and his inheritance.

In the discussion in 2:9a he mentions as particular hardship cases the defenseless women (widows) who are driven from their houses. Nothing indicates that the sayings of the second chapter are proclaimed in Jerusalem. Rather, at this point we must think of the more proximate homeland of Micah.The town of Moresheth, which was already mentioned in the Amarna texts along with Lachish,[10] lay in the West Judaean hill country approximately 35 kilometers southwest of Jerusalem, 15 kilometers east of Gath (ᶜarāk el-menšije) and a good 30 kilometers west of Tekoa, the home of Amos; it is the present day ed-ǧudēde,[11] situated approximately 400 meters above sea level, along the edge of the Shephelah. It is worth noting that no less than five of the fortress towns founded by Rehoboam (2 Chr 11:7-9) lie near Moresheth within a radius of less than 10 kilometers, specifically Asekah to the north, Socoh to the northeast, Adullam to the east, Mareshah to the south and Lachish to the southwest. These secure the accesses to Jerusalem from the coastal road and from the Philistine plain. That means, however, that in the immediate vicinity of Moresheth, Jerusalemite officials were going and coming (cf. 2 Chr 19:5). These people are not called by Micah "my people" but rather "this people" (העם הזה, 2:11). One can imagine how they attempted to commandeer with official force the nicest pieces of property and houses in and around Moresheth for their private or even official uses. In Jerusalem the flogs of the ruling people fall directly on the persons obligated to work. In Mic 3:3, Micah says of those responsible in Jerusalem: "They devour the flesh of my people." From the rural towns construction workers and others bound to serve were probably frequently brought into the capital (cf. Mic 3:10). There they had to suffer under their masters. Micah was probably calling his compatriots in the narrower sense "my people" in Mic 3:3 as well as in Mic 2:9.

As an elder of the land he is attached to them in the first place and he has now committed himself to them as a prophet with special authority, while they are also being exploited by the Jerusalem prophets (Mic 3:5, 11). Thus, Micah's official function as an "elder of the land" can make comprehensible his appearance in Jerusalem as well as the reference to his compatriots as "my people" in contrast to the circles of officers and officials in the residential city and in the fortification towns in the vicinity of Moresheth.

It is striking that Micah never once calls his tormented compatriots poor (אביון), helpless (דל) or oppressed (עני), as is quite often done by Amos (Amos 2:6-7; 4:1; 5:11-12; 8:4, 6) and not infrequently by Isaiah (Isa 3:14-15; 10:2; 14:32), although Micah sees, just as those prophets, that they are being overpowered and punished to the point of bleeding (Mic 2:2, 8-9, 3:2-3, 10). Obviously, however, Micah visualizes in them more the free men (Mic 2:2, איש־גבר) in the קהל יהוה (Mic 2:5) who have to suffer under the Jerusalem office holders. His use of language is quite comprehensible from the standpoint of an elder of the land who is quite closely attached to his fellow citizens.

(4) The crudity of the figurative language of Micah has frequently been pointed out. He speaks especially drastically in Mic 3:2-3 of the Jerusalem officials who tear the skin and flesh from the bones of his people of his nation, cut in pieces their flesh for the pot and break their bones. There is a trace here of close proximity to the life of peasants. Certainly, he is a "man from the country."[12] However, from that it is not to be concluded that he himself was a "poor peasant" or an "agricultural worker,"[13] no more than he is to be categorized on the other hand as a cult prophet.[14]

(5) Micah's adoption of typical forms of the mourning ceremony as it was practiced within the clans and rural settlements further helps us determine his cultural background more precisely.

Here the exclamation of woe in Mic 2:1 must be mentioned first of all. The הוי is followed by a plural participle which characterizes this form, as the following verbal sentences with "Woe!" illustrate. Research is still undecided between two attempts at a solution based on the history of forms with regard to the origin of the woe-cry. Did Amos (Amos 5:18; 6:1) for the first time use the woe-cry for the dead (1 Kgs 13:30; Jer 22:18; 34:5) and metaphorically, with the הוי speak to those mentioned as persons figuratively already dead?[15] Then Isaiah (cf. esp. Isa 5:8-24; 10:1-4) and Micah would perhaps be dependent on him by the mediation of his Judaean school. Or do the prophetic exclamations of woe join sapiential forms which, parallel to the אשרי exclamations, teach the difference between the way to life and the way to death in the clans of the rural communities—especially amongst the elders in the gate?[16] Then the reference to living persons would be readily understandable, as well as the special closeness of Isaiah to sapiential traditions and the approximately simultaneous appearance of the woe-cries in the case of Amos, Isaiah and Micah. However, precedents are lacking in the proverb collections of wisdom.[17] In any case, the exclamation of woe originally belongs to the mourning ceremony within the rural communities.[18]

A similar setting is even more clearly indicated of the mourning lament as it is intoned by the prophet: in Mic 1:8 he uses the mourning lament as his own and in Mic 2:4 he invents a quotation for the hour of coming disaster. In Mic 1:8 he commences his lament of destruction[19] especially for the villages of the land of Judah (vss. 9-16):

> For this I will lament and wail;
>   I will go stripped and naked;
> I will make lamentation like the jackals,
>   and mourning like the ostriches. (Mic 1:8)

Neither this opening nor that which follows is reminiscent of a cultic lament. An invocation to Yahweh, as is inadmissible in the case of a lament of destruction in the sanctuary, does not follow. Thus, here too the voice of the priests is not fitting (cf., e.g., Joel 2:17), but rather the voice of those knowledgeable in lamentation—in the country towns.[20] The place of such lamentation is the streets and squares of the town, not a sanctuary.[21] Also the song of lamentation given in Mic 2:4 (נהי, which can also read משל!) is a profane song of the destruction, which probably originally consisted only of a single stichos in a 2 + 2 meter:[22]

> We are fully ruined
> our fields divided.

Both form and content belong to the profaneness of the rural community in which Micah is at home. It is noteworthy that in Jer 9:16 those who are knowledgeable in lamentation are also considered to be the wise men. The lamenting prophet Micah participates in such wisdom.

(6) Much more in the sayings of Micah might remind us of the wisdom of the elders in the rural communities. Additionally, I mention only the disputation style in Mic 2:6-11 (cf. Amos 3:3-8) and the antithetical explication of injustice in Mic 3:2a reminiscent of Amos 5:14-15: "hate the good and love the evil."[23]

It has been correctly pointed out that such individual observations are not absolutely conclusive as proof of an "ancient Israelite clan wisdom."[24] Nevertheless, I have sought in the present essay to point out with specific reference to Micah the use of a form of wisdom, as it was administered by the elders in the gates of the country towns and as it is to be found in a related form in the case of Amos and his earliest transmitters.[25] According to that which has been handed down from Micah, he is more distant from the world of the cult than Amos, who can draw upon, and occasionally parody, the priestly forms of speech of sanctuaries in the northern kingdom.

The discussion concerning Amos' intellectual background may also be enriched if we look for the intellectual background of Micah in the sphere of life of the elders in Judah. Such a conclusion is in accord with the observations we have made above concerning his language, the world as he viewed it and his manner of thinking. He is familiar with that which an elder has to do in a Judaean country town, in the judicial process in the gate and in the instruction of youth. Above all, he has knowledge of "justice," but also of the forms of the local mourning lament. In addition to the form of the exclamations of woe and the occasional disputation style, along with Amos and Isaiah he is associated especially with three themes which are also familiar to the proverb wisdom of Israel: oppression of free citizens,[26] corrupt judging[27] and undisciplined drinking.[28] His prophetic authority enables him to assail injustice with special force, to announce the disastrous consequences with extreme sharpness, to register complaint as well as threat beyond the boundaries of his immediate homeland as far as the capital, Jerusalem.

For the judgment of the passages of the Book of Micah, the authenticity of which is questioned, the following criterion will be useful: can they be interpreted as having come from the linguistic sphere of an elder in a Judaean country town in the last third of the eighth century B.C.?

*The items referred to in Professor Wolff's *Grusswort* are as follows: S. Terrien, "Amos and Wisdom," *Israel's Prophetic Heritage: Essays in Honor of James Muilenburg* (eds. B. W. Anderson and W. Harrelson; New York: Harper & Bros., 1962) 108-15; H. W. Wolff, *Amos' geistige Heimat* (WMANT 18; Neukirchen-Vluyn: Neukirchener Verlag, 1964); Engl. *Amos the Prophet* (Philadelpha: Fortress, 1973). On the last mentioned commentary, see n. 2 below [Ed.]

[1] Cf. J. L. Mays, *Micah* (OTL; Philadelphia: Westminster, 1976) 15.

[2] Cf. H. W. Wolff, *Joel and Amos* (Hermeneia; Philadelphia: Fortress, 1977) 108-11.

[3] Cf. 2 Chr 19: 5-11 and G. Chr. Macholz, "Zur Geschichte der Justizorganisation in Juda" *ZAW* 84 (1972) 314-40, esp. 317-24.

[4] H. J. Boecker, *Recht und Gesetz im Alten Testament und im Alten Orient* (Neukirchen-Vluyn: Neukirchener Verlag, 1976) 39-40.

[5] Cf. 2 Chr. 19:8 and Macholz, *ZAW* 84 (1972) 325.

[6] The messenger's formula כה אמר יהוה (2:3, 3:5) is encountered only twice, while it is perhaps editorial in 3:5, thus Th. Lescow, "Redaktionsgeschichtliche Analyse von Micha 1-5," *ZAW* 84 (1972) 46-84, esp. p. 48.

[7] 2:4aβ must be viewed as secondary; cf. Jörg Jeremias, "Die Deutung der Gerichtsworte Michas in der Exilszeit," *ZAW* 83 (1971) 330-54, esp. p. 334. 2:8a is textually uncertain.

[8] This is the interpretation of W. Rudolph, *Micha-Nahum-Habakuk-Zephanja* (KAT 13/3; Gütersloh: Mohn, 1975) 43 and J. L. Mays, *Micah*, 55.

[9] This is the interpretation of A. Alt, *Kleine Schriften zur Geschichte des Volkes Israel* (3 vols.;Munich: Beck, 1953) 2. 243 and A. S. van der Woude, *Micha: De Prediking van het Oude Testament* (Nijkerk: Callenbach, 1976) 45-46.

[10] The town mentioned is *Muḫrašti*; see J. A. Knudtzon (ed.), *Die El-Amarna-Tafeln* (Vorderasiatische Bibliotek; 2 vols.; Leipzig: Hinrichs, 1915; reprinted Aalen: Zeller, 1964) 2.1356 (Letter EA 335, lines 16-17).

[11] Joachim Jeremias, "Moreseth-Gath, die Heimat des Propheten Micha," *PJB* 29 (1933) 42-53.

[12] W. Rudolph, *Micha*, 23.

[13] Ibid., 22.

[14] W. Rudolph, (ibid., 24) is surely right in this regard as opposed to A. S. Kapelrud, "Eschatology in the Book of Micah," *VT* 11 (1961) 392-405, and W. Beyerlin, *Die Kulttraditionen*

*in der Verkündigung des Propheten Micha* (FRLANT 72; Göttingen: Vandenhoeck & Ruprecht, 1959).

[15] This was the conclusion of Chr. Hardmeier, "Kritik der Formgeschichte auf texttheoretischer Basis am Beispiel der prophetischen Weheworte," (Diss. Heidelberg, 1975) 382-91.

[16] E. Gerstenberger, "The Woe-Oracles of the Prophets," *JBL* 81 (1962) 249-63; W. Schottroff, *Der altrisraelitische Fluchspruch* (WMANT 30; Neukirchen-Vluyn: Neukirchener Verlag, 1969) 110-12, 117-20; H. W. Wolff, *Joel and Amos*, 242-45.

[17] K. Koch et al., *Amos — untersucht mit den Methoden einer strukturalen Formgeschichte* (Alter Orient und Altes Testament 30; Neukirchen-Vluyn: Kevelaer, 1976) 286.

[18] Cf. Amos 5:16-17 and H. W. Wolff, *Joel and Amos*, 249.

[19] For the basic work on this form, see now the dissertation of Chr. Hardmeier referred to in n. 15 above.

[20] Cf. Amos 5:17 יודעי נהי as well as אבל and מספד and Mic 1:8b; cf. also Jer 9:16-19.

[21] In the light of Amos 5:17 the assumption by A. S. van der Woude *Micha* 21 that Micah 1:2-16 was pronounced in the sanctuary of Lachish is not convincing. Crucial is the fact that ספד and מספד do not occur in the whole Book of Psalms; on the exception, Ps. 30:12, see Hardmeier, "Kritik der Formgeschichte," p. 203 n. 107.

[22] On the expansion of the text see the article by Jörg Jeremias, referred to in n. 7 above. Note also the similar wording in Jer 9:18.

[23] Cf. H. W. Wolff, *Amos the Prophet*, 6-16, 67-76; J. W. Whedbee, *Isaiah and Wisdom* (New York: Abingdon, 1971) 104; cf. Isa 5:20.

[24] H. H. Schmid, "Amos. Zur Frage nach der 'geistigen Heimat' des Propheten," *Wort und Dienst* 10 (1969) 85-103 = *Altorientalische Welt in der alttestamentlichen Theologie* (Zürich: Theologischer Verlag, [1974] 121-44. The elders who give advice (Ezek 7:26) are called wise men in Jer 18:18.

[25] As I indicated in the dedicatory note, the decisive stimulus for my study of the prophetic appropriation of sapiential forms I owe to Samuel Terrien, who is being honored here, and his essay, "Amos and Wisdom." The impulses toward research which his provocative essay generated cannot be turned back.

[26] See Mic 2:2; 3:3, 10; see also Amos 2:6-7; 4:1; 8:4-6; Isa 3:15; 10:2; Prov 14:31; 22:16, 22; 28:3.

[27] See Mic 3:11; see also Amos 5:7, 12; Isa 1:23; 5:23; Prov 17:15; 18:5; 24:23.

[28] See Mic 2:11; see also Amos 4:1; 6:4-6; Isa 5:11-12, 22; Prov 20:1; 21:17; 23:20-21, 29-35; 31:4-7.

# THE EPISTEMOLOGICAL CRISIS OF
# ISRAEL'S TWO HISTORIES (Jer 9:22-23)

WALTER A. BRUEGGEMANN

EDEN THEOLOGICAL SEMINARY, WEBSTER GROVES, MISSOURI 63119

## I

TWO developments in recent OT scholarship, when brought together, may illuminate the words and ministry of Jeremiah. First, recent emphasis on wisdom studies has shown that the sapiential tradition is not at all peripheral to the reflective life of Israel.[1] Wisdom studies are vexed by difficult questions, largely definitional in character. Depending on definitions, we may broadly locate wisdom influence at many points in the OT, or with Crenshaw,[2] we may take a narrow view and resist the notion that sapiential influences can be identified outside conventional wisdom literature.

This paper does not intend to engage those sticky debates in relation to Jeremiah. While attention has been given to the possibility of wisdom influences in Amos and Isaiah,[3] only the most surface attention has thus far been given to Jeremiah.[4] It seems likely that Jeremiah himself utilized the style and/or imagery of the wisdom teachers.[5] But lacking definitions, that will not be insisted upon here.

More important is the awareness that the appearance of wisdom influences (wherever they appear) of necessity raises important epistemological issues. When the conventions of a society seem to function, when life is coherent and manageable, when all the definers of reality agree on their perception, epistemological questions are screened out and need not even be raised, much less agreed upon.[6] It is likely that most of the wisdom teachers, at least the ones usually stereotyped by that label, function with such an epistemological consensus. And predictably, their teaching need not be very risky nor very profound. They could work from "assured results."

It is when the conventions of society collapse, the consensus disappears, and life is experienced as incoherent, that the community is pressed to reexamine its epistemological presuppositions and deal with the fundamental issues of how the known is known and what is known.[7] It is the suggestion of this paper that Jeremiah lived precisely in a time of collapse of the consensus when the epistemological issues were most raw. The wisdom tradition which he apparently criticizes likely belonged to the royal definers of reality who continued to operate by a now discredited consensus. And conversely, Jeremiah (perhaps characteristically for a prophet) insists that epistemological questions must be raised which will seriously challenge the illusionary regnant consensus and the royal definition of reality.[8] Thus, I suggest, we may circumvent the problem of an adequate definition of wisdom if we discern the clash between those who presume an epistemological consensus (wisdom teachers, perhaps, but surely royal ideologues) and those who press the hard, unanswered epistemological issues (Jeremiah and, in my view, the prophets generally).[9]

If wisdom is characterized in some way as the deposit of the best observations coming from a long history of reflection on experience, then it is likely that this epistemology will settle for things which enhance continuity.[10] The substance of such a deposit will inevitably be conservative in its support of things as they are.[11] It is the task of the prophet, in such a context, not simply to protest such a deposit, but to raise fresh epistemological questions which may have been screened out by the not disinterested tradition of perception.[12]

## II

Second, in addition to the widespread attention to wisdom in the OT, it is also clear from recent study that we may identify two histories in the community of Israel, each powered by a different memory, each providing a different lens through which life may be experienced. One such history we may characterize as *Mosaic-covenantal.* It focused upon the radical intrusion of Yahweh through saving events on behalf of the historically powerless. That history is of course borne by the great succession of Moses, Joshua and Samuel, and continued to inform the prophets. That history experienced and presented the God of Israel as an intruder who was continually calling establishment reality into question. The tradition referred consistently to his intention for freedom and justice which characterized his coming to Israel. George Mendenhall has articulated this in sociological categories to suggest that this history powered a people's revolt against tyrannical urban government.[13] It represented a radical critique which prevented the absolutizing of the present arrangement. It also yielded a promise that an alternative social arrangement is yet to be given.

The other history we may characterize as *Davidic-royal.* It was shaped by the conviction of Yahweh's abiding, sustaining presence in behalf of legitimated political-cultural institutions, especially the royal house and derivatively the royal temple. Whereas the first history is radically concerned for *justice*, this royal history is more concerned for *order* ("peace and prosperity") and it relies on the institutions which are designed to create and maintain that order.

This Davidic-royal history can be assessed in more than one way. Read positively from a political perspective, the development of enduring social institutions enabled Israel to survive and develop as a responsible historical entity. Theologically, it permitted an institution to be a vehicle for a vision of a messianic reality expressed, e.g., in Psalm 72. This monarchial reality provided a guarantee of a humane order in a social world of hostility and threat. Such an institutionally self-conscious order of course needed a management mentality to sustain itself and to preside over its resources. It also needed protection (might), resources (riches), and technical skill (wisdom) to accomplish its goals.[14]

This same history can also be assessed negatively. Mendenhall most critically has characterized this history as "the paganization of Israel."[15] The development of bureaucracy, harem, standing army, tax districts and temple are not only institutions which concretize a social vision. They are also ways by which pagan, i.e., non-covenantal, patterns of life were adapted from Israel's neighbors.[16] This radical adaptation caused the abandonment of a certain vision of history, the loss of a covenantal notion of God and humanity and a forgetting of the messianic vision the monarchy was intended to guarantee. In short, all the epistemological questions were settled in terms of self-serving continuity. Proper protection became a way of authoritarian management. Necessary skill in governance became a way of preventing change. The consensus of the new institution created a context in which human questions could no longer be raised.[17]

Now it may be that Mendenhall has overstated the case. It is likely that this Jerusalem version of history and reality also has a more positive value as the only possibility of cultural continuity and creativity in Israel. But we may not miss the high cost in terms of human freedom and justice.[18]

These two histories, Mosaic-covenantal and Davidic-royal, continue in tension with each other all through Israel's story. During the period of the United Monarchy, it is likely that the rival priestly orders carry these rival traditions. Frank M. Cross[19] has indicated that the Aaronite order, perhaps linked to Hebron and Bethel, was in conflict with the Mushite order associated perhaps with Nob and Shiloh.[20]

In the period of the divided monarchy, it seems likely that the same two consciousnesses are in tension, borne by the dynasty and the prophets.[21] The enduring conflict between them surfaces in the unresolved epistemological question of what is known and how it is known. The royal (sapiential)[22] tradition, inevitably conservative, fashions a life-world which is essentially settled. What is valued, i.e., true and life-giving, consists in the resources managed by the king and his retinue. Alternatively, the Mosaic-covenantal tradition is characteristically in tension, as it finds the core of a legitimate epistemology in the Exodos-sojourn-Sinai memories, stories of intervention by Yahweh on behalf of the politically, historically disenfranchised against the Egyptian royal reality. The royal consciousness developed a consensus which screened out such an unbearable concern. It was unbearable because, on the one hand, it kept raising to consciousness those very elements in society which had been declared non-existent.[23] On the other hand, it was unbearable because it articulated a freedom and sovereignty for God which would not be domesticated by the royal apparatus.

This sustained tension between the two histories, as Paul Hanson has now shown,[24] continues into Israel's later history. Hanson has labeled the two opinions as "pragmatic" and "visionary." As he characterizes the two, they are radically distinguished by their epistemology. The pragmatists are those who benefit from the way things currently are. They give religious legitimacy to the present arrangement of realized eschatology. The visionaries are the "world-weary" who have been treated unfairly and so dare to risk and hope. They hold together the tragedy of human denial with a conviction of God's sovereign freedom which will lead to a new future, calling the present into question.

Not in any of these instances – not in the United Monarchy with Zadok and Abiathar, not in the divided monarchy with kings and prophets, not in the later period with the accommodators and hopers – is the issue resolved. It is always a question of *singular reliance* on Yahweh or a more *prudent*[25] embrace of the gifts of culture which seem more secure and which are not always obviously incompatible with Yahweh. The question of *prudence* and *singular reliance* focuses the epistemological issue. It is that issue which is addressed in this discussion of Jeremiah and wisdom in Jer 9:22-23.

### III

Jeremiah is placed at a critical juncture in the on-going tension between these two histories. The international history of the time suggested radical changes and disappearance of the old certainties. The internal political history of Judah is characterized by vacillation in foreign policy, with unrelieved fascination with Egypt, by an extraordinary sequence of kings who could not develop a sustained policy, and by a peculiar reform movement which impacted at least the king and no doubt his very particular constituency.

Jeremiah's perception of his people and his leaders is that things had gone utterly sour. Or in our terms, the Davidic-royal history had reached a point of irredeemable failure. The very consciousness which appeared dominant and seemed to have coopted the Mosaic tradition had failed. The prophet is repelled by what he sees. For him, it is a question whether the royal consciousness can be penetrated at all. The royal consciousness, secure in its own illusionary perceptual consensus, continued its risky game of self-deception (cf. 6:14, 8:11), engaging in the traditional royal ploys of purchased justice, denied humanness, double-tongued diplomacy. In that make-believe world, the royal apparatus could finally overcome or outlast every threat and question. While the royal arrangement potentially may have been the vehicle for a peculiar social vision, it had by this time become concerned only for self-securing and self-justification, and indeed, for survival.

Jeremiah's sense of the history of his people with Yahweh was so different that he could hardly communicate. He raised questions which lay outside the grasp of his royal contemporaries. Informed by a tradition of the freedom and sovereignty of God who could create and destroy, who could begin things and end things,[26] he took as his program that Yahweh will "build/plant, tear down/pluck up."[27] Kings in Israel seldom recognized that there had been beginnings when God would plant and build – because the royal reality appeared to be ordained forever. The royal perception was that there was no history before it, because it is the source of history. And surely there could be no ending, never plucking up and tearing down, because royal reality will endure. The royal arrangement fully contains history and things will continue to be as they have been. Jeremiah insists that there are radical turns, pasts to move from and futures to embrace. Kings know no past or future, but only "now" is to be defended and celebrated.

Jeremiah translated his alternative covenantal vision into an alternative political reality. Babylon is called and ordained by Yahweh to cause an end to a royal history which presumed it would go on forever:

> Behold, I will send for all the tribes of the north, says the Lord, and for Nebuchadnezzar, the King of Babylon, my servant, and I will bring them against this land and its inhabitants, and against all these nations round about. (Jer 25:9)[28]

That of course is more than kings can take and more than the royal consciousness can ever receive. It must be dismissed as a "weakening of the hands" of the king (38:4).

So the issue is joined between the two histories. It is joined visibly, for Jeremiah is in deathly conflict and great danger from those who cannot bear his word (11:21-23).[29] It is also joined internally, for Jeremiah knows in his person the wrenching of the two histories in conflict.[30] In his person there is anguish over valuing what is, deeper anguish over abandoning it for the sake of Yahweh's freedom and sovereignty. Jeremiah anguishes because he himself is not sure which history is true history. He cannot easily walk away from royal reality which must at times appear to be the only real history.[31] And yet he is deeply sure that that epistemology is based on an unreality. That wisdom is based on a consensus which has no correspondence to reality.

## IV

It is the suggestion of this essay that in 9:22-23 these two issues, (a) the problem of wisdom and the epistemological crisis, and (b) the two alternative histories in Israel, come together and provide in this text a focal point[32] from which the work of Jeremiah can be discerned. In these verses Jeremiah voices in sharpest form the hard epistemological questions facing Judah, the royal consciousness notwithstanding. In these verses, the two histories collide and are sorted out, in a way characteristic for the prophets and in a way quite unacceptable to the royal consciousness.[33]

Only in a most general way can anything be determined about the present placement of the verses in the text. It is possible that the unit is displaced here.[34] In the general movement of 8:4 – 10:25, we may note the recurrent reference to themes of "know and "wisdom":

My people does not *know* the ordinance of the Lord. (8:7)

How can you say "we are *wise*." . . . .

Behold the *false* pen of the scribes have made it a *lie*.[35]

The *wise* men shall be put to shame . . .

and what *wisdom* is in them? (8:8-9)

They did not *know* how to blush. (8:12b)[36]

They do not *know* me, says the Lord. (9:2b)

They refuse to *know* me, says the Lord. (9:5b)

Who is the man so *wise* that he can *understand* this? (9:11)

Send for the *wise* women to come. . . . (9:16b)[37]

I *know*, O Lord, that the way of man is not in himself,

that it is not in man who walks to direct his steps,

Correct me, O Lord. . . . (10:23-24a)[38]

Pour out thy wrath upon the nations that *know* thee not. (10:25a)

Two problems must be acknowledged in such a listing. First, it is likely that this is a collection of various fragments which have no original coherence. Nonetheless, they have been brought together, and it may well be that our themes of *knowing* and *wisdom* have been the guide for bringing them together.[39] Second, it is obvious that the words italicized have a variety of different nuances, exploring a whole field of meanings. But perhaps even with this recognition, it is not too much to conclude that in all of them the poetry means to pose the central epistemological question which Jeremiah discerned at the end of royal history. The ones who claim to know do not know. There is no knowledge of the Torah (8:7), nor of how to blush (8:12), nor of Yahweh (9:2, 5; 10:25). The only positive knowing (10:23-24) is done by Jeremiah himself in a statement suggesting that he knows what the others do not know. Thus, even the positive statement is another way of asserting that the others do not know. Most of all, what they do not know is that man (= king) is not self-reliant. Jeremiah's knowledge is contrasted with the non-covenantal foolishness of the royal consciousness.[40] This climactic statement recognizes that human well-being is not derived from human capacity.

Thus 10:23-24 speak of true wisdom. But the wisdom of Judah, presumably held by members of the other history in the royal circle, is a joke (cf. 8:8-9), because in all their pretension, they cannot do what must be done. The wise men have failed (9:11) and the only wisdom now valued is that which knows how to weep (9:16), i.e., those who do not pursue their self-deception continuously but who have the sensitivity to respond appropriately to death.[41] That is, the real wisdom appropriate to the moment is to recognize the end that surely has come upon this people. There is no other wisdom in Judah which now can make any difference.

The entire "unit" uses images which are at least reminiscent of wisdom teaching. It employs analogy (8:6-7), rhetorical questions (8:4-5, 8-9, 12, 19, 23, 9:11)[42] as well as admonition (9:3-4). Thus the style of the unit, if it may be regarded now as a unit, raises the question of knowing and wisdom in a context of painful ending and death. True knowing consists in facing Yahweh's remarkable freedom. Real wisdom consists in acknowledging death and responding appropriately (9:20). The foolishness of the so-called wise is to have business as usual. The lie they speak (8:8, 9:2, 4), the deception they practice (9:4-5) is that they continue in the illusion of the royal history which knows no end or beginning but only cherishes šālôm (8:11, 15) and anticipates healing (8:22)[43] but cannot recognize that this history is finished. It is the other history, of planting and building, of plucking up and tearing down, in which Judah must now participate. Kings cannot do that.

So the epistemological issue is joined. It is not a theoretical issue of experience and authority. It is a question of having defined reality in ways which keep what is real from ever surfacing. And Jeremiah must now use his best imagination to show that it is history with a covenant-making God that is the only history. Every other history is an illusion and a deception.

## V

Thus 9:22-23 is not inappropriate to its present context which concerns wisdom/foolishness on the way to death. Jeremiah had discerned that while the royal consciousness presumed its own continued well-being, that history was already destined for death. The form of this saying is likely sapiential,[44] but that is difficult to sustain in light of our fuzzy definitions. The messenger formula at the beginning seems inappropriate to its style but it may be imposed on this saying in order to claim authority in the harsh conflicts of epistemologies. (In chapters 8 – 10, the messenger formula occurs elsewhere only in 9:6, 16). The concluding formula, "něᵓum yahweh," also occurs in 8:17, 9:2, 5, 8, 21, 24, but seems to recur in various settings without impacting the rhetoric.[45]

Thus both formulae seem to be extraneous and may be discounted. Without them the saying appears to be a didactic statement, consisting in two parts, first three negative admonitions, then a contrasting positive with three members together with a motivational clause:

> Let not (ᵓal)[46] the wise one glory in his wisdom, and
> Let not (ᵓal) the mighty one glory in his might
> Let not (ᵓal) the rich one glory in his riches
> But (kîᵓim) let him who glories, glory in this,
>           that he understands and knows me.
> Surely (kî) I am Yahweh who does kindness,
>           justice, and
>           righteousness in the land.
> Surely (kî) in them I delight.

The three negatives, all modifying yithallēl,[47] introduce a triad. The reflexive verb serves here to turn the subject back on himself.[48] What is prohibited by the negative plus the reflexive is preoccupation with self and self's resources.[49] The alternative is sharply presented by the abrupt *kî ʾim*. The same verb is used, but the object now is not self-resources. The boast now concerns Yahweh.

The two motivational clauses, both introduced by *kî*, serve to delineate further this recommended choice so sharply contrasted with the previous objects of wisdom, might and riches. Yahweh is not to be confused with or associated with wisdom, might or riches. He is differently characterized, again by a triad, *ḥesed, mišpaṭ* and *ṣĕdāqâ*. That triad is surely deliberately cast in parallel form but radically contrasted in substance. The second *kî* clause further identifies what is legitimate for approval and celebration.

The form is clearly didactic, but not strenuously hortatory.[50] The *kî ʾim* is too common a form to be identified as sapiential. But we may note a peculiarly close parallel in Prov 23:17-18a:

> Let not (*ʾal*) your heart envy sinners
>> But (*kî ʾim*) continue in the fear of the Lord all the day.
> Surely (*kî ʾim*) there is a future
>> and your hope is not cut off.[51]

The parallel in form is close, but not total in the three parts: *ʾal, kî ʾim, kî ʾim*. But the second *kî ʾim* in the proverb does not function as a disjunctive as does the first but in fact serves as a motivational clause. With that provision, the form is a striking parallel to the passage under consideration which has *ʾal, kî ʾim, kî*. The rhetorical stress of our unit falls on *kî ʾim* which serves to contrast the two triads. The *kî ʾim* is used broadly and is not the monopoly of any circle of tradition. While it serves to contrast, it may also serve to introduce a radical call to a certain kind of behavior:

> And now, Israel what does the Lord require of you,
>> but (*kî ʾim*) to fear . . . to walk . . . to love,
>>> to serve . . . to keep . . .? (Deut 10:12-13)

> And what does the Lord require of you
>> but (*kî ʾim*) to do justice,
>> to love kindness, and
>> to walk humbly with your God? (Mic 6:8)[52]

It may be used to introduce a new teaching which replaces the old:

> In those days they shall no longer say:
>> "The fathers have eaten sour grapes,
>> and the children's teeth are set on edge."
> But (*kî ʾim*) every one shall die for his own sin;
>> each man who eats sour grapes,
>> his teeth shall set on edge. (Jer 31:29-30)[53]

It may be used to contrast what is in quantity but of indifferent value and what is rare but precious:

> But (*kî ʾim*) the poor man had nothing but one
>      little ewe lamb
>      which he had bought. (2 Sam 12:3)[54]

It serves to create an opening for new behavior:

> The Lord made a covenant with them, and commanded them,
> "You shall not fear other gods or bow yourselves to
>      them or serve them or sacrifice to them;
> But (*kî ʾim*) you shall fear the Lord . . .
>      You shall not serve other gods
> But (*kî ʾim*) you shall fear the Lord your God . . ." (2 Kgs 17:35-36, 38-39)[55]

These parallel uses make clear the radical contrast Jeremiah draws between the two triads, which are not simply lists of virtues and vices but which embody the core of the two histories and which provide the parameters of contrasting epistemologies. The form itself would suggest that there is a deathly way and a life-giving way for Israel. Jeremiah's context is one in which the death-choosers think their way will lead to life. His anguish is that he has discerned its sure end in death.

## VI

The first triad—*wisdom, might, riches*—characterizes one history in Israel, the royal history. These three terms occur nowhere else together. The prophet has constructed a new triad which intends to summarize the whole royal history which has continually reassured and deceived its key actors, but which has now brought Judah to the point of death. One could not imagine a more radical critique of the royal consciousness, for Jeremiah disposes in one stroke of all the sources of security and well-being upon which the royal establishment is built.

His critique is of course more radical than the older proverbial wisdom. That reflective tradition had been aware of the temptation of riches (Prov 11:28, 23:4, 28:20). It saw the positive good of riches but believed they are gifts which will be given and are not to be pursued for themselves (Prov 3:16, 8:18, 10:4, 22, 22:4, 28:25).

Even that tradition is radical enough to see that riches deceive and are finally linked to foolishness which will destroy:

> A rich man is wise in his own eyes
>      but a poor man who has understanding (*bîn*) will find him out. (Prov 28:11)[56]

But we are still in the area of relatively simple virtue in a quid-pro-quo world. In that world there is little reflection at all upon the problem of might. It is not particularly celebrated and other things are better (Prov 16:32), but it is scarcely an item of interest. And certainly wisdom receives no critique, except as noted, when one is "wise in his own eyes." In that world, *might* is of little concern, *wisdom* is to be valued, and only *riches* are seen as a danger.

Thus Jeremiah's polemic does not grow out of that tradition in any direct sense. It is only when these matters are discerned in royal history that they are a threat. That history, beginning with Solomon,[57] has turned these three matters into a way of life which is self-securing and finally numbing, both toward human need as well as divine purpose. While Jeremiah may draw upon wisdom teaching, he fashions this negative summary out of a direct response to royal history which seemed utterly secure and yet which now had led to death. That he adds wisdom and might to the sapiential warning on riches indicates how he has deepened the critique to an epistemological level:

(1) Riches are of course a royal prerogative. They are the gift to the king (1 Kgs 3:11, 13, 2 Chron 1:12, Dan 11:2, Esth 1:41, 5:11). They are an identifying mark of a good king (of David, 1 Chron 29:12, 28; of Solomon, 1 Kgs 10:23, 2 Chron 9:22; of Jehoshaphat, 2 Chron 17:5, 18:1; of Hezekiah, 2 Chron 32:27). They are the king's to give (1 Sam 17:25). Riches belong precisely to royal awareness.

(2) Might does not refer here simply to the fullness of manhood as it sometimes does. Here it refers to the capacity of the royal establishment to work its will by human power before which none may issue a challenge. *Gbr* is the peculiar claim of the king (2 Sam 10:7, 16:6, 20:7, 23:9-22). The regime managed to order its own universe and combine the mythic power of virility together with the hardware of a war machine.[58]

(3) And wisdom in such a context is no longer the power to discern, but the capacity to manage and control, to reduce everything to royal proportions. By placing wisdom in the context of this triad, Jeremiah has defined and nuanced it in a harshly critical way. Wisdom is presented as self-serving. The form itself makes wisdom negative.

The triad as a whole speaks of placing trust in places from which can come no health, but the king never knows it. The critique of Jeremiah thus may be related to several other passages. (1) Psalm 49, often associated with the sapiential tradition of Israel,[59] reflects on men who trust in their wealth and who boast of the abundance of their riches.

> Yes, he shall see even the wise die . . .
>     and leave their wealth to another
> Man cannot abide in his pomp (*yqr*). . . .
>     This is the fate of those who have foolish confidence. . . .
>     (vss. 11, 13, 14a; cf. 17-18, 21 [Engl. 10-13a; cf. 16-17, 20])

The psalm discerns the boundary of self-securing. These apparent sources of long life and well-being can promise nothing.[60] (2) Ps 52, not inappropriately assigned in the superscription against royal power, begins with an attack on a mighty man who boasts (*tithallēl*) (vs. 3) and who trusts in the abundance of his riches and who seeks refuge in his wealth (vs. 9). The psalm concludes with a contrast of the well-being of the one who eschews might and riches and trusts the goodness of God. Thus David and Saul are presented as models of the two histories, David being the one who trusts and Saul the one who secures his own way and must surely come to ruin. (3) Isa 5:21-23 in turn presents a radical critique of those who are,

> *wise* in their own eyes (cf. Prov 28:11)
> *mighty* in drinking and
> takers of *bribes.*

While the third member of the triad is not quite "riches," the triad is very close to that of our verse in Jeremiah.[61] The criticism of Isaiah turns each element so that it must be negative: not wise, but wise *in their own eyes*, not mighty, but mighty *in drinking*, not rich, but only *in bribes*.

None of these texts, Pss 49, 52 or Isa 5:21-23, contains our triad. But the various configurations suggest a pattern of critique against the most elemental values of the royal-urban consciousness which by the time of Josiah was bringing Judah to death. Each of these texts has affinities with what is commonly thought to be a wisdom teaching. Jeremiah challenges the foundations of the establishment credo.[62] In 5:27-28 he appears to appeal to a tradition of such criticism which likely is rooted in and derived from sapiential circles. But he has recast it in more radical ways. His critique characteristically is not interested in either inner attitudes or in conduct per se, but in the inevitable price paid in terms of human injustice. Thus he links deceit and oppression to refusal to know Yahweh (9:5).[63] The practice of self-deception expresses itself in terms of oppression. That brings death, and Jeremiah had seen it clearly even though the royal mentality continued to deny it.

## VII

The alternative history is expressed in two ways. First, to "know Yahweh." We have already noted the references in chs. 8-10 on this theme. See also 2:8, 4:22, 5:4, 28-29, 7:5-6, 22:3, 16, 24:7, 31:34. The theme of knowing Yahweh has been well explored and requires no additional comment here. Wolff[64] has established that it means knowledge of the mighty deeds and the torah claims. Huffmon[65] has shown that it refers to acknowledgment of covenantal sovereignty and required allegiance. Thus the "refusal to know" is the fundamental critique against the royal consciousness because it could not embrace the serious impact of covenantal reality without giving up its claims and pretensions. Thus in contrast to the first triad, Jeremiah announces his primary theme which serves to discredit and dismantle the epistemology of the regime.

Jeremiah asserts that if Judah will have something of legitimate pride, she must terminate the royal history which leads to death and embrace the history of the covenant. That history, of course, is always precarious, never yields stately mansions, but in inscrutable ways brings life.[66]

In terse fashion the prophet inquires about national priorities in relation to national well-being. As in the more expansive statement of 22:13-17,[67] he lays out the life/death issues:

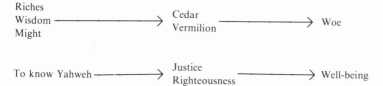

The anguish of the prophet is that he knows, cognitively and covenantally, what the royal community in its congenital stupidity could not learn.

Second, this alternative history is summarized in an equally powerful triad, ḥesed, mišpāṭ, ṣĕdāqâ. As in the first triad, the prophet has shrewdly expressed the central issue, namely, solidarity not only between person (king) and God, but in the community, the very solidarity against which wisdom/riches/might militate.[68]

This second triad occurs, to my knowledge, only in one other text, Hos 2:21-22, upon which Jeremiah is likely dependent.[69] It occurs only in these two prophets most deeply sensitive to the pathos of God[70] as articulated in covenant and most knowing about the deathly course of Israel. Only these two dare to entertain the alternative "knowing Yahweh," which will bring new life. Jeremiah has recited the entire history of death (riches, wisdom, might). Hosea has in parallel fashion reviewed the history of fickleness and betrayal. Incredibly, both of them can now use this triad to speak of an alternative history with the radically faithful one who can bring newness where death seemed final.[71] It is not very helpful to try to identify what in this comes from the traditions of wisdom or covenant or prophets. The epistemological crisis does not concern simply circles of tradition but the change made in all perceptions (of every tradition) by radical Yahwistic faith. Every epistemology is called into question when knowing begins in the faithfulness of Yahweh which requires and evokes a responding faithfulness from Israel. Hosea and Jeremiah believed that a new history was possible, but on quite different grounds.

## VIII

The two triads set the choice Israel must make. These triads, contrasted by the emphatic kî ᵓim, set in juxtaposition the two histories, the one of self-glorification, the other of vulnerable fidelity. By setting the two histories together as indeed they had finally collided in his time, Jeremiah sets the choice Israel must now make. We may learn more of the prophet's intent by noting the two envelope words, hithallēl and ḥāpēṣ. The crisis in Israel's history concerns a cause for glorification. Since Solomon, Israel had sought a cause for glory and since Solomon had been glorying in deathly things.

The act of boasting in and of itself is not bad. When it is addressed away from self toward God, it is of course approved and we may call it "praise"(Ps 34:3, cf. Jer 4:2, Ps 64:11). The problem for Jeremiah is not boasting, but it is boasting turned toward self, i.e., toward royal history as the generator of its own life, meaning and security. Again we may note the affinities with the psalms already cited:

> Men who *trust* (*bāṭaḥ*) in their wealth
>     and *boast* of the abundance of their riches. (Ps 49:7)

> Why do you *boast*, O mighty man. . . .
> See the man who would not make God his refuge,
>     but *trusted* (*bāṭaḥ*) in the abundance of his riches
>     and sought refuge in his wealth. (Ps 52:3, 9)

In both texts the term *tithallēl* is parallel to *bāṭaḥ*. Boasting thus is understood as misplaced trust. The word *bāṭaḥ* occurs in various contexts, 5:17, 7:4, 8:13, 9:3, 13:25 and Isa 31:1. See especially the harsh declaration of Jer 2:37:

> Surely the Lord has rejected those in whom you *trust*,

and the contrast:

> Cursed is the man who *trusts* in man. . . .
> Blessed is the man who *trusts* in the Lord
>     whose *trust* is in the Lord. (17:5a, 7)

Again the two histories are clearly contrasted.

Concerning the formula used in our text, we may learn from the defiant statement of the king of Israel to the taunting Ben-Hadad:

> Let not him that girds on his armor boast himself (*yithallēl*)[72]
> as he that puts it off. (1 Kgs 20:11)

Probably this was a sapiential saying which warned against claiming too much in prospect, in contrast to legitimate claims in retrospect.[73] Thus it is a warning against presuming too much for one's own powers in a situation likely to be beyond one's control. But it is now used in this narrative as a defiant affirmation of trust in Yahweh against enormous odds. On the basis of this parallel, Jeremiah may be understood as throwing down the gauntlet of radical faith against enormous odds, i.e., of trusting and obeying Yahweh's covenantal gifts and demands in the face of external threat and internal collapse. In the same defiant manner as 1 Kgs 20:11, Jeremiah asserts that the power of riches, wisdom and might, the substance of royal history, is a poor match against *ḥesed, mišpāṭ* and *ṣĕdāqâ* in determining what will finally shape history.

Attention may also be called to David's defiance of Goliath.[74] While not a wisdom saying, it also makes a defiant contrast in the face of the enemy. The two-part assertion is not unlike that of our text:

> You come to me with a sword
>         with a spear and
>         with a javelin[75]

> but I come to you in the name of the Lord of hosts
> the God of the armies of Israel
> whom you have defied. (1 Sam 17:45)[76]

Again we are offered an assertion of the power of Yahweh against the apparent power of Goliath. The giant is mismatched because David's presuppositions lie outside Philistine awareness and call into question that entire understanding of reality.

In both 1 Kgs 20:11 and 1 Sam 17:45, sharply contrasting views of reality are presented in the context of war and in the face of a major threat. In both cases reliance on Yahweh calls into question the presuppositions of the other party. In a similar way Jeremiah uses what appears to be a sapiential form, perhaps honed by usage in a context of defiance against a stronger military power, to call Judah to a new history in covenant.[77] The Israelites whom Jeremiah addresses are as misinformed about reality as are Goliath and Ben-Hadad. A wisdom teacher might declare what is proper for boasting and what is not. A war story might turn this against an arrogant enemy. But the form has been radicalized by Jeremiah to carry the fundamental challenge to royal presuppositions, and this against his own king. If that is a correct way of understanding the text, we may better understand the promise to Jeremiah (1:17-19) that he will be a safe man of war against the odds, for the risky proposition of Jeremiah against his contemporaries is at least as bold and risky as David against Goliath or Ahab against Ben-Hadad.[78]

The term of self-congratulations, *tithallēl*, is balanced by the concluding term *ḥāpēṣ* in our text.[79] Its climactic position gives its stress, so that the entire saying contrasts the self-congratulations of the royal managers and the unfailing desires of Yahweh. The prophet clearly means to assert that the history of Israel and her risky future will not be determined by self-securing but by his purposes. *Ḥāpēṣ* cannot be assigned to any circle of tradition in particular. It is used for acceptance of cultic offerings, in wisdom instruction and in interpersonal relations.

Applied to Yahweh, several stresses are important: (1) The term is used to assert Yahweh's radical freedom to do what he wills (Pss 115:3, 135:6, Jonah 1:14). (2) In his radical freedom he may reject (Pss 65:12; 66:4; 5:5) and even will death (Judg 12:23, 1 Sam 2:24, Ezek 18:23). (3) His characteristic action is that he wills life and not death (Ezek 18:32, 33:11), but the gift of life requires radical turning. Thus the word bears the good news that Yahweh wills covenanted living. (In this regard as in so many, Jeremiah has affinities with Ezekiel and holds out the promise of life.) (4) The substance of his desiring of life is the triad of the alternative history of *ḥesed, mišpāṭ, ṣĕdāqâ*. When this is practiced, life comes. When it is not, death comes. This understanding of the will of Yahweh is twice articulated:

> Surely I DESIRE *ḥesed* and not sacrifice
> *knowledge of God* rather than burnt offerings.
> (Hos 6:6, cf. 1 Sam 15:22-23)[80]

He does not retain his anger forever
because he DELIGHTS in ḥesed. (Mic 7:18)

The dramatic teaching thus presents a good news/bad news pattern which surely will lead to life or death.

## IX

It is not too much to suggest that 9:22-23 might provide a screen through which Jeremiah can be understood more generally. It is not at all, as Duhm suggested, "a harmless, meaningless text." Rather it articulates the basic issues that finally cannot be avoided in Judah, especially in the seventh to the sixth centuries. Our analysis suggests that Jeremiah spoke out of a complex relation with Israel's sapiential tradition. On the one hand he utilized a speech form and manner of instruction which is likely sapiential. On the other hand, he polemicizes against a self-contained wisdom which will bring death. The presumed wisdom of Israel has turned out to be a foolishness to death. Conversely, the foolishness of the fragile purposes of Yahweh[81] which seems of little note finally will bring life.

In categories of Christian faith, Jeremiah here presents a theology of the cross in protest against a theology of glory. In that way, the use of this saying by Paul in 1 Cor 1:26-31 is seen to be not casually or incidentally related. Rather in dealing with the scandal of the gospel, Paul has discerned that Jeremiah rightly presented the scandal which violates royal history.[82] The wisdom of kings is foolishness. The strength of kings is weakness. The riches of kings is poverty (cf. 2 Cor 8:9). What Paul discerned in Jesus of Nazareth[83] Jeremiah has seen about Judah's death gasp in his time. Things are not as they seem, especially to kings (cf. Prov 25:2). That is what wisdom always sought, to find out how things are. God's capacity to hide things outdistances the capacity of the kings to find out.

---

[1] The literature is extensive and well known. See the bibliography by J. Crenshaw, *Studies in Ancient Israelite Wisdom* (New York: Ktav, 1976) 46-60. Special note should be taken of the work of Crenshaw, Murphy, von Rad and Zimmerli and of the phrase of N. Whybray, "The Intellectual Tradition of Israel."

[2] Crenshaw, "Method in Determining Wisdom Influence upon 'Historical' Literature," *JBL* 88 (1969) 129-42; reprinted in *Studies in Ancient Israelite Wisdom*, 481-94.

[3] See S. Terrien, "Amos and Wisdom," *Israel's Prophetic Heritage* (eds. B. W. Anderson and W. Harrelson; New York: Harper & Bros., 1962) 108-15, H. W. Wolff, *Amos the Prophet* (Philadelphia: Fortress, 1973) and W. Whedbee, *Isaiah and Wisdom* (New York: Abingdon, 1971).

[4] See the sparse suggestions of J. Lindblom, "Wisdom in the Old Testament Prophets," *Wisdom in Israel and in the Ancient Near East* (VTSup 3; H. H. Rowley Festschrift; eds. M. Noth and D. W. Thomas; Leiden: Brill, 1955) 193-200.

[5] See the essay by Professor McKane in this volume. Several matters will require a quite new perspective on the question: (a) J. Muilenburg ("Baruch the Scribe," *Proclamation and Presence* [eds. J. I. Durham and J. R. Porter; London: SCM, 1970] 215-38) has opened new possibilities in

understanding those parts of Jeremiah which may be tilted toward sapiential influences. More radically, G. Wanke (*Untersuchungen zur sogenannten Baruchschrift*; BZAW 122, 1971) has called into question our usual presuppositions about Baruch; (b) the matter of Jeremiah's relation to Deuteronomic circles of tradition must be rethought in light of the work of M. Weinfeld (*Deuteronomy and the Deuteronomic School* [Oxford: Clarendon, 1972]) with the prospect of wisdom influences; (c) it is now clear that the rigid distinction of categories among various traditions cannot be sustained in the neat manner of Mowinckel. For all these reasons, new categories of interpretation will need to be found for Jeremiah studies which, among other things, take wisdom influences into account.

⁶ In the following references to epistemological issues, I am working with the constructs especially articulated by P. Berger, *The Sacred Canopy* (Garden City, NY: Doubleday, 1969), Thomas Luckmann, *The Invisible Religion* (New York: Macmillan, 1967) and Berger and Luckmann, *The Social Construction of Reality* (Garden City, NY: Doubleday, 1966). Pertinent also is the notion of "life-world" from Alfred Schutz, *The Structures of the Life-World* (Evanston: Northwestern University, 1973). The wisdom teachers reflected in the positive teaching of proverbs presumed a life-world in which there was a major consensus which needed to be neither challenged nor defended.

⁷ See the discussion of *anomie* by Robert Merton, *Social Theory and Social Structure* (Glencoe, IL: Free, 1957) chapters 4 and 5. Jeremiah clearly spoke in a context of anomie which was derived from Israel's ineffective ways of knowing. Crenshaw has been especially sensitive to these matters in his concern for wisdom and theodicy.

⁸ K. Underwood, *The Church, the University and Social Policy* (2 vols.; Middletown, CT: Wesleyan University, 1969) has shown how the crucial task of ministry is the raising of epistemological issues. It means to be concerned with "systems of knowledge and power"(1. 126). It is clear that this was the crucial task in the time of Jeremiah as in the present time, when the old consensus has collapsed. It may well be that Hosea and Jeremiah, both of whom stress "knowing," are the very ones who have in Israel discerned the depth of the crisis and are aware that any lesser question is futile.

⁹ I do not intend to utilize any narrow, precise definition of "wisdom" nor do I presume any necessarily close relation between royal court and an identifiable wisdom school. Rather I am concerned more broadly with the whole way in which an established community of opinion preserves, discerns, knows and decides. Wisdom both affirms and presents a critique of this unexamined intellectual climate. It is my impression that scholarship may miss these urgent issues if it focuses on narrow and precise definitions and misses the epistemological crisis. My approach here addresses what Crenshaw calls "wisdom thinking." This approach enables us to take seriously the stress on falseness, so well underscored by T. Overholt, *The Threat of Falsehood* (SBT 2/16; London: SCM, 1970). Šqr does not refer to concrete acts, but to a wrong discernment of all of life.

¹⁰ N Whybray, *The Intellectual Tradition in the Old Testament* (BZAW 135; New York: de Gruyter, 1974) has advanced the discussion by speaking more inclusively of an "intellectual tradition" rather than a wisdom movement. This paper urges that wisdom be recognized as the consensus by which established order sustains and legitimates itself. Dennis McCarthy has suggested the phrase, "intellectual patrimony" (oral communication).

¹¹ See R. Gordis, "The Social Background of Wisdom Literature," *Poets, Prophets, and Sages* (Bloomington: Indiana University, 1971) 160-97, and B. Kovacs, "Is There a Class-Ethic in Proverbs?" *Essays in Old Testament Ethics* (eds. J. Crenshaw and J. T. Willis; New York: Ktav, 1974) 173-89.

¹² On the discussion of the relation of interest and perception in heremeneutics, see F. Herzog, "Liberation Hermeneutic as Ideology Critique?" *Int* 28 (1974) 387-403, J. Miranda, *Marx and the Bible* (Maryknoll, NY: Orbis, 1974) and Roy Sano, "Neo-Orthodoxy and Ethnic Liberation Theology," *Christianity and Crisis*, 35 (1975) 258-64.

¹³ His programmatic statement is in *The Tenth Generation* (Baltimore: The Johns Hopkins University, 1973) but he had indicated the major line of his argument already in "The Hebrew

Conquest of Palestine," *BA* 25 (1962) 66-87; reprinted in *The Biblical Archaeologist Reader* 3 (Garden City, NY: Doubleday, 1970) 100-20.

[14] That list is not so different from the conclusion of Mendenhall, "The Monarchy," *Int* 29 (1975) 156, ". . . in any given culture, ideology, social organization and technology" are both essential and interrelated. The triad of Jer 9:22 must be understood not in terms of moral virtues, but in terms of sociological realities.

[15] Cf. "The Monarchy," 160, and "Samuel's Broken Rib," *No Famine in the Land* (eds. J. Flanagan and A. Robinson; Missoula, MT: Scholars, 1975) 67.

[16] See the primary evidence and example of I. Mendelsohn, "Samuel's Denunciation of Kingship in Light of the Akkadian Documents from Ugarit," *BASOR* 143 (1956) 17-22.

[17] See the statement of N. Gottwald, "Biblical Theology or Biblical Sociology?" *Radical Religion* 2 (1975) 42-57, showing the political implications of some forms of religious consensus.

[18] The royal consciousness is never primarily concerned about such matters. In that context one might observe the "interest" served in the program of B. F. Skinner, *Beyond Freedom and Dignity* (New York: Knopf, 1971).

[19] Frank M. Cross, *Canaanite Myth and Hebrew Epic* (Cambridge: Harvard University, 1973) 195-215.

[20] See the development from Cross' suggestion by B. Halpern, "Levitic Participation in the Reform Cult of Jereboam I," *JBL* 95 (1976) 31-42.

[21] See R. Rendtorff, "Reflections on the Early History of Prophecy in Israel," *History and Hermeneutic* (ed. R. W. Funk; *JTC* 4 [New York: Harper & Row, 1967]) 14-34, who explores the dialectical relation of king and prophet.

[22] It is my judgment and presupposition in this paper that sapiential tendencies, broadly identified, can best be understood in relation to the royal consciousness. For the purposes of this paper, I do not regard the more precise and technical issues of definition to be pertinent. Nor do I wish to deny the force of the "clan hypothesis." But it seems clear that so far as Jeremiah is concerned, he deals with a royal phenomenon.

[23] On the royal attitude to peasant, see the unpublished paper by J. M. Halligan, "The Role of the Peasant in the Amarna Period," *SBL Seminar Papers* (Missoula, MT: Scholars, 1976) 155-71. The power of the throne is enormous in denying history to the powerless.

[24] Paul D. Hanson, *The Dawn of Apocalyptic* (Philadelphia: Fortress, 1975).

[25] There can be little doubt that "prudence" is crucial to a sapiential approach to life. What is apparent in the sociological studies cited is that such prudence is never poltically or socially disinterested. Prudence is concerned not to disturb the present ordering. (Amos 5:13 is characteristic in that regard.)

[26] There can be little doubt that Jeremiah belongs to the circle of northern tradition fed by Mosaic memories and expressed in the traditions of Hosea and Deuteronomy.

[27] Variations on the theme occur in 1:10, 12:14-17, 18:7-9, 24:6, 31:28, 32:10, 42:10, 45:4. Cf. Robert Bach, "Bauen und Pflanzen," *Studien zur Theologie der alttestamentlichen Überlieferungen*, (eds. R. Rendtorff and K. Koch; Neukirchen: Neukirchener Verlag, 1961) 7-32.

[28] See also 27:6 and 43:10. While it may be that textual problems can lessen the claim of these particular texts as W. Lemke ("Nebuchadnezzar, My Servant," *CBQ* 28[1966] 45-50) has argued, there is little question that this expectation from Babylon is central to Jeremiah's discernment of Yahweh's will for Judah. Cf. T. W. Overholt, "King Nebuchadnezzar in the Jeremiah Tradition," *CBQ* 30 (1968) 39-48.

[29] In an unpublished paper, "Jeremiah and the 'Men of Anatot'," S. Dean McBride, Jr. has suggested that the men of Anathoth are not among the villagers of his home community but must be located "within the Jerusalem establishment of the prophet's day, particularly among prominent Temple personnel." Such a judgment would strengthen the intensity of the conflict between the two perceptions of reality.

[30] It is not necessary to pursue the question of the meaning of Jeremiah's "laments" here. Even if H. G. Reventlow (*Liturgie und prophetisches Ich bei Jeremia* [Gütersloh: Mohn, 1963] 205-57) is not correct in their being public liturgical pieces, he is surely correct in seeing that the struggle

concerns not a private problem but anguish over the course and end of Israel's public life. On that anguish as it reflects an alternative consciousness, cf. A. J. Heschel, *The Prophets* (New York: Harper & Row, 1962) esp. 108-27.

[31] That issue is clearest in the encounter with Hananiah, Jer 27-28. Cf. H. J. Kraus, *Prophetie in der Krisis* (Neukirchen: Neukirchener Verlag, 1964) 82-104.

[32] Duhm, *Das Buch Jeremia*, 1901, 97, had dismissed the text as "ein harmlos unbedeutender Spruch." On the contrary, this paper suggests that it may provide a decisive point of entry to understand the tensions and intent of the tradition of Jeremiah.

[33] The verses contain no textual problems which need detain us. Perhaps the last negative of vs. 22 might have an added conjunction to parallel the second, but it is not necessary. In vs. 23, the LXX has a conjunction before the second object of the participle, but that also is unnecessary.

The authenticity of the saying has been challenged by Duhm and recently by W. Holladay, *Jeremiah: Spokesman Out of Time* (Philadelphia: United Church, 1974) 59.

The following, however, retain it: F. Giesebrecht, *Das Buch Jeremia* (Göttinger Handkommentar zum Alten Testament; Göttingen: Vandenhoeck & Ruprecht, 1907) 61-63; W. Rudolph, *Jeremia* (HAT 12; 2d ed.; Tübingen; Mohr [Siebeck], 1958) 63; J. Bright, *Jeremiah* (AB 21; Garden City, NY: Doubleday, 1965) 75-80. There seems no compelling reason to regard the words as other than those of Jeremiah.

[34] So A. S. Peake, *Jeremiah and Lamentations* (2 vols.; The Century Bible; Edinburgh: Jack, 1910-11) 1. 169; A. W. Streane, *Jeremiah* (Cambridge Bible; Cambridge University, 1913) 68.

[35] On *šqr* here and characteristically, see Overholt, *The Threat of Falsehood*, 74-82. The lie refers to a fundamental misconception of covenantal reality.

[36] On forgetting how to blush, see the remarkable words of Heschel, *Who is Man?* (Stanford: Stanford University, 1965) 112-14. He quotes our verse in making the contrast between self-glorification and "a sense of ultimate embarrassment."

[37] Clearly the term refers to skill and so is not theologically important. Cf. 4:22 for a similar use. Nonetheless, it adds to the semantic field being explored by the prophet.

[38] This saying clearly echoes sayings in the book of Proverbs. Cf. von Rad, *Old Testament Theology* (2 vols.; New York: Harper & Bros., 1962) 1. 439, and his comment on Prov 16:9, 19:21, 21:2, 16:2, 20:24, 21:30-31. Each raises the issue both of this passage and of our primary text. The plea for correction with the word *yāsar* suggests a sapiential-educational tradition. Cf. H. J. Kraus, "Geschichte als Erziehung," *Probleme Biblischer Theologie* (ed. H. W. Wolff; Munich: Kaiser, 1971) 267-71. Note the importance of the word to Hosea. Whybray (*Intellectual Tradition in the OT*, 128), while suggesting the term belongs to the sphere of education, denies it specifically to wisdom.

[39] Westermann, *Jeremia* (Stuttgart: Calwer, 1967) 36, suggests the principle of *Stichwort*.

[40] See Donald Gowan (*When Man Becomes God* [Pittsburgh: Pickwick, 1975]) on the problem of hybris as it shapes royal consciousness. See W. McKane (*Prophets and Wise Men* [SBT 44; Naperville, IL: Allenson, 1965] 89-90) who speaks of "self-contained . . . sagacity," and helpfully relates our passage to a trajectory of related passages.

[41] Cf. Amos 5:16. Perhaps the same motif is present in Matt 5:4, surely a sapiential form. The blessed are the ones who are wise enough to know the appropriate response to the proper time. Royal consciousness is likely not attentive to the times, because the establishment believes only in managed time. Cf. Jer 8:7 on not knowing the times, surely not the time for repentance and death, and von Rad, *Wisdom in Israel* (New York and Nashville: Abingdon, 1972) 138-43.

[42] In my article, "Jeremiah's Use of Rhetorical Questions," *JBL* 92 (1973) 358-74, I have shown that Jeremiah's use of the form serves to call into question conventional presuppositions and conclusions, a very different function from the usual wisdom teaching.

[43] See J. Muilenburg, "The Terminology of Adversity in Jeremiah," *Translating and Understanding the Old Testament* (eds. H. T. Frank and W. L. Reed; New York: Abingdon, 1970) 46, 50, 57 and *passim*.

[44] So Weiser, *Der Prophet Jeremia* (ATD 20; Göttingen: Vandenhoeck & Ruprecht, 1960) 89; Von Rad, *Wisdom*, 102-03; and R. B. Y. Scott, *Proverbs and Ecclesiastes* (AB 18; Garden City, NY: Doubleday, 1965) xxxv. This saying apparently meets the requirements of Crenshaw as

well. Dürr (*Erziehung*, 182) has not only linked our passage to wisdom but has explicitly related it to Prov 3:7. Gerstenberger in turn has found Prov 3:7 to be a summary and motto for wisdom instruction generally; cf. E. Gerstenberger, *Wesen und Herkunft des "Apodiktischen Rechts"* (WMANT 20; Neukirchen-Vluyn: Neukirchener Verlag, 1965) 49. If both Dürr and Gerstenberger are correct, as seems likely, then our passage may indeed express a central wisdom teaching. However, the teaching is much more concrete than is Prov 3:7. The warning is not only against "evil," but wisdom, riches and power. The urging is not only toward fear of Yahweh but also toward very specific covenantal factors.

45 Cf. R. Rendtorff, "Zum Gebrauch der Formel 'nĕʾum Jahwe' im Jeremiabuch," *ZAW* 66 (1954) 27-37, and F. S. North, "The Expression The Oracle of Yahweh as an Aid to Critical Analysis," *JBL* 71 (1952) x. The form is apparently not integral to this unit, as is also the case in a number of passages in Jeremiah.

46 It is worth noting that the negative is not *lōʾ* as might be expected, but ʾal, which might also stress the sapiential connection, as Gerstenberger would argue.

47 The hithpael form of *hll* is not used often. In Proverbs it is used three times negatively (30:14, 25:14, 27:1) and once positively (31:30). Elsewhere, it is used for praise to Yahweh (Pss 34:3, 63:12, 64:11, 105:3, 106:5, 1 Chron 16:10, Isa 41:16, 45:25, and especially to be noted Jer 4:2). It is used negatively in Pss 49:7, 52:3, 97:7. Outside of these poetic passages, it is used only in 1 Kgs 20:11, on which comment will be made below.

48 Too much should not be made of the grammatical form in claiming this. Its usage simply shows two primary functions, (a) in praise of Yahweh and (b) inordinate celebration of something else, often implying pride and self-preoccupation. Mendenhall suggests the form means "saying hallelu to self" (oral communication).

49 In such uses it is the very opposite of the affirmation of Jer 10:23-24, also a wisdom saying.

50 The tone is not unlike the "summary-appraisal form" identified by B. Childs, *Isaiah and the Assyrian Crisis* (SBT 2/3; Naperville, IL: Allenson, 1967) 128-36. Our form contains a number of conclusions not dissimilar to the climactic conclusion of Childs' form. Similarly, these conclusions do not urge a specific action but simply make a non-discussable judgment about conduct and consequences.

51 The form with this particle serves to make a sharp, unqualified distinction between sinners and fearers of the Lord. Characteristically in such parallelisms, it serves to contrast.

52 While this teaching is now set in a prophetic context, it also echoes a sapiential concern. Note the address to "man," in contrast to Deut 10:12 where the same address is to Israel. Note also that the items urged are similar to those urged in our verses.

53 In a way similar to the rhetorical question, the particle challenges conventional wisdom expressed in the proverb and sets out an alternative.

54 It is not necessary to insist that this parabolic form is sapiential, but its structure and intent do make a contrast in what is to be valued in a way that is surely congenial to wisdom teaching.

55 The contrast set forth by the Dtr is surely didactic. Given the suggestions of Weinfeld, we may suggest that the contrast here between service to Yahweh and to the other gods is not unlike the sharp sapiential contrast or Prov 8:32-36, which presents ways to life and death.

56 W. McKane, *Proverbs* (Philadelphia: Westminster, 1970) 621, has observed that this saying equates wealth and impiety, poverty and piety. The fool is one who will not submit to Yahweh and to Torah. McKane observes that the question of theodicy has surfaced, surely an issue that came to full expression in the pathos of Jeremiah. This saying on wisdom is more radical than most in Proverbs and reflects the tradition to which Jeremiah appeals.

57 Mendenhall, *The Tenth Generation*, 121, refers to our saying in identifying the meaning of Solomon. There can be little doubt that in his regime, this alien ideology which Jeremiah resists became legitimated in Israel.

58 Lewis Mumford, *The Myth of the Machine* (New York: Harcourt, 1970) has in a general way shown the dialectical development of technology and mythic claims. More specifically related to Israel, see Mendenhall and Gottwald in the works cited.

59 There can be little doubt that this psalm is informed by wisdom traditions. Cf. S. Mowinckel, "Psalms and Wisdom," *Wisdom in Israel and in the Ancient Near East* (VTSup 3;

1955) 213-15 and R. Murphy, "A Consideration of the Classification 'Wisdom Psalms'," *Congress Volume, Bonn 1962* (VTSup 9; Leiden: Brill, 1963) 161-63.

[60] These verses have much in common with the general tenor of Ecclesiastes. Cf. J. Williams, "What Does it Profit a Man?" *Studies in Ancient Israelite Wisdom*, 375-89. Jeremiah seems to refer to such a tradition. The difference is that he has, as they do not, a positive alternative to urge. On the triad, see esp. Qoh 9:11. Ecclesiastes asserts that neither might, riches, nor wisdom—the very items named in our passage—finally have any significance.

[61] See Whedbee, *Isaiah and Wisdom*, 82-110, for a full discussion.

[62] His radical critique is apparent in many places, but note especially 5:27-28. The prophet describes: (a) their self-deluding prosperity, (b) the disregard of order and boundary, and (c) the social consequences. In the political implications of the epistemology, see Abraham Katsh, "The Religious Tradition or Traditions in a Traditionless Age," *Christian Action and Openness to The World* (ed. J. Papen; Villanova, PA: Villanova, 1970) 213-17. Katsh shows how this tradition leads to democratic society and its absence to oppressive class society.

[63] The text is difficult, but cf. Bright, *Jeremiah*, 66-72.

[64] "'Wissen um Gott' bei Hosea als Urform von Theologie," *EvTh* 12 (1952/53) 533, 554; reprinted in *Gesammelte Studien zum Alten Testament* (ThB 22; Munich: Kaiser, 1964) 182-205.

[65] Herbert Huffmon, "The Treaty Background of Hebrew *Yādaᶜ*," *BASOR* 181 (1966) 31-37, Huffmon and S. B. Parker, "A Further Note on the Treaty Background of Hebrew *Yādaᶜ*," *BASOR* 184 (1966) 36-38.

[66] On the inscrutable source of life as it relates to wisdom teaching, see R. Murphy, "The Kerygma of Proverbs," *Int* 20 (1966) 3-14, and Prov 8:32-36 on the gift of life from wisdom.

[67] On this text as a central one for our hypothesis of two histories, see H. W. Wolff, *Anthropology of the Old Testament* (Philadelphia: Fortress, 1974) 195-96.

[68] Radical liberation theology is helping us discover that these phenomena are inherently against solidarity. This is the insight of the prophet, that riches, might and that kind of wisdom belong inevitably to the consciousness which practices domination and oppression and so destroys community.

[69] On the relation of Hosea and Jeremiah, see H. Wildberger, *Jahwes Eigenstumsvolk* (Zürich: Zwingli, 1960) 112, and K. Gross, "Hoseas Einfluss auf Jeremias Anschauungen," *NKZ* 42 (1931) 241-56, 327-43. More recent tradition-critical study confirms this connection. More than any other they sensed the depth of the tragedy of Israel's royal consciousness. On "knowing" in Hosea, cf. 4:1, 6, 5:4, 6:4, 8:2.

[70] On the pathos of God into which the prophets entered, see Heschel, *The Prophets*. On the ways in which the other consciousness leads to apathy, see J. Moltmann, *The Experiment Hope* (Philadelphia: Fortress, 1975) 69-84, and D. Sölle, *Suffering* (Philadelphia: Fortress, 1975).

[71] Yahweh is not only in favor of these things, but he *does* them. His doing them makes clear that he has freedom to act against and in spite of the royal management which attempted to circumscribe his action. The saying asserts that Yahweh will work his will in spite of all the ideological commitment to wisdom, riches and power which try to prevent it. This is in contrast to the mood of the time expressed in Zeph 1:12. On Yahweh as doer cf. P. Volz (*Der Prophet Jeremia* [KAT 10; Leipzig and Erlangen: Deichert, 1922] 118), as well as Isa 9:6. On the participial form, see Job 9:9-12 with the double verb plus the concluding rhetorical question, and Amos 4:8. Thus the form is likely sapiential. The substance concerns his royal authority in the face of those who deny or circumscribe it. On the royal motif, see Jer 23:5, Pss 99:4, 103:7 and on wisdom formulation Exod 34:7, with R. C. Dentan, "The Literary Affinities of Exodus XXXIV 6f." *VT* 18 (1963) 34-51; see also Giesebrecht, *Das Buch Jeremia*, 62.

[72] This is the only text in the *narrative* traditions of the OT in which the hithpael occurs. It is a remarkable passage which contrasts the boasting of Syria and the confidence in Yahweh expressed by Israel. On the formulae of the chapter as assertions of faith, see Zimmerli, "Das Wort des Gottlichen Selbsterweises," *Gottes Offenbarung* (*ThB* 19) 129.

[73] Cf. John Gray, *I & II Kings* (Philadelphia: Westminster, 1963) 376, and H.-J. Hermisson, *Studien zur israelitischen Spruchweisheit* (WMANT 28; Neukirchen-Vluyn: Neukirchener Verlag, 1968) 43.

[74] See the comment of Hermisson, ibid.

[75] Note the triad. Too much should not be made of the triad, but perhaps it illuminates the pair of triads in our passage. The same historical consciousness is reflected in the triad sword/spear/javelin as in the triad riches/might/wisdom.

[76] Attention might be drawn in this connection to 1 Sam 16:18 where David is presented as the one with the true wisdom and capacity to cope with the boaster. In that text he may well be a paradigm of the way in which wisdom and faith are held together. The critique of Jeremiah is that wisdom and its companion properties have displaced faith. Cf. Hermisson, *Studien zur israelitischen Spruchweisheit*, 125.

[77] After this essay was completed, I became aware of the analysis of Jeremianic texts by Wm. Holladay, *The Architecture of Jeremiah 1 — 20*, (London: Associated University, 1976). In his analysis of Jer 4-6, 8, Holladay suggests "there is a steady movement in each of these sections from battle scenes to wisdom preoccupations . . . the battle is a *lesson* to the people" (pp. 67, 85). See pp. 110-13 for a parallel comment on 8:14 – 9:8. What Holladay discerns in a larger structural analysis is indicated also concerning our verses.

[78] On war themes in Jeremiah, see Robert Bach, *Die Aufforderungen zur Flucht und zum Kampf im Alttestamentlichen Prophetenspruch* (Neukirchen: Moers, 1962) and P. D. Miller, Jr., "The Divine Counsel and the Prophetic Call to War," *VT* 18 (1968) 100-07.

[79] Holladay, *op. cit.*, 123, comments on *ḥpṣ* in this text by observing the structural link to 6:10 which is the only previous occurrence.

[80] Note that in 1 Sam 15:22-23, along with delight, there is also rejection, a point worth noting in the context of Jeremiah's crisis.

[81] Cf. Isa 55:8-9. In what is likely a sapiential motif, the poet insists God's purposes are different from those of his people. That contrast is fundamental to faithful wisdom, but never honored by kings who wish to monopolize wisdom and identify the regime with the purposes of God.

[82] See the analysis of K. E. Bailey, "Poetic Structure of I Cor. 1:17-2:2" *Nov T* 17 (1975) 268-96.

[83] Volz (*Der Prophet Jeremia*, 118-19) notes a derivative motif also in James 1:9-10; see also 2 Cor 10:27.

# JEREMIAH 13:12-14: A PROBLEMATIC PROVERB

WILLIAM McKANE

UNIVERSITY OF ST. ANDREWS, ST. ANDREWS, SCOTLAND KY 16 9JU

It gives me much pleasure to participate in a volume which does honour to Professor Terrien, and which celebrates his devotion to biblical scholarship. I have valued highly his contributions to the study of the Wisdom Literature of the Old Testament, and I recall particularly how impressed I was with his presence on the occasion when he read his paper on Job at the Geneva Congress in 1965.

## I

You will speak this word to them. This is what Yahweh, God of Israel, has to say: "Every jar (skin) is filled with wine." They will say to you: "Do you suppose we do not know that every jar (skin) is filled with wine?" You will say to them. This is what Yahweh has to say: "I shall make all the inhabitants of this land drunk, the kings who sit on David's throne, the priests, the prophets and all the inhabitants of Jerusalem. I shall smash them against each other, fathers against sons. I shall not spare them; I shall not pity them nor show mercy to them, so as to stop short of destroying them." This is what Yahweh says. (Jer 13:12-14)

THE most difficult and interesting philological problem in the passage is constituted by *nēbel* which is shown by Brown–Driver–Briggs[1] to mean either "skin" or "jar" and by Koehler-Baumgartner[2] to mean "earthenware jar." The uncertainty over *nēbel* has had a long history in Hebrew lexicography. AbuʾL Walīd Marwān ibn Janāh in his Hebrew-Arabic dictionary, *The Book of Hebrew Roots* (c. 1050 A.D.),[3] cites the proverb in Jer 13:12 ("Every *nēbel* is filled with wine") and glosses *nēbel* with *ziqqun* "skin." He attaches the same sense to *nēbel* in 1 Sam 10:3 and Job 38:37, where he supposes that *nibēlê šāmayim* is an expression for "clouds." On the other hand, he recognizes that the sense must be "earthenware vessel" in Isa 30:14 in view of the phrase *nēbel yôṣĕrîm* and the presence of *šbr*, and also in Jer 48:12 in view of the presence of *npṣ*. Sebastian Muenster in his *Book of Roots* or *Dictionarium Hebraicum* (1539),[4] derived from Rabbinic sources and especially from David Kimchi, apparently regards "skin" (*nōʾd; uter*) as the primary sense of *nēbel*, but he also notes the sense "earthenware flask" (*lagena*) and remarks, "a vessel made either of skin or of clay." He suggest that *nēbel* in Job 38:37 may have the sense *gešem* "rain-waters" and that this usage is perhaps to be correlated with *mabbûl* "flood."

Johannis Buxtorf (1631)[5] indicates both "skin" and "earthenware flask" for Jer 13:12 and he gives the sense "skin" for two passages (Jer 48:12; Lam 4:2), where "earthenware vessel" must be right. Like Ibn Janāh he understands Job 38:37 ("skins of heaven") to be a circumlocution for "clouds." J. D. Michaelis (1784-1792)[6] gives the sense of *nēbel* as "skin," "clay pot," "stone pot." He states that the sense "skin" is not appropriate at Isa 30:14, Jer 13:12 and Jer 48:12. He notes that none of the cognate languages except Ethiopic has the Hebrew sense of *nēbel* and he conjectures an association with Arabic *nabalun* "stone." The precise sense of *nēbel* is "stone vessel," but the word was used of a clay vessel and even of a skin container of liquid.

This view of the semantic development of *nēbel* is contradicted by W. Gesenius in his *Thesaurus* (1840).[7] Gesenius divides his entry into two sections: under "skin" he cites 1 Sam 1:24, 10:3, 25:18 and Jer 13:12, but he observes that all of these usages could be fitted into his second section where the sense "earthenware vessel" is posited for *nēbel*. Thus only in the case of Job 38:37, where he takes *nibělê šāmayim* ("skins of heaven") to mean "clouds" (agreeing with Ibn Janāh and Buxtorf), does he suppose that the sense "skin" is certainly established. He cites Kimchi to the effect that *nēbel* is either a leather bottle or an earthenware pot and this shows that the similar remark of Muenster is derived from Kimchi. Gesenius' view of the semantic development of *nēbel* has exercised considerable influence on subsequent lexicographers and commentators: *Quum autem aquae, lacti, vino condendis portandisque utplurimum utres adhibere solerent prisci homines hoc nomen dein translatum est ad cuiuscunque generis vasa aquaria:* "Since, however, ancient men were, for the most part, accustomed to use skins for containing and carrying water, milk and wine, this name was then transferred to any kind of water-vessel."[8] The classification of Gesenius is preserved in Brown-Driver-Briggs,[9] where there is an incoherence between the meaning ("skin") attached to *nēbel* in Jer 13:12 and the meaning ("smash") attached to *npṣ* in Jer 12:14, unless it is supposed that Jer 13:12-14 does not constitute an original unity (see section III.3 below). A. M. Honeyman, in his definitive article on the pottery vessels of the Old Testament, reproduces Gesenius' view of the semantic development of *nēbel*: "Originally the *nēbel* was a skin bottle and throughout the Biblical period wine was regularly stored in these, e.g. 1 Sam i 24, Matt ix 17. It was from this container that the *nēbel yôṣěrîm* (Isa xxx 14) took its name, on account of the similarity either of shape or of capacity."[10] Honeyman has a note on Jer 13:12 in which he remarks: "That an earthen vessel is here intended is more than a possibility, as Gesenius s.v. states. The verb refers not to the deflating of a skin but to the smashing of pottery, as in Judges vii 19."[11]

The following are the occurrences where the meaning "earthenware pot" or the like appears to be well-established for *nēbel*:

(a) *kělê hanněbālîm*, "earthenware vessels," Isa 22:24.
(b) *kěšēber nēbel yôṣěrîm*, "like the shattering of a vessel made by a potter," Isa 30:14.

(c) *nēbel* with *npṣ,* "shatter," if Jer 13:12-14 is a unity (see section III.3 below).
(d) *wĕnibĕlêhem yĕnappēṣû,* "and they will shatter their pots," Jer 48:12.
(e) *nibĕlê ḥereś,* "earthenware vessels," Lam 4:2.

The sense "skin" is not well-founded for *nēbel,* although it is given by Gesenius[12] and Brown–Driver–Briggs[13] in respect of 1 Sam 1:24, 10:3, 25:18, 2 Sam 16:1 and Job 38:37. Only with Job 38:37 is there any contextual help: the parallelism of *nibĕlê šāmayim* with *šĕḥāqîm* "clouds" might be thought to point to "skins." Koehler-Baumgartner[14] associates *nēbel* in *nibĕlê šāmayim* with *mabbûl* "flood" and this becomes more probable if *mabbûl* means strictly the ocean above the firmament, as Albright[15] and Stolz[16] suppose. In that case it is understandable that *nibĕlê šāmayim* should be an expression for "rain-waters," that is, waters released from the upper ocean through the "windows" of heaven. My provisional conclusion is that the meaning "earthenware pot" or the like can be gathered with certainty from some passages and that a contextual indication in favor of "skin" is given only in Job 38:37, although *nibĕlê šāmayim* may be a reference to rain-waters. I turn now to the versions to see what light they throw on the matter.

## II

The following table shows how the versions handled the rendering of *nēbel* in those passages where a decision about its meaning is difficult.

### *The Treatment of* nēbel *in the Versions*

|            | LXX     | Aquila    | Symmachus | Theodotion | Vulgate   | Peshitta | Targum |
|------------|---------|-----------|-----------|------------|-----------|----------|--------|
| 1 Sam 1:24 | *nebel* |           |           |            | *amphora* | *grb*ᵓ   | *grb*  |
| 1 Sam 10:3 | *askon* | *amphorea*| *nebel*   |            | *lagenam* | *grb*ᵓ   | *grb*  |
| 1 Sam 25:18| *aggeia*| *amphoreis*| *askous* | *nibel*    | *utres*   | *grbyn*  | *grb*  |
| 2 Sam 16:1 | *nebel* |           |           |            | *utre*    | *zq*ᵓ    | *grb*  |
| Job 38:37  | *ouranon* | *aporreonta ouranou* | *organa ouranou* | *organa ouranou* | *concentum caeli* | ᶜ*mwd*ᵓ | *zyqy*ᵓ |

The device of transliteration adopted by LXX at 1 Sam 1:24 and 2 Sam 16:1, by Symmachus at 1 Sam 10:3 and by Theodotion at 1 Sam 25:18 may be an indication of uncertainty how to translate (see the next paragraph below on Jer 13:12). It will be seen that there is no agreement among the Greek versions in respect of the occurrences which are transliterated. Peshitta *grb*ᵓ and Targum *grb* do not allow us to decide with certainty whether "jar" or "skin" is intended, though it is probably the former. Peshitta *zq*ᵓ (2 Sam 16:1) is certainly "skin." The random character of the renderings in the versions and the absence of a consensus is striking. Vulgate uses two words for "jar" or "flask" (*amphora* and *lagenam*) and Aquila uses the first of these (*amphorea* and *amphoreis*). But where Vulgate (*lagenam*) and Aquila (*amphorea*) opt for "jar" at 1 Sam 10:3, LXX indicates "skin" (*askon*) and Symmachus transliterates *nebel.* At 1 Sam 25:18 LXX (*aggeia*) and Aquila (*amphoreis*) indicate "jars" or the like, but Vulgate *utres* and Symmachus *askous* indicate "skins," while Theodotion transliterates *nibel*. At 2 Sam 16:1 LXX transliterates (*nebel*), while Vulgate *utre* and Peshitta *zq⁾* represent "skin." The mystification of the versions deepens at Job 38:37, where LXX evades the difficulty of *nibĕlê šāmayim* with the rendering *ouranon*. Symmachus and Theodotion (*organa ouranou*) and Vulgate (*concentum caeli*) have identified *nibĕlê* with *nēbel* "musical instrument" and supposed a reference to a kind of harmony of the spheres. Peshitta's translation, "And who raised the pillars of heaven," is far removed from the Hebrew. The most interesting renderings are those of Aquila and Targum. Aquila's *aporreonta ouranou*, "overflowing waters of heaven," shows that he connected *nibĕlê* with *mabbûl*, so that this understanding of *nibĕlê šāmayim* (see above at the end of Section I) is supported by an early witness. Targum, on the other hand, gives explicit support to the view that *nibĕlê šāmayim* means "skins of heaven": "And the clouds which are like skins of heaven."

When we turn to Jer 13:12 (where it seems to me, for reasons which will appear below, that it is worthwhile raising the question whether *nēbel* means "jar" or "skin") we find the same kind of disarray in the versions. "Skin" is represented by LXX *askos* and "jar" or the like by Vulgate *lagnuncula*. Peshitta *grb⁾* and Targum *grb* probably indicate "jar." The variations in the later Greek versions are noted by Jerome:[17] *verbum Hebraicum nebel Aquilae prima editio lagunculam, secundum ipsum nebel, Symmachus craterem, LXX utrem, Theodotio vas interpretati sunt* (cf. Ziegler,[18] who also notes Josephus, *koramion* "pitcher," "pot"). Hence Aquila having hazarded "jar" or "pitcher" (*hydria*) as a translation would seem to have retreated to a transliteration (cf. the suggestion made in the previous paragraph that transliterations may arise from an uncertainty how to translate). Symmachus (*kratēr*) supposes that *nēbel* is the bowl in which wine was mixed with water preparatory to serving it and Theodotion (*aggeion*) clearly indicates a pottery vessel and not a skin.

The lexicographical inquiry has shown that there is no usage of *nēbel* in biblical Hebrew for which the sense "skin" is certainly established. This may be the sense in Job 38:37, although there is the attractive alternative "rain-waters" which I have discussed. I shall leave open the possibility that "skin" may have been the sense of *nēbel* in the proverb *kol nēbel yimmālē⁾ yāyin* (Jer 13:12), although all the versions except LXX indicate a pottery vessel rather than a skin, and the commentators are almost unanimously in favor of "jar" or the like.[19]

### III

I move on to a consideration of the exegesis of Jer 13:12-14 and, first of all, to an assessment of the contribution of the versions and of Rashi and Kimchi. The clash between *nēbel* rendered as *askos* "skin" and *wĕnippaṣtîm*, (vs. 14) "smash" is avoided by LXX because of the translation adopted for *wĕnippaṣtîm*, namely, *diaskorpiō* "scatter." It would be unwise to assume that it was necessarily an awareness of the incongruity between "skin" and "smash" which led to the translation as a kind of relieving device. Thus Vulgate has "jar" in vs. 12 and yet it too renders *wĕnippaṣtîm* as "disperse" (*dispergam*), as also does Peshitta (ʾ*bdr*). There are two ways in which these translations might be accounted for:

(a) *npṣ* might have been understood as a variant root of *pwṣ* "scatter."

(b) The renderings of LXX, Vulgate and Peshitta contain an element of interpretation and "smashing" is interpreted as dispersion and exile. At any rate the element of interpretation is clearly present in Targum: "I shall fill [them] . . . with *šikkarôn*" (vs. 13) of the Hebrew is spelt out as "I shall fill them with distress and they will be like drunk men," while *wĕnippaṣtîm* (vs. 14) is explained as "and I shall incite them" (*wgrynwn*). On this view the "smashing" refers to a process of divine incitement which will set members of the same family at one another's throats and will create bitter divisions between older and younger generations.

The general view of both Rashi and Kimchi[20] is that *nēbel* (vs. 12) means "earthenware vessel" (*kĕlî hereś*) and that *wĕnippaṣtîm* (vs. 14) means "smash." The unity of vss. 12-14 and the functioning of the *māšāl* are thought to require this correlation of "earthenware vessel" and "smash." On vs. 14 Rashi comments: "I shall strike one against the other, until they are broken in minute pieces."[21] This would seem to me to be a correct interpretation both of ʾ*iš* ʾ*el* ʾ*āḥîw* and of *wĕhāʾābôt wĕhabbānîm yaḥdāw*. In the latter case he has the support of Ehrlich[22] who explains *yaḥdāw* as a reciprocal pronoun, "fathers and sons against each other," but this view of the matter is contradicted by Giesebrecht[23] who argues that *yaḥdāw* is not compatible with a reference to internecine strife and that the meaning must be, "fathers and sons together."

Kimchi's[24] exegesis is more elaborate than that of Rashi: *nēbel* has two proverbial nuances:

(a) Just as the entire capacity of a jar is taken up with the wine that fills it, so Judah will be entirely filled with *šikkarôn* (explained as great distress and tribulation); and just as a drunk person is no longer fully aware of what he is doing, so they, under the pressure of privations and sufferings, will become bewildered and confused.

(b) The Judaeans are likened to a *nēbel* because when one jar is struck against another, both are broken in pieces, and so *nēbel* is similarly used with *npṣ* in Jer 48:12. There will be strife in the community because of the extent of its sufferings, and this civil strife within families and between older and younger generations will lead to a total disintegration. It will so weaken them that external enemies will have an easy job to finish them off—they will be destroyed ʿ*al yad hāʾôyĕbîm wĕ* ʿ*al yad* ʿ*aṣmām*.

Most of the exegetical issues raised in subsequent commentaries have been, at least, touched on in the versions and in Rashi and Kimchi. I take these in what I regard as an ascending order of importance and discuss each in turn:

1. *Inner and Outer Aspects of Yahweh's Judgment.* Different definitions of the segmentation of "outer" and "inner" appear in the commentaries:

(a) The thought that the judgment on Judah will finally be carried out by external enemies who will find their task easy in view of the inner disintegration of the community is implied in the references to dispersion and exile in LXX, Vulgate and Peshitta and is explicit in the exegesis of Kimchi. It is represented also by Venema,[25] *Judaeos prae stupiditate et desperatione in se invicem collidendos esse et ea ratione occasionem hostibus daturus plenariae destructionis*; and Volz,[26] who has a different definition of "inner" judgment, comprehends internecine feuds and external enemies in his understanding of "outer" judgment. He equates inner judgment with the "intoxicated" condition of the individual members of the community and with reference to this loss of reason and will for self-destruction he adds: "Thereby will come the outer judgment: they will be reduced to internecine conflict. The word of the prophet was fulfilled through the catastrophe of 587/6." Naegelsbach[27] and Peake[28] differ from Volz in this respect only, that they do not introduce the thought of external enemies into their differentiation of inner and outer. Thus Naegelsbach says: "*šikkarôn* designates the immediate subjective effect of the wine of fury . . . of which the further objective effect is collision and breaking into pieces."[29]

(b) The outer aspect of judgment is emphasized in quite a different way by many commentators who connect vs. 13 with those passages where Yahweh is represented as giving his own people or the Gentile nations a cup of wine to drink, and where their resulting intoxication is an aspect of the fury of his judgment. The cup of wine is the cup of wrath which he requires them to drink (Jer 48:26; 49:12, 51:57, Isa 19:14, 51:17, Nah 3:11, Hab 2:16, Lam 4:21, Rev 14:10, 16:19). "Outer" judgment in the sense that it is a judgment executed by Yahweh against his people is stressed by a number of scholars.[30] This thought is pressed furthest by Hitzig who urges that the significance of *šikkarôn* is exhausted by the "cup of wrath" interpretation and that no weight should be attached to the aspect of "inner" intoxication. The figure is intended simply to convey Yahweh's wrath as he judges his people and should not be developed in the direction of an "inner" intoxication—a state of confusion, irrationality and socially destructive behavior which dissolves the fabric of the community. This is a limitation which can hardly be right and which should not be accepted.

(c) The commentators are divided as to whether or not there is a reference to civil war in vs. 14 (Yes: Calvin, Naegelsbach, Elliott Binns, Volz; No: Graf, Hitzig, Keil, Plumptre, Giesebrecht, van Selms).[31] There is not much at stake exegetically here, although what is intended by vs. 14 is probably a disruptive and destructive disunity; something less than civil war, but something which amounts to unnatural and suicidal factions and feuds in families and between generations which will inevitably lead to social and political disintegration.

2. *The meaning of the Proverb, "Every jar (skin) is filled with wine."* At least three explanations are offered and I arrange these in what I regard as an ascending order of probability:

(a) The proverb is expressive of a false sense of security and of a belief that prosperity will be enjoyed without interruption. The prophet handles it in such a way that he produces a shocking reversal of a tenacious, popular attitude.[32] Thus according to Elliott Binns the prophet is combating the influence of a popular proverb which was the vehicle of an easy optimism: "Just as wine bottles are liable to be filled with wine in the normal course of events, so Judah in due course will be rewarded by Yahweh." Jeremiah directs the proverb towards a contrary conclusion: "Just as a jar is filled with wine, so will the men of Judah be filled with the wine of God's wrath and made 'drunken'."

(b) "Every jar is filled with wine" is a *māšāl*[33] or "dark saying"[34] adopted or coined by the prophet in order to communicate his message of God's cup of wrath and the imminent "shattering" of the community. Where the saying is envisaged as a popular proverb which Jeremiah has taken up,[35] it is thought to mean something like "Every vessel receives the contents for which it is intended" or "Everything has its right use." It is appropriated at this level by those who hear it and this is explained by the commentators mentioned above as either an accidental or willful misconstruction of the prophet's words. The manner in which Jeremiah's *māšāl* is misunderstood is variously described by the commentators. Henderson remarks: "The Jews either did not or pretended not to know to what the prophet referred, and responded by adverting to the fact with which every one was acquainted that after the vintage the wine was preserved in leathern bottles."[36] Lowth says: "God that knew the profaneness of their hearts foretells the reply they will make to this threatening (i.e., 'Every jar is filled with wine') and taking it in a literal sense they will make a jest of it, as if the words were intended to encourage intemperance, either they did not or would not understand the drift of them."[37] This is similar to the exegesis which is offered by Bright[38] who supposes that a popular proverb which means "Everything has its right use" is twisted by those who hear it into a toper's jest and then developed by the prophet as a threat of judgment in terms of a cup of wrath and the shattering of wine jars. Yet another account is given by Blayney:

> The answer . . . seems to imply that by a wilful mistake they would put a literal construction upon his words as if he had meant to tell them of a plentiful vintage that was coming on, which would fill all their wine vessels; and of this they claim to be as good judges as he from the promising appearance of the vineyards. 'Do you tell us this as a piece of news or supernatural discovery? Is it not evident to us as well as you?'[39]

Blayney's view of the matter is that the situation in Jer 13:12-14 is similar to that of Nathan's "parable" in 2 Samuel 12. The first attempt to communicate parabolically is thwarted by the failure of the audience to grasp the parable (just as David failed to understand the meaning and application of Nathan's words), and it then becomes necessary for the prophet to spell the matter out. Thus Blayney continues: "But the prophet is directed to deal more plainly with them and to tell them that the wine he meant was not so much as would exhilarate but such as would intoxicate; being no other than would be poured out of the wine cup of God's fury to the subversion of all ranks and orders of men among them."[40]

(c) The distinction between (b) and (c) cannot be established absolutely, but there is a difference of emphasis which is significant. The commentators who are assembled under (c)[41] make particular use of the thought that the opening saying, "Every jar is filled with wine," is commonplace or banal, that this banality is deliberate and that it triggers the process of communication. It is true that such commentators as Naegelsbach, Keil and Plumptre (listed under b) also refer to the ordinariness of the opening saying, but they are, for the most part, making a different point. They are saying that "Every jar is filled with wine" is an attempt by Jeremiah to communicate proverbially which is thwarted by the circumstance that it appears to be obvious to those who hear it and is misunderstood as commonplace and pedestrian. The other point of view, which I am now trying to articulate is that Jeremiah was purposely banal, that "Every jar is filled with wine" is in the first instance not to be understood as a serious attempt to communicate proverbially, but as a saying by a prophet of such ordinariness that those who hear it are struck by its incongruity on his lips and are jolted into attention. From this point of view Giesebrecht[42] argues that the longer text of MT in vs. 12, which represents "Every jar is filled with wine" as a word of Yahweh, increases the element of incongruity and enhances the effectiveness of the device, and so is superior to the shorter text of LXX ("And you will say to this people, 'Every skin is filled with wine'"). On the other hand, it has been argued[43] that since "Every jar is filled with wine" is a popular proverb, it ought not to be introduced by "Thus says Yahweh, God of Israel," that the word of Yahweh makes its entrance at vs. 13 and that the shorter text of LXX is to be preferred at vs. 12. This view is supported by Janzen[44] who supposes that the secondary insertion of "Thus says Yahweh, God of Israel," at vs. 12 is accounted for by the circumstance that the formula often follows upon *wĕᵓāmartāᵓēl* in the Book of Jeremiah (cf. 13:13).

A very graphic representation of the manner in which the banality of the opening saying may be supposed to have awakened the attention of the audience is given by Calvin:

The general introduction might have appeared to be of no weight, for what instruction does this contain. "Every bottle shall be filled with wine." It is as if one were to say that a tankard is made to carry wine and that bowls are made for drinking; this is well known even to children. And then it might have been said that this was unworthy of a prophet: "What do you say? You say that bottles are the receptacles of wine, even as a hat is made to cover the head, or clothes to keep off the cold—you seem to mock us with childish trifles."[45]

A more specialized application of this mode of interpretation is associated with the assumption that the proverb "Every jar (skin) is filled with wine" is a toper's witticism[46] and that the occasion is a drinking-bout, perhaps an abuse associated with a cultic occasion.[47] Thus Volz remarks:

Jar after jar is filled with wine by the publican. The prophet looks on. The first words are purposely banal; precisely thereby is attention awakened. By all possible means the prophet sought to secure recognition in the throng. . . . Resounding laughter followed—so had the prophet won the ear of the hard-drinker and was in a position to speak his prophetic word.[48]

3. *Intoxication and Fragility.* I now consider the relation between "intoxication" and "shattering," and how these two ideas are thought of as combining or interacting in the functioning of the proverb.

(a) There are those who, so far as I can see, have not been greatly exercised to demonstrate that the proverb has a complex unity and have been content to assume that Jer 13:12-14 contains two images of judgment ("intoxication" and "shattering") which are perhaps loosely connected, in so far as the vessels which are shattered are wine jars, but which function more or less independently, the second reinforcing the first.[49] Thus Lowth comments on vs. 14: "I will confound and destroy them all, as earthen vessels are broken to pieces, when they are dashed one against another. The words allude to earthen bottles which were to be filled with wine."[50] Hitzig[51] holds that the fragility of an earthenware vessel is the thought on which vs. 14 hinges, although he supposes that there is also an allusion to the manner in which drunk men stagger and bump against each other. Plumptre[52] simply comments that vs. 14 points to the "crash of a falling kingdom when all bonds that keep society together are broken." The dissociation of the two images of "intoxication" and "shattering" is most pronounced in van Selms[53] who introduces the thought of an earthquake as the background to the image of shattering: the tremor causes jars which are stacked in rows to break against each other.

(b) There are those who have explained vss. 12-14 on the assumption that "intoxication" and "shattering" are inter-connected images which contribute to a complex proverbial or parabolic unity.[54] That this relation between "intoxication" and "shattering" in the functioning of the proverb is difficult to explain is shown by the ambiguity in some of these accounts.[55] In particular, if the thought that drunk men (who are full wine jars) is present in vs. 14, *wĕnippaṣtîm* does not seem to be appropriate, because the shattering ought to result from the collisions of drunkards (full wine jars) and ought not to be described as a further act of Yahweh. On this difficulty Peake comments: "Since the drunkenness is caused by Yahweh, he is said to dash them against each other, though strictly we may suppose that they stumble against each other."[56] The fullest expression of this type of exegesis is found in Volz[57] who specifies the two parts of the parable and the manner in which they are related: (a) As a jar filled with wine, so will the Judaeans be filled with drunkenness by Yahweh, so that they will be like full jars. (b) As drunken topers shatter their wine jars against those of their fellow-topers—this thought may also be present in Graf's[58] exposition—so will Yahweh shatter the Judaeans (who are full wine jars) against each other. The inconcinnity of *wĕnippaṣtîm* is fully exposed in this exegesis. For Volz the primary explanation of "shattering" derives from "intoxication" (just as they break their wine jars one against the other, so they will break themselves against each other); and, finally, in order to explain *wĕnippaṣtîm* Volz has to suppose that vs. 14 contains both an image of "shattering" which hangs together with the "intoxication" of vs. 13 and an explanation of that image ("so Yahweh will shatter the Judaeans" etc.).

## IV

Some reference to higher critical matters is necessary, though so far I have avoided this in order to concentrate on the language and grammar of the proverb, and I do not intend now to be drawn into a general consideration of the prose in the Book of Jeremiah. So far as Jer 13:12-14 is concerned two of the most recent studies point in different directions: Thiel[59] concludes that the unit is deuteronomic, that particular deuteronomic features are the specification of leading classes in the community (vs. 13; cf. Berridge)[60] and the three-fold assertion that Yahweh will not relent nor allow thoughts of mercy and love to weaken his determination, until the work of judgment is completed and nothing remains but fragments (at the end of vs. 14). The general tendency of Weippert's[61] book, on the other hand, is to reclaim the prose of the book of Jeremiah for the prophet Jeremiah, and this is true for Jer 13:12-14 in particular. Rudolph[62] explains the passage on the assumption that the historical background is in the time of the prophet Jeremiah, during the reign of Zedekiah, while Weiser[63] maintains that since the threat is a future one and since it was fulfilled in the civil strife of Zedekiah's reign, it must have been issued in an earlier period. Rudolph understands the passage not only as the issuing of a threat of civil strife and disintegration which is to eventuate in the future, but also as a description of existing conditions and a search for self-understanding on the part of the prophet. The irrationality and self-destructiveness of the behavior of the community and especially of its leaders in the reign of Zedekiah is not capable of any ordinary explanation. The pressures of historical circumstances do not themselves account for it and it is explicable only as the manifestation of an intoxication or madness with which Yahweh himself has afflicted his community. Jeremiah saw the beginnings of the end in the reign of Zedekiah and was concerned to understand the source of the madness which was carrying the community to destruction, as well as to issue a threat of complete fragmentation.

My dissatisfaction with Rudolph's exegesis, which has admirable features, arises from my doubt whether the images of "intoxication" and "shattering" can be combined so as to create a credible unity out of vss. 12-14. This point was put by Duhm[64] with characteristic sharpness and it is this consideration, together with others which he raised, which inclines me to the conclusion that vss. 12-14 are not an original unity and that they derive from an understanding of Jeremiah's life and ministry held by exilic men—this is the implication of Thiel's criticism—or postexilic men, rather than from the times of the prophet himself. Duhm argues that the two images of "intoxication" and "shattering" do not properly cohere. If the Judaeans are jars, they can shatter themselves against each other without being filled with wine. The thought of the "wine of wrath," such as is worked out in Jer 25:27, probably hovered before the mind of the author, but he employed it unskillfully. If he had simply said, "They will shatter themselves against each other," he would have given expression to a threat of destruction without duplication. Duhm's view that 13:12-14 is removed from the age of the prophet Jeremiah is connected with his observation that the detailed instructions given to the prophet create an unreal situation: "Yahweh tells Jeremiah not only what he is to say, but what the people will reply. Everything goes like clockwork."[65] The author deals with Jeremiah's relationship to Yahweh as if he were "a small boy who has a message to deliver." Hence Duhm supposes that the passage is a kind of *midrash*, but that the creators of such edifying narratives had no gift for invention, no sense of real life, no deep inner life.

I do not lay much emphasis on my critical preferences in the present connection, since my principal concern is with the exegesis of the proverb or parable in 13:12-14, and my contention that vss. 12-14 do not properly cohere can be made whether the constituents of these verses are attributable to the prophet Jeremiah or whether they derive from later creators of prophetic legends. My argument is that vss. 12-13 constitute a proverbial unit and that vs. 14, which has been tacked on secondarily and which introduces the idea of "shattering," does not integrate satisfactorily with this unit. That it should have been tacked on is understandable, for if the proverb in vs. 12 is taken to mean "Every jar is filled with wine," the fragility of these jars supplies a *point d'appui* for the thought of "shattering." Nevertheless, this produces a distortion of the main thrust of the proverb in vss. 12-13, and if we were not distracted by the introduction of the idea of "shattering," we would see that what really follows from "Every jar (skin) is filled with wine" is the threat of "intoxication": Yahweh will give his people a cup of wrath to drink, they will be "intoxicated" and will behave irrationally and self-destructively. Hence the area of thought in which vss. 12-13 are located is that of the "cup of wrath" (see the passages cited above in section III 1b): the banqueting-cup is changed to a cup of poison, or, perhaps, the chalice brings curse instead of blessing and induces suicidal behavior.

If the point of departure in vss. 12-13 is a toper's slogan, and if there is an allusion in it to the distended belly of the toper (so Rudolph),[66] there is something to be said for rendering the proverb "every skin is filled with wine," since the correspondence of the full wine-skin and the full belly of the toper has greater proverbial acuteness than that between the full wine jar and full belly of the toper. If vss. 12-14 are not an original unity, the argument that there is an incongruence between "skin" and "shatter" no longer applies. The pattern of usage in biblical Hebrew points to "jar" or the like, but the possibility that *nēbel* means "skin" should be kept open for Job 38:37 and Jer 13:12. However, the argument that vss. 12-13 are the original proverbial unit, with which vs. 14 imperfectly coheres, does not depend on the assumption that *nēbel* in vs. 12 means "skin" and is compatible with the assumption that *nēbel* in vs. 12 means "jar." The argument in relation to vs. 14 (as indicated above) would then be that whoever was responsible for this exegetical development of vss. 12-13 correctly understood *nēbel* in vs. 12 as "jar" and redirected it towards "shattering" rather than "intoxication" in terms of the fragility of wine jars.

[1] BDB (Oxford: Clarendon, 1907; reprinted with corrections, 1966) 614.

[2] KB² (Leiden: Brill, 1958) 589.

[3] AbuᵓL Walīd Marwān ibn Janāh, *The Book of Hebrew Roots* (ed. A. Neubauer; Oxford: Clarendon, 1875; reprinted, Amsterdam: Philo, 1968) 402.

[4] S. Muenster, *Dictionarium Hebraicum* (Basel: Froben, 1539) 239.

[5] J. Buxtorf, *Lexicon Hebraicum et Chaldaicum* (4th ed.; Basel: Ludovic König, 1631; rev. ed., London: Whittaker Treacher, 1833) 258.

[6] J. D. Michaelis, *Supplementa ad Lexica Hebraica* (ed. T. C. Tychsen; Göttingen; 1784-1792) 1588-89.

[7] W. Gesenius, *Thesaurus Philologicus Criticus Linguae Hebraeae et Chaldaeae Veteris Testamenti* (3 vols.; Leipzig: Fr. Chr. Guil. Vogel, 1829-42) 2. (1840) 844.

[8] Ibid. 844.

[9] BDB, 614.

[10] A. M. Honeyman, "The Pottery Vessels of the Old Testament," *PEQ* (1939) 85.

[11] Ibid., 85 n. 1.

[12] W. Gesenius, *Thesaurus Philologicus Criticus*, 2. 844.

[13] BDB, 614.

[14] KB², 589; cf. S. Muenster, *Dictionarium Hebraicum*, 239.

[15] W. F. Albright, "The Babylonian Matter in the Pre-Deuteronomic Primeval History (JE) in Gen 1-11," *JBL* 58 (1939) 98.

[16] F. Stolz, *Strukturen und Figuren im Kult von Jerusalem: zur altorientalischen vor- und frühisraelitischen Religion* (BZAW 118, 1970, 165).

[17] Hieronymi Sancti Eusebii, *In Hieremiam Prophetam* (CSEL 59; ed. S. Reiter; Leipzig: G. Freytag, 1913) 163.

¹⁸ J. Ziegler (ed.), *Septuaginta Vetus Testamentum Graecum Auctoritate Societatis Litterarum Gottingensis editum* 15: *Ieremias, Baruch, Threni, Epistula Ieremiae* (Göttingen: Vandenhoeck & Ruprecht, 1957) 215.

¹⁹ J. Calvin, *Praelectiones in Librum Prophetiarum Ieremia et Lamentationes* (3d ed.; Geneva: Haered Evstath Vignon, 1589) 108; W. Lowth, *A Commentary upon the Prophecy and Lamentations of Jeremiah* (London: R. Knaplock, 1718) 122; H. Venema, *Commentarius ad Librum Prophetiarum Ieremiae* (2 vols. Leeuwarden: H. A. de Chalmot, 1765) 1.357; K. H. Graf, *Der Prophet Jeremia* (Leipzig: T. O. Weigel, 1862) 200; F. Hitzig, *Der Prophet Jeremia* (Kurzgefasstes exegetisches Handbuch zum Alten Testament 3; 2d ed.; Leipzig: S. Hirzel, 1866) 102; C. W. E. Naegelsbach, *The Book of the Prophet Jeremiah* (A Commentary on the Holy Scriptures, Critical, Doctrinal and Homiletical 12; ed. J. P. Lange; Edinburgh: Clark, 1871) 141; C. F. Keil, *The Prophecies of Jeremiah* (Clark's Foreign Theological Library, 4th Series 40-41; 2 vols.; Edinburgh: Clark, 1873-74) 1.235; C. von Orelli, *The Prophecies of Jeremiah* (Clark's Foreign Theological Library, New Series 39; Edinburgh: Clark, 1889) 115; C. von Orelli, *Der Prophet Jeremia* (Kurzgefasster Kommentar zu den heiligen Schriften Alten und Neuen Testamentes A.4.2; Munich: Oskar Beck, 1905) 65; F. Giesebrecht, *Das Buch Jeremia* (HKAT 3.2.1 Göttingen: Vandenhoeck & Ruprecht, 1894) 79; B. Duhm, *Das Buch Jeremia* (Kurzer Hand Commentar zum Alten Testament 11; Tübingen and Leipzig: Mohr [Siebeck], 1901) 122; A. S. Peake, *Jeremiah and Lamentations* (2 vols.; The Century Bible, Edinburgh and London: T and E. Jack, 1910-1911) 1.195. L. Elliott Binns, *The Book of the Prophet Jeremiah* (Westminster Commentaries; London: Methuen, 1919) 117; P. Volz *Der Prophet Jeremia* (KAT 10; 2d ed.; Leipzig: D. Weiner Scholl, 1928) 152; W. Rudolph, *Jeremia* (HAT 12; 2d ed.; Tübingen: Mohr, 1958) 87-88; A. Weiser, *Das Buch Jeremia* (ATD 20-21; 6th ed.; Göttingen: Vandenhoeck & Ruprecht, 1969) 113-15. J. Bright, *Jeremiah: Introduction, Translation and Notes* (AB 21; New York: Doubleday, 1965) 94; N.C. Habel, *Jeremiah, Lamentations* (Concordia Commentary; Saint Louis and London: Concordia Publishing House, 1968) 130; A. van Selms, *Jeremia* (De Prediking Van Het Oude Testament; Nijkerk: G. F. Callenbach, 1972) 193; E. W. Nicholson, *The Book of the Prophet Jeremiah, 1-25* (Cambridge Bible Commentary on the New English Bible; Cambridge: Cambridge University, 1973) 123.

²⁰ *Miqrā᾽ôt Gĕdôlôt Nĕbî᾽îm ᾽ahărônîm* (Tel Aviv: Schocken, 1959) 134.

²¹ Ibid. 154.

²² A. B. Ehrlich, *Randglossen zur Hebräischen Bibel 4: Jesaia, Jeremia* (Leipzig: Hinrichs, 1912; photographically reproduced, Hildesheim: Olms, 1968) 278.

²³ F. Giesebrecht, *Das Buch Jeremia*, 79.

²⁴ *Miqrā᾽ôt Gĕdôlôt*, 154.

²⁵ H. Venema, *Commentarius ad Librum Prophetiarum Ieremiae*, 359.

²⁶ P. Volz, *Der Prophet Jeremia*, 152.

²⁷ C. W. E. Naegelsbach, *The Book of the Prophet Jeremiah*, 141.

²⁸ A. S. Peake, *Jeremiah and Lamentations*, 195.

²⁹ C. W. E. Naegelsbach, *The Book of the Prophet Jeremiah*, 141.

³⁰ W. Lowth, *A Commentary*, 122; H. Venema, *Commentarius*, 358-59; B. Blayney, *Jeremiah and Lamentations: A New Translation with Notes critical, philological and explanatory* (Oxford: Clarendon, 1784) 88; E. Henderson, *The Book of the Prophet Jeremiah and that of the Lamentations* (London: Hamilton Adams, 1851) 84-85; K. H. Graf, *Der Prophet Jeremia*, 200-01; F. Hitzig, *Der Prophet Jeremia*, 102; E. H. Plumptre, *Jeremiah–Malachi* (An Old Testament Commentary for English Readers 5; ed. C. J. Ellicott; London: Cassell, 1884) 51; C. von Orelli, *The Prophecies of Jeremiah*, 115; F. Giesebrecht, *Das Buch Jeremia*, 79; B. Duhm, *Das Buch Jeremia*, 122; A. S. Peake, *Jeremiah and Lamentations*, 195; P. Volz, *Der Prophet Jeremia*, 152.

³¹ J. Calvin, *Praelectiones*, 108; C. W. E. Naegelsbach, *Jeremiah*, 141; L. Elliott Binns, *Jeremiah*, 117; P. Volz, *Der Prophet Jeremia*, 152; K. H. Graf, *Der Prophet Jeremia*, 201; F. Hitzig, *Der Prophet Jeremia*, 102; C. F. Keil, *Prophecies of Jeremiah*, 1.236; E. H. Plumptre, *Jeremiah–Malachi*, 52; F. Giesebrecht, *Das Buch Jeremia*, 79; A. van Selms, *Jeremia*, 193.

³² So L. Elliott Binns, *Jeremiah*, 117 and N. C. Habel, *Jeremiah, Lamentations*, 130.

[33] So W. Lowth, *A Commentary*, 122; B. Blayney, *Jeremiah and Lamentations*, 88; E. Henderson, *Book of the Prophet Jeremiah*, 84-85; K. H. Graf, *Der Prophet Jeremia,* 200; F. Hitzig, *Der Prophet Jeremia*, 102; C. F. Keil, *Prophecies of Jeremiah*, 1.235; C. von Orelli, *Der Prophet Jeremia*, 65; A. van Selms, *Jeremia*, 193; E. W. Nicholson, *Jeremiah 1-25*, 123.

[34] E. H. Plumptre, *Jeremiah-Malachi*, 51.

[35] C. von Orelli, *Prophecies of Jeremiah*, 115; J. Bright, *Jeremiah*, 94; A. van Selms, *Jeremia*, 193; E. W. Nicholson, *Jeremiah 1-25*, 123.

[36] E. Henderson, *Book of the Prophet Jeremiah,* 85.

[37] W. Lowth, *A Commentary*, 122.

[38] J. Bright, *Jeremiah*, 94.

[39] B. Blayney, *Jeremiah and Lamentations*, 88.

[40] Ibid. 88.

[41] J. Calvin, *Praelectiones*, 108; F. Giesebrecht, *Das Buch Jeremia*, 79; B. Duhm, *Das Buch Jeremia*, 122; A. S. Peake, *Jeremiah and Lamentations*, 195; P. Volz, *Der Prophet Jeremia*, 152; W. Rudolph, *Jeremia*, 88; A. Weiser, *Das Buch Jeremia*, 114.

[42] F. Giesebrecht, *Das Buch Jeremia*, 79.

[43] F. Hitzig, *Der Prophet Jeremia*, 102; P. Volz, *Der Prophet Jeremia*, 152; W. Rudolph, *Jeremia*, 84; J. Bright, *Jeremiah*, 92; A. van Selms, *Jeremia*, 193.

[44] J. G. Janzen, *Studies in the Text of Jeremiah* (HSM 6; Cambridge, MA: Harvard University, 1973) 85.

[45] J. Calvin, *Praelectiones*, 108.

[46] F. Giesebrecht, *Das Buch Jeremia*, 79; B. Duhm, *Das Buch Jeremia*, 122; W. Rudolph, *Jeremia*, 88.

[47] A. S. Peake, *Jeremiah and Lamentations*, 195; P. Volz, *Der Prophet Jeremia*, 152; W. Rudolph, *Jeremia*, 88; A. Weiser, *Das Buch Jeremia*, 114.

[48] P. Volz, *Der Prophet Jeremia*, 152.

[49] W. Lowth, *A Commentary*, 122; F. Hitzig, *Der Prophet Jeremia*, 102; E. H. Plumptre, *Jeremiah-Malachi*, 51-52.

[50] W. Lowth, *A Commentary*, 122.

[51] F. Hitzig, *Der Prophet Jeremia*, 102.

[52] E. H. Plumptre, *Jeremiah-Malachi*, 52.

[53] A. van Selms, *Jeremia*, 193.

[54] K. H. Graf, *Der Prophet Jeremia*, 200-0ḵ; C. F. Keil, *Prophecies of Jeremiah*, 1.235-36; C. von Orelli, *Der Prophet Jeremia*, 65; F. Giesebrecht, *Das Buch Jeremia*, 79; A. S. Peake, *Jeremiah and Lamentations*, 195; P. Volz, *Der Prophet Jeremia*, 152-53.

[55] C. F. Keil, *Prophecies of Jeremiah*, 1.235-36; C. von Orelli, *Der Prophet Jeremia*, 65; F. Giesebrecht, *Das Buch Jeremia*, 79.

[56] A. S. Peake, *Jeremiah and Lamentations*, 195.

[57] P. Volz, *Der Prophet Jeremia*, 152-53.

[58] K. H. Graf, *Der Prophet Jeremia*, 200.

[59] W. Thiel, *Die deuteronomistische Redaktion von Jeremia 1-25* (WMANT 41; Neukirchen-Vluyn, Neukirchener Verlag, 1973) 77-78, 205, 234, 246.

[60] J. M. Berridge, *Prophet, People and the Word of Yahweh* (Basel Studies of Theology 4; Zürich: EVZ-Verlag, 1970) 212.

[61] H. Weippert, *Die Prosareden des Jeremia Buches (BZAW 132, 1973) 83.*

[62] W. Rudolph, *Jeremia*, 88.

[63] A. Weiser, *Das Buch Jeremia*, 114-15.

[64] B. Duhm, *Das Buch Jeremia*, 122.

[65] Ibid 122.

[66] W. Rudolph, *Jeremia*, 88.

# THE SERVANT'S KNOWLEDGE IN ISAIAH 40-55

JAMES M. WARD

PERKINS SCHOOL OF THEOLOGY, SOUTHERN METHODIST UNIVERSITY,
DALLAS, TEXAS 75275

FOR a long time modern critics of the OT gave priority to the prophets when considering the literary relations of their writings to those of the historians, lawgivers, psalmists, and wise men of ancient Israel. Where affinities in language and idea were observed, the prophets more often than not were credited with the original creativity and the others were regarded as imitators, although the complexity of the literary history of the canon and the likelihood of interdependence among the literary traditions were acknowledged.

This older scholarly consensus began to give way about two generations ago, and it is now dissolved. First it was the relationship between the prophets and the Pentateuch. Today it is widely agreed that the dominant religious traditions reflected in the Pentateuch—though not, of course, the later editorial work of the Deuteronomic and priestly schools—assumed definitive shape before the emergence of the great, canonical prophets, and that the prophets accepted these traditions as the foundation of their work.

Next it was the prophets and the psalms. Most critics today date the development of the main literary types, as well as the main religious convictions, exhibited in the Psalter, before the time of the canonical prophets. Where affinities exist between the psalms and the prophetic books, priority is usually assigned to the psalms. This is true, for example, in the case of the similarity between the complaints of Jeremiah and the individual complaint psalms of the Psalter, and in that between the creation-theology of Second Isaiah and that of the enthronement psalms.

Now it is the prophets and wisdom. Interest in the subject is not entirely new, for Samuel Terrien had already addressed himself to one aspect of it in 1954,[1] as had J. Fichtner in 1949.[2] Indeed, J. Lindblom had produced a brief, general treatment of the subject as early as 1955.[3] Nevertheless, it is only within the last few years, when wisdom studies generally have moved toward the fore, that the subject to which these scholars gave the initial impetus has gained widespread attention. Today we have a number of major studies of the issue.[4]

The conclusions reached in most of the published analyses of the prophets and wisdom resemble those of the earlier analysis of the relation of the prophetic traditions to the Torah and the psalms, that is, the prophets are viewed as dependent upon the wisdom tradition at those points where literary dependency seems likely. This conclusion presupposes the prior judgment that the wisdom tradition reflected in the OT was not a late, postexilic phenomenon, as was once commonly believed, but an ancient one, in the Near East generally and in Israel specifically. Furthermore, it is argued—or assumed—by many of those writing on the subject, the wisdom tradition in Israel was borne by a succession of formally trained wise men, who were recognized as a distinct group, and who may have held professional offices within the royal establishment during the whole era of the Israelite monarchy. This group, or class, as it is sometimes called, would thus have existed long before the time of the literary prophets, and, therefore, it is reasonable to expect the language, ideas, and literary forms cultivated by this highly placed group to be reflected in the writings of the prophets. If the prophets borrowed standard words, ideas, and forms from the legal/covenantal and liturgical traditions of Israel, then it is likely that they borrowed from the wisdom tradition, too.

The chief difficulty with the argument is that the evidence for the existence of a distinct group of professional teachers of wisdom in Israel during the monarchy is scanty and ambiguous. R. N. Whybray's recent effort to refute the widespread belief that there was such a group has demonstrated how uncertain the hypothesis is, even if it has failed to disprove it.[5] Moreover, even if there were such teachers of wisdom in Israel during and before the time of the canonical prophets, we cannot be certain whether their teachings resembled those contained in the extant wisdom writings, namely, Proverbs, Job, Ecclesiastes, and the wisdom psalms. Therefore, any conclusions drawn concerning the influence upon prophetic thought and speech of a distinctive group of wise men must remain tentative. This does not mean that comparative study of prophetic and wisdom thought is impossible or unfruitful. Indeed, such study is possible on the basis of the existing texts, and it may be more important in the end than the effort to determine the origin of the shared concepts and literary forms.

The present essay falls within this area of comparative study, but only in a general way. It is an attempt to examine a major dimension of Second Isaiah's thought, which seems to be a response to an intellectual outlook exhibited most fully in the Book of Job—and later in Ecclesiastes. Our concern is not to trace in Isaiah 40–55 specific terms, propositions, or literary forms that are deemed characteristic of the wisdom literature itself, much less to search for traces of the influence of an alleged "wisdom school."[6] We are concerned here only with the general intellectual situation which is mirrored in the canonical wisdom books.

## A Response to Scepticism

This situation was marked by scepticism concerning traditional Yahwistic faith. Popular scepticism toward Yahwism, mixed with idolatrous worship of other gods, had been known in Israel from the beginning of her history, but the rigorous scepticism exhibited in the Book of Job—and later in Ecclesiastes—was a new development in Israel's recorded tradition. It was rational, comprehensive, and self-conscious. Unconvinced by parochial dogmas, it demanded confirmation of inherited beliefs through personal experience and broad observation of human life. Although it would be anachronistic to identify this mentality with modern, scientific empiricism, it is "modern" in the sense that it appeals today to readers who are sceptical of traditional theism. Scepticism of this kind may have existed in the minds of some individuals in Israel prior to the exile, perhaps among teachers of wisdom. However, it was apparently only after the fall of the Israelite monarchy, during the Babylonian exile and afterwards that it became a serious threat to corporate faith.

The loss of faith encountered by Second Isaiah (as well as Jeremiah and Ezekiel) in some quarters was what we would call practical atheism, in the sense that, while it probably did not involve the direct denial of the existence of God, as Israel had known him, it did deny his effective involvement in the concerns of the Israelite people, as well as his power to shape and control their destiny. The Israelites must have been impressed greatly by the power of Babylon and its gods, and correspondingly embarrassed by the insignificance of Yahweh. Their covenantal history would have lost its importance when compared to the grandeur of Babylon's world empire.

And yet, it is difficult to believe that all thoughtful Israelites shifted their loyalty at once to the gods of Babylon. After all, these gods were not new to them. Babylonian gods, and others like them, had been prominent in the environment of Israel for centuries, and they had been disdained by many Israelites in spite of the disproportionate power of their devotees. It seems likely that some Israelites of the exile, instead of moving opportunistically from one national cult to another, would have become disillusioned with all the gods as effective benefactors and masters of human destiny. They would have been practical atheists, viewing all conventional religious ideologies with a sceptical eye and waiting for some new word to interpret the course of history and give meaning to their lives. Such scepticism would have been an important factor in the religious situation of Second Isaiah, in addition to that simple apostasy to alien gods which was the most obvious alternative to traditional Yahwism for discouraged Israelites.

## In Defense of Divine Wisdom

A full exposition of Second Isaiah's response to the intellectual situation of the exile would require treatment of the entire series of his prophetic poems. However, the essentials of his response to the kind of intellectual currents we have been describing may be seen in a group of selected passages, to which we now turn.

In the middle of the opening poem (Isaiah 40), immediately after the announcement of the imminent revelation of the glory of Yahweh and the salvation of his people (40:1-11), there is this remarkable apologia for "the only wise God":

> Who measures the spirit of Yahweh,
>     or what counselor instructs him?
> With whom does he take counsel that he
>     might give Him understanding,
>     or teach Him the way of justice?
> Who teaches Him knowledge,
>     or instructs Him in the way of understanding? (40:13-14)

The questions asked here are reminiscent of those in Job 38:1-42:6. Both writers are addressing the problem of divine and human knowledge in a situation where traditional theological formulations have been challenged, and both combine the affirmation of God's understanding with the assertion of his sovereign power in creation (Isa 40:12, 15, 22, 26). The issue is not whether Israel's national deity is concerned with her welfare and able to secure it against the gods of other nations, but whether there is, in and behind the world, as it is known and inhabited by all peoples, a benevolent mind and righteous purpose, and whether this purpose can be expected to manifest itself within the course of human affairs. This is the really serious question. Matching idols is mere foolishness (40:18ff.).

There is an unusual concentration of terms for learning, knowing, and understanding in 40:13-14: know (*yāda<sup>c</sup>*, vss. 13b, 14b), knowledge (*da<sup>c</sup>at*, vs. 14b), counsel (verb *yā<sup>c</sup>aṣ*, vs. 14a, and noun, *<sup>c</sup>ēṣâ*, vs. 13b), teach (*lāmad*, vs. 14a, 14b), understand (*bîn*, vs. 14a), and understanding (*tĕbûnâ*, vs. 14b). If we trace these terms throughout Isaiah 40-55, we discover a pattern of ideas which provides a coherent, and morally empowering, response to religious scepticism and idolatry, although in the nature of the case it cannot be a demonstrative one. After everything has been said, the mystery of God's being remains: "For as the heavens are higher than the earth, so are my ways higher than your ways and my thoughts than your thoughts" (55:9).

The counsel—or purpose—of God could be understood only by interpreting present events on a world-scale and in the light of Israel's whole prior history. The content of this counsel was universal justice. Its agents were two, the world conqueror, Cyrus, and the religious messenger, Israel. Its necessary condition was faith in the one, transcendent, just creator, which faith entailed the permanent rejection of all forms of idolatry. Achievement of this purpose required breaking the oppressive power of Babylon and releasing the peoples captive to her. This was Cyrus' role. But beyond the forceful suppression of tyranny there was the necessity of disseminating the knowledge of God, the only foundation of true faith. This was Israel's role.

The wisdom associated with idolatry and divination was scorned by Second Isaiah (40:20; 44:25), as was the vainglorious wisdom of Babylon (47:10). These references constitute his total use of the technical term for wisdom (the adjectival form, *ḥākām*, in 40:20 and 44:25, and the nominal form, *ḥokmâ*, in 47:10), as we are familiar with it from the canonical wisdom books. He never uses it positively. We may wonder whether it had only negative connotations for him. That it did is suggested by the three-fold parallelism, liars/diviners/wise men, in 44:25, but perhaps we should not infer too much from this one allusion.

In any case, this last text (44:24-26) sets forth a central theme of the prophet's message concerning true knowledge. Yahweh, who by himself created the heavens and the earth, frustrates the wisdom of diviners (vs. 25) but "confirms the word of his servant and performs the counsel of his messengers" (vs. 25). In this case the divine purpose involves the restoration of Jerusalem and Judah (vs. 26). Further, Yahweh, who takes counsel from none (40:13-14), gives it to Israel, his servant, and also to Cyrus, so that Yahweh's own counsel/purpose may be accomplished (46:10-11; 44:28). By contrast, the counsel of idolaters (45:21), and especially the great tyrant Babylon (47:13), proves empty. Yet, it is not enough merely to assert the emptiness of a rival religion and the superiority of one's own. A reasoned apologetic is required to elicit an informed response.

## Israel's Unique Understanding

Second Isaiah's defense of Yahwism centers upon the continuity of prophetic interpretation of history and the absence of any corresponding witness among the other nations. This point is made with great force in the dramatic trial of the nations described in ch. 41 (vss. 22-23), and it is reiterated in subsequent poems (43:9; 44:9, 18-19; 45:20-21). The assertion is not simply that Israel's prophets are superior to alien diviners in foreseeing future events. Divination as a mark of human wisdom is repudiated by the writer, whether it be foreign (47:13) or domestic (48:6-8). This last passage contains a sharp word of caution against any facile "argument from prophecy." It declares that God's saving acts are full of surprises, not only for others but also for Israel, and that any boast Israel might make of prior knowledge is bound to be set at naught by her perennial failure to fulfill the moral responsibility incumbent upon those who claim to discern God's purpose in history. This linking of knowledge and responsibility, an issue to which we will return below, is rooted in the very character of God himself, in whom knowledge and understanding serve "the way of justice" (40:14). Therefore, knowing God rightly necessarily involves seeking justice.

The superiority of Israel's witness, then, lies not in greater skill at divining the future, but in a unique understanding of history as the scene of God's working for justice. Israel's own story as a people provides the principal clue to this conception of God's activity, so the prophet repeatedly calls Israel to reflect on this story (41:8-9; 42:24; 43:15-17, 26-28; 51:2, 11; 55:3-4). However, what has happened in the past is mere prelude to the fulfillment of God's just purpose; therefore, Israel is not to be preoccupied with "the former things," not even the formative event of the Exodus (43:16-18). It is the new act of God's justice that is to command her attention (43:19).

The true meaning of God's new act cannot be comprehended in terms of the ideology of paganism, but only in terms of the justice of God, as defined by Israel's tradition. Therefore, Second Isaiah plays repeatedly upon the theme of the unknowing of idolaters (43:9, etc.). Even Cyrus, an agent of Yahweh's justice, does not know Yahweh (45:4-5) and, therefore, cannot know the ultimate purpose of his own deeds. His world conquest is part of God's plan for the universal dissemination of religious knowledge, that is, the truth about God. It is made possible by God, so that throughout the world "men may know" the one God, the creator and Lord (45:6-7; cf. 41:20, 26).

The announcement of Cyrus' conquest beforetime (41:26) was not the mere prediction some months or years before the fact by a prophet of Yahweh of this or that military victory of Cyrus, as has often been thought. A divinatory act of that sort could not have elicited the proper acknowledgement of Yahweh. The point is not that Yahweh has better forecasters of future events than other gods, and therefore must be a superior deity, but that the one God, who is creator of all things and judge of all nations, has provided a unique witness to himself through Israel, throughout the generations (40:21-23; 41:4; 43:12). Understanding the significance of Cyrus' conquest is a matter, not simply of remembering a prediction made by an Israelite prophet, but of setting a world-historical event in the context of the purpose of God, as it has been declared "from ancient times" (46:10). This point is made unmistakably in 46:8-11 (if indeed the "bird of prey/man of my counsel" in vs. 11 is Cyrus, as is now all but universally supposed),[7] and it is confirmed by 41:4, where Yahweh's "calling the generations from the beginning" is mentioned in the same sentence as his empowering of the world conqueror (41:2-4). The prophet's case rests not on an argument from a particular prophecy but upon the ancient, and continually renewed, Israelite testimony to the purpose and character of God.

Cyrus' conquest of the Babylonian Empire fulfills a double purpose. First of all it brings the righteous judgment of God upon a nation that has terrorized and oppressed many peoples (47:1-15; 48:14). Secondly, it makes possible the release of Babylon's prisoners, and the repatriation of exiled peoples, including of course Israelites (45:13; 48:20; 49:9). The restoration of Jerusalem and Judah is part of this repatriation (40:1-2, 9-11; 44:26; 49:14-21; 51:3, 11, 16-23; 52:1-2, 7-12). Therefore, the prophet can say that Cyrus' triumph is "for the sake of my servant Jacob, and Israel my chosen" (45:4). However, it is so, only in order that Israel may proclaim the truth about God, and thus make it possible for the peoples to know him truly (45:6-7). Everything that takes place in the world drama which is about to unfold is ultimately meant to serve this purpose.

There are several vivid descriptions in the book of the reversal of fortunes which is to take place between Israel and other powers (41:11-12; 43:3-4; 45:14; 49:7, 22-26; 51:21-23). It has recently been argued, primarily on the basis of these passages, that Second Isaiah, far from being the universalist he has commonly been supposed to be, was a fierce nationalist.[8] Undeniably, a certain national pride is displayed in these passages. However, most of the imagery is that of the traditional Israelite cult;[9] therefore, it cannot be taken merely as an expression of the writer's personal sentiment. Some of it (43:3-4) is exodus imagery, used in conjunction with the proclamation of a new Exodus (43:1-2). For the most part, however, these are pictures of the humiliation of kings who have oppressed the peoples of the world tyranically (49:22-26; 51:21-23). These images express the prophet's fierce passion for justice more than any nationalism. And they do not contradict the many expressions of universalism found elsewhere in the book. Indeed, by manifesting the justice of God, "who brings princes to nought" (40:23), the humbling of oppressor kings will contribute to the recognition of the divine purpose behind such events (45:22-25; 49:26). Israel's "threshing of mountains" in the time to come has one end, namely "that men may see and know, may consider and understand together, that the hand of Yahweh has done this" (41:14-20).

These events require interpretation in order to be revelatory. Therefore, the agency of Cyrus as conqueror must be coupled with the agency of Israel as interpreter. The glory of God, embodied in the world transformations about to be observed by all men (40:3-5), can be recognized as the glory of *God* only as the *word* of God (40:8) makes sense of it. This word, known by Israel "from the beginning" (40:21,28), is once again to be proclaimed by Israel, the messenger of God. In contrast to the gods of the nations, which have no witnesses to interpret world history (41:21-24, 28-29), Yahweh has a witness in his servant, the one who will bring justice to the nations through his teaching (*tôrâ*, 42:1-4), As bearer of this teaching, the servant is to be a light to the nations (42:6-8; 49:6). There can be no doubt that the justice, teaching, and light which the servant mediates to the nations are Yahweh's own. The three terms, used to describe the servant's work in 42:1-6, appear together again in a single line, in 51:4, as the elements of Yahweh's saving work. It is he, who "forms light and creates darkness, makes weal and creates woe" (45:7), who turns the darkness to light[10] for the blind (42:16) and inspires his servant as an agent in this work (42:1).

The problem with Israel's performing as bearer of light/teaching/justice lies in first bringing Israel itself to full and confident acknowledgement of Yahweh. The teacher must also be taught. In the past Israel has failed to discern the hand of God in the judgments of history, and failed to take God's discipline to heart (42:25). In the present Israel misunderstands her way as being hidden from God (40:27). She is the blind messenger of God (42:18-20), the discouraged servant (49:4). Therefore, her commissioning as teacher is first of all to enable herself to learn. " 'You are my witnesses,' says Yahweh, 'so that you may know, and believe me, and understand that I am He' " (43:10). The teacher learns in teaching others. The servant is instructed every morning, so that he may fulfill his commission (50:4).

Interestingly, the commission is not described in this last passage as teaching, but as the sustaining of the weary. The content of God's salvation is not merely correct ideas about God, but the moral and personal rejuvenation of those who are worn out and discouraged (cf. 40:29-31). The implication of these lines corresponds to that of 40:14, where knowledge and justice are mentioned together as attributes of God, and of 42:1-4, where the servant's work is described in terms of both justice and teaching (*tôrâ*).

## The Servant's Knowledge

We come finally to the text alluded to in the title of this essay, namely 53:11. In the Authorized English tradition the crucial line is rendered, "By his knowledge shall the righteous one, my servant, make many to be accounted righteous" (*RSV*). If this is correct, it means that the servant's knowledge is the decisive factor in bringing many to a state of righteousness, that is to say, it is the decisive factor in the whole process of transformation described in Isa 52:13-53:12. What might this knowledge be?

Before attempting to answer this question we must discuss the translation of vs. 11, for the version we have quoted is no longer universally accepted by scholars.

The New English Bible has adopted the suggestion of D. W. Thomas that *da$^c$at* in 53:11 is not "knowledge," from the *pê-yôd* verb *yāda$^c$*, but "humiliation," from a properly *pê-wāw* verb *wāda$^c$* ("to be quiet, submissive").[11] Thus, *NEB* reads, "After his *disgrace* he shall be fully vindicated" (italics added). This translation of *da$^c$at* is perhaps possible, since the root adduced by Thomas does seem to occur a number of times in the OT.[12] However, Thomas was not able to cite another occurrence of the noun *da$^c$at* in the sense of humiliation. Therefore, the usual meaning, "knowledge," is much more probable in our text, unless of course it makes nonsense of the verse.[13] It should be noted that *da$^c$at* occurs four more times in Isaiah 40-55, each time with the usual meaning (40:14; 44:19, 25; and 47:10). The verb *wāda$^c$* (*NEB*, "humbled") may be present in 53:3, and, if so, it is the best evidence available to support Thomas' theory, occurring as it does in the same poem as 53:11. However, the verb *yāda$^c$*, "to know," is a common and central word in Second Isaiah, as we have already observed.[14]

To understand the second clause of 53:11 properly, one must deal also with the first. The MT reads, literally, "From (or, after) the travail of his life (or, soul) he shall see . . ."; but the older text from Qumran (both Isaiah scrolls), which is supported by the Greek translation, is clearly preferable. Therefore, it is unnecessary to struggle with the MT, as *RSV*, for example, has done (". . . he shall see the fruit of the travail of his soul"). The preferred text, which is now receiving general acceptance,[15] has "light" as the object of the verb *see*. Thus, we may translate the verse as follows:

Out of his mortal travail he shall see light;
  he shall be satisfied by his knowledge.

The righteous one, my servant, shall make
    many righteous,
    and shall bear their iniquities.

An alternative division of clauses, which is supported by the Masoretic accentuation, yields this reading:

Out of his mortal travail he shall see light
    and be satisfied;
By his knowledge the righteous one,[16] my servant,
    shall make many righteous
    and bear their iniquities.

Both translations make good sense. Both achieve satisfactory poetic parallelism (the first, a double synthetic, and the second, a single synthetic parallelism). The lines of the first have better balance in length (six and seven words) than those of the second (five and eight words),[17] though this consideration is hardly decisive. The choice is difficult; indeed, it cannot be made on objective grounds alone. Therefore, as we try to explicate the meaning of the verse, we are forced to take both alternatives into account.

The argument that we will present in the remainder of this essay may be stated briefly in the following way: the servant's knowledge, by which he is ultimately satisfied, or, alternatively, makes many righteous, is the knowledge of God—of God's oneness, power, righteousness, sovereignty, benevolence, and saving activity. This truth about God, in contrast to all scepticism or idolatry, is the final, indispensable factor in the transformation of human life, which it is the servant's/Israel's mission to assist, and the prophet's to proclaim. Without an acknowledgement of the truth about God, the significance of the servant's sacrifice could not be grasped by those who observed his fate – the speakers of 53:1-10. That is to say, without the peoples' knowledge of the truth about God, the servant could not be vindicated, and the purpose of God, which the servant's life was meant to accomplish, could not be fulfilled.

Before proceeding further, we must state several exegetical conclusions concerning Isaiah 40–55 which our argument presupposes, but which cannot be defended within the compass of this essay. (1) All four of the so-called servant songs are integral parts of the work. (2) The servant in the songs (42:1-4; 49:1-6; 50:4-9; and 52:13-53:12) is representative of Israel as the bearer—and agent—of God's word, teaching, and justice. He is not a particular historical person, but a symbolic figure in the poetic drama of Isaiah 40–55. He represents an office which any Israelite may fill, and which Israel, understood not as a political entity but as the people of God, must fulfill, however imperfectly, in order to maintain her identity. (3) Whatever contradiction there appears to be between the attributes and behavior of the servant in the songs, and those of the servant-Israel outside the songs, arises out of the difference between commission and performance within the religious community. (4) The fourth song includes 52:13–53:12 and not merely 53:1-12.

## The Peoples' New Perception

According to the central section (53:1-9) of the climactic fourth song, the servant has been despised, persecuted, and condemned by others. They have regarded him as a criminal, and thus rationalized his suffering as the punishment of God (53:4). But now in retrospect the observers of his fate express a totally different estimate of the man. It is they, not he, who deserved such affliction, as a punishment for their own iniquity. Nevertheless, what happened to him was what God willed to happen, not for the apparent reason, but in order to benefit them. They have been made whole as a result of his experience (53:5-6). This confession is confirmed by the concluding speech of God: the servant's suffering has indeed been undeserved, but it has been willed by God in order to bring others into right relationship with him (53:11). Therefore, "the many" will soon behold the Lord's exaltation of his servant (vs. 12; cf. 52:13-15).

The speakers are not identified explicitly in 53:1-9, but the clue to their identity is provided by the opening speech of Yahweh (52:13-15). There it is said that "many peoples . . . kings" will be amazed at the eventual reversal of the servant's lot. Therefore, since the very next statement in the dialogue is a confession of surprise over the discovery of the true meaning of the servant's life (53:1), the speakers can be none other than the "many peoples/kings" of 52:15. To the extent that the servant is here the representative of a prophetic and teaching office, a kind of parabolic figure in the poetic drama of Isaiah 40-55, to this extent the chorus of speakers in 53:1-9 may include Israelites, for, although all Israel is called to be the servant people (43:10; 44:1-2; 45:4; 49:3), not all in Israel respond equally and at all times, and many require to be instructed by those who do fulfill the servant's ministry. Consequently, I see no reason to restrict the role of the speakers in ch. 53 to non-Israelites. However, we must surely think of them first of all as Gentiles. "Many peoples" can hardly mean less than this, and the "kings" cannot be Israelites. The primary purpose of this servant song is to prophesy the conversion of the peoples of the world to faith in Israel's God. The scope of the prophet's intention is universal.

The picture of foreign peoples and kings turning toward Israel and Yahweh has appeared before in Second Isaiah, and yet a profound inner development has taken place in the course of its recurrence. Twice before the writer has employed the image of a triumphal procession to proclaim the humbling of the oppressors and their final acknowledgement of Yahweh (45:14-15 and 49:22-26; cf. 49:7). The fortunes of the nations and their kings are to be reversed, their idols, repudiated, and the injustices done to Israel, redressed. But this humbling of kings is in fact a humiliation, and this vindication of Israel is an exaltation that smacks of the very pride previously displayed by the rulers who have been displaced. Thus, using the image of a triumphal procession—an image drawn from the actual practice of ancient kings—carries certain ethical liabilities, although it is a vivid dramatic device.

In the fourth servant song there is no humiliation of peoples, but only the emergence of a new perception on their part. They ponder the inner meaning of the servant's oppression in relation to their own behavior, and reach a new understanding of the moral dynamics of human existence. They anticipate the exaltation of the servant, but not at the expense of others (53:10-12). From this point to the end of the book (Isaiah 55) there is no recurrence of the earlier note of vindictiveness.[18] The nations will gather around Israel and her new "David" in the eschatological celebration (55:5), but they will not be put to shame. In the present time, according to the testimony of the speakers in 53:1-9, it is the servant who is abased and not themselves, although, according to their own admission, his behavior has not justified such treatment (53:9), while their own behavior has been laden with guilt (53:5-6). What are we to make of this confession and the related statements in the following lines of the poem?

First of all, we must take full account of the poetic character of this text. Like all of Isaiah 40-55, it is filled with poetic images and metaphors. Levels of meaning overlap. One image fades into another. At times the identity of the speaker(s) is unclear.[19] Therefore, we must be careful not to press any one metaphor too far, nor stress any one level of meaning as the sole key to the author's intention, for example, the metaphor of the trespass-offering in 53:10, or that of the criminal in vss. 8-9, or that of the victorious warrior in vs. 12. There is a virtual riot of images in this passage, and the possible implications of such a mixture are numerous indeed. The interpretive suggestions offered here, then, are not meant to be exclusive or exhaustive.

The work that God accomplishes through the life of the servant is full of surprises—reversals of human value and expectation. The weak and ugly one, deemed a deserving object of divine punishment, is ultimately exalted and vindicated, while those who have despised and condemned him discover their own guilt and unworthiness. But at the same time—this is the miracle—they find themselves in a new situation before God, one of wholeness (vs. 5) and righteousness (vs. 11), which is brought about precisely by the servant's obedience.

## The Kind of Obedience

This obedience, which is unto death, is likened to the traditional trespass-offering (the ʾāšām). This metaphor is an intriguing and highly suggestive one, but, because we know so little about the meaning—that is the interior, moral meaning—of the trespass-offering in the minds of ancient Israelite worshippers, the writer's purpose in using it is not fully clear to us. By and large in the OT the ʾāšām is a sacrifice made over and above the material compensation offered for a measurable offence (Lev 5:14-16). As such it does not suffice in itself to effect atonement for the offender, but provides a necessary ritual accompaniment of the restitution. However, there are circumstances in which the ʾāšām alone is deemed instrumental in atoning for sin and bringing about forgiveness (e.g., Lev 19:20-22). Since we do not know which of these circumstances, if either, was in the mind of Second Isaiah, we should not press either analogy too far in the case of Isa 53:10.

We do not know why there lay deep in the consciousness of ancient man the conviction—nay, the assumption—that a broken relationship between himself and God could not be restored without a ritual of sacrifice. The literary sources do not explain the conviction, probably because it was far older than the literature. The fragmentary clues provided by the Bible, e.g., "the blood is the life" (Lev 17:11, 14; Deut 12:23; cf. Gen 9:4), are not enough to dispel the cloud of our ignorance. If the blood is the life, does this mean that blood sacrifice establishes a living relationship between the worshipper and God through the means of a third—or substitute—life? We simply lack sufficient evidence to penetrate the mystery. Perhaps it was also a mystery to the Israelites in historical times, an inherited, immemorial ritual that they themselves did not fully understand. Nevertheless, they performed sacrifice, and deemed it an effective means of bringing about or restoring a vital relationship with God, or, at the very least, of marking publicly their acknowledgement of responsibility for sin, gratitude for forgiveness, and obligation for future obedience. These are the fruits of the servant's sacrifice, as is made clear in the confession in 53:1-9. Therefore, we may see an analogy between his life of obedience unto death and the obligatory ritual of the trespass offering. And yet, *for us* the servant's offering clarifies the meaning of the ʾāšām more than it is clarified by it. Whatever this offering meant in Israel before Isaiah 40–55 was written, for every reader of this great poem it has come to mean the self-conscious offering of one's life for the sake of others, in obedience to the word of God.

Whether 53:4-12 depicts the servant as actually dying or as merely being led to the point of death (or of willingness to die) is a much debated question today. We can determine *what* the servant accomplished for others, which is the principal theme of this essay, without answering this question, but we cannot determine *how* he accomplished it, without doing so. Therefore, we must deal with the issue, however briefly.

The verb to die is not explicitly predicated of the servant in the MT; therefore, it is possible to regard him as being brought to the point of death but not actually dying.[20] The analogy commonly cited in support of this interpretation is that of the pious sufferer in the psalms of lamentation, whose affliction is likened to being in, or in the power of, the pit, or Sheol, that is, the realm of death (e.g., Pss 18:4-5; 30:3; and 88:3-6). On the other hand, the clause, "he was cut off from the land of the living," in Isa 53:8 certainly implies that he has died, and this meaning is confirmed by an examination of the other OT passages where the phrase "land of the living" is employed.[21] In my judgment, the issue is settled by the use of the phrase in Jer 11:19. In this passage the prophet complains to God of a plot by his enemies to murder him, and it is clear that the clause "cut him off from the land of the living" here means to kill him, in the ordinary sense of the word. It is interesting to note that the same metaphor of the sheep being led to slaughter is used both in Jer 11:18-19 and in Isa 53:7-9[22] Furthermore, both Jeremiah and the servant are prophetic figures. Surely the use of the metaphor of the trespass-offering also implies that the servant died, since the usual ʾāšām was a ram that was slaughtered (cf. Lev 5:15, 18; 7:1-5; 14:10-13). The evidence is not absolutely unambiguous, but it is clear enough, it seems to me, to make probable the conclusion that the servant's fate, as described in 53:7-10, includes his death.

### The Servant's Vindication and Accomplishment

The servant's ignominious condemnation and death are not the last word, for the prophet looks forward to his glorious revival and vindication by God (53:10-12, cf. 52:13). Since the servant is a symbolic, or parabolic, figure in the poetic drama, and not an historical person, it is unnecessary to decide whether the prophet could have expected the physical resurrection of an individual human being after his death. It is enough to realize that he could have *imagined* such an event. This is proved by Job 14:7-17, which is roughly contemporary with Isaiah 40–55.[23] Although Job laments the fact that men do not return to life after death, he is certainly able to imagine such an event, and even to wish for it. So there is nothing inherently incredible about Second Isaiah's use of similar imagery in his poem.

What, then, does the servant accomplish for others? The people confess (53:1-9) that they have wholly misunderstood the servant's relationship to God, as well as their own, and that they now see these relationships in an entirely different light. They now perceive that they have been in the wrong, and the servant in the right, about their behavior and its consequences, about God and his justice, about good and evil, reward and punishment, life and death. A changed perception of this sort constitutes a religious and moral conversion. The people have been brought into a new relationship with God— justified. This is the meaning of the climactic affirmation in vs. 11: "The righteous one, my servant, shall make many (to be accounted) righteous." His life, teaching, and example have been the indispensable elements in the transformation of the people at the level that matters most, that is, their moral consciousness and their knowledge of God.

The conversion of the people is the essential content of the servant's exaltation. His triumph is to see light from his travail (53:11a)—the success of his ministry, his teaching, and his "intercession for transgressors" (vs. 12). There is nothing else that need be added to this. Anything else would be extraneous and irrelevant to the entire purpose of his vocation. The "spoils" he is to receive are in reality nothing more—and nothing less!—than the people's proper acknowledgement of the ways of God and of valid service to him.

In the poetic drama of the fourth song the people already acknowledge the meaning of the servant's life and its consequences for the many, but in the actual world of the writer this success of "the servant's" mission was yet to come. Therefore, he spoke of the servant's exaltation as lying in the future (52:12; 53:11-12). When it came, its essential content would be the same as the people's confession in the prophetic drama, namely, the transformation of people's moral and religious understanding. This conversion would be not merely a response to the servant's exaltation but the very exaltation itself.

## The Knowledge of God

The only possible way in which the people could learn that the servant was right was by discerning the truth of his teaching, which was exemplified in his life. This is the meaning of 53:8. The servant's knowledge, which can only be the knowledge of God,[24] is the decisive factor in the eventual success of his life and work. It is the truth of his teaching, for which he is willing to die, and for which the people are initially determined to reject and persecute him. It is his proclamation about God, as the creator and source of all natural blessing, and the judge of all nations, who demands justice among people as the condition of life, who forgives former transgressions in order to bring about new possibilities, and who commissions his servants to serve people, at last, without resort to violence. This message, and the life that exemplifies it, are the very antitheses of the convictions and behavior of the peoples of the world, and, therefore, the fundamental cause of their persecution of the messenger.

The poet does not make clear what it was that triggered the reversal of the people's judgment about the servant, that is, its immediate cause. What made them acknowledge finally what they had spurned initially? In part, at least, it seems to have been the servant's death, or his willingness to die, for the sake of his message and vocation. And yet, the death of the servant—or his faithfulness unto death—could not by itself validate the truth of his teaching. There have been countless martyrs for false causes. In the last analysis the knowledge of God, which was the foundation and substance of the servant's teaching, could only be authenticated by itself. The servant's suffering and death at the hands of the people may have been the occasion which shocked them into reexamining his life, and their own, but it alone could not explain why they now interpreted his life in an entirely new way.

It is of decisive importance to realize that the life, suffering, and death which can bring about the people's atonement—their right relation to God— are those of a particular kind of servant, who is the witness to God. What he was and what he was doing when he died make all the difference, for it is only when his special work and his prophetic proclamation are acknowledged and accepted by others, including those who persecuted him, that they are brought into a redemptive relation to God. This relation involves knowledge, commitment, and faith. No merely mechanical (or forensic) transfer of penalty from one to another could produce this kind of atonement. The transaction is thoroughly moral and religious—a matter of the mind, the will, and the affections. This, it seems to me, is the meaning of Isa 53:8, which thus stands out as the central verse in the fourth, climactic servant song.

The servant's knowledge, which is the knowledge of God and of God's unfolding purpose for the peoples of the world, and which requires the commitment of faith, not only to be fulfilled but also to be fully understood, is the wisdom set by the prophet against the scepticism of his time.

---

[1] In a paper entitled "Amos and Chokmah," read before the Society of Biblical Literature and subsequently published in *Israel's Prophetic Heritage* (eds. B. W. Anderson and W. Harrelson; New York: Harper & Bros., 1962) 108-15.

[2] "Jesaja unter den Weisen," *TLZ* 74 (1949) 75-80.

[3] "Wisdom in the Old Testament Prophets," *Wisdom in Israel and the Ancient Near East* (VTSup 3; H. H. Rowley Festschrift; eds. M. Noth and D. W. Thomas; Leiden: Brill, 1955) 192-204.

[4] Among these are W. McKane, *Prophets and Wise Men* (SBT 44; London: SCM, 1965), J. W. Whedbee, *Isaiah and Wisdom* (Nashville: Abingdon, 1971), and Joseph Jensen, *The Use of* tôrâ *by Isaiah: His Debate with the Wisdom Tradition* (CBQMS 3; Washington, DC: Catholic Biblical Association of America, 1973). The relation of the prose traditions of the book of Jeremiah to the circles of the wise is treated in Moshe Weinfeld, *Deuteronomy and the Deuteronomic School* (Oxford: Clarendon, 1972); see, especially, pp. 138-46.

[5] *The Intellectual Tradition in the Old Testament* (BZAW 135; Berlin: de Gruyter, 1974).

[6] The specific question of the literary relation of Second Isaiah to the Book of Job has been treated admirably in Samuel Terrien, "Quelques remarques sur les affinités de Job avec le Deutéro-Esaïe," *Volume du Congrès, Genève 1965* (VTSup 15; Leiden: Brill, 1966) 295-310.

[7] C. C. Torrey regarded the mention of Cyrus in 44:28 and 45:1 as a scribal gloss and the original conquering figure in 41:2, 25, and elsewhere as an Israelite messiah, identical with the servant of Yahweh (see, *The Second Isaiah* [New York: Scribner, 1928] 38-52, 135-50). James Smart has taken a similar position more recently (see, *History and Theology in Second Isaiah* [Philadelphia: Westminster, 1965] 115-30). Their argument deserves to be taken seriously. One can certainly make good sense of Isaiah 40-55 on the theory that there was originally only one, unnamed servant/messiah in the prophet's mind. However, no theory can stand in the face of the clear naming of Cyrus in all the extant ancient versions. It must remain a scholarly hypothesis and not the basis of positive exegesis.

[8] See, H. M. Orlinsky and N. H. Snaith, *Studies on the Second Part of the Book of Isaiah* (VTSup 14; Leiden: Brill, 1967); and F. Holmgren, *With Wings as Eagles: Isaiah 40/55: An Interpretation* (Chappaqua, NY: Biblical Scholars, 1973).

[9] See, especially, the royal psalms (Pss 2, 18, 72, 89, 110, 118, etc.).

[10] The use of the term "light" in these texts, in association with the reference to the servant's mission, tends to confirm the reading of the LXX and the Qumran Isaiah scrolls in 53:11 ("he shall see light"), against the MT, which lacks the word "light" there. We must take this evidence into account in dealing with 53:11, below.

[11] D. W. Thomas, "More Notes on the Root $yd^c$ in Hebrew," *JTS* 38 (1937) 404-05. See also his earlier articles on the same root in *JTS* 35 (1934) 298-306; 36 (1935) 409-12; and 37 (1936) 59-60; and further, "A Consideration of Isaiah XIII in the Light of Recent Textual and Philological Study," *De Mari à Qumran. Hommage à Mgr. J. Coppens* (BETL 24/2; ed. H. Cazelles; Gembloux: J. Duculot, 1969) 119-26.

[12] Judg 8:16 and 16:9 are perhaps the clearest examples (see Thomas, *JTS* 35, 298-306), although *NEB* is the only one of the major, recent English versions to adopt the proposed reading in these passages. *RSV, JB,* and *NAB* do not. Other occurrences are less clear (e.g. Prov 10:9; Jer 31:19; and Isa 53:3).

[13] *JB* and *NAB* read "suffering(s)" in 53:11, but not as a translation of *da^c at*. Both emend to *ra^c at*, on the slim evidence of one Hebrew ms. This procedure is unconvincing.

[14] It appears thirty-two times (not counting 53:3): 40:13, 14, 21, 28; 41:20, 22, 23, 26; 42:16, 16, 25; 43:10; 44:8, 9, 18; 45:4, 5, 6, 20, 21; 47:11, 13; 48:4, 6, 7, 8; 49:23, 26; 50:4, 7; 51:7; 55:5 (52:6 is a gloss).

[15] See *NAB, JB, NEB*, and J. Muilenburg ("Isaiah 40-46: Introduction and Exegesis," *IB* 5 [New York and Nashville: Abingdon, 1956] 630), C. R. North (*The Second Isaiah* [Oxford: Clarendon, 1964] 233), J. L. McKenzie (*Second Isaiah* [AB 20; Garden City, NY: Doubleday, 1968] 130; C. Westermann (*Isaiah 40–66: A Commentary* [Philadelphia: Westminster, 1969] 255).

[16] Many scholars have considered this word (*ṣaddîq*) to be either a dittograph of the preceding one (*yaṣdîq*) or a misplaced element of the second clause, and, accordingly, have either omitted it or moved it. Either procedure seems subjective to me, although the omission does not change the sense materially. If the word is moved to the first line, however, a different translation is required. The discrepancies among the translations proposed on this basis (see, e.g., Torrey [*Second Isaiah*, 254] and *NEB*) confirm one's doubt over the correctness of the move.

[17] The second has five and seven words, if *ṣaddîq* is deleted as a dittograph. Thus, e.g., McKenzie, whose translation is almost identical to our second version (see, *Second Isaiah*, 131). On the other hand Muilenburg regarded the first treatment of vs. 11a as the better one (IB 5, 630).

[18] Isa 54:2-3 is not an exception. The picture here is of a restored Israel repopulating the cities and lands from which she was previously exiled. Cf. *JPSV* (1973), footnote.

[19] Are 53:7-9 spoken by the same persons as 53:1-6, or by someone else? The text of vs. 8 makes it uncertain. MT reads: ". . . the blow upon him (was) for the transgression of my people." IQIsa^a has "his people", the LXX, "for the iniquities of my people he was led to death." Emendations have been proposed, for example, ". . . because of our sins" (Westermann), but the uncertainty remains. Again, who is the speaker in 53:10? Is it the chorus, which speaks in 53:1-9, or Yahweh, who speaks in 53:11-12? The reference to Yahweh in the third person in vs. 10 suggests the former, while the structure of the poem and the movement of thought suggest the latter. We prefer the second alternative, since it is not uncommon in Hebrew poetry for the speaker to refer to himself in the third person (e.g., Isa 54:13, 17; 55:3, 13). Nevertheless, the question remains open.

[20] See, e.g., Torrey (*Second Isaiah*, 420-21); G. R. Driver ("Isaiah 52:13-53:12: The Servant of the Lord," *In Memoriam Paul Kahle* [BZAW 103; eds. M. Black and G. Fohrer; Berlin: Töplemann, 1968] 104-05); and H. M. Orlinsky, *Studies*, 59-63.

[21] The full list is Pss 27:13; 52:7; 116:9; 142:6; Job 28:13; Isa 38:11; Jer 11:19; and Ezek 26:24; 32:23, 24, 25, 26, 27, and 32. Note especially Pss 52:7; 116:9; Isa 38:11; Jer 11:19; and the texts in Ezekiel. In all of these "the land of the living" means life as opposed to death, in the literal sense.

[22] Orlinsky cites Jer 11:19 to support his view that the servant does not die in Isa 53:8, on the ground that Jeremiah did not die (*Studies*, 60-61). But this observation is completely beside the point. Jeremiah refers to his enemies' intention to kill him. That they failed to do so is irrelevant to the meaning of his statement.

J. Alberto Soggin argues in a recent article that the verb *nigzar* ("cut off") in Isa 53:8 refers hyperbolically to the hopeless situation of one in the power of death, while the verb *nikrat* ("cut off") in Jer 11:19 to actual death ("Tod und Auferstehung des leidenden Gottesknechtes, Jesaja 53:8-10," *ZAW* 87/3 [1975] 346-55). However, an examination of all twelve occurrences of *gzr* in the OT (thirteen if *gzr* is read for *grz* in Ps 31:23) shows that the verb has the same range of meanings as *krt*, and that only the context determines whether it is used literally or figuratively, in reference to dying. Note, e.g., Ps 88:6 (Engl. 5), where being cut off (*gzr*) from Yahweh's hand is being like the dead. The severance denoted by *gzr* is no less complete than that denoted by *krt* (cf. 2 Kgs 6:4; Isa 9:19; Hab 3:17; 2 Chr 26:21).

[23] On the dating of the poetic dialogue in the Book of Job in the sixth (or fifth) century B.C., see the discussion by James Sanders in this volume ("Comparative Wisdom: L'Oeuvre Terrien," sec. I), M. Pope, *Job* (AB 15, 3d ed.; Garden City, NY: Doubleday, 1974) xxxiv-xxv, and S. Terrien, "The Book of Job: Introduction and Exegesis, " *IB* 3 (New York and Nashville: Abingdon, 1954) 888-90.

[24] McKenzie, *Second Isaiah*, 132.

# JONAH: A *MĀŠĀL*?

GEORGE M. LANDES

UNION THEOLOGICAL SEMINARY, NEW YORK, NEW YORK 10027

URING the oral defense of her dissertation on the Book of Jonah at Columbia University in the spring of 1963, in response to a question on whether the literary category of Jonah might possibly be a *māšāl* in view of the many commentators who had labeled it a parable, Ms. Phyllis Trible responded, as I recall, by reiterating her support for Karl Budde's old suggestion,[1] subsequently followed by a number of other scholars,[2] that Jonah was an early example of a midrash inspired by 2 Kgs 14:25. In her opinion this seemed a much more plausible and less problematic designation for Jonah's literary genre than a *māšāl*, and in this judgment she was vigorously supported by two of her mentors on the examining committee, Professors James Muilenburg and Isaac Mendelsohn, who were not only openly critical of calling Jonah a *māšāl*, but even quite disdainful of such a suggestion. Now most recently, in connection with his study of the date and purpose of Genesis 3, George E. Mendenhall has boldly asserted that in addition to texts normally so considered, also Genesis 3 and the Book of Jonah should be reckoned among the OT examples of *māšāl*.[3] However, because his main concern was another issue, Mendenhall did not endeavor to show how one might arrive at this conclusion based upon a thorough study of the usage of the term *māšāl* in the OT. It will be the burden of this investigation to engage in such a study, as well as to explore in light of it what implications might be forthcoming concerning the circle from which the author of Jonah may have come. In view of Professor Terrien's long-standing literary concerns, especially focusing on the Book of Job, which interestingly was sometimes called a *māšāl* in rabbinic and later Jewish sources,[4] it would seem altogether appropriate, in a volume of essays celebrating Dr. Terrien's most distinguished teaching and scholarly career at Union Theological Seminary, to present and dedicate to him a study on this theme.

## Parable and Māšāl

At first glance, the skeptical reactions of Muilenburg and Mendelsohn would seem to be quite justified. Obviously Jonah is not called a *māšāl* in the OT itself, nor, as far as I have been able to determine, did rabbinic or later Jewish sources ever propose *māšāl* as its literary type. Moreover, in all the commentaries, monographs and articles on Jonah which I have surveyed wherein the book is called a parable,[5] no writer has at the same time brought this latter term into conjunction with the Hebrew word *māšāl* to indicate that by parable a form of *māšāl* was meant. The rather widespread agreement that Jonah is a parable, combined with the equally pervasive and remarkable hesitation to associate the word parable in this case with its assumed Hebrew reflex, has to my knowledge never been explained, though perhaps two considerations are pertinent. First, the conceptual definition of a parable, as applied to various OT instances of the genre, would seem to have been shaped less by examples actually drawn from the OT or ancient Near Eastern sources than from those found in the NT Synoptic Gospels and rabbinic literature, so that the models upon which OT literary pericopes defined as parables were based, have been derived primarily from later rather than contemporary or earlier literary prototypes. Secondly, a careful study of all the OT passages where the text of a *māšāl* is clearly presented turns up few if any that appear even remotely to resemble the Book of Jonah.

Does this mean, then, that the English translation "parable" for Hebrew *māšāl*, as the latter is used in the OT, is rarely if ever a proper rendering of the term, and if so, that the specification of Jonah as a *māšāl* should be ruled out, even though it may be quite legitimate from a broad literary perspective to call the book a parable on the basis of later literary examples? Apparently supporting an affirmative response to this question is the often made observation that most of the prime examples of the parable form in the OT are not referred to as *měšālîm*,[6] while on the other hand, among the great variety of literary types that actually receive the name *māšāl*, only a very few qualify as possible parables.[7] It does not necessarily follow, however, that what we define in the OT today as a parable could not have been thought of as a *māšāl* by the biblical writer, but it does raise a question we should be able to answer before addressing the issue of whether or not the Book of Jonah might properly qualify as a *māšāl*: what characteristics, criteria, special features, or situation was necessary for a biblical author to label a saying, song, speech, oracle or story a *māšāl*?

### *General Characteristics and Definition of* Māšāl[8]

A study of those passages in the OT where a clear instance of a *māšāl* appears shows that it was not characterized by a more or less fixed literary form. Though generally poetic, it could also be in prose.[9] In terms of length, it could be extremely brief (as few as two words in Ezek 16:44) or relatively long (the *māšāl* that begins in Job 29:1 extends through 96 verses, divided into three chapters in the present edition of the Hebrew text). Finally, it could be formulated in one of several literary types: a popular proverb[10] (cf. 1 Sam 10:12; 24:14; Ezek 12:22; 16:44; Prov 10:5; 13:4, 7-8, etc.); various kinds of poems: taunting-satirical (Isa 14:4b-21; Mic 2:4; Hab 2:6; Num 21:27-30),[11] oracular (Num 23:7; 24:3, 15, 20-24),[12] didactic (Pss 49 and 78), including a didactic autobiographical peroration (Job 29-31);[13] or a parable in the form of an allegorizing fable (Ezek 17:1-10; 21:2-5 [Engl. 20:45-49]).[14] It was therefore not the oral or written form (in prose or poetry), its length, or the type of saying that determined whether or not it was called a *māšāl*, but rather its content and function.[15]

The meaning of the word *māšāl* gives an important clue to the content it specifies. Although traditionally associated with two distinct homographic etymons, *MŠL*, "to be like," and *MŠL*, "to rule,"[16] from the standpoint of etymology as well as content and usage, it is now clear that *māšāl* must be derived from the former and not the latter. Though in the Old Aramaic Sefire inscriptions (cf. III, 9), the root *MŠL* (not *MTL*) occurs in the sense of "to rule, have authority over,"[17] unfortunately this does not furnish the decisive philological evidence needed to demonstrate that etymologically *MŠL* (⟨*MTL*⟩), "to be like," and *MŠL*, "to rule," do indeed represent originally separate roots, since in Old Aramaic Proto Semitic *tha* is regularly represented by *š* rather than by *t*, as in later Aramaic. Nonetheless, McKane's conclusion is probably correct: it is "a mistaken enterprise to try to establish a semantic relationship between the two meanings. . . ."[18] Hence the proposal that *māšāl* means basically something like "sovereign saying" or "word of power," and on this understanding was used to indicate symbolic actions and machinations associated with sympathetic magic, should be abandoned.[19]

A *māšāl*, then, is related to the ideas of likeness, resemblance, and comparison. In whatever it refers to, these ideas should somehow be present in or connected with the referent.[20] Now in the OT, two fundamental referents are attested for *māšāl*: the first and most widespread is to something that is spoken, a speech form, but one which, as already indicated, may manifest itself in any of a variety of literary types; the second, closely related to the first, is to a person, people, nation, or object which either functions as a *māšāl*, i.e. represents in what has been done (or not done!) that which can also be exemplified through a speech-form, or becomes the subject or object of a *māšāl*, i.e. the thematic motif about which or against which a *māšāl* is delivered. When one studies these usages in the OT, it quickly becomes evident that there really is no single English word which does justice precisely to what the Hebrew conveys in and through its term *māšāl*.[21] Not even within the technical terminology of literary critical analysis does there seem to be a suitable English term appropriately defining *māšāl* as a literary category.[22] Nonetheless, it should be possible to be more precise about what the term signifies, even if we often encounter difficulty finding the right word to translate it.

## The Principal Māšāl *Genres in the Old Testament*

In each of the following types (with the exception of the first, which is only summarily treated) we shall keep to those texts where the biblical author or editor has either directly indicated the piece in question to be a *māšāl*, or strongly inferred such to be the case.

1. *The popular proverb.* Historically it is not unlikely that this represents the earliest form of *māšāl*, based upon a comparison or analogy expressed either quite explicitly or by implication, for the purpose of conveying a model, exemplar, or paradigm. This could be rendered simply as an insightful or perceptive observation, or in a more elaborate expression, usually to serve as a guide to prudential thinking and action. This is essentially the conclusion McKane[23] has reached in his study of most of the OT examples of popular proverb both outside and within the Book of Proverbs, and for details one should simply refer to his discussion.[24] As we shall now go on to show, this basic meaning, which defines a saying as a *māšāl*, is never lost in the various other genres in the OT to which the name *māšāl* is applied.

2. *Satirical taunt poems.*[25] Basically four examples occur (Isa 14:4b-21; Mic 2:4, Hab 2:6ff., and Num 21:27-30), though a number of passages where usually a person or people are called a *māšāl* (cf. 1 Kgs 9:7 [also 2 Chr 7:20], Deut 28:37; Jer 24:9; Pss 44:15 [Engl. 14]; 69:12 [Engl. 11]; Ezek 14:8; and Job 17:6, as emended) would also seem to be related to this category and therefore should be included under this rubric.[26]

In Isa 14:4b-21, what the prophet or editor[27] has introduced as a *māšāl*, most modern scholars are agreed is an impressive and striking illustration of a taunt poem or prophetic mocking dirge.[28] However, its *māšāl*-character is probably not epitomized so much by the derisive and dirge-like tone[29] as by what would seem to be the basic purpose of the poem, viz., to portray through the figure of an oppressive and powerful ruler the outcome of arrogant pride and overreaching *hybris* as a negative public example. Running throughout the poem is a comparison in the form of a contrast between the mighty power and state of ascendancy of the ruler (cf. vss. 4b, 6, 13-14, 16-17, 20aβ) and his devastating fall and complete humiliation at the hands of Yahweh (vss. 7-12, 15, 18-20aα). Moreover, this is presented not simply as an object lesson for the edification of the hearers, but also to motivate them to take measures to guard against the situation happening again (vss. 20b-21). Thus, through the poem's contrasting images and figures, those addressed are given a vivid exemplar of the divine judgment on human pride, applicable to more than one set of circumstances, but set forth as a model to be prevented and rejected whenever conditions allow for its appearance.

The *māšāl* in Mic 2:4 is much briefer than the one in Isaiah 14, and considerably more difficult to interpret, though careful study of it in its context (Mic 2:1-5) shows some striking thematic similarities to Isaiah 14. First of all, the term *nĕhî,* "lament," used only here in parallelism with *māšāl*, clearly indicates the dirge-like character of the saying. Secondly, the content of the *māšāl* expresses an ironically pertinent divine judgment suffered by the "devisers of wrong and practitioners of evil" mentioned in vs. 1, whose ruthless acquisition of property (vs. 2) and unseemly pride (*tēlĕkû rômâ,* vs. 3bβ) shall come only to ruin (*šādôd nĕšaddunû,* vs. 4a) and humiliation (*lĕsôbēb śādênû yĕḥallēq,* vs. 4b). Once again a contrasting comparison is set up, but now not wholly confined to the *māšāl* itself, but expressed through the *māšāl* and its context, in which the former and latter estate of the powerfully arrogant are juxtaposed in order to make the experience of these ruined oppressors an object lesson to the prophet's audience. Those whose evil (*raᶜ*, vs. 1) has been effectively countered by the divine evil (*rāᶜâ*, vs. 3a, defined as judgment) are an example to be avoided because their conduct can only lead to an ignominious end.[30]

Also in the *māšāl* of Hab 2:6-19, we find a similar thematic pattern expressed, only now in a series of woe pronouncements,[31] which present the content of the *māšāl* (vs. 6), here further defined by the additional words *ûmĕlîṣâ ḥîdôt*, "and an ambiguous allusion"(?).[32] Again, the subject of the *māšāl* is an example of an arrogant abuse of power (cf. *geber yāhîr*, "an arrogant man," vs. 5), whose conduct will be judged by punishments[33] that appropriately fit each crime. As one scholar has aptly put it, "Hab. 2:6f. might be summed up, 'The spoiler is spoiled, the robber robbed, and the usurer will pay usury.'"[34] Thus, those who proclaim the *māšāl*, i.e. the victims of the Chaldeans' oppressive power, see in what will happen to their oppressors an exemplar of the unjust and violent receiving their retributive due.

Though the poem in Num 21:27-30 is not actually called a *māšāl*, the biblical editor's attribution of it to the *mōšĕlîm*, i.e. those who utter *mĕšālîm*, the *māšāl*-sayers,[35] makes it a likely candidate for this category, and it is generally so considered. However, its literary type is perhaps better described as a Victory Song than as a satirical taunt poem, though the expression of mockery and ridicule is not foreign to the Victory Song,[36] and the presence of the woe pronouncement in vs. 29, a form which Hab 2:6-19 associates with a *māšāl* with taunting intonation, suggests the connection of at least that part of the song to the mocking genre. I am persuaded by Hanson's study of this text that it was originally an Amorite Victory Song composed to celebrate the rebuilding of Heshbon and its establishment as capital of the new dynasty of Sihon after the Amorites had defeated and expelled the Moabites.[37] But in what sense could this song be understood as a *māšāl*, and by whom? The Amorites? The Israelites? Both? Unfortunately, the biblical writer does not make clear to what group the *mōšĕlîm* may have belonged. On one level he has quoted the poem to add credence to the historical datum cited in vs. 26[38] that "Heshbon was the city of Sihon the king of the Amorites, and he fought against the former (or, first?) king of Moab and took all his land out of his hand as far as the Arnon." But this seems hardly the reason for calling the song a *māšāl*. In light of the *mĕšālîm* already studied, is it possible to suggest a rationale for considering the Song of Heshbon as a *māšāl?*

We note first that there are two subjects in the Song which are contrasted: on the one hand, the victorious Amorites, symbolized by their soon to be rebuilt capital at Heshbon; on the other, the defeated Moabites, exemplified by desolate cities "from Heshbon as far as Dibon . . . from Nophah as far as Medeba" (vs. 30).[39] However, the Moabites' set-back is not viewed as due simply to Amorite military prowess. It is also because Kemosh, Moab's national god, "has given up his sons as fugitives, his daughters as the captives of Sihon" (vs. 29).[40] In other words, Moab is the object of Kemosh's wrath, and as a consequence, has lost her territory north of the Arnon. Unlike the *měšālîm* already considered in this category, no reason is given for the divine anger. No Moabite deeds are cited as the ground for Kemosh's fury, and hence the people are not being set up as a paradigm to show how certain crimes are divinely punished. Rather they are the example of a people who have lost the favor of their god, an example to serve not a Moabite but an Amorite purpose originally, viz., to justify Amorite expansion into Moabite territory. If, then, Num 21:27-30 once functioned as an Amorite *māšāl*, it was to legitimize Sihon's new hegemony over the land north of the Arnon. In its present biblical setting, of course, the Song of Heshbon serves a somewhat different though related purpose. According to Num 21:23-25, it is now Israel who has defeated Sihon and moved into much of the same territory that he had once taken away from Moab. The Moabite people still remain as an example of a people doomed by their god, but now to justify Israel's claim to a southern extension of Gad's territory beginning at Heshbon (cf. Josh 13:24-28, esp. vss. 26-27) against possible future Moabite threats. This interpretation is admittedly conjectural, but if the biblical writer thought of the Song of Heshbon as a *māšāl*, which seems likely, this is a plausible explanation for its understanding.

While on the subject of the satirical taunt poem genre, a word should be said about those related passages where no oral or literary *Gattung* is given, but instead a nation, group of people, individual or object is called a *māšāl*.[41] As a study of these texts shows, it is clearly the meaning of *māšāl* that underlies its usage in these particular instances, and the words that are found in close association with it indicate its uniformly pejorative connotation. The two terms most commonly linked here with *māšāl* are *šěnînâ*, "barbed scorn,"[42] and *ḥerpâ*, "reproach."[43] The person, group, or object who become, are made or established as a *māšāl*,[44] receive this appellation most frequently as the result of divine punitive action for conduct offensive to the Deity. Indeed it is usually Yahweh himself who is seen as the one most directly applying the term,[45] though of course with the understanding that it would be mediated through the mouths of those witnessing the divine punishment for the opprobrious conduct which together—conduct and punishment— provoked this name in the first place. In the majority of texts where this usage occurs, it is Israel or a group or individual from among Yahweh's people[46] who become or are made a *māšāl* as the result of a judgment for sins of disobedience and idolatry.[47] Thus for Israel or an Israelite to be a *māšāl* does not simply mean to become an object of reproach or mockery, or even the subject of a satirical taunt poem, but to stand forth as an example, an indisputable test case, in light of which all who witness it may measure their own conduct and thereby determine whether or not they also are in danger of the divine punishment.[48]

3. *Prophetic-type oracular poems descriptive of weal or woe.* Since it is not necessary for our present purpose to argue the appropriateness of this genre

designation for the so-called Oracles of Balaam in Numbers 23–24,[49] let it suffice to say that although these poems are much older and manifest a more archaic language and poetic style than is typical for most oracles of the OT classical prophets, they nonetheless do have a prophetic ring to them, and as oracular pronouncements of weal or woe, they would seem to represent an early form of the treatment of these themes prior to their subsequent appearance in somewhat different forms in later prophetic literature. However that may be, nowhere else in the OT do we have oracles of this type bearing the title *māšāl*, and though it is likely the latter stems from the biblical redactor and not the original poet, it is still important to ask what understanding was presupposed in calling them by this name.[50]

The principal subject of Balaam's oracles is the people of Israel, but Israel portrayed as blessed and favored by Yahweh through a series of effective metaphors and similies.[51] Over against this picture of Yahweh's blessed people is set a contrasting one, viz., of those cursed peoples who have threatened and opposed Israel, and hence refused to bless her. In the second half of the concluding oracle (or series of oracles, Num 24:17bγ-24) several of Israel's traditional enemies are cited, and with the exception of Moab and Edom, a special oracle is devoted to each, indicating the final determination of their situation under curse (Num 24:20-24), thereby providing a concrete illustration of the last half of the formula which concludes the third oracle, "Blessed be every one who blesses you, and cursed be every one who curses you" (Num 24:9). In their present prose context, which is also what defines them as *māšāl* (Num 23:7; 24:3, 15, 20-21, 23), the oracles are presented to Balak, the Moabite king who has hired Balaam to curse Israel. Thus to Balak the oracles represent a reversal of his request, as well as give to him a vivid exemplar of why his intention will not be fulfilled: the people whom Yahweh has blessed will not be effectively cursed; those who try to curse Yahweh's people will themselves suffer cursing. Considered as *māšāl*, then, Balaam's oracles present a paradigm case of peoples blessed and cursed by Yahweh, and the contingent interrelation between the two, in order to impart a guide for conduct to the hearer (in this case, Balak). After hearing the curse-like sayings against Israel's adversaries, including Moab (Num 24:17-24), Balak apparently learns the lesson: he lets Balaam return to his place, and he also goes his own way (Num 24:25).

4. *Didactic poems.* Psalms 49 and 78, usually classified as wisdom psalms, are the only two of whatever type in the Psalter whose texts infer the inclusion of a *māšāl* (cf. 49:5 [Engl. 4]; 78:2). They are clearly didactic poems, though with its long survey of Israel's history from the reception of the *tôrâ* at Sinai until the establishment of the Davidic kingdom, Psalm 78 may be more precisely categorized as a didactic historical poem. In both psalms the actual text of the *māšāl* (49:6-21 [Engl. 5-20]; 78:5-72) begins after a brief introduction, in which the psalmist summons the audience to hear, indicates specifically that what follows is a *māšāl* (qualified in both instances by the

noun *ḥîdâ*), while in the case of Psalm 78 a summary statement is added epitomizing the content of the *māšāl* to follow (vss. 3-4).

In Psalm 49 the subject of the *māšāl* is a problem (hence the appropriate association of *ḥîdâ* with *māšāl*), viz., the ultimate destiny of human life, and the relationship between the object in which one trusts and the character of that destiny. In essence, the psalmist compares two types of faith and the differing fates to which each leads. On the one hand there is the faith that trusts primarily in wealth (vs. 7 [6]) whose permanent destiny is Sheol (vs. 15 [14]); on the other, there is the faith that trusts in God leading finally to an existence beyond Sheol (vs. 16 [15]). Though no one can escape death (vss. 8-10 [7-9]), those who rely upon the abundance of their possessions can anticipate only Sheol as their eternal home, while those whose confidence is God can look forward to a divine deliverance from the permanent imprisoning hold of Sheol's power. In almost identical refrains (vss. 13 [12], 21 [20]) marking the mid-point and conclusion of the *māšāl*, respectively, the psalmist focuses on the negative faith-type, presumably to get his hearers to compare it with their own and to emphasize the example that should be avoided.[52] The psalmist's own faith-model, expressed only once, and then very tersely without further development, is obviously the solution he offers to the problem posed by the *māšāl*, leaving the impression that whatever response was made by those hearing the *māšāl* was based more upon the extended description of the *via negativa* than its opposite.

The *māšāl* in Psalm 78 conveys a lesson which takes its point of departure from two model-types presented in vss. 7-8. Both arise as reactions to the divine initiative which has "established a covenant agreement (*ᶜēdût*) in Jacob and set covenant teaching (*tôrâ*) in Israel" (vs. 5), which the ancestors are to teach their children so that they might know and perpetuate it through succeeding generations (vs. 6). The first model-response describes those who set their confidence in God, who do not forget his deeds, and keep his covenant stipulations (vs. 7), while the second imitates the ancestors who became "a stubborn and refractory generation, a generation whose heart was not steadfast, whose spirit was not faithful to God" (vs. 8). With these paradigms in mind, the psalmist proceeds to sketch the history of principally the Joseph tribes' response[53] to the Sinai covenant, a history from which a constantly recurring pattern emerges: despite their experience of God's grace and powerful deliverances (vss. 9, 12-16, 23-29, 38-39, 42b-55), Jacob-Israel has persistently refused to keep his covenant, forgotten his deeds, and rebelled against him (vss. 10-11, 17-20, 32, 36-37, 40-42a, 56-58), and even though judged for their recalcitrance and lack of faith (vss. 21, 31, 33, 59-66), such judgment sometimes provoking repentance (vss. 34-35), adherence to the negative model continued, in spite of a marvelous renewal of the divine compassion (vss. 38-39 following upon 34-37; cf. also vss. 12-16, following 10-11; 23-30 following 21-22; 42b-55 following 40-41).[54] But then in the concluding section of his poem, the psalmist indicates something new has happened in God's dealings with his people. Though the "tent of Joseph" (vs.

67) has been rejected, the divine election love and grace has not ceased; it has only shifted its focus to the tribe of Judah, to Mt. Zion with its sanctuary, and to David, the new and promising shepherd of Jacob-Israel (vss. 68-72). At this point, the poem abruptly ends, with no indication of how the people responded to this fresh manifestation of the divine mercy and care. It would appear, then, that as a result of the new hope created by the founding of David's kingdom,[55] it was the psalmist's purpose to challenge the people to break with the disastrous pattern of their ancestors' behavior so vividly depicted throughout the *māšāl*, and move them to embrace the model originally intended by Yahweh (vs. 7), promoted and encouraged by the paradigm of the divine actions.

A quite different type of didactic poem is found in Job 29-31, which might be called a didactic autobiographical peroration, but which the redactor introduces as a *māšāl* doubtless because of the content of this concluding speech.[56] For it is here that Job sums up his case, first by surveying the happiness of his life before its calamitous affliction (ch. 29), then contrasting this with his current miserable existence in which he is the object of punishment, reproach, and humiliation by both God and men (ch. 30), concluding with a solemn reaffirmation of his innocence and a final plea to confront God as an equal in a fair and vindicating encounter (ch. 31). Through this long speech Job sets himself up as an example,[57] a typical case of horrendous injustice which implicitly calls for a moral judgment on the part of those who witness it. Job's contrast of his former happy life with his present unhappy estate has an instructive purpose: to impel his hearers to make their own comparison between his case and similar ones they have known or experienced, in order to decide whether the analysis Job has made of his situation and its implications for the working of God in the world is substantially correct, or whether the perspectives argued by his adversaries do not present a more adequate assessment of what has happened. In all of this there emerges the typical features of a *māšāl*: the description of a representative case or object lesson,[58] often focused in the experience of an individual and implemented by one or more comparisons from which those addressed are expected to make an analogy that will effect some reassessment in their thinking and conduct.

5. *Allegorizing parabolic fables.* Among the examples of the fables that occur in the Old Testament,[59] it is only in Ezekiel where we find three specified as types of *māšāl*: Ezek 17:3-10, 21:1-4 [Engl. 20:45-48],[60] 24:3-5.[61] In each of these instances the figure of an animal, plant (or a combination of both), or inanimate objects is employed in usually a poetic narrative[62] to represent human personages and events in connection with Ezekiel's prediction about the forthcoming siege and fall of Jerusalem and its aftermath. Appended to these *mĕšālîm* is an indication of the way the prophet intended each figure and the actions related to it to be interpreted, since standing alone, without any such interpretive explanation, the *māšāl* was susceptible to more than one interpretation, or perhaps even in danger of remaining inexplicable.[63] A study

of these interpretations quickly shows the allegorizing character of the prophet's understanding of each *māšāl*,[64] a feature previously not encountered among the *mĕšālîm* so far examined. Yet it is primarily through these interpretations, when compared with the fables themselves, that we see how the latter could be typed as *mĕšālîm*, for the interpretations make clear the analogies Ezekiel wanted his audience to draw between the fable images and the persons and events they were intended to symbolize. And for what purpose? Certainly first of all to inform the people of the precariousness of their situation, to pique their attention and make them vividly aware that Yahweh will perform what he has spoken: Jerusalem *will* fall; many will suffer and perish, both the righteous and the wicked; but exile will not be the end of the matter. And secondly, to be prepared for disaster, not so much to avert it, for the hour was already too late for that, but to accept it and make the most of it. Thus once again we see the *māšāl* functioning to get its hearers to draw a comparison between the situation adumbrated in its content and their own relation to that situation in order to respond in some appropriate way.

In light of the understanding of *māšāl* that has emerged from this extended survey of its principal examples in the OT, it should now be possible to test the hypothesis that the Book of Jonah may have been composed as a type of *māšāl*.

### Jonah as a Māšāl

Within OT literature, or even more broadly among ancient Near Eastern literary sources in general, the Book of Jonah as a work of literary art comes close to being *sui generis*. Aside from the story of the nameless Judean man of God in 1 Kgs 12:33–13:32,[65] there is really no other literary work in the OT that has the same genre and employs similar motifs and structural features as we find in the Book of Jonah,[66] and even regarding the story in 1 Kgs 12:33ff., there is no assurance that it was an account of this kind that furnished a prototype for the author of Jonah. But Jonah's rather unique literary character does not preclude it from the outset from being considered as a *māšāl*. As we have seen above, the term *māšāl* does not refer to a particular literary form, but rather to the manner in which a variety of forms could be shaped to serve a special didactic purpose or function.

While commentators on the Book of Jonah have reached no common agreement as to its literary form, there is a fairly widespread consensus, embracing several different formal possibilities, that the book was created with an intentional didactic *Tendenz*. What is important to observe for our present concern is how the author chose to express that *Tendenz* through his literary artistry. Close rhetorical analysis of his work suggests that he did this chiefly in three ways: through a special twofold structural arrangement of the content and themes; through the probable assignment of an emblematic function to several features in the content; and through the frequent employment of questions as a distinctive rhetorical device.

There are two important aspects to the structural arrangement of Jonah:

first, the overall parallelism between each event in the narrative sequence in parts one (chs. 1–2) and two (chs. 3–4), up through vs. 8b of chapter 4;[67] and second, the inner thematic parallelism between the central motifs within chapters 1–2, on the one hand, and chapters 3–4, on the other.[68] Through the larger parallelism between the events in the two halves of the story, the author indicates certain congruities between two quite diverse settings and event sequences. Not only is the Jonah and what he does of chapters 1–2 to be compared with the Jonah and his actions of chapters 3–4, but the same also applies to the sailors and the Ninevites. Moreover, this arrangement inspires a similar comparison regarding the relation of God to both Jonah and the sailors in the first half of the story, and to Jonah and the Ninevites in the second half. The abrupt end to the parallelism at 4:8b would then serve two purposes: to heighten the climax of the book, where the author brings home the lesson he wants to convey, by making the ending independent of or outside the parallel structure of the story as a whole; and to underline by contrast how Jonah's response differs from that of the two major *dramatis personae* (the Ninevites and God) in the second half of the book. Thus, while in chapters 1–2 the major motifs applied to the sailors and Jonah are congruent (they both are threatened by death; they respond ultimately with prayer to Yahweh, who then moves to deliver them; they end up worshipping Yahweh through offering sacrifices and making vows), in chapters 3–4, those assigned to the Ninevites and Jonah are not (each is confronted by a different crisis, and though they both respond to Yahweh, it is in quite different ways: the Ninevites with faith and repentance, Jonah with anger, complaint, and request for death; Yahweh's final reaction to each also varies: to the Ninevites he changes his mind about destroying their city and graciously withholds judgment, while to Jonah, after graciously offering the *qîqāyôn*-plant without achieving its intended result, he "appoints" various punitive measures to move the prophet to do what both the Ninevites and God have done, i.e., change one's mind). In the end, Jonah remains unchanged, isolated, full of self-pity, wishing for death. The structural arrangement highlights the difference between Jonah and the other actors in the second half of the story, especially that between Jonah and God.

There are several prominent elements in the content of the Jonah story to which it would seem the author attributed an emblematic significance, in keeping with his overriding didactic purpose in writing.[69] Two are of particular importance: Nineveh and the Ninevites,[70] who represent the large, evil, and threatening world of people outside Israel who do not venerate Yahweh, yet who potentially can be brought to turn to him in prayer and repentance; and Jonah, who stands for that group in Israel whose attitudes and conduct reflected in the rebellious, unrepenting prophet the author wanted his audience to see as a mirror of their own. What we have here, then, are two models, the one exemplary and worthy of emulation, the other reprehensible and something to be avoided. The wholehearted and universal response of the Ninevites — not simply in cultic rituals but also in genuine amendment of life (3:5-10) — to the announcement of their impending destruction, is clearly viewed with approval by the author, and set forth as an example to be followed, while Jonah, though not completely without some redeeming features (he does call upon Yahweh in his distress and receive the divine deliverance, as well as reverse his futile flight to Tarshish to accept at last his commission and proceed obediently to Nineveh (2:3 [Eng. 2]–3:4) is ultimately seen as improper in his refusal to change his mind about what God has done for Nineveh. When the readers compare the two, it is obvious they are to be guided by the former, not the latter.

Finally, the author's didactic purpose is further implemented by a series of questions he causes to be directed at Jonah throughout the story, first by the captain of the ship (1:6), then by the sailors (1:8, 10, 11), at last by God (4:4, 9, 11). Though Jonah responds explicitly to only three of them (1:9, 12; 4:9b),[71] each answer gives evidence to some inadequacy in his thinking and attitude, which lends support to this portrayal as an essentially negative model. Of even greater significance are the questions to which he gives no answer at all, as they are left open to, and indeed are aimed at the readers' response, especially the question with which the book ends (4:11). It is through this final question that the writer drives home with telling impact the principal teaching for which he has written his story. The question implies that the primary model the readers are to follow is embodied both in the attitude and conduct of the Ninevites and in what God has done in response to their acts of contrition and repentance. The readers are invited to acknowledge what Jonah has refused to accept: that they cannot be continuing recipients of the divine delivering grace without manifesting the fruits of repentance, and also, they must show compassion for all those whose evil deserves punishment if such "turn from their evil way and from the lawlessness that is in their hands" (3:8b).[72] Only by rejecting the model of Jonah and following that of the Ninevites and God can they avoid destruction and receive deliverance.

We have no way of knowing what Hebrew term, if any, the author of Jonah may have had in mind for the work created. In the foregoing discussion we have endeavored to explore the possibility that it might have been thought of as a *māšāl*, even though none of the examples specifically called a *māšāl* in the OT closely resembles what we have here in Jonah. Possibly the nearest we come is in the parabolic fables of Ezekiel, but a formal comparison of these with Jonah does not indicate a very close relationship. Nonetheless, our survey of the main types of *māšāl* in the OT has suggested criteria that seem to be essential for defining a *māšāl*, no matter what its particular literary form. From what has been said above, it can be seen that most of these criteria are met in the Book of Jonah. Structurally arranged to depict comparisons between Jonah and the other protagonists in the story, with the overall purpose of presenting paradigmatic types of conduct or ways of thinking for the readers either to reject or embrace, the Book of Jonah seems designed to function as a *māšāl*, a *māšāl* in the form of an example story (*Beispielerzählung*),[73] whether or not the author may have had this term in mind when he wrote. Moreover, the emblematic use of the figure of Jonah to stand for Israel or a particular group within Israel as a negative model is reminiscent of those texts where Israel is called a *māšāl*.[74] In this sense, the character of Jonah himself can be seen as a *māšāl*, representing an object lesson in reproachable conduct.[75] On the other hand, just as in Psalm 78, the portrayal of God in the Book of Jonah also comes across as a *māšāl*, but in a positive sense, as a model of thought and action to be replicated.

## Product of a Sapiential, or a Prophetic Circle?

Assuming that it is conceivable and plausible to consider Jonah as a *māšāl*, does this point to a particular circle out of which the book may have come? From the *māšāl*-texts we have surveyed, it would appear that the vast majority stem from two sources: wisdom teachers and prophets. Because of its obvious didactic impulse, its manifestation of a more broadly universalistic over a narrow nationalistic outlook, its focus on moral rather than more specifically religio-theological sins (at least for the Ninevites), and its author's breadth and diversity of knowledge, encompassing sea and nature lore, along with themes from myth and fable, the Book of Jonah has sometimes been thought to come from a milieu under wisdom influence, if indeed it is not itself a specimen of wisdom didactic story.[76] As a putative *māšāl*, it is perhaps worth noting that the book employs several content elements—the great fish (2:1,11 [Engl. 1:17, 2:10]), the animals (3:7-8, 4:11), the *qîqāyôn*-plant (4:6-7), and the worm (4:7)—that are either identical with or comparable to those said to have been used by Solomon in the composition of 3000 *mĕšālîm*, evidencing his great wisdom (cf. 1 Kgs 5:9-13, esp. vs. 13 [Engl. 4:29-33, esp. vs. 33]). Moreover, there are several other themes and details in the subject matter that doubtless would have appealed to the wisdom teachers: the expression of the "fear of Yahweh" on the part of both Jonah and the sailors (1:9, 16; for the wise this was "the beginning of wisdom," cf. Prov 1:7; 9:10; Ps 111:10; Job 28:28); the pursuit of measures against "evil" (*ra^c, rā^câ*, 1:2, 3:8,10; 4:6; cf. Prov 2:12; 3:7; 4:27; 8:13; 11:21; 16:6; 19:23; 20:8, 30; 22:3); Yahweh's responding to the prayer of the righteous[77] (1:14-15; 2:3, 7-8 [Engl. 2:2, 6-7]; 3:8-10; cf. Prov 15:29); God's controlling power over both the creatures and forces of nature (1:4,15; 2:1 [Engl. 1:17], 11 [10]; 4:6-8; cf. Prov 3:19-20; Job 38–41); a negative attitude toward the strong expression of human anger (4:1-4,9; cf. Prov 14:29; 15:18; 16:32; 19:11, 19; 29:8; 30:33); certain conceptions about both the divine and human relationship to Sheol (2:3-10 [Engl. 2-9]; cf. Prov 15:11a, 24; and esp. vs. 16 [Engl. 15] in the *māšāl* of Ps 49), as well as about the meaning or understanding behind lot-casting (1:7; cf. Prov 16:33). Yet none of these features alone nor all of them together make a persuasive case for considering the Book of Jonah as a wisdom work, or as a *māšāl* written by a wisdom teacher. Many of the characteristics enumerated above can often be just as easily found in non-wisdom sources,[78] while some of the thematic motifs mentioned may have been understood by the author of Jonah in a way somewhat different from that construed by the wise. So the most that can be said is that Jonah's creator may have drawn some of his material from wisdom works or from contacts with wisdom thinkers.[79] But if we follow the helpful criteria Crenshaw[80] has proposed for deciding whether or not a biblical work falls within the wisdom orbit, the Book of Jonah would not seem seriously to qualify, either in terms of meeting a proper definition of wisdom or any of its levels (natural, juridical, practical, theological), or in terms of giving evidence of "a stylistic or ideological peculiarity found primarily in wisdom literature" and with essentially the same meaning as in the latter.[81] Though the Book of Jonah indicates no animus, explicit or implicit, against wisdom themes or concerns, its vocabulary and chief interests are not typical of what we usually encounter in what are commonly acknowledged as wisdom books. Indeed the principal teaching of the Book of Jonah would seem to cohere more closely with what we find in prophetic and deuteronomic writings than in wisdom.

Since the *māšāl* is well attested within prophetic literature and the Book of Jonah is a story about a prophet, was redacted within the prophetic corpus in its final form,[82] and laid stress on concerns that receive particular prominence in prophetic writings, especially those of Jeremiah, Ezekiel, and Joel,[83] it is pertinent to raise the question whether Jonah, assuming the book was intended to be a *māšāl*, was the *māšāl* of a prophet, or at least influenced by prophetic interests.[84] Unfortunately, though it has often been suggested,[85] we have no way of demonstrating that the author of Jonah was himself a prophet. He of course does not identify himself as such, and the clues we derive from the story itself are not sufficient to confirm prophetic authorship. Moreover, as already observed, there is no portion of a prophetic work labeled *māšāl* that is of the same literary genre as the Book of Jonah. This leaves us with the message of Jonah, which though it does not provide us with decisive support for the prophetic origin of the book, does seem to point in that direction. The emphasis on the compassionate Yahweh who may withhold his punishment in the face of genuine repentance, and who offers his delivering grace to any— non-Israelite as well as Israelite—who turn to him in prayer and contrition, seems to be more at home within prophetic than in other types of Israelite thinking, whether wisdom, priestly, scribal, or deuteronomic. It is tempting to view the author of Jonah as was Ezekiel, i.e., as one who was called "a maker of *měšālîm*" (Ezek 21:5 [Engl. 20:49]), who, like the great exilic prophet, took a form not otherwise designated as *māšāl*[86] among the prophetic or other OT writings, yet which clearly manifested the thought pattern and intention of the *měšālîm* found elsewhere, and using emblematic-allegorical features to show Israel as a negative model, sought to bring about a change in Israelite thinking that the people might live and be saved.

---

[1] First made in his article, "Vermutungen zum 'Midrasch des Buches der Könige,'" *ZAW* 12 (1892) 37-51, esp. 40-43. Cf. also P. Trible, "Studies in the Book of Jonah" (Ph.D. dissertation,

Columbia University, 1963), esp. pp. 161-68. I understand that Prof. Trible has now prepared her dissertation for publication by Scholars Press, to appear shortly.

[2] Cf. e.g. the commentaries or monographs on the book of Jonah by R. F. Horton and S. R. Driver, *The Minor Prophets* (The Century Bible; Edinburgh and London: Jack, 1904)1. 198; J. Wellhausen, *Skizzen und Vorarbeiten* 5: *Die kleinen Propheten* (2d ed.; Berlin: Reimer, 1898) 211; J. Bewer, *A Critical and Exegetical Commentary on Jonah* (ICC; Edinburgh: Clark, 1912) 9; C. Steuernagel, *Lehrbuch der Einleitung in das Alte Testament* (Tübingen: Mohr, 1912) 442; J. Steinmann, *Le livre de consolation d'Israël et les prophètes du retour de l'exil* (Paris: Les Editions de Cerf, 1960) 286; O. Loretz, *Gotteswort und menschliche Erfahrung* (Freiburg: Herder, 1963) 14-15; H. W. Wolff, *Studien zum Jonabuch* (Neukirchen-Vluyn: Neukirchener Verlag, 1965) 56-57; G. F. A. Knight, *Ruth and Jonah* (Torch Bible Commentaries; London, SCM, 1950) 51-52.

[3] G. E. Mendenhall, "The Shady Side of Wisdom: The Date and Purpose of Genesis 3," in *A Light Unto My Path: Old Testament Studies in Honor of Jacob M. Myers* (Philadelphia: Temple University, 1974) 326.

[4] For references, see E. Dhorme, *Le livre de Job* (Paris: Gabalda, 1926) xiv; Engl., *A Commentary on the Book of Job* (London: Nelson, 1967) xv.

[5] For a recent comprehensive defense of Jonah as a parable, see L. C. Allen, *The Books of Joel, Obadiah, Jonah and Micah* (NICOT; Grand Rapids: Eerdmans, 1976) 175-81.

[6] E.g., 2 Sam 12:1-4; 14:4-21; 1 Kgs 20:39-42; 2 Kgs 14:9; Isa 5:2-7; 28:23-29.

[7] Cf. Ezek 17:2-10; 21:1-5 [Engl. 20:45-49]; 24:3-5. For a more precise definition of the genre involved with these passages, see below.

[8] Among the most comprehensive and important scholarly studies of *māšāl* in the Old Testament are the following: M.-J. Lagrange, "La parabole en dehors de l'Evangile," *RB* 6 (1909) II, 342-67; O. Eissfeldt, *Der Maschal im Alten Testament* (BZAW 24; Giessen: Töpelmann, 1913); A. H. Godbey, "The Hebrew *MAŠAL*," *AJSL* 39 (1922-23) 89-108; J. Schmidt, *Studien zur Stilistik der alttestamentlichen Spruchliteratur* (Münster: Aschendorffsche Verlagsbuchhandlung, 1936); M. Hermaniuk, *La parabole evangélique: enquête exégétique et critique* (Bruges-Paris et Louvain: Desclée, de Brouwer, et Bibliotheca Alfonsiana, 1947) 62-189; J. Pirot, "Le 'Mâšâl' dans l'Ancien Testament," *RSR* 37 (1950) 566-80; A. S. Herbert, "The 'Parable' (*MĀŠĀL*) in the Old Testament," *SJT* 7 (1954) 180-96; F. Hauck, *"Parabolē," TDNT* 5 (1967) 744-61; A. R. Johnson, *"Māšāl,"* Wisdom in Israel and in the Ancient Near East (VTSup 3; Leiden: Brill, 1955) 162-69; W. McKane, "The Meaning of Māšāl," *Proverbs, A New Approach* (OTL; Philadelphia: Westminster, 1970) 22-33.

[9] See 1 Sam 10:12 (cf. 19:24); 24:14; Ezek 12:22; 16:44. Eissfeldt (*Der Maschal*, 48) thought the earliest *mĕšālîm* were composed in prose rather than poetry, though the data for supporting such a judgment are no longer extant. In the OT, it would appear that the oldest datable *māšāl*, at least in its original oral form, is the one preserved in Num 21:27-30 (for a discussion of its *māšāl*-character, see the section below, entitled "Satirical taunt poems"), and it is clearly poetic. Note also Marvin Pope, when he writes: ". . . the term *māšāl* is about as near as we come — leaving aside the words that denote song or musical accompaniment — to the range of meaning carried by our word 'poem' . . . and a poem, like a *māšāl*, can be long or short as 'even one lone verse sometimes makes a perfect poem' (Ben Jonson)" *Job* [AB 15; 3d ed.; Garden City, NY: Doubleday, 1973] 190). But translated into the Hebrew phenomenon, it is questionable that a poetic verse was ever constituted by only a single colon or stichos, for without parallelism, one can hardly speak of a poem in Hebrew. "Poem," therefore, would not appear to be a very good rendering for *māšāl*.

[10] In the technical sense described by McKane, *Proverbs*, 32.

[11] Among the commentators these texts are customarily called "songs," though in the context of each there is no explicit indication that they were sung, and the Hebrew word for "song" (*šîr, šîrâ*) is never used in association or parallelism with *māšāl*. However, singing or chanting as the mode of presentation cannot be ruled out, and would seem most likely. In Num 21:27, the ensuing *māšāl* is referred to as being "said" (*yōʾmĕrû*) by the *mōšĕlîm*, a term variously rendered in English by "balladsingers" (*RSV*), "bards" (*JPSV, NEB*), or "poets" (*JB, NAB, The Good News Bible*), while in Mic 2:4, *māšāl* is associated with *nĕhî*, "lament," something obviously given in a wailing song-like style.

[12] Presumably the most ancient designation for Balaam's oracles was *nĕ'um*, "oracle, word, utterance, message, declaration" (cf. Num 24:3-4, 15-16), while it was the editor who set these poems in their present prose context who called each a *māšāl* (23:18; 24:3, 15, 20, 21, 23).

[13] An appropriate English rendering for *māšāl* in Job 29:1 is very difficult. Each of the standard translations seem much too broad or otherwise inadequate: "discourse" (*RSV, JB*), "theme" (*NAB*), "parable" (*KJV*), "poem" (Pope, *Job*, 207, with discussion on pp. 189-90). The suggestion made here is not entirely satisfactory, but it does attempt to specify the form and content of Job 29-31.

[14] Because the subjects in these passages are not humans but animals, plants, or inanimate objects, they are best classified as fables, and as their appended interpretations indicate, they consist of extended metaphors pointing to an allegorizing understanding of the subject matter. See our discussion below on "Allegorizing parabolic fables." For a recent most helpful discussion of the parable as a literary class and its relation to allegory, see M. Boucher, *The Mysterious Parable: A Literary Study* (*CBQ MS* 6; Washington, DC: The Catholic Biblical Association of America, 1977) esp. 11-25.

[15] Cf. Pirot, "Le 'Māšāl'. . .," 566: ". . . mâšâl n'a pas désigné dès l'abord une *forme* littéraire mais un *contenue.*"

[16] Schmidt (*Studien zur Stilistik*, 1-2) endeavored to show that both meanings can quite plausibly be explained as derivatives from a common root, and out of the several meanings of the cognate Arabic *MTL*, he selected "to stand before" as the one from which developed the meaning "to rule," which he thought also had the nuance "to stand for," from which came the ideas most commonly associated with the Arabic *Grundstamm* of *MTL*, viz., "to resemble, imitate, compare." However, neither the meaning "to rule" nor "to stand for" is ever actually attested for *MTL*. Nonetheless, a number of scholars have gone along with Schmidt's contention that the definitions "to be like" and "to rule" represent developments within a single rather than different Semitic roots, without, however, necessarily adopting the specifics of Schmidt's Arabic etymological conjectures. Cf. most notably Godbey, "The Hebrew *MAŠAL*," 107; A. Bentzen, *Introduction to the Old Testament* (2d ed.; Copenhagen: Gad, 1958) 1. 168 (citing Boström); and most recently, J. L. Crenshaw, "Wisdom," *Old Testament Form Criticism* (ed. J. H. Hayes; San Antonio: Trinity University, 1974) 230.

[17] Cf. J. A. Fitzmyer, *The Aramaic Inscriptions of Sefîre* (Biblica et Orientalia 19; Rome: Pontifical Biblical Institute, 1967) 95-96, 187.

[18] McKane, *Proverbs*, 25. Cf. also Herbert, "The 'Parable'. . .," 180, 189.

[19] See also in this regard the strictures of Herbert (ibid., 195), particularly against Godbey's vigorous attempt to link *māšāl* with the performance of symbolical and magical action, though in the end, Herbert still seems to find it difficult to give up the possible origin of the term in magical practices.

[20] Hermaniuk's observation (*La parabole evangélique*, 115) that the comparative element in a *māšāl* is secondary and supplemental because in most examples no comparison is involved (p. 118) would seem to be based on too narrow a definition of comparison, limited to explicit formal expressions. Clearly his own suggestion that the fundamental element in a *māšāl* is the idea of representation (ibid.) must rest upon an implicit comparison, so that whether or not the content of a *māšāl* expresses a formal comparison, the understanding of a comparison remains basic.

[21] Hence Mendenhall ("The Shady Side of Wisdom," 326-27) defines *māšāl* as "a constant device of ancient thought . . . a thought pattern . . . a form of thought that primarily classifies, such classification [being] used for a number of purposes other than upbraiding or persuading, even though this is the clearest usage of the form. A *mashal* may serve as a ground, precedent, as justification of existing reality—similar to the category of myth in ancient pagan cultures." It is of course not crucial that one find a common English rendering for *māšāl*, but important to recognize to what extent this may or may not be possible. In some cases, at least, *māšāl* is like such Hebrew terms as *ḥesed, nepeš,* and *hinnēh,* for which the right English equivalent is frequently difficult if not impossible to find. One should also keep in mind that meanings do change and differ, both synchronically in terms of varying contexts and situations, and diachronically in different historical periods. Interestingly, the history of the usage of *māšāl* does not seem to display any marked diachronic shifts in its meaning (contrast Eissfeldt, *Der Maschal*, 26-28),

unless in agreement with McKane (*Proverbs*, 32), we see it becoming less precise and particular when applied to the wisdom sentences in Proverbs (see further on this below, n. 24). However that may be, by the time of the rabbinic period, instead of becoming more diverse and of a wider applicability in its meanings, *māšāl* seems to have been used in a much more restricted fashion, encompassing only a few of the literary types attested in the OT (for details, see Hermaniuk, *La parabole evangélique*, 153-89).

22 Note the remarks of McKane, *Proverbs*, 24. For want of a better term, I have arbitrarily chosen to define *māšāl* in general as a speech or literary category, deliberately avoiding such words as form, *Gattung*, and genre, which are most often used to specify literary types, something a *māšāl* does not do. I am unaware whether in literary theory there may be an appropriate technical term which does justice to the meaning of *māšāl*.

23 W. McKane, *Proverbs*, 22-33, esp. p. 26. For a more refined description of the various patterns in which popular proverbs and wisdom sentences were shaped, see R. B. Y. Scott, *Proverbs. Ecclesiastes* (AB 18; Garden City, NY: Doubleday, 1965) 5-9.

24 However, McKane's opinion (*Proverbs*, 32) that the application of *māšāl* to the instruction genre (Proverbs 1-9; 22:17-24:22; 31:1-9) and wisdom sentences (Proverbs 10:1-22:16; 24:23-34; 25-29) which make up the bulk of the Book of Proverbs shows that the term has lost its precision and particularity in these genres, perhaps needs further reflection. Though I would agree that an oral or literary speech-form may become a *māšāl* "when it transcends a simple particularity and its representative potential is intuited" (ibid., 31), it would also seem that many of the commands and sentences in Proverbs, from whose particularities one draws a guide for conduct by analogy or comparison, could be viewed as falling within the category of *māšāl*, while even the poems and numerical sayings in Proverbs 30 and 31:10-31 (esp. the latter, presenting a paradigmatic model for an *ʾēšet ḥayil*) are not as remotely related to the signification of *māšāl* as might first be thought.

25 For Pirot ("Le 'Mâšâl'. . .") the prevailing type of content characteristic of most *mĕšālîm* in the OT is a sense of satire, mockery, sarcasm, or reproach (cf. pp. 566, 572), the principal exception being the sapiential use of the term, where these tones have been attenuated into at most remonstrance, or simple moral discourse or lessons (p. 576). Though the expression of a taunting, ridiculing, or satirical spirit does seem to distinguish many *mĕšālîm*, including some which are not ordinarily typed as taunts (e.g. the Oracles of Balaam and the proverbial expressions in 1 Sam 10:12, Ezek 16:44, 18:2-3), and especially in those cases where a person or nation is called a *māšāl*, it would seem too much to say that this spirit expresses the constant value of a *māšāl* in all but wisdom texts (p. 572).

26 Obviously there are many other passages in the OT where mockery or ridicule is expressed, and where the biblical writer or redactor might have specified a *māšāl*, but for whatever reason, did not.

27 Whether or not it was the 8th century prophet Isaiah or some later redactor who characterized this piece as a *māšāl* is of no great importance for the present discussion.

28 So O. Eissfeldt, *The Old Testament: An Introduction* (Oxford: Basil Blackwell, 1965) 97, who discerns here the form of the funeral dirge combined with the mood of the mocking song.

29 Cf. Johnson, *"Māšāl,"* 166, who sees the mood of mockery or derision as quite secondary, and Hermaniuk, *La parabole evangélique*, who objects to the poem's being called a satire, viewing it himself as basically a prophetic oracle.

30 Cf. esp. L. C. Allen's commentary, *Joel, Obadiah, Jonah and Micah*, 290. Allen's largely successful effort to interpret Mic 2:1-5, in particular vs. 4, without resorting to radical emendations or highly conjectural reconstructions is most persuasive, and underlies the interpretation followed here. See also W. Janzen, *Mourning Cry and Woe Oracle* (Berlin: de Gruyter, 1972) 62-64, and esp. n. 81, p. 63. On the other hand, if Mays and other commentators are correct that Mic 2:1-5 has experienced redactoral retouching to extend the application of the oracle to all Israel in a much later situation than that of the 8th century prophet, the exemplary character of the *māšāl* in vs. 4 still holds true. See J. L. Mays, *Micah: A Commentary* (OTL; Philadelphia: Westminster, 1976) 60-66.

31 See Janzen, *Mourning Cry*, 64-70, who also calls attention to the same woe formula introducing Mic 2:1 (n. 84, p. 64).

[32] The meaning of these two terms together is not certain, and there is almost no unanimity among the translations as to how to render them. They occur together elsewhere (only not immediately contiguous as here) only in Prov 1:6 (on which see McKane, *Proverbs*, 267; Janzen, *Mourning Cry*, 65, who thinks Hab 2:6a may have been formed under the influence of Prov 1:6, but this is problematic). Were two separate categories intended (as perhaps understood by the Syriac which reads the conjunction before the second term) or only one (i.e. a kind of hendiadys, but without the conjunction, or with a construct chain, as in the reading of 1 QpHab, *wmlyṣy ḥydwt*)? As we shall see below, the noun *ḥîdâ* is found a number of times in association with *māšāl*, suggesting the latter's enigmatic or ambiguous character, i.e., its susceptibility to more than one interpretation, or its applicability to more than one situation, and hence requiring careful study and reflection so as to grasp its meaning (note further Janzen on this, *Mourning Cry*, 66 and n. 91). Neither *mělîṣâ* nor *ḥîdâ* alone seem to indicate taunting or ridicule, so these ideas emerge primarily from the tone in which it is assumed the woes were delivered or spoken.

[33] Probably to be understood as divine, though sometimes executed through human instruments (cf. vs. 8 with vss. 13, 16).

[34] Herbert, "The 'Parable' . . . ," 190. The last woe against idolators (vss. 18-19), where the verses seem to be in reverse order and the *idem per idem* retributive pattern is abandoned, may be secondary, though it is conceivable that the prophet thought that the failure of an expected revelation to come from the dumb and lifeless idol was a sufficient counter to its maker's creative efforts.

[35] I am assuming, of course, that *mōšělîm* is best construed here as the qal active participle, used nominally, derived from the denominative of *māšāl*, and having the nuance, "to say a *māšāl*," rather than the same form from the root *MŠL*, "to rule" (so Godbey, "The Hebrew MAŠAL," 91). Though the latter is not impossible, the present context seems to weigh more heavily in the direction of the first interpretation. I also render the form by "to utter or say a *māšāl*," instead of by "to compose or make a *māšāl*" (cf. Eissfeldt, *The Old Testament*, 93; G. B. Gray, *A Critical and Exegetical Commentary on Numbers* [ICC; Edinburgh: Clark, 1903] 299), since it would appear that the piel would have been employed if the latter meaning had been intended (as in Ezek 21:5 [Engl. 20:49]).

[36] Cf. Eissfeldt, *The Old Testament*, 99-101, and Gray, *Numbers*, 300-01.

[37] See P. D. Hanson, "The Song of Heshbon and David's *NÎR*," *HTR* 61 (1968) 297-320, esp. pp. 299, 308. For a somewhat different reconstruction of the historical background, see J. R. Bartlett, "The Historical Reference of Numbers XXI.27-30," *PEQ* 101 (1969) 94-100.

[38] Hanson, "The Song of Heshbon," 307.

[39] Vs. 30 has obviously suffered from corruption during the long history of its textual transmission. I follow the tentative but attractive reconstruction of Hanson, "The Song of Heshbon," 300-01.

[40] Again, following the translation of Hanson, ibid.

[41] Only in 2 Chr 7:20 is an object labeled a *māšāl*, viz., the Jerusalem temple. For a more or less detailed discussion of these texts, see esp. Eissfeldt, *Der Maschal*, 8-10; Hermaniuk, *La parabole evangélique*, 66-75; Herbert, "The 'Parable' . . . ," 186.

[42] From ŠNN, "to sharpen," I follow the apt rendering of the *NAB* at Deut 28:37. Other English translations render *šěnînâ* as "byword" (RSV, JB, NAB), "object lesson" (*NEB*), "taunt" (*RSV, NAB*), and "laughing stock" (*JB*). The pertinent texts are 1 Kgs 9:7, 2 Chr 7:20, Deut 28:37 and Jer 24:9. In each of these passages, which are the only ones where *šěnînâ* occurs in the OT, it always immediately follows *māšāl*.

[43] See Jer 24:9, Pss 44:15 [Engl. 14]; 69:12 [Engl. 11]. Other terms closely conjoined with *māšāl* are *šammâ* (Deut 28:37); *zawǎᶜâ, raᶜâ, qělālâ* (Jer 24:9); *laᶜag wāqeles, měnôd rōᵓš* (Ps 44:14f. [Engl. 13f.]); *ᵓôt* (Ezek 14:8); and *tōpet lěpānîm* (Job 17:6).

[44] The expressions are *hāyâ lěmāšāl* (1 Kgs 9:7; Deut 28:37; Ps 69:12 [11]); *nātan lěmāšāl* (2 Chr 7:20; Jer 24:9); *śām lěmāšāl* (Ps 44:15 [14]; Ezek 14:8); *yāṣag lěmāšāl* (Job 17:6, assuming that MT *limšōl* should read *lěmāšāl*, as now generally accepted).

[45] The exceptions are Deut 28:37, where it is Moses who says the people will become a *māšāl*, and Ps 69:12 [11], where it is the psalmist who applies it to himself.

[46] The principal exception being the non-Israelite Job (17:6).

[47] Note, however, that sometimes the individual involved is perplexed as to the reason he and his people have been made a *māšāl*, and leaves the impression that such an application is undeserved if not also unjust. Cf. Pss 44:18-23 [Engl. 17-22]; 69:5-13 [Engl. 4-12]. Presumably this would also be the case with Job, though the context of 17:6 does not bring this out.

[48] Cf. Herbert, "The 'Parable' . . . ," 188, 196.

[49] Pirot ("Le 'Mâšâl' . . . ," 572) would apparently classify them under the rubric we have just considered, i.e. as satirical taunt poems, because they express sarcasm on the vanquished. But though it is possible, even plausible, to hear a sarcastic tone running through the oracles, this feature alone was not sufficient to warrant the name *māšāl*.

[50] For various scholarly efforts to address this question, none of them entirely satisfactory in the present writer's opinion, cf. Gray, *Numbers*, 344; Hermaniuk, *La parabole evangélique*, 76-81; Herbert, "The Parable' . . . ," 189; Johnson, *"Māšāl,"* 167.

[51] Though from a strict form-critical perspective, the oracles are not blessings, they do describe the situation of Yahweh's people as divinely blessed, and hence were possibly understood to function as blessings by the biblical editor. One could argue that the latter half of the concluding oracle contains a series of curses against various nations opposing Israel, though here too the special curse formula is not employed.

[52] It is interesting that these refrains contain the only place in an OT *māšāl* where its denominative verbal root is used, *MŠL*, "to be like."

[53] Note the names: *běnê ʾeprayim*, vs. 9; *yôsēp* and *šebeṭ ʾeprayim*, vs. 67, while the parallel pair "Jacob-Israel" (vss. 5, 21, 71) may possibly have the sense of its original reference to the northern tribes.

[54] The *ḥîdôt*-character of this *māšāl* (vs. 2) is perhaps to be explained not only by the inexplicable, indeed irrational rebellion of Jacob-Israel (cf. A. Weiser, *Die Psalmen* [ATD 15; 4th ed; Göttingen: Vandenhoeck & Ruprecht, 1955] 366), but also by the equally mysterious renewal of the divine grace, despite such rebellion.

[55] Though the psalm may not have originated during David's monarchy, the psalmist would seem to have imaginatively presupposed such a historical setting, at least if the content and thrust of vss. 67-72 indicate a proper guide to this. Of course the implications for Israel's conduct would be relevant as long as the ideal of the Davidic dynasty persisted, thus beyond the fall of Judah and Jerusalem in the early 6th century B.C. which failed to squelch hopes of a Davidic reincarnation in the restored Jewish community of the postexilic era.

[56] In the present MT of Job 27:1, the term *māšāl* is also used by the editor to introduce another Joban speech, but because there clearly has been some displacement from the original order of the speeches in chs. 24–27, as well as loss of or simple failure to include some of the rubrics indicating which speech should be assigned to which speaker, 27:1 may no longer be in its right place, or in any case, may represent a secondary insertion under the influence of 29:1, where the words "take up again" seem more appropriate following the obviously secondary interpolation of ch. 28. In his recent translation, Pope (*Job*, xx, 189), places 27:1 before 26:1, and considers Job's reply to Bildad's speech in ch. 25, 26:5-14 as consisting of 26:1-4; 27:2-7. For the problems posed by the textual arrangement and various solutions that have been offered, see the commentaries on Job, esp. Dhorme, *A Commentary on the Book of Job*, xlviii-xlix, 377; S. R. Driver and G. B. Gray, *A Critical and Exegetical Commentary on The Book of Job* (2 vols.; ICC; New York: Scribner, 1921) 1. xxxvii-xl; S. Terrien, *Job* (CAT 13; Neuchâtel: Delauchaux et Niestlé, 1963) 22-23.

[57] For the interpretation followed here, cf. Hermaniuk, *La parabole evangélique*, 88-90; Herbert, "The 'Parable' . . . ," 187-88.

[58] Thus the rabbinical opinion that Job himself was a *māšāl* (cf. n. 4 above), by which was meant a human type as over against an historical personage, was clearly in the right direction, though of course to be a *māšāl* does not necessarily preclude historical existence.

[59] Cf. Judg 9:8-15; 2 Kgs 14:9, and probably also 2 Sam 12:1-4 and Isa 5:1-7, where human subjects are associated with either animals or plants.

[60] Actually the *māšāl* designation of this fable must be inferred from vs. 5 [Engl. 20:49], where the prophet confesses before Yahweh that the people are reproaching him as a "composer of

*měšālîm,*" in light of which the identification seems fairly assured. The similarity of some of the imagery here and in 17:3-10 with that in ch. 15 suggests the presence of another *māšāl in nuce* in 15:6. Moreover, the casting of 24:3-5 in the form of a summons to perform certain symbolic actions suggests the possibility, at least, that other symbolic deeds or their oral or written description, with reference to Ezekiel and other prophets, most notably Jeremiah, may have been considered a form of *māšāl* (cf. Ezek 4:1-17; Jer 13:1-11; 19:1-12; 27:2-15; 28:10-4, and Godbey, "The Hebrew *MAŠAL,*" 103).

[61] W. Eichrodt (*Ezekiel: A Commentary* [OTL; Philadelphia: Westminster, 1970] 338) types this pericope as "a working song, sung while carrying out some particular piece of work (cf. Num 21:17f.)," rather than a fable, and this may possibly be a better genre description since the pot is not portrayed in a human role. However, what is placed in the pot certainly stands for human characters, and the whole passage represents human activity (cf. 24:2), so that the fable genre should not too hastily be precluded. See also W. Zimmerli, *Ezekiel* (BKAT 13; Neukirchen-Vluyn: Neukirchener Verlag, 1969) 559 and references. For a more or less detailed treatment of all these Ezekiel texts, see Hermaniuk, *La parabole evangélique,* 92-95; Herbert, "The 'Parable' . . . ," 190-93; Johnson "*Māšāl*" 168, and G. A. Cooke, *A Critical and Exegetical Commentary on the Book of Ezekiel* (ICC; 2 vols.; New York: Scribner, 1937).

[62] Only 21:1-4 [Engl. 20:45-48] does not appear to be poetry in its present form, though it may have been originally.

[63] Hence the probable reason for *ḥîdâ* in association with *māšāl* in 17:2 and elsewhere (cf. above, n. 32). A *māšāl* of this type had a mysterious or enigmatic character to it which was difficult to penetrate without accompanying interpretation.

[64] However, this does not mean they should be understood as thorough-going allegories, for as Herbert ("The 'Parable' . . . ," 191) has shown, not every feature in each of these *měšālîm* has its counterpart in the following interpretation, or vice versa.

[65] For a study of this story together with a comparison of it with Jonah, see A. Rofé, "Classes in the Prophetical Stories: Didactic Legenda and Parable," *Studies on Prophecy* (VTSup 26; Leiden: Brill, 1974) 143-64, esp. pp. 153-163.

[66] Though a number of scholars have assigned the Book of Jonah to the category of prophetic legend, comparing it especially to the Elijah-Elisha stories in 1-2 Kings, a careful study of the latter shows striking differences from Jonah. Moreover, the *Gattung* of legend is really not an appropriate categorization for the book as a whole, since the distinctive feature of legend is the portrayal of the principal character as an object of devotion or veneration, precisely the reverse of the way Jonah is presented. The genre of prophetic biographical narrative, like those found within Isaiah 36-39 and Jeremiah 37-44, also does not fit the Book of Jonah, in which it is clear that the author was not concerned to give an excerpt from the actual career of the 8th century prophet of the same name. For a recent survey and critical evaluation of the various scholarly proposals for the literary form of the Book of Jonah, see M. Burrows, "The Literary Category of the Book of Jonah," *Translating and Understanding the Old Testament* (eds. H. T. Frank and W. L. Reed; Nashville and New York: Abingdon, 1970) 80-107.

[67] For details, see Trible, "Studies in the Book of Jonah," 186-92, where, however, she excludes the psalm in Jonah 2 from the structural and symmetrical arrangement. For my own analysis, which incorporates the psalm, see G. M. Landes, "The Kerygma of the Book of Jonah," *Int* 21 (1967) 3-31, esp. p. 16.

[68] Ibid., 25-31.

[69] For an extended discussion, see Wolff, *Studien zum Jonabuch,* 48-54.

[70] The sailors also in ch. 1 should probably be seen as possessing a similar emblematic or exemplary character.

[71] It is possible to interpret 4:5 as Jonah's non-verbal response to Yahweh's question in 4:4, thereby suggesting that the prophet had misunderstood the divine purpose behind the question. According to this interpretation, Jonah would correctly perceive that through the question Yahweh was trying to tell him there was no cause to be angry, but not because Yahweh had done a good thing in sparing the Ninevites, but rather because the destruction of the city was still to come.

But it is also possible that 4:5 functions in another way, viz., to indicate where Jonah went immediately after he delivered his terse message of doom (3:4), and where he was to remain for the subsequent events in the story. With this interpretation, the verbs in 4:5 would have to be construed as having pluperfect tense meaning, but this poses no problem, as the author has employed this meaning several times before in his narrative (cf. Wolff, *Studien zum Jonabuch*, 47). He thus would have intentionally delayed giving any details about Jonah's location until this point in the narrative sequence in order to stress the prophet's isolated situation outside the gates of Nineveh where Yahweh will deal with him for the last time.

It should perhaps also be noted that it is only after 4:5 that Yahweh resumes his action toward Jonah as described by the verb *wayman*. When this verb first occurs in 2:1, it is likewise only after Jonah has been isolated from everyone else. In any event, the overall parallel structural arrangement of the book would seem to indicate that 4:5 is in its originally intended position (against Trible, "Studies in the Book of Jonah," 187, 198, 200-02), i.e. parallel to 2:11, so that Jonah's departure from the fish to resume his mission stands over against his departure from Nineveh to witness the results of that mission.

72 A. Rofé ("Classes in the Prophetical Stories") has argued against the interpretation followed here, one that is in accord with a traditional Jewish understanding of Jonah that views the book as mainly "a sermon on the value of repentance" (p. 155). He avers that "this view does not do justice to Chapter IV where the issue is not the conduct of men but the qualities of God" (p. 156), and that if human repentance were the overriding issue of the book, the latter should have ended with ch. 3 and not as it does with ch. 4, where a different problem is reflected. Rofé thinks the author's concern is with a tension that had developed within Israelite circles by the early post-exilic period—a tension between the expectation of a more or less literal fulfillment of the prophesied word of God and the gracious and merciful quality of the divine nature that in certain circumstances can move the Deity not to keep his word. It is not impossible that the author of the Book of Jonah was aware of this tension, but I do not think ch. 4 indicates that this was the key issue which motivated him to write the book.

73 Cf. E. Haller, *Die Erzählung von dem Propheten Jona* (Theologische Existenz Heute NF 65; Munich: Kaiser, 1958), 50.

74 Cf. above the last paragraph in the section on "Satirical taunt poems."

75 As also the king of Babylon in the *māšāl* of Isa 14:4b-21, the "arrogant man" of Hab 2:5, and the idolator of Ezek 14:8. Though a satiric tone of reproach and ridicule is not a necessary component of a *māšāl*, it is frequently associated with forms that are called *māšāl*, and it also characterizes the style of Jonah. Burrows ("The Literary Character of the Book of Jonah," 95) has been sufficiently impressed by this to define the literary category of Jonah as a satire, but in light of our discussion, it is perhaps better to think of Jonah as a *māšāl* with satiric features rather than as a satire as such. Miles, on the other hand, has wanted to see Jonah as a parody, "that breed of satire in which the standardized behavior to be exposed is literary" (cf. J. A. Miles, "Laughing at the Bible: Jonah as Parody," *JQR* 65 [1974-75] 168). Aside from the fact that I think the author of Jonah had a different purpose in writing from the one Miles proposes, one wonders if the prophetic career-stereotypes he sees parodied in Jonah had already achieved widely known *literary* currency by the time the Book of Jonah was written. I am assuming that Jonah had been written no later than the 6th century B.C. (for this dating, see provisionally my comments in "Jonah, Book of," *IDBSup* [1976] 490).

76 See e.g., R. E. Clements, "The Purpose of the Book of Jonah," in *VTSup* 26 (1975) 17; Haller, *Die Erzählung von dem Propheten Jona*, 8-11; E. Kraeling, *Commentary on the Prophets* (Camden, NJ: Nelson, 1966) 2. 191; W. Rudolf, *Joel-Amos-Obadja-Jona* (KAT 13/2; Gütersloh: Mohn, 1971) 325; H. W. Wolff, "Jonabuch," *RGG*³ Tübingen: Mohr [Siebeck], 1959) 3. 854.

77 Though Jonah is hardly portrayed as righteous in terms of his negative response to Yahweh's commission, his praying to Yahweh from the sea is certainly deemed the right thing for him to do in that situation, and Yahweh grants him his request for deliverance. For an attempt to show that the psalm in Jonah 2 was a part of the original content of the book, see my study, "The Kerygma of the Book of Jonah."

78 For the fear of Yahweh/God, cf. Gen 20:11; 2 Sam 23:3; Isa 11:2-3, 33:6; Neh 5:15; also Gen

42:18; 1 Kgs 18:3, 12; 2 Kgs 17:25; Deut 25:18, 31:12; Lev 19:14, 32; 25:17, 36, 43; Neh 7:2, etc. On counteracting evil, cf. Gen 6:5-7; 38:7; 48:16; Amos 5:14-15; Mic 2:1, 3; Isa 13:11, etc. For the divine control of nature and its creatures, cf. the Genesis flood narrative, the Egyptian plagues in Exodus 7-11, and the account of the Reed Sea event in Exodus 14-15. Of course a work written to teach something and composed in a didactic style need not be confined to wisdom literature (cf. the work of the Deuteronomist, the oracles of many of the prophets, etc.). Moreover, a universalistic perspective, when it is attested in the OT, most often turns up in texts not associated with wisdom writing (cf. e.g., Gen 12:3b; Amos 9:7; Isa 2:2-4; Mic 4:1-4; Isa 19:19-25; 42:1-4, 6; 45:22-23; 49:6; Ps 145:9, etc.), while the use of mythic and fabulist motifs occur in many places outside of wisdom sources. For knowledge of ships and the sea, cf. Ezekiel 27 and Ps 107:23-32.

[79] In his monograph on Jonah, Haller (*Die Erzählung von dem Propheten Jona*, 7-11) has speculated that the author may have been a member of a *sôd*, a group of people who met together to share their experiences, tell stories, sing songs, propound riddles, recite maxims, and reflect on the sacred history of their people. From such a *sôd* would come not only wisdom sayings, but also the creative impulse for composing psalms and stories and serious meditations on the issues of the day. Though there is no way of demonstrating that the author of Jonah may have been influenced by such a setting, it is an interesting and attractive hypothesis.

[80] J. L. Crenshaw, "Method in Determining Wisdom Influence Upon 'Historical' Literature," *JBL* 88 (1969) 129-42.

[81] Ibid., 132-33.

[82] The reason for its placement here rather than among the Writings (like Daniel) is not really known, but if it was not simply because of the coherence of its message and spirit with that of other prophets (so Bewer, *Jonah*, 11), it may also have been because to the editor of the prophetic corpus the "hero" of this book was the same Jonah ben Amittai of 2 Kgs 14:25, and thus deemed to be just as genuine a historical figure as the other eleven minor prophets. In the opinion of my OT colleague, Gerald T. Sheppard, the decision to include Jonah among the Twelve, despite its different literary genre, could indicate the redactor's historicizing judgment with regard to the book, in line with the editorial superscriptions that introduce several of the other minor prophets' works (cf. Hos 1:1; Amos 1:1; Mic 1:1; Zeph 1:1; Hag 1:1; Zech 1:1; the superscriptions to Joel, Obadiah, Nahum, Habakkuk, and Malachi give virtually no historical information). The significance of this remains to be explored.

[83] Cf. esp. Jer 18:7-17; Ezek 33:11; Joel 2:13-14. For further references and extended discussion, see A. Feuillet, "Les sources du livre de Jonas," *RB* 54 (1947) esp. 170-81, and for Jeremiah, cf. Wolff, *Studien zum Jonabuch*, 16-20.

[84] Cf. Mendenhall's comment, "The Shady Side of Wisdom," 326: "It is not at all surprising that the *mashal* is most unpopular among elite circles and, at the same time, a favorite device of minority movements such as prophets."

[85] Cf. e.g., G. E. Wright, and R. H. Fuller, *The Book of the Acts of God* (Garden City, NY: Doubleday, 1957) 168.

[86] The thesis submitted here does not necessarily preclude the understanding of Jonah as a midrash, as there would appear to be nothing *a priori* to prevent a midrash from functioning as a *māšāl*, or vice versa. Though it is likely that the literary category of midrash was in existence when the author of Jonah wrote, it is not at all certain that in its fundamental features it resembled the form it took later among the rabbis (that it did not has been argued forcefully by S. Zeitlin, "Midrash, A Historical Study," *JQR* 44 [1953-54] 21-36). In any case, if Jonah should prove to be an early (if not the earliest) form of a midrash, the portion of sacred tradition which inspired it was not limited to Exod 34:6-7, as often stated, but reflected the entire tradition about the merciful God, which at the time Jonah was written, had taken the same form as in Joel 2:13. It is not clear whether the author of Jonah was dependent upon Joel for this, or the other way around, or whether both drew upon a common understanding of this theologumenon at the time they wrote. For arguments supporting an early 6th century dating for Joel, and thus, in my view, to place him as a contemporary or near contemporary of the author of Jonah, see Rudolf, *Joel-Amos-Obadja-Jona*, 25-28.

IV
ON THE PROVENANCE, ETHICS
AND THEOLOGY OF
THE PSALMS, PROVERBS, QOHELETH AND JOB

# PSALM 73

JAMES F. ROSS

VIRGINIA THEOLOGICAL SEMINARY, ALEXANDRIA, VIRGINIA 22304

Samuel Lucien Terrien introduced me to both the psalms and the wisdom literature, and it is appropriate that I should choose to deal with a work which many think to combine the two traditions.

P SALM 73 has received almost universal approbation as one of the greatest of the OT psalms. Staerk, for example, ascribes to its author "the deepest religious knowledge of pre-Christian ethical monotheism,"[1] and Weiser claims that the poem "occupies a foremost place among the more mature fruits borne by the struggles through which the OT faith had to pass."[2] Terrien, having said that Psalm 139 is "in some respects the greatest prayer of the psalter" goes on to remark that "Ps. 73 takes us one step further."[3]

For both Staerk and Terrien this "one step further" is the allusion to an afterlife which they find in vs. 24. For others the chief interest of the psalm is its connection with the problems raised in the Book of Job; some even see it as coming out of the "Joban school," if not from the author of Job himself.[4] More commonly, however, interpreters are attracted to Psalm 73 because of its obvious associations with the wisdom traditions of the OT as a whole.[5] In this essay I will attempt to classify this psalm by examining its structure and certain distinctive expressions.

## 1. Translation

1  Yet indeed ‹God is good to the upright›,[6]
      ‹Yahweh›[7] to the pure in heart.

2  But as for me, my feet had nearly turned aside (from the way),[8]
      my steps had almost slipped,[9]

3  because I was jealous of the boasters;
      I begrudged[10] the prosperity of the wicked.

4  For [11]‹they›[11] are in no pain;[12]
      their bodies[13] are [11]‹sound›[11] and fat.

5  They are not involved in the troubles of mortals,
      nor stricken with (others of) mankind.

6  Therefore pride serves as their necklace;
      violence, the robe with which they wrap themselves.

7  Their ⟨iniquity⟩[14] proceeds from fatness;
      the imaginations of (their) hearts are excessive.[15]

8  They mock and speak of evil;
      from on high they talk of oppression.[16]

9  They set their mouth in the heavens
      and their tongue goes about in the earth.[17]

10  Therefore ⟨my⟩ people turn ⟨to them
      and find no blemish⟩ in them.[18]

11  And they say, "How could God know?
      Is there knowledge in the Most High?"

12  Behold, these are the wicked: ⟨they prosper;
      the evildoers⟩:[19] they increase wealth.

13  But in vain have I made my heart clean
      and washed my hands in innocence.

14  For all day long have I been stricken
      and ⟨chastened⟩[20] every morning.

---

15  If I were to say, "Let me speak thus . . .,"[21]
      behold, I would betray the generation of your children.

16  So I took thought to know this;
      it seemed troublesome to me

17  until I went to the sanctuaries of God:
      then I discerned the outcome (of) their (deeds).[22]

18  Indeed you have put (their feet) on slippery places;
      you have made them fall down in ruins.[23]

19  How suddenly have they become a wasteland,
      come to a complete end in terrors!

20  Like a dream when one awakes, ⟨they are nothing⟩;[24]
      when you arise,[25] (O God,) you will despise their phantoms.

21  When my heart was sour
      and I was pained in my innermost parts,

22  then I was stupid, and did not know —
      a beast; (but) I was with you![26]

23  But as for me, I am always with you;
      you have grasped my right hand.

24  You lead me in your counsel,
      and afterwards will receive me ⟨in⟩[27] honor.

25  Whom have I in heaven ⟨beside you⟩?[28]
      And, being with you, I desire nothing on the earth.

26  Even though my flesh and my heart may fail,
      God is ⟨my strength⟩[29] and my portion forever.

27  For behold, those who are far from you shall perish;
      you annihilate everyone who is unfaithful to you.

28  But as for me, being near to God is good for me;
      I have made ⟨    ⟩[30] Yahweh my refuge,
    that I may tell of all your works
      ⟨in the gates of the daughter of Zion⟩.[31]

## 2. Individual or Corporate?

Most interpreters of Psalm 73 regard it as a composition of a pious Israelite who compared his lot with that of the wicked, and, after going through a period when he was tempted to "speak thus," received a revelation of some sort in which the fate of the enemies was made known and the psalmist's continuing support by God affirmed. The psalm is said to be intensely personal; "the poet . . . speaks of himself and his own struggles."[32] His problem is his own; how can he maintain his faith when the wicked prosper?

But even in what might be called the "pre-Gunkel" period of psalm criticism, there were some who saw in the psalm a "corporate" or "national" dimension, transcending the concerns of the individual. F. Hitzig envisioned a situation in which, during the reign of Antiochus IV Epiphanes, a great many Israelites fell away from the faith when they were misled by the good fortune of their heathen overlords.[33] And in recent years, when such interpretations of even the most individualistic psalms have again become popular, Psalm 73 has been taken to be "corporate" in its *basic* intent; the poet is merely symbolic of the nation as a whole.[34] Würthwein not only regards the pagans as the enemy, but also thinks that the author is really a king who received an "oracle of assurance" in the temple.[35] Ringgren, with some reservations, also identifies the psalmist with a king who is ritually humiliated at a certain moment of the New Year's festival in the temple.[36] And Caquot is convinced that the psalm as a whole is a meditation on the fate of those Israelites left behind in Palestine during the exilic period, and that the poet speaks "in the name of all," even though he may not have had an official position.[37]

But the identification of the psalmist's enemies as "pagan overlords," whether Babylonian or Seleucid, is scarcely enough reason to interpret the entire psalm as "corporate," let alone to identify the author with a king.[38] To be sure every psalmist speaks "in the name of all," which accounts for the very preservation of the "individual" psalms of lament and thanksgiving. Yet it is going too far to say that such "individuals" are merely symbolic of a group. And this would seem to be especially the case with our poet. He seems to make a great effort to *distinguish* himself from others. God is indeed good to the upright/ to Israel (depending upon the reading in vs. 1). But as for *me* —[39] I nearly fell away when I saw the prosperity of the wicked. Some of the people turn to "the boasters," and I was once tempted to do so, until I saw what would happen. In retrospect, I would have betrayed my fellow Israelites if I had, like many of them and their friends, doubted the knowledge and power of God. And so I will now tell of all God's works (including my own salvation) "in the gates of the daughter of Zion" (so the LXX). This psalmist hardly personifies Israel; he stands over against her (especially if vs. 10 refers to apostate fellow countrymen) and speaks to her. Therefore I believe that we must return to a primarily "individual" interpretation of the poem, recognizing that the experiences and insights found therein transcend the concerns of the author himself.

### 3. Structure

Since there is general agreement on the structure of the psalm,[40] only a few details need to be discussed here.

Verse 1 stands by itself. It is an "anticipated conclusion" of the work as a whole, and at the same time an assertion that, in spite of appearances (which are then to be detailed), God is good to those who are "pure in heart."[41] Verses 2 and 3 then introduce the theme of the psalmist's jealousy and envy.

The description of the wicked falls into three parts. In the first (vss. 4-5) their physical well-being is emphasized; in the second (vss. 6-7), the psalmist speaks more generally of their presumptuous, violent character.[42] In the third (vss. 8-9) he characterizes their mocking language.

Verses 10 and 11 seem to introduce a new note, if our understanding of the text is correct.[43] Here we are introduced to the psalmist's countrymen, who are all too eager to repeat the mocking words of the "boasters." Verses 12-14 are in the style of a "coda" in which the author summarizes his observations of the wicked and remembers his feelings of frustration[44] and pain.

Now we have a major break in the text, as is usually recognized.[45] The psalmist had been nearly (cf. vs. 2) at the point of saying words such as those of his enemies. Yet he "took thought." This was "troublesome,"[46] until finally he entered the sanctuaries of God and understood what would happen to the unrighteous because of their deeds. Verse 17 is the conclusion of this turning-point in the psalm; the particle $^c ad$ "until" connects it with the foregoing, not the following. This is particularly obvious when one considers the first word of vs. 18: $^{\jmath} ak$ "nevertheless," "on the contrary," "in spite of one's expectations (or previous temptations)."[47]

In vss. 18-20 the poet tells us of the results of his inquiries "in the sanctuaries of God." The "outcome" of the deeds of the wicked is that, in spite of their own expectations, they will suddenly fall "on slippery places," "in ruins"; in only a short time they will be like a wasteland, completely consumed in terrors.[48]

Verses 21-22 are a parenthetical "flashback" with an affirmation of the author's present confidence in God. He remembers once again his previous condition, how "sour," "stupid" and ignorant he was—just a "beast"—when he was inclined to follow the wicked and the apostates (cf. vs. 15). But because of the new insight received in the "sanctuaries of God" he now sees that he is truly "with you (God)";[49] the former temptations are in the past.

Now, after all of these ups and downs, we are ready for the poet's final affirmation (vss. 23-26). He begins, as in vs. 2, with $wa^{\jmath} \check{a}n\hat{\imath}$, "But as for me. . . ." Contrary to what I had thought, I am always with you—you hold me, guide me, and receive me in honor. There is no one else in heaven or on earth; no matter what may happen to my physical being, God is always "my strength and my portion."[50]

So the author repeats the conclusion which he had already expressed (somewhat tentatively?) in vs. 1. All those who "go a-whoring from you," whether pagans or their imitators, will perish—that is the "outcome" realized in vs. 17. But as for *me* (again!—see vss. 2, 22, 23), nearness to God[51] is good. So I have made Yahweh my refuge (a common word in the psalms of lament and thanksgiving). Therefore I will tell of his works, not only the "mighty acts" of the past but also his deeds on my behalf, "in the gates of the daughter of Zion" (vss. 27-28).

The analysis may be outlined as follows:

| | | |
|---|---|---|
| 1 | | Anticipated conclusion |
| 2-3 | | My jealousy |
| 4-9 | | The wicked |
| | 4-5 | Their well-being |
| | 6-7 | Their character |
| | 8-9 | Their words |
| 10-11 | | Apostasy of my countrymen |
| 12-14 | | My former thoughts |
| | 12 | Thus the wicked . . . |
| | 13 | My frustration |
| | 14 | My pains |

| | | |
|---|---|---|
| | | My conversion |
| | 15 | Turning away from temptation |
| | 16 | What does it mean? |
| | 17 | I went to the sanctuaries . . . |
| 18-20 | | The fate of the wicked |
| 21-22 | | The "flashback" |
| | 21-22a | "I was stupid . . . |
| | 22b | but with you!" |
| 23-26 | | The final affirmation |
| 27-28 | | Conclusions |
| | 27 | The fate of the wicked again |
| | 28a | My nearness to God |
| | 28b | My testimony to his works |

## 4. The Meaning of vs. 17

Even if one might have some questions about the details of the analysis, the significance of vss. 15-17 as the "pivot" of the psalm is still clear.[52] The author experienced something in the "sanctuaries of God." What was it? An answer to this question may help us to understand not only the psalm as a whole, but also its significance in the history of the religion of Israel.

Certain interpretations of vs. 17 may be rejected out of hand. Gunkel simply emends MT's *miqděšê* "sanctuaries of . . ." to *môqěšê* "snares of . . .," supposing that the psalmist saw, in some fashion, the traps which God had laid for the wicked.[53] Equally unlikely is Birkeland's suggestion that we have here a reference to the psalmist's visit to the ruins of certain illegitimate sanctuaries left over after the centralization of sacrifice in Jerusalem; he also interprets vss. 18-20 as criticisms of such *places*, not the wicked in general.[54] Nor may we be so imaginative as Schmidt, who supposes that our author saw one of the wicked struck by a heart-attack on the stones of the temple court.[55]

A somewhat more popular view is that the *miqděšê ʾēl* are not places, but ideas or concepts. Ever since Hitzig it has been suggested that we have a parallel in the Wisdom of Solomon. There we read that "ungodly men," caught up in their own follies, propose to "test" the righteous one by condemning him to death (1:16–2:20). But they were led astray because "they did not know the mysteries of God" (*mystēria theou*) and so did not see the "prize of holiness" (2:22). The meaning of the Wisdom passage is not entirely clear (as with all mysteries!); *RSV*, for example, translates *mystēria* as "secret purposes," whereas *NEB* has "hidden plan." However this may be, those who accept the parallel use it to explain Ps 73:17 in a variety of ways.[56] Kittel thinks that the psalmist not only meditated on the divine decisions, but also experienced a "mystische Versenkung in Gott."[57] Similarly Oesterley can refer to "the *holy places* of God's heart, not merely in the outward temple, but in that inner shrine of the spirit where God and man may most surely meet."[58] Eichrodt concludes that vs. 17 refers to esoteric knowledge, "holy places into which the profane cannot enter, areas of God's dealings with men which are open only to the one who humbly seeks refuge in Yahweh."[59] And some hold that the reference is to mysteries of the future, those of an afterlife[60] which will take place in heaven.[61]

One suspects that "spiritual" interpretations of this sort, whether or not based on the Wisdom parallel, proceed in part from an assumption that the psalmist's experience could not have occurred in any kind of real temple.[62] This may also be connected with the conviction, once popular in psalm research, that works such as Psalm 73 and many others are quite late, even Maccabean.[63] But since Gunkel, and especially Mowinckel, such views have come under serious attack. Therefore it is not surprising that many recent scholars, freed from the necessity of ascribing the psalmist's experience to some sort of non-physical "sanctuaries," have taken the words *miqdĕšê ʾēl* quite literally: "(earthly) sanctuaries of God." Unfortunately scholars are equally divided on what this may mean.

As noted above, Ringgren holds that the poet saw the enemies of God defeated in a ritual battle which took place in the course of a cultic drama in the temple, probably in connection with a New Year's or throne ascension festival.[64] Others are also inclined to posit one of the annual festivals as the context of the experience. Weiser, as might be expected, says that the psalmist had an "encounter with his God that was brought about by the theophany, assumed to have taken place in the cult of the Covenant Festival. . . ."[65] It is more common, however, to interpret the temple experience as of a more particular sort, such as the psalmist's observation of a "divine judgment in a sacral process of law"[66] or even a special service related to the present desperate circumstances caused by the nation's enemies, in the course of which an oracle mediated by a cultic prophet was received.[67] And perhaps this was only a "recitation of the *Heilsgeschichte*"[68] or some sort of meditation in the temple on the "holy ordinances" of God.[69]

Yet when one remembers the individualistic tone of the psalm ("but as for *me . . .*") such interpretations, which ascribe the author's "conversion" to participation in or observation of a normal temple ritual, are somewhat dissatisfying. This feeling seems even to be shared by Würthwein, who, as we have just seen, thinks that the "psalmist-king" received a special cultic oracle. Others are even more sure that the psalmist had an intensely personal experience. Mowinckel believes that the author was really sick (thus he interprets vs. 4) and went to the temple for the "usual purification rites," in the course of which he received a new understanding of God and his righteousness.[70] Terrien may have something similar in mind when he says that the "sanctuary of God" was where the psalmist "poured out his anguish before the divine face": he said a prayer of lament.[71]

Still, are even these interpretations sufficient to account for the new *knowledge* gained by the psalmist—". . . it seemed troublesome to me . . . until I went to the sanctuaries of God: then I discerned. . ."? Some think not, and believe that the author, although really in the temple, took part in deliberations of the wisdom schools, where discussions of problems of theodicy took place.[72] The likelihood of this interpretation is enhanced by the fact that throughout Israel's history there was a close connection between wisdom and the cult. Even though we may not assume that all wisdom literature had its origin in cultic forms, the existence of temple schools cannot be denied, and it is most probable that these became one of the centers in which wisdom was cultivated.[73] This conclusion is based in part upon analogies from the cultures of Israel's neighbors. Temple schools certainly are to be found in Egypt,[74] Sumer,[75] and Babylon,[76] and may also have existed at ancient Ugarit.[77] Some, to be sure, have doubted the relevance of these parallels for Israelite religion,[78] but this view seems to be overly cautious. In spite of the fact that the first explicit reference to Israelite schools seems to be in Sirach (51:23: *bêt midrāš*) we may be fairly confident that the institution had existed from ancient times, and was closely connected with the temple. Nor can it be seriously questioned that such schools were among the places where ancient Israelite wisdom was at home.[79]

The thesis that the psalmist's inspiration derived from the wisdom schools seems also to be supported by the distinctive character of his words, many of which find close parallels in wisdom literature. Both his lament and his thanksgiving are echoed in wisdom language. The affirmation of vs. 1 reminds one of the terminology of Job 11:4 (both use the word *bar* "pure"); the author's description of his feet as "turning aside" is very similar to Job 31:7. The motif of jealousy in vs. 3 (*qinnēʾ*) is, of course, to be found often in the OT, but in this sense occurs frequently in Proverbs (3:31; 23:17; 24:1, 19) and a wisdom psalm (37:1). The description of the wicked in vs. 7 uses the rare word *maskît* ("imagination") which is found in this context only in Prov 18:11. Their haughty speaking (vs. 8) is reflected in Prov 24:2b, and their actual words (vs. 11) in a speech of Job ascribed to him by Eliphaz (22:13). The psalmist, vainly making his heart clean (vs. 13), seems almost to be mocked in Prov 20:9 (both *zikkâ lēb[āb]*). And his "troublesome" search for

understanding (vs. 16) is also that of Qoheleth (Qoh 8:17, also using the root ᶜ-
*m-l,* otherwise very frequent in that book). So also the author's final
realization of the fate of the wicked: "then I discerned their outcome
(*ʾăharît*)"—the same word is used in a positive sense in Prov 23:18 (cf. also 5:4;
14:12 = 16:25; 20:21; 23:32; 29:21; and Sir 38:20). The "terrors" (*ballāhôt*) to
be visited upon the unrighteous (vs. 19) are frequently mentioned in Job
(18:11, 14; 24:17; 27:20; 30:15), often in a very similar context. And the
insubstantial character of the evildoers, "like a dream when one awakes," (vs.
20) is a motif in Job 20:8 (also *kahălôm*); see also, using a different image, Job
21:18. A term in the psalmist's self-description—"then I was stupid, and did
not know, a beast (*běhēmôt*) . . ." (vs. 22)—recurs in Bildad's angry retort to
Job, 18:3.[80] Note also the similarity between the psalmist's question, "Whom
have I in heaven ‹beside you›" (vs. 25), and Eliphaz' taunt to Job: "Call now; is
there any one who will answer you? / To which of the holy ones will you turn?"
(5:1).[81] Perhaps even the poet's remark, "Though my flesh and my heart may
fail . . .," (vs. 26) has a distant parallel in Job 19:27b, "my innermost parts fail
within my bosom."[82]

Nevertheless it cannot be claimed that the expressions of Psalm 73 have
parallels *only* in the wisdom literature. Many of the words and phrases
discussed in the previous paragraph have equally impressive attestation in the
psalms themselves, particularly those ordinarily classified as "individual
laments." Furthermore our poet has some things to say which are distinctively
characteristic of the psalmodic, not wisdom, tradition. This is especially
the case with vs. 28, typical of the affirmations and vows often to be found at
the ends of laments (Pss 7:18 [Engl. 17]; 13:6b; 22:23-26 [Engl. 22-25]; 32:11;
35:28; 41:14 [Engl. 13]; 56:13-14 [Engl. 12-13]; etc.). Indeed some might claim
that the conversion of the psalmist can be explained solely on the basis that he
had heard such psalms of lament in the temple, and had taken heart from the
experiences of his fellow worshippers. This is not likely to be the case—there is
sufficient wisdom terminology in the poem to make us fairly confident that
the work was inspired, at least in part, by the wisdom schools, presumably
those associated with the temple. How are we to account for this mixture of
psalm and wisdom motifs?

I submit that we have been dealing all along with a false alternative—cultic
versus non-cultic, psalmodic versus wisdom. This is due to our natural
tendency to conceive ancient Israelite religion in water-tight compartments—
either this or that. Rather we must imagine the experience of the average
person to have taken place in a variety of places and contexts not mutually
exclusive of each other—both the temple *and* the school, both those who
lamented *and* those who pondered the question of the fate of righteous and
wicked. In other words, I suggest that we can have it both ways. There is
support for this view in the actual spelling of one word of the psalm: *miqděšê.*

The author says that "it [the good fortune of the wicked or the process of
thinking about the same] seemed troublesome to me / until I went to the
sanctuar*ies* of God" (vss. 16b-17a). Ever since the LXX (*hagiostērion*) the

word *miqdĕšê* (by form a plural construct) has been taken as singular, either (1) a "plural of amplification," "intensity," "majesty," or (2) a singular with a *yod* compaginis.[83] But it is to be noted that there are a good many other places in the OT where one finds plurals in designations of cultic buildings, and surely not all can be so easily explained. Our particular word or a similar form occurs in Lev 21:23 (a priest with a blemish shall not approach the altar so as to "profane my sanctuaries" [*miqdāšay*]); Jer 51:51 (strangers have come to the "sanctuaries of the house of Yahweh" [*miqdĕšê bêt yhwh*]);[84] Ezek 21:7 (Engl. 2; the prophet is to preach against the "sanctuaries" [*miqdāšîm*] in Jerusalem);[85] and Ps 68:36 (Engl. 35; God is to be feared "from your sanctuaries" [*mimmiqdāšêkā*]).[86] Other Hebrew terms with a similar meaning also occur frequently in the plural. *Miškĕnôt* "dwelling places" apparently refers to the temple area in Ps 43:3 (Yahweh's light and truth are to lead the psalmist "to your holy mountain and to your dwelling places" [*wĕᵓel miškĕnôtêkā*]); 84:2 (Engl. 1; how lovely are "your dwelling places" [*miškĕnôtêkā*]); 132:5 (David promises to find a place for Yahweh, "dwelling places" [*miškānôt*] for the Mighty One of Jacob); and 132:7 (let us go to his "dwelling places" [*miškĕnôtāyw*]).[87] Note also that *môᶜădîm* "meeting places" occurs in Ps 74:4 (the enemies roared in the midst of "your meeting places" [*môᶜădekā*]) and 74:8 (they burned all the "meeting places of God" [*môᶜădê ᵓēl*] in the land).[88]

Even though some of the references above can be explained as "plurals of majesty" or the like, this cannot be the case with all of them. Nor is it likely that we have here merely a "Canaanite poetic practice of using a plural form of names of buildings to express the singular," as Dahood would have us believe.[89] Rather it is most likely that at least some of these plurals are references to "a single sanctuary with its precincts," as G. A. Cooke remarks in a comment on Ezek 28:18.[90] And if these "precincts" included buildings used by the wisdom schools, as one could assume on the basis of parallel phenomena in the cultures of Israel's neighbors,[91] we may suggest that the psalmist's visit to the *miqdĕšê ᵓēl* was not only to the temple proper, but also to buildings where the wisdom teachers discussed the problems of good and evil, life and death. On one and the same day in a closely connected series of structures he may have participated in a public service, heard a psalm of lament and its closing affirmation, and encountered teachers such as Eliphaz, Bildad, Zophar, and the elders who have left us the Book of Proverbs (with perhaps rebuttals by "Job" and "Qoheleth"!). And having now seen the fate of the wicked, he promises to tell of all Yahweh's works, including his own revelation, in the gates of the daughter of Zion.[92]

## 5. Classification

So, to return to our original question: is Psalm 73 really a wisdom psalm, as is so often claimed? Some have replied in the negative, saying that the psalmist's concern with the question of theodicy is not enough to justify that classification.[93] And it is often noted that the motifs of thanksgiving, praise, and trust are prominent, also diverging (so it is thought) from the usual wisdom categories.[94] But the didactic character of the work cannot be ignored,[95] and this would seem to support the usual view. Again the answer seems to be "both/and." If my suppositions are correct, the psalmist solved his problems *both* by visiting the temple *and* by participating in the discussions of the nearby wisdom schools. Our problem is only one of our own making, as we try to draw lines unknown to the ancient Israelites. Psalm 73 is *both* a wisdom psalm *and* a psalm of lament, trust, and thanksgiving. It anticipates the synthesis of Sirach, who, after his poetic personification of Wisdom, says, "All this is the book of the covenant of the Most High God, / the law which Moses commanded us . . ." (24:23).

---

[1] W. Staerk, *Lyrik* (SAT 3/1; 2d ed.; Göttingen: Vandenhoeck & Ruprecht, 1920) 229.

[2] A. Weiser, *The Psalms* (OTL; Philadelphia, 1962) 507.

[3] S. Terrien, *The Psalms and Their Meaning for Today* (Indianapolis and New York: Bobbs-Merrill, 1952) 254.

[4] See, for example, W. O. E. Oesterley (*The Psalms* [London: SPCK, 1959] 344): "In a sense, this psalm is an epitome of the book of *Job* [italics in original]," and M. Buttenwieser (*The Psalms* [Chicago: University of Chicago, 1938] 530): "Without a question, Psalm 73 is a poem worthy of the author of the Job drama." Buttenwieser makes similar remarks about Psalms 39 and 139. Terrien (*Psalms* 240) is content to ascribe Psalms 73 and 139 to "men who belonged to the same school of thinking as that which produced the masterpiece of Job."

[5] B. W. Anderson (*Out of the Depths: Studies into the Meaning of the Book of Psalms* [New York: United Methodist Church, 1970] 154) regards it as "the greatest of the wisdom psalms."

[6] Reading *layāšār ʾēl* with B. Duhm (*Die Psalmen* [Kurzer HKAT 14; Tübingen: Mohr, 1922] 278), H. Gunkel (*Die Psalmen* [Göttinger HKAT 2/2; 4th ed.; Göttingen: Vandenhoeck & Ruprecht, 1926] 316), H.-J. Kraus (*Psalmen* [BKAT 15; Neukirchen Kr. Moers: Neukirchener Verlag, 1961] 502) and many others, for MT's *lĕyiśrāʾēl* "to Israel," retained by A. Caquot ("Le Psaume LXXIII," *Sem* 21 [1971] 33), Weiser (*Psalms* 505), M. Buber (*Right and Wrong: An Interpretation of Some Psalms* [London: SCM, 1952] 35-36) et al. The question is one of the balance of the verse and an understanding of the psalmist's intent; see section 4 below and n. 34.

[7] Restoring the tetragrammaton in the Elohistic collection.

[8] Following the *qĕrēʾ* and taking "my feet" as the subject of the verb; the *kĕtîb* (a passive participle) would have to be rendered "(I) was turned aside (in respect to) my feet."

[9] Again following the *qĕrēʾ* (plural) against the *kĕtîb* (singular). The verb (a pual of the root *š-p-k*, "to pour out") is never elsewhere used with "feet, steps" or the like as a subject, and is here translated by context (cf. Ezek 7:17); for another suggestion see Caquot, "Psaume LXXIII" 35.

[10] For this meaning of *rāʾâ* see M. Dahood, *Psalms* (AB 17; Garden City: Doubleday, 1968) 2. 188.

[11-11] Reading, with most commentators, *lāmô / tām*. MT has *lĕmôtām* "to their death," which is retained by those who are inclined to see here a possible reference to the Canaanite god Môt (M. Mannati, "Les adorateurs de Môt dans le Psaume LXXIII," *VT* 22 [1972] 424-25; cf. also H. Ringgren, "Einige Bemerkungen zum lxxiii. Psalm," *VT* 3 [1953] 266, and, with some reservation, Caquot, "Psaume LXXIII" 36).

[12] The word (plural of *harṣubbâ*) usually means "bond, fetter," but is connected with "wickedness" in Isa 58:16. The literal meaning is kept by B. Eerdmans (*The Hebrew Book of Psalms* [OTS 4; Leiden: Brill, 1947] 347-48), who translates "they were not noosed to death."

¹³ The Hebrew word has a cognate in Ugaritic (ʾul) which seems to mean "(military) force" (CTA [Gordon Krt] 88) or "strong one" (CTA 2, IV [Gordon 68] 5).

¹⁴ Reading ᶜăwônāmô with support from the LXX and the Peshitta; MT has ᶜênēmô "their eyes." For the pejorative sense of "fatness" see Job 15:27.

¹⁵ The verb is intransitive; see Caquot, "Psaume LXXIII" 38.

¹⁶ Regarding ᶜōšeq "oppression" as the first word of the second stichos; cf. LXX and Aquila.

¹⁷ Many find in this verse an allusion to or echo of the Ugaritic text CTA 23 (Gordon 52) 61-62, "a lip to earth and a lip to the heavens," describing the appetite of the "gracious gods" (cf. also CTA 5 [Gordon 67], II, 2-3); the connection was made independently by R. O'Callaghan ("Echoes of Canaanite Literature in the Psalms," VT 4 [1954] 169) and Ringgren ("lxxiii. Psalm" 267-68). Others are more doubtful; see especially H. Donner, "Ugaritismen in der Psalmenforschung," ZAW 79 (1967) 336, and P. A. H. de Boer, "The Meaning of Psalm LXXIII 9," VT 18 (1968) 260-64.

¹⁸ The MT of this vs. is undoubtedly corrupt; a literal translation would be "Therefore his people return (qĕrēʾ; kĕtîb "therefore he returns his people") hither, and waters of fullness are drained out for them." Of the many suggested emendations the best seems to be that proposed originally by Duhm (Psalmen 280, with slight variations): lākēn yāšûb ᶜammî lāhem / ûmûm lōʾ yimṣĕʾû lāmô, followed by the NEB and, for the most part, by RSV. Some, e.g. E. Würthwein ("Erwägungen zu Psalm 73," Festschrift Alfred Bertholet [ed. W. Baumgartner, O. Eissfeldt, et al.; Tübingen: Mohr, 1950] 543) and L. Sabourin (The Psalms [Staten Island, NY: Alba House, 1969] 2. 271), regard the verse as a taunt of the evildoers: "So he brings his people to such a pass that they have not even water!" (NAB; cf. also JPSV).

¹⁹ Reading with G. R. Driver (cited in A. Anderson, Psalms [New Century Bible; London: Oliphants, 1972] 2. 532) yišlāyû / ᶜăwwālîm; the MT has no verb in the first stichos, and takes wĕšalwê ᶜôlām ("and, always prosperous . . .") as the subject of the second.

²⁰ Reading a hophal perfect wĕhûkahtî for MT wĕtôkahtî "and my chastisement"; for another suggestion, which does not involve a change of the text, see Dahood, Psalms 2. 191.

²¹ Many commentators add an object such as "them" or "that" after MT's kĕmô, "like," but the word can be construed as an adverb; see F. Delitzsch, Commentary on the Psalms (Edinburgh: Clark, 1861) 2. 316, and Dahood, Psalms 2. 191, citing Ugaritic usage.

²² Rather than "end" or "future"; see C. A. and E. G. Briggs, The Book of Psalms (ICC; New York: Scribner's, 1906) 2. 146, and the general discussion by H. Seebass, "ʾAhărît," TDOT 1 (1974) 207, 210.

²³ MT's maššûʾôt seems to mean "deceptions," and so several scholars emend to mĕšôʾôt. The change may not be necessary, however; see Caquot, "Psaume LXXIII" 47, and Delitzsch, Psalms 2. 318.

²⁴ Reading ʾênām for MT's ʾădōnāy "O Lord"; so Terrien (Psalms 255) and others.

²⁵ bāᶜîr = bĕhāᶜîr; see GKC § 53q, and the Targum here.

²⁶ For this understanding of the verse see the suggestion of Mannati, "Sur le quadruple avec toi de Ps. LXXIII 21-26," VT 21 (1971) 59-67, which obviates the necessity of inserting vss. 21-22 after vs. 15 or elsewhere; see my comments below on vss. 21-22 in section 3.

²⁷ Reading bĕkābōd, with possible support from the LXX (meta doxēs); see Dahood, Psalms 2. 195. On the verse as a whole see below n. 92.

²⁸ Adding zûlātĕkā, both for reasons of sense and meter; see Mannati, "Avec toi," 65-66, who himself prefers ᶜimmĕkā/ᶜimmāk, as do some others. There is possible support in the Targum.

²⁹ Reading merely ṣûrî for MT's ṣûr lĕbābî ("rock of my heart").

³⁰ Omitting ʾădōnāy ("Lord") with the LXX and the Peshitta (an error of dictation?).

³¹ The second stichos is missing in the MT, and is supplied (with the NAB) from the LXX; see Ps 9:15 (Engl. 14: bĕšaᶜărê bat ṣiyyôn). Others solve the problem by simply omitting the last line of the MT.

³² Gunkel, Psalmen 312.

³³ Cited by Würthwein, "Psalm 73" 532-33; cf. also Caquot, "Psaume LXXIII" 31, who, like Würthwein, ascribes this view also to J. Olshausen.

³⁴ Those who hold this opinion are also inclined to retain MT's lĕyiśrāʾēl in vs. 1.

<sup>35</sup> "Psalm 73" 542-49; see also below in section 4 the text prior to n. 67.

<sup>36</sup> "lxxiii. Psalm" 270-72; he regards "the generation of your children" in vs. 15 as the cultic community (269, 272). See also H. Birkeland, "The Chief Problems of Ps 73:17ff.," ZAW 67 (1955) 101 (largely repeated in his The Evildoers in the Book of Psalms [Oslo: J. Dybwad, 1955] 36), who says that "the individual is a representative of the people." See below in section 4 the text prior to n. 54 for Birkeland's interpretation of vs. 17. His general view is summarized and criticized by G. W. Anderson, "Enemies and Evildoers in the Psalms," BJRL 48 (1965/66) 18-29.

<sup>37</sup> "Psaume LXXIII" 54. It should be noted that Caquot regards several verses to be anticipations of a future restoration. He understands vs. 10 to refer to a time when "he (Yahweh) will bring his people back here" (to Palestine, after the exile); vs. 11 means "What! God knew! There is knowledge in the Most High!" (in spite of what we had thought); vs. 17 speaks of the forthcoming entry by the psalmist into the restored temple, after which the events of vss. 18-20 will take place. For a somewhat similar view see Buber, Right and Wrong 39.

<sup>38</sup> See especially S. Mowinckel, The Psalms in Israel's Worship (New York and Nashville: Abingdon, 1962) 1. 207, 213; 2. 36 and n. 13.

<sup>39</sup> wa<sup>ɔ</sup>ānî; for this use of the adversative wāw and first person pronoun introducing a motif of distress or sorrow, see especially Pss 30:7 (Engl. 6); 31:23 (Engl. 22); 35:13; 38:14 (Engl. 13); 40:18 (Engl. 17; cf. 70:6 [Engl. 5]); 69:30 (Engl. 29); 88:14 (Engl. 13); 102:12 (Engl. 11); 109:25.

<sup>40</sup> The most elaborate discussion is that of E. Baumann ("Struktur-Untersuchungen im Psalter II," ZAW 62 [1950] 126-32), who places great emphasis on particles such as adverbs, pronouns, and conjunctions.

<sup>41</sup> See especially Caquot ("Psaume LXXIII" 34), who affirms Snaith's understanding of the particle <sup>ɔ</sup>ak as "nevertheless" (N. H. Snaith, "The Meaning of the Hebrew אך," VT 14 [1964] 221-25, esp. 223; Hymns of the Temple [London: SCM, 1951] 102). For a similar view see also Briggs, Psalms 2. 142, and A. Anderson, Psalms 2. 529. R. Kittel (Die Psalmen [KAT 13; Leipzig and Erlangen: Deichert, 1922] 241) calls the psalm "das grosse 'Dennoch'!"

<sup>42</sup> Note the position of lākēn "therefore" at the beginning of vs. 6; Baumann, "Struktur-Untersuchungen" 127.

<sup>43</sup> See above n. 18 for other suggestions.

<sup>44</sup> For a close parallel to rîq "in vain" see Isa 49:4.

<sup>45</sup> See, for example, Terrien's arrangement of the text (Psalms 254-55), contra Briggs, Psalms 2. 141-42.

<sup>46</sup> The reference may be either to the actual process of trying to understand what "this" all means, or to the object of reflection, namely the prosperity of the wicked; see Caquot, "Psaume LXXIII" 45.

<sup>47</sup> See above n. 41 for the meaning of this word. Baumann missed the break here because of his (in my opinion mistaken) conviction that vss. 21-22 belong after vs. 16 ("Struktur-Untersuchungen" 128-29).

<sup>48</sup> For the "suddenness" of the fall see Ps 6:11 (Engl. 10); 37:36.

<sup>49</sup> Following Mannati's suggestion; see above n. 26.

<sup>50</sup> On the basis of the latter word (ḥēleq) some have thought that the author was a Levite, since that tribe had no real "portion" in the land (Deut 10:9; 18:1-2 and elsewhere); see, for example, P. Munch, "Das Problem des Reichtums in den Ps 37; 49; 73," ZAW 55 (1937) 41-43. But surely this is pushing the expression too far.

<sup>51</sup> qirbat <sup>ɔ</sup>ĕlōhîm, whether the first word is construed as a construct noun or as an infinitive construct, could mean "God's being near"; see Caquot, "Psaume LXXIII" 53-54. Parallels elsewhere suggest the interpretation offered in my translation; see Isa 58:2 (pace Caquot); Ps 65:5 (Engl. 4). For a somewhat different view see S. H. Blank, "The Nearness of God and Psalm Seventy-three," To Do & To Teach: Essays in Honor of Charles Lynn Pratt (ed. R. M. Pierson; Lexington: College of the Bible, 1953) 1-13. This verse is especially emphasized by L. Delekat, who thinks that the whole work is an "asylum psalm" (Asylie und Schutzorakel am Zionheiligtum. Eine Untersuchung zu den privaten Feindpsalmen [Leiden: Brill, 1967] 250-53).

<sup>52</sup> So Caquot, "Psaume LXXIII" 32, whose opinion, however, differs from mine in that he thinks the psalmist anticipated a return to the temple after the exile (p. 46); see above n. 37.

53 *Psalmen* 314, 318. Gunkel's suggestion brought forth the clever rejoinder by Kittel (*Geschichte des Volkes Israel* [2d ed.; Stuttgart: Kohlhammer, 1927-29] 3. 714) who hoped that none of Gunkel's students would be caught in their teacher's "snare."

54 "Ps 73:17ff." 100, and *Evildoers* 37. To my knowledge Birkeland has been followed only by R. Tournay in a note to Ps 73:17 in *La Bible de Jérusalem* (rev. ed.; Paris: Cerf, 1973) 793; see below n. 62 for his earlier opinion.

55 H. Schmidt, *Die Psalmen* (HAT 15; Tübingen: Mohr, 1934) 139-40. As Würthwein notes ("Psalm 73" 547), this is merely a "hübsche Geschichte."

56 Many cite Wisdom without extensive further remark; see, for example, Staerk, *Lyrik* 228-29; J. Calès, *Le Livre des Psaumes* (Paris: Beauchesne, 1936) 2. 6, 9; H. Lamparter, *Das Buch der Psalmen* (Die Botschaft des Alten Testaments 15; Stuttgart: Calwer, 1959) 2. 14, 19-20; see also Buber, *Right and Wrong* 42.

57 *Psalmen* 245-46.

58 *Psalms* 2. 344 (italics in original).

59 W. Eichrodt, *Theology of the Old Testament* (OTL; London: SCM, 1967) 2. 253 n. 1. He translates "holy counsels or mysteries of God" and finds a parallel in Ps 25:14 ("the *sōd* [special knowledge] of Yahweh is (only) for those who fear him").

60 Duhm, *Psalmen* 281-82, who also considers it possible that the poet was initiated into mystery cults similar to those of the Greeks; against this see E. Podechard, *Le Psautier* (Bibliothèque de la Faculté Catholique de Théologie de Lyon 3; Lyon: Facultés Catholiques, 1949) 1. 318.

61 Dahood (*Psalms* 2. 192) makes a direct claim that "God's sanctuary" means heaven, where "the glaring inconsistencies of this life will become intelligible to the psalmist in the hereafter," citing also Ps 68:36 (Engl. 35) and his interpretation of Ps 53:7 (ibid. 21).

62 So explicitly Duhm, *Psalmen* 281. This is also the opinion of A. Deissler (*Die Psalmen* [Die Welt der Bibel; Düsseldorf: Patmos, 1963] 2. 116), who then goes on to say that the "mysteries" are really the teaching of holy scripture, a view shared by Sabourin (*Psalms* 2. 273) and, at one time, by Tournay (note to Ps 73:17 in the *JB*; for his later opinion see above n. 54). All three claim that holy scripture is the "house of wisdom" in Prov 9:1-6; Sir 14:23-25.

63 See, for example, Hitzig's opinion cited above in section 2, second paragraph.

64 "lxxiii. Psalm" 270.

65 *Psalms* 511; Weiser here refers back to his general remarks on this festival (ibid. 37-44, 72-73) in which Ps 73:17 is cited. W. S. McCullough is content to refer merely to "one of the annual festivals, when memories of God's great mercies in the past were revived . . ." (*IB* 4. [1955] 390).

66 G. von Rad, *Wisdom in Israel* (London: SCM, 1972) 205.

67 Würthwein, "Psalm 73" 546-48; as noted above, Würthwein has a "corporate" interpretation of the psalm as a whole and thinks that the author is really a king.

68 A. Maillot and A. Lelièvre, *Les Psaumes* (Geneva: Labor et Fides, 1966) 2. 138 (see also below n. 72 end); A. Anderson, *Psalms* 2. 534. So also E. J. Kissane (*The Book of Psalms* [Dublin: Browne and Nolan, 1955] 7) says that the psalmist recovered his faith by "considering [the] downfall of Israel's past enemies" (the real "mysteries of God") and Briggs, *Psalms* 2. 140-41, 145. For the latter, however, vss. 17-20 are a gloss intended to correct the solution of the psalmist himself found in vss. 21-26.

69 Munch, "Problem des Reichtums" 42, in accord with his thesis that the author was a Levite.

70 *Psalmenstudien* (Amsterdam: P. Schippers, 1961 [reprint; original 1921]) 1. 127, 131. See also his *Psalms* 2. 36.

71 *Psalms* 257.

72 To my knowledge this was first suggested by H. L. Jansen (*Die spätjüdische Psalmendichtung. Ihr Entstehungskreis und ihr "Sitz im Leben"* [Skrifter utgitt av Det Norske Videnskaps-Akademi i Oslo II. Hist.-Filos. Klasse, 1937, No. 3; Oslo: J. Dybwad, 1937] 138, 140). He was followed, with some slight reservations, by H.-J. Hermisson (*Sprache und Ritus im altisraelitischen Kult. Zur "Spiritualisierung" der Kultbegriffe im Alten Testament* [WMANT 19; Neukirchen-Vluyn: Neukirchener Verlag, 1965] 146, 156 and *Studien zur israelitischen Spruchweisheit* [WMANT 28; Neukirchen-Vluyn: Neukirchener Verlag, 1968] 132). Note also

that Eerdmans, although he claims that the plural form *miqdĕšê* shows that we cannot have a reference to the temple in Jerusalem, thinks that the poet found some place "where religious problems [were] discussed or religious thoughts were recited" (*Psalms* 349-50). So Maillot and Lelièvre say that in addition to reciting the *Heilsgeschichte* (see above n. 68) the author may have engaged in catechetical classes (*Psaumes* 2. 138).

⁷³ See especially A. Bentzen, *Introduction to the Old Testament* (4th ed.; Copenhagen: G. E. C. Gad, 1958) 1. 171, 174-75, criticizing the extreme view of Engell. On the general question see also Jansen, *Psalmendichtung* 60; Hermisson, *Spruchweisheit* 129-33; W. Richter, *Recht und Ethos. Versuch einer Ortung des weisheitlichen Mahnspruches* (Studien zum Alten und Neuen Testament 15; Munich: Kösel, 1966) 182-89; G. Östborn, *Tōrā in the Old Testament: A Semantic Study* (Lund: Ohlsson, 1945) 113; Mowinckel, "Psalms and Wisdom," *Wisdom in Israel and in the Ancient Near East* (ed. M. Noth and D. W. Thomas; VTSup 3; Leiden: E. J. Brill, 1955) 207; P. Volz, *Hiob und Weisheit* (SAT 3/2; 2d ed.; Göttingen: Vandenhoeck & Ruprecht, 1921) 103-06; and J. Muilenburg, "Baruch the Scribe," *Proclamation and Presence* (ed. J. Durham and J. Porter; Richmond: John Knox, 1970) 228-30 and works cited there.

⁷⁴ E. Otto, "Bildung und Ausbildung im alten Ägypten," *Zeitschrift für ägyptische Sprache und Altertumskunde* 81 (1956) 42; see also H. Brunner, *Altägyptische Erziehung* (Wiesbaden: Harrassowitz, 1957) 28-29.

⁷⁵ Hermisson, *Spruchweisheit* 109; see ibid. 97-133 for a valuable study of the whole question of schools in Israel and elsewhere.

⁷⁶ B. Meissner, *Babylonien und Assyrien* (Kulturgeschichtliche Bibliothek 1/4; Heidelberg: C. Winter, 1925) 2. 325, 331. See also L. Dürr, *Das Erziehungswesen im Alten Testament und im Antiken Orient* (Mitteilungen der vorderasiatisch-ägyptischen Gesellschaft 36/2; Leipzig: Hinrichs, 1932) 69 (still the classic work on the subject).

⁷⁷ Hermisson, *Spruchweisheit* 116 n. 2, and C. F. A. Schaeffer, *The Cuneiform Texts of Ras Shamra-Ugarit* (Schweich Lectures; London: Oxford, 1939) 34-35.

⁷⁸ R. N. Whybray, *The Intellectual Tradition in the Old Testament* (BZAW 135; Berlin and New York: de Gruyter, 1974) 33-43.

⁷⁹ J. L. McKenzie is most explicit here: "We know that wisdom literature is associated with scribal schools in Egypt and Mesopotamia, and we can assume that the same association existed in Israel" ("Reflections on Wisdom," *JBL* 86 [1967] 4).

⁸⁰ It is common to emend the Hebrew word to a singular, but this seems to be unnecessary. Another term used here, *baᶜar* "stupid," is thought even by Whybray to be a clue that the psalm is from the wisdom tradition (*Intellectual Tradition* 145, 153-54).

⁸¹ On this motif see my "Job 33:14-30: The Phenomenology of Lament," *JBL* 94 (1975) 42-43.

⁸² The operative verb (*kālâ* "to fail") is relatively rare in this particular sense. On Job's "innermost parts" (*kilyôt*), probably from the same root, see also Ps 73:21.

⁸³ Respectively (1) *GKC* § 124*b*; Briggs, *Psalms* 2. 146; A. Anderson, *Psalms* 2. 534 and (2) Delekat, *Asylie* 252 n. 1. Presumably many others hold such an opinion, without special note.

⁸⁴ LXX apparently read *miqdĕšênû* (*eis ta hagia hēmōn, eis oikon kyriou*).

⁸⁵ See also 28:18, where Ezekiel says that Tyre profaned her sanctuaries.

⁸⁶ Dahood (*Psalms* 2. 152) thinks that the reference here is to the "celestial shrine," i. e., heaven; this is also his understanding of Ps 73:17 (see above n. 61).

⁸⁷ See also the secular use of this term in Job 18:21; 39:6.

⁸⁸ In vs. 4 the manuscripts vary; B19a, the standard text used in *BHK*, has the suffix written defectively (as one can see from the plural construct form in vs. 8), whereas other manuscripts noted in the critical apparatus have the full form. The situation is reversed in Ezek 28:16: manuscripts defective, B19a full. For similar cases see *GKC* § 91*n*.

⁸⁹ *Psalms* 2. 111 with cross references to his discussions elsewhere.

⁹⁰ *The Book of Ezekiel* (ICC; New York: Scribner's, 1937) 2. 324 and ibid. 1. 228, where there is an explicit reference to Ps 73:17. A similar opinion is held by J. H. Eaton (*Psalms* [Torch Bible Commentaries; London: SCM, 1967] 185 n. 2) who wrongly cites *GKC* § 124*b*. It is difficult to

understand how Dahood (*Psalms* 2. 192) can cite Cooke as supporting his opinion. On the general question of the temple buildings see K. Galling, "Die Halle des Schreibers," *PJB* 27 (1931) 51-58, and L. Fisher, "The Temple Quarter," *JSS* 8 (1963) 34-41.

[91] See my discussion above in this section and nn. 72-79.

[92] A similar view is held by Jansen (*Psalmendichtung* 140). For the text of the last stichos see above n. 31.

A brief note on the vexed question of whether or not we have a reference to an afterlife in vs. 24 may be in order here. (1) The text is by no means secure (for various suggestions see S. Jellicoe, "The Interpretation of Psalm lxxiii, 24," *ExpTim* 67 [1955/56] 209-10), (2) the meaning of the individual words is uncertain (e. g., Does *lāqaḥ* "receive" really mean "translate [to heaven]" as in Gen 5:24; 2 Kgs 2:3, 5, 9? See especially J. van der Ploeg, "Notes sur le Psaume XLIX," *Studies on Psalms* [OTS 13; Leiden: Brill, 1963] 159), and (3) the parallel with Zech 2:12 proposed by Eerdmans (*Psalms* 350), Ringgren ("lxxiii. Psalm" 270-71), Delekat (*Asylie* 252 n. 4), and Caquot ("Psaume LXIII" 51-52) is dubious—Th. C. Vriezen thinks 2:12 is merely a gloss explaining the proper arrangement of Zechariah 2 ("Two Old Cruces," *OTS* 5 [1948] 88-91)! Given these difficulties, it is not surprising that while many scholars still affirm that the psalmist anticipated some sort of communion with Yahweh after death, others claim that vs. 24 is really only a strong affirmation of the *present* and *continuing* "nearness of God" expressed elsewhere in the psalm (so especially Snaith, *Hymns* 106, 113; Mowinckel, "Psalms and Wisdom" 215 and n. 3; *Psalms* 2. 128 and n. 4; and C. Barth, *Die Errettung vom Tode in den individuellen Klage- und Dankliedern des Alten Testaments* [Zollikon: Evangelischer Verlag, 1947] 161-63). My understanding of the psalm would tend to support this latter opinion.

[93] R. E. Murphy, "A Consideration of the Classification 'Wisdom Psalms'," *Congress Volume, Bonn 1962* (VTSup 9; Leiden: Brill, 1963) 164; so also Bentzen, *Introduction* 1. 161.

[94] This is especially emphasized by Mowinckel (*Psalmenstudien* 1. 127-28, 131-33; 6. 65-66; *Psalms* 2. 17-18); see also C. Westermann, *Der Psalter* (Stuttgart: Calwer, 1967) 95-96.

[95] So Deissler, *Psalmen* 2. 115; A. Anderson, *Psalms* 2. 529; Eaton, *Psalms* 184 and many others. See even Mowinckel, "Psalms and Wisdom" 208.

# THE MOTIF OF THE WISE COURTIER
# IN THE BOOK OF PROVERBS

W. LEE HUMPHREYS
THE UNIVERSITY OF TENNESSEE, KNOXVILLE, TENNESSEE 37916

THE developmental history of the materials that make up the Book of Proverbs—from individual sayings through smaller and larger collections to the book itself—might be likened to several rivers which are fed by smaller streams and which come together in time to form a large body of water. The sources and upper reaches of the smaller streams have been charted only in part, if at all.[1] And they come together into rivers that flow through terrain that is also not wholly mapped out. Yet, it has been a widespread assumption in biblical studies that a most formative area through which these rivers passed was the royal court. Specifically, it is asserted that much of the material in Proverbs 10–29 served a didactic function, used in the education of young men who would enter various branches of service in the royal establishment, providing instruction not only in the fundamentals of writing, but serving to inculcate a style of life, a set of values, aspirations, goals, and loyalties.[2]

However, direct evidence for an educational establishment in the royal courts of Israel or Judah is sparse, if not totally lacking. The archaeologist has failed to uncover traces of any schools, a situation in striking contrast to that in Egypt, Mesopotamia, and even Canaanite Syria-Palestine. And there are few if any clear references to court schools in the Hebrew Bible.[3] Apparently, it is the perceived need for some sort of training program for the body of officials in royal service, and the available model for such in the surrounding Near East, that leads to their suggested existence in Israel as well.[4] Beyond this, and granting the existence of some such training centers linked to the court, the basis for placing the collections in Proverbs 10–29 in this context must be examined. While the designation ḥākām is applied to royal officials, both foreign (Gen 41:8, 33, 39; Exod 7:11; Isa 19:11; 44:25; etc.) and native (Jer 18:18),[5] it is in no way restricted to such usage, and does not provide a basis for ascribing to these figures the collections in Proverbs, nor suggesting that they are the primary addressees of these sayings. Although tradition does state that Solomon possessed wisdom greater than any other man, and his name is linked with Proverbs (Prov 1:1; 10:1), this ascription seems based on the assertions presented in 1 Kgs 2:6, 9; 5:9-14; 10:1-10, 13, 23-24, and critical assessment finds them to be quite vague, mixed, and of late date.[6] Even the designation *mišlê šĕlōmōh* is not itself without ambiguity.[7] The firmest link between the collections in Proverbs 10–29 and activity of the royal court is perhaps found in the notice in Prov 25:1. All this, however, provides little solid foundation for linking Proverbs 10–29 with a supposed school for future courtiers and its literary activity.

In this essay we propose to assess this theory from another angle. If all or a part of Proverbs 10–29 served as a core curriculum in the training of future courtiers, such a setting and function should leave its imprint on both the content and form of presentation of the collections. In this respect a comparison with a body of Egyptian materials that are universally designated wisdom and are often compared with Proverbs will be useful. The so-called "Instructions" of ancient Egypt are collections of admonitions by aged courtiers or rulers for their sons and/or successors. They impart to the next generation their distilled wisdom, based in ancient tradition and full lives. In such Instructions, copied again and again by the youths in the court schools, there is an informing motif that binds the varied sayings together into a unified and distinct literary type. This can be designated "the motif of the wise courtier," for it develops an ideal portrait of one whose life is devoted to royal service, who would stand in the presence of kings. If this motif is found, the clear imprint of a courtly-didactic *Sitz im Leben* may be posited.

It is our purpose in this essay first to examine this motif as it is developed in the Egyptian Instructions in terms of its salient features, literary function, and theological potential. Then we shall turn to the several collections in Proverbs 10–29 to see where and how this motif is developed therein.

## I. *The Motif of the Wise Courtier in Egyptian Instructions*

Four of the Instructions survive in sufficient extent to allow us to construct an overview of the motif. From the Old Kingdom come the "Instruction of Ptahhotep" and the "Instructions from Kagemni." From the New Kingdom come the "Instruction of Ani" and the "Instruction of Amenemope."[8]

The wise courtier is humble before his superiors, taking care to please them through a controlled and mild demeanor and careful observation of the rules of procedure that apply in the "vestibule of the great." "Thou shouldst not sit when another who is older than thou is standing, or one who has been raised higher in his rank. . . . Go every day according to the prescribed way, that thou mayest walk (with regard to) procedure" (Ani 29; see also Amenemope chs. 26–27). In service of another, for example as a messenger, the wise courtier is faithful in fulfillment of his duties.

To petitioners he gives an attentive hearing, for he knows that "the victim of wrong prefers the venting of his feelings to the performance of that for which he has come" (Ptahhotep 17). He keeps clients satisfied, for they shall remain faithful in troubled times. His attitude toward those below him is further tempered by the knowledge that wisdom and good speech are fully in no man's possession (Ptahhotep 1). He acts with the certainty that "truth is great and its effectiveness endures" (Ptahhotep 5). Amenemope warns repeatedly against oppression or official corruption: "Do not displace the surveyor's marker . . . nor overturn the boundaries of a widow" (ch. 6); "Make not for yourself a measure of two capacities. . . . Do not enter into collusion with the grain measurer" (ch. 17); "Do not corrupt the people of the law court. . . . Take not the gift of the strong man" (ch. 20).

The wise courtier is a solid family man because a wife is a source of profit (Ptahhotep 10), comfort, and support (Ani 49-50). In the home of another he is wary of the women, for they offer a road to death (Ptahhotep 18; Ani 49). Friendship is valued.

He is a silent man and knows both the difficulty and the value of effective speech (Ptahhotep 24). The Instructions are c: lled "maxims of good speech" (Ptahhotep, Intro.). Silence and effective speech are bound together, for silence is recognized on occasion as the most forceful form of communication: "Let your (good) name go forth, while you are silent in your speech, and you will be summoned" (Kagemni 2. 1; see also 1. 1; Ani 1. 7; Amenemope chs. 3, 9, 10). There is a silence that reveals strength, a quiet confidence that the world is ordered and comprehensible, so that attunement is possible.[9] The silent man is the tranquil man (Eg. gr), one who does not take up much living space. He avoids the passionate or hot man (Eg. smm), whose appetites consume so much (Kagemni 1. 5). "Do not fraternize with the hot-tempered man, nor approach him to converse" (Amenemope ch. 9).

The wise courtier is a hearer of instructions offered. The concluding unit in Ptahhotep includes a play on the word "hear." He who in his youth hears the instructions of elders and who orders his life about their teaching shall become himself a hearer, that is, one who in a place of authority hears the cases of others (Ptahhotep 38-42).

While there is much in the Instructions that can be applied to situations other and more general than that of the courtier per se, they are clearly and primarily directed to one who would serve the king. This is reinforced by the framework in which the individual admonitions are presented. They are words of successful and wise courtiers to those who would succeed them, "a good example to the children of the magistrates." Ptahhotep is a "hereditary noble and Count, God's father, beloved of the god, eldest bodily son of the king, the City Governor and Vizier." The author of the Instruction for Kagemni was Vizier, and his son was made "overseer of the residence town and Vizier." Amenemope presents his offices and titles at greater length, even though they indicate that his office was on a lower level. Yet, his words are also a "guide for well-being," offering "all the principles of official procedure, the duties of the courtiers." Both Ani and his son are called simply "scribes." In spite of differences in rank the overarching structure of admonitions from courtiers to future courtiers binds the individual sayings of each collection together and stamps the Instructions with a quite distinctive character.

A number of the motivating clauses in the Instructions have a pragmatic thrust, leading some to pronounce them "the gospel of the 'go-getter,' the bald rules for a young man who is on the make."[10] Others are critical of what they call the "pragmatic misinterpretation,"[11] and in their critique the theological potential of the motif as developed in the Egyptian context becomes clear. For not only is a sharp distinction between this-worldly success and rewards and an ethical thrust artificial, but there are motivating clauses that stress obedience to and the pleasing of the god(s). At points it is not clear whether the reference is to a particular deity or to the Pharaoh, for, of course, the king of Egypt was divine, and often simply called "the god" or "the good god." The distinction is in one way not crucial, for service of the king was service of the deities. In fact, royal service rooted the courtier in the ongoing activity that sustained the created universe itself. The Pharaoh was vitally linked with the creative process itself. He was the son of the creator, and the creator was the first Pharaoh. He was the image through whom all deities functioned to preserve and sustain the created order that in its many facets is denoted by the term "*maat*."[12] For the courtier, the king was the sole source of life and, as such, the focus of his life. In the words of the Vizier of Thutmose III: "What is the king of Upper and Lower Egypt? He is a god by whose dealings one lives, the father and mother of all men."[13]

Pharaoh was the state, the god-king, son of the creator, establisher of *maat*. Thus, it was upon *maat* that the courtier founded his life, upon that which defined and informed the created universe itself. He avoided the passionate man who had lost sight of the created order. The silent man is one whose life is in harmony with the foundations of creation; the man given to appetites and lust transgresses *maat*. This is the ideal held up by Ptahhotep at the end of his instruction: "I have passed 110 years of life through what the king gave to me, favors over and above those who went before, because of acting rightly for the king until the blessed state."

Within Egypt the ideal set forth in this motif of the wise courtier was designed for one who served not only a human ruler but the totality of the gods. In this is expressed the ultimate Egyptian vision of the good life. The motif informed material designed primarily for those who would enter court service, but it could have a wider appeal in Egypt as well, for every man was a servant of the king.

## II. *The Motif of the Wise Courtier in Proverbs 10–29*

In this essay we shall confine our attention to the five collections isolated in Proverbs 10–29 on the basis of formal structure, headings, and content: 10:1–15:33; 16:1–22:16; 22:17–24:34; 25:1–27:27; 28:1–29:27. A majority of scholars assert that the collections are pre-exilic.[14] This division of the material and this dating will be assumed without further discussion. With the exception of Proverbs 22:17–24:34, these collections do not have extended introductory and concluding statements, which in the case of the Egyptian Instructions identify the material as words of a courtier addressed to future courtiers. With no such overarching structure in Proverbs, any evidence for a motif of the wise courtier must come from the content of the sayings themselves. We need first to consider those king-sayings that speak directly of the situation of the courtier. Then other sayings that seem to speak of the courtier's situation and/or that treat themes found in conjunction with the motif in the Egyptian Instructions will be noted. Since aspects of this motif can have an application beyond the courtier per se, only limited weight can be given to the latter, unless the king-sayings indicate that a collection is possibly addressed to the courtier.

1. *Proverbs 10:1–15:33*. This collection is composed almost entirely of statements (*Aussage*), most cast in two lines in antithetical parallelism. Only two make reference to a king. While 14:28 is a general observation, 14:35 seems to speak of the courtier:

> The favor of a king is upon one who deals discreetly,
> but his wrath is upon one who acts shamefully.

Two others speak of the value of counsel and of the need for *yōcesîm* (11:14; 15:22). Beyond this no further sayings seem specifically addressed to the courtier. Some themes associated with the motif of the wise courtier in the Egyptian Instructions are found here:[15] a faithful messenger is praised (13:17);[16] companions are to be selected with care (13:20, reading with Q); a good wife is her husband's crown (12:1, 4), but women are also a source of potential danger (11:22; cf. 11:16). Careful and effective speech is valued (10:20; 12:18; 15:1, 2, 7, 23), and silence is seen as at times the way of discretion (10:19). The apt word can enliven (10:11, 14, 21, 31-32; 12:14; 13:2, 3; 14:3; 15:4). In 15:18 the *ʾîš hēmâ*, the "heated man," is compared to the *ʾerek ʾappayīm*, the one who can "bridle his anger." It is suggested that we find here the equivalent of the Egyptian *smm* and *gr* (see also 10:12; 11:2; 14:17, 29-30).[17]

Skladny and Schmid call attention to signs of systematic structuring of this collection.[18] It is clear, however, that sayings developing the motif of the wise courtier play no significant role in this. In only a few isolated units is the motif possibly present, and these in no way provide a governing thrust within the collection.

2. *Proverbs 16:1–22:16*. The situation is strikingly different in the second sub-collection within the material designated as "proverbs of Solomon." In this collection stress is placed on the apt word, on effective speech and self-mastery (16:5, 18, 19, 29, 32; 17:9, 27; 18:6, 12; 19:11, 19a; 20:3, 22; 22:4, 11). Self-control extends to the physical appetites as in the Egyptian Instructions (20:1; 21:17). In all of Proverbs 10–29 the theme is most fully developed in this collection. Concern is shown for the poor and defenseless (19:17; 21:23; 22:9); a good wife is treasured (18:22; 19:14), while a shrew is a plague (21:9, 19) and the strange woman a snare (22:14). These additional sayings with the few

address-clauses seem to suggest a ruling, urban, and upper class (see 17:26; 18:11, 18; 19:1, 6, 10; 22:7, 16).

In chs. 16 and 20–21 are found groups of king-sayings. These reflect the situation of one who might experience the wrath or favor of a ruler, one whose life is devoted to royal service and whose existence is bound intimately to royal favor. Prov 16:12-15 is prefaced by 16:10, a statement that sets the king on a very high level:

> Divine utterances (*qesem*) come from the lips of a king;
>> his mouth does not err in judgment.
> The doing of evil is an abomination to kings,
>> for the throne is fixed in righteousness.
> Righteous lips win the favor of a king,[19]
>> and he who speaks what is right he loves.
> The wrath of a king is a messenger of death;
>> the wise man will appease it.
> In the light of a king's face is life,
>> and his favor is like the clouds that bring spring rain.   (Prov 16:10, 12-15)

The use of *qesem* in Prov 16:10 without a condemnatory notice is unique in the Hebrew Bible (cf. Deut 18:10; 2 Sam 18:23; 23:1-2; 1 Kgs 3:28; Isa 2:6).[20] The king is placed within a supra-human sphere here, as in Prov 20:8, 26,[21] where it is almost with superhuman knowledge that he judges the wicked.

Also to be noted is the image of the throne supported by righteousness in 16:12 (see also 20:28).[22] H. Brunner notes that the throne of the Egyptian Pharaoh was depicted standing on a pedestal that is in the form of the sign for *maat*, and that this throne base was also thought to symbolize the hillock of creation in Egyptian tradition. The royal throne thus stood upon the locus of creation, upon *maat*, as a force for the preservation of the natural and social orders. *Ṣĕdāqâ* is in its range of usage and meaning the closest Hebrew concept to the Egyptian *maat*. Thus, Brunner suggests, "the idea . . . that *ṣĕdāqâ* could be the foundation, *mākôm*, of the throne, goes back to Egyptian conceptions and was taken over presumably with the form of the king's throne in the time of Solomon."[23]

Preceding and interlocked with the king-sayings in chapter 16 are others (16:1-9, 11) that deal with Yahweh and human relations with him. In 20:22-21:3 another group of mixed Yahweh-sayings and king-sayings is found.

It has been suggested that in the king-sayings the term *melek* could be replaced with "Yahweh."[24] This linking of king-sayings with those that speak of Yahweh's powers and judgment and his ultimate incomprehensibility places the ruler in a sphere above other human beings. The two are not interchangeable, however, for while "the king manifestly belongs more to the divine than to the human sphere . . . nevertheless the distance which still exists between the mightiest and the Almighty was clearly and impressively described."[25] Prov 21:1 and 21:30-1 are most striking instances of the latter point. This disclaimer should not obscure, however, the vantage point from which the ruler is presented. It is that of the courtier who would most immediately experience the power, the life-and-death authority, of the ruler, and who would at the same time view this from a perspective of admiration and approval. For the king is in no way viewed critically in this.

> The king (the LXX reads *kyrios* [ Yahweh]!) loves the pure in heart;
> the man of elegant speech is his friend. (Prov 22:11)[26]

Skladny has observed that 16:1-15 and 20:22–21:3 (both mixed Yahweh- and king-sayings) are the only large complexes in this collection. In them it receives its focus and thrust.[27] The significant placement of the combined Yahweh- and king-sayings at the head and toward the end of the collection suggests that it received its shape from the hands of those concerned with the training of future courtiers.[28]

3. *Proverbs 22:17–24:34*. Since it was first demonstrated by A. Erman in 1924, the dependency of Proverbs 22:17–24:22 upon the Egyptian Instruction of Amenemope has been widely accepted. While only the first third of the collection has any direct correspondence to the Egyptian material, the whole is patterned in thirty chapters as is Amenemope.[29] In this segment of Proverbs 10–29 we encounter a preponderance of admonitory forms, and the collection has an introductory notice as well.

For our purposes 22:29 is of particular interest:

> You see a man skilled (*māhîr*) in his work:
> before kings he stands!
> He stands not before the obscure.

With this we can compare the concluding lines of Amenemope (Amenemope ch. 30):

> As to a scribe who is experienced (*mahir*) in his position,
> he will find himself worthy of being a courtier.

We should note that while Amenemope speaks of a scribe, Prov 22:29 is more general. And this saying in Amenemope stands at the conclusion, providing motivation, having a summary force, and giving specific orientation thereby to the material as a whole. In Proverbs 22:17–24:22 this saying stands simply as one among others. Beyond this, Prov 24:5-6 might well refer to the situation of the courtier, and, not surprisingly, themes associated with the wise courtier in Egyptian materials are found in this collection as well. The harlot is a deep pit (23:27-8); social justice receives strong emphasis (22:22-23, 28; 23:10-11; 24:11-12, 15-18). Effective speech is not mentioned, but the passionate man is said to be a danger (22:24-25; 23:20-22; 23:27-28, 29-35).

Two further sayings call for attention:

> If you sit to dine with a ruler (*môšēl*),
> observe with care what is before you;
> you should put a knife to your throat,

> if you are a man of desires (ba‵al nepeš).
> Desire not his delicacies,
>     for they are a food of deceptions.
>
> Fear Yahweh, my son, and the king,
>     associate not with those of high rank;[30]
> for ruin from them arises suddenly;
>     the destruction from those of high rank,
>     who can comprehend it!   (23:1; 24:21-22)

In the first saying the court is presented as a place of danger, a complex and slippery setting, where appearances can be deceptive. It is striking in the latter saying to find Yahweh and the king spoken of as almost equal. Again, it is the dangers involved in association with them that are stressed. The perspective here seems to be that of the courtier, and certainly later courtier tales dwelt with intense delight on the possibilities for sudden rise or fall and the ever present dangers and intrigues in the royal court (see, for example, the tales of Esther and Mordecai, of Daniel and his companions, and of Aḥiqar). The position here is perhaps that of a lesser official more removed from the centers of power, for there is not here the certainty of mastery of life that is found elsewhere, but this could be a direct result of influence from Amenemope.

While the author speaks in the first person in an introductory admonition, he does not identify himself, as does Amenemope, and it is not stated that he is a courtier, nor does his introductory unit set forth the future courtier as the one primarily addressed. It appears that we have in this collection a group of sayings formed in part under the influence of the Instruction of Amenemope, and that traces of the motif of the wise courtier remain from this source. But the motif is no longer controlling. In fact, themes linked with the motif elsewhere have here been extended in application to apply to a broader group than those who might actually stand before kings. In this respect the collection stands between Proverbs 10:1–15:33, in which the motif appears only in a most fragmentary and isolated manner, if at all, and Proverbs 16:1–22:16, in which it provides the informing and controlling thrust.

4. *Proverbs 25–27*. This collection begins with a pairing of two sayings linked through the use of the root *ḥqr*:

> The glory of God is to hide things,
>     and the glory of kings is to search out (ḥăqōr) things.
>
> As the heavens are high and the nether world deep,
>     so the mind of kings is unsearchable (᾽ên ḥeqer).

In the first the divine and royal spheres are clearly distinguished. In the second the king is set apart from other human beings, and set on an exceedingly high level, as in Proverbs 16:1–22:17, for the incomprehensibility of the universe itself is called upon for comparison.

To these sayings are added two others:

> Remove the dross from silver,
>    and the smith has material for a vessel.
> Remove the wicked from the king's presence,
>    and his throne is set upon righteousness.[31]
>
> Do not exalt yourself in the king's presence;
>    nor assume the place of the great;
> for it is better to be told, "Come up here,"
>    than being set down in the presence of the princes.    (25:4-7b)

The primary addressee seems clearly to be the courtier. Other themes associated with the wise courtier elsewhere are found in this collection: self-mastery and clever speech are highly regarded (25:11, 15; 26:16, 24-26); a faithful messenger is valued (25:13); friendship and loyalty are encouraged (25:18, 19); self-control is an ideal set against the braggart and the conceited (27:1; 26:12).

On the whole, however, there is a wide range of material found in this collection, and it is difficult, even with the controlling position occupied by 25:2-7b, to comprehend the three chapters under a single motif. Yet, G. E. Bryce has proposed on the basis of both content and structure that in 25:2-27 we have a short set of instructions addressed specifically to the future courtier and utilized in his education.[32] His arguments need not be reviewed here in detail; they are, on the whole, compelling, and his suggestion is attractive. If Prov 25:2-27 is a small collection addressed to the future courtier, it can be set beside Proverbs 16:1–22:16, and the depiction of the ruler in this collection (25:2-3) suggests that this might well be the case. It was later incorporated into a larger collection of varied materials by the men of Hezekiah (25:1). In its new setting 25:2-27 lost its restricted focus and found expanded reference in the larger and quite diverse collection of Proverbs 25–29.

5. *Proverbs 28–29.* A number of sayings in this collection deal with the king (28:15, 16; 29:4, 14; etc.). But the perspective is quite different from that encountered heretofore. The king is suddenly the one addressed; these are sayings for, and not about the ruler.[33] And it is a ruler who clearly stands under the authority of the deity:

> Many seek the face of a ruler,
>    but from Yahweh a man gets justice.

The concern for justice rings through the collection (28:3, 8, 15, 21, 27; 29:7, 14). This is a theme linked elsewhere with royal wisdom (2 Sam 14:16-20; 15:1-6; 1 Kgs 3:9, 11, 16-28),[34] especially in the deuteronomistic tradition. We can also recall the Egyptian Instruction for Meri-ka-Re, which purports to be written by a king for his son. There, as well, stress is placed on the need for royal oversight of justice. In Meri-ka-Re, as in this collection, the king appears as a more human figure than in the Instructions by courtiers and even than in Proverbs 16:1–22:16 and 25:2-27.

### III. *Conclusions*

The motif of the wise courtier plays a limited role in the collections in Proverbs 10–29. Only in Proverbs 16:1–22:16 and 25:2-27, if this latter can be defined as a once separate unit, does the motif occupy a governing position. With the exception of these collections, Proverbs 10–29 does not seem to be primarily addressed to the courtier. What traces of influence from Egyptian Instructions are found in the remaining collections—e.g., in Proverbs 22:17–24:22, in the image of the founding of the throne on righteousness, the weighing of the heart, the silent man opposed to the heated man—are a residue in materials now addressing a more generalized audience.[35]

1. *The wise courtier and the king.* The sole focus of the courtier's life and activity in the Egyptian Instructions was the king. This was directly expressed in the introductory and concluding notices in Ptahhotep and Amenemope. It was from the king that the courtier received authority, status, and even life itself. But in so orienting his life, the Egyptian courtier centered his existence upon the divine sphere as well, for the king was a deity, in direct line with the creator god himself. Royal service was devotion of one's life to the divine sustenance of the ordered cosmos. The motif of the wise courtier presented the highest ideal of the good and pious life within the Egyptian context. The theological potential of this motif was immense and was realized by the ancient Egyptians.

In the Israelite religious setting, however, this potential was severely restricted, for within Yahwism the royal and divine spheres were distinct. Thus, there was the possibility of tension for the courtier who was also a Yahwist. In Prov 16:10 and 25:3, for example, the king is clearly elevated above the level of other mortals, and the image of the throne founded in righteousness developed in 16:12; 20:28; 25:5, has its origin in connection with the divine king of Egypt. In Psalm 97:2 the same image is used of Yahweh. Life and death are in the hands of the king (Prov 16:14-5). Yet, in none of this is the king divine, and it is precisely in these collections that the sphere of God and that of king are sharply distinguished (21:1, 30-1; 25:2). The attitude toward the king is not negative, but the possibility of a tension between loyalties must be acknowledged. Unlike his Egyptian counterpart, the courtier who was a Yahwist had to acknowledge that royalty and deity were distinct.

The primary and secondary loyalties of the Israelite courtier were kept separate.[36] Yet, they were also permitted to coexist, for the tension that was potential between them was never actualized. A situation in which the courtier must choose between deity and king is not presented in this material. In this respect we need take notice of the later development of this motif in the tales of Esther and Mordecai and of Daniel and his companions. In the former the tension in loyalties is touched upon as questions of ultimate allegiance arise (e.g., Esth 4:10-17; 7:4) even if they are resolved in a manner that allows the courtier to serve both the pagan king and people. In the latter the tension breaks forth into a crisis of decision: the courtier must choose whom he will serve (see especially Dan 3:16-18), even if in the end all works out for the best. But miracles are needed (Dan 2:24-25; 6:21-22) and, in some instances, even the conversion of the pagan king (Dan 2:46-47; 3:28-29; 4:31-34 [Engl. 4:34-37]; 6:25-27).[37]

2. *The wise courtier and Yahweh.* The Yahwist as courtier, therefore, had a double focus in his life: the king and the deity. In Prov 16:1-15 and 20:22-21:3 king- and Yahweh-sayings are intertwined. Some of these speak of a divinely established order that supports and preserves life (16:3-5, 7, 11; 20:23, 27; 21:3).[38] The king is the upholder *par excellence* of this order, and as this is a divinely founded order, the king is more firmly associated than other mortals with the divine sphere.[39] At times the limits of human knowledge of this order are stressed (16:2, 25), and there are also sayings in which Yahweh's freedom over against this order is established, sayings that take us into the mysterious depths of the freedom of Yahweh to act even in ways that seem to shatter all structures (16:1, 9, 33; 20:24; 21:2, 30-31).[40] It is again to be noted that these sayings all appear in the very same collections in which the motif of the wise courtier is most fully developed as an overarching frame of reference.

In Israel, as in Mesopotamia,[41] the king was the first of courtiers, the highest servant of the divine sovereign. And those who served the human sovereign demonstrated that they did not lose sight of the fact that their royal master stood as well under life-and-death authority. The king was a courtier of the deity; he was not divine. Yahweh stood beyond all created order, and in Proverbs 16:1-22:16 there is recognized a wide area of experience that could not be subsumed by any concept of universal order. In Egypt *maat* was established at creation, and the gods, including the divine Pharaoh, sustained it. In Israelite tradition Yahweh was not bound to the order he established. This radical divine freedom is what H. Gese calls the *Sondergut* of Israelite wisdom.[42] And it seems that it was precisely in the recognition of the double focus for the courtier's life that this received recognition and full expression.

3. *The limited utilization of the motif in Proverbs.* Within Yahwism the motif of the wise courtier was limited in its potential for theological expression. Of the 538 sayings in Proverbs 10-29, only about 30 have the courtier as the primary addressee. There may have been material in the royal Israelite court that developed the motif more fully, but little of this has survived in Proverbs. Thus, while a court establishment for the training of courtiers may have played a role in the development of a limited segment of this material, the restricted use of the motif suggests that other areas of life be considered as well in the developmental history of Proverbs, and that the role of the royal court has been greatly exaggerated. There may have been specific centers for training of courtiers—and possibly royal sons as well (2 Kgs 10:1-11)—and probably Proverbs 16:1-22:16 and 25:2-27 were shaped for them.[43] But the probability must be considered that circles other than a court educational center played formative roles in the middle stages of the development of the book. Like the upper reaches and sources, the middle

courses of this process are not as clearly charted as we seem to suppose.[44] Furthermore, if, as seems likely, the Book of Proverbs received its final form in the postexilic period, when the Judean royal court was no more, some use of this motif would have been weeded out (cf., however, Qoh 5:8-9 and 8:2-5, to which Qoheleth gives his unique twist in 8:6-9). Basically, however, the theological potential of this motif was restricted within Yahwistic circles, especially in comparison to its use in Egypt. Among Israelites and their early Jewish heirs this motif—with total devotion and loyalty to the king as its formative theme—would possess limited value for the development and expression of an understanding of the interrelations between humankind and Yahweh. In this setting the theological and ethical potential of the motif of the wise courtier was decidedly restricted.

[1] Cf. the attempts of E. Gerstenberger, *Wesen und Herkunft des "apodiktischen Rechts"* (WMANT 20; Neukirchen-Vluyn: Neukirchener Verlag, 1965), and W. Richter, *Recht und Ethos: Versuch eines Ortung des weisheitlichen Mahnspruches* (Munich: Kösel-Verlag, 1966).

[2] See especially the influential observation of G. von Rad: "Nevertheless the older collections (Prov x-xxix) — permeated as they are by proverbs about the king, and about behaviour at court, etc. — were no doubt edited at the royal court in Jerusalem. . . . They . . . served there in the education and schooling of the rising generation of officials." G. von Rad, *Old Testament Theology* (2 vols.; New York: Harper, 1962) 1. 430; idem., "Die ältere Weisheit Israels," *Kerygma und Dogma* 2 (Göttingen: Vandenhoeck & Ruprecht, 1956) 54-72; cf. the more cautious statements in idem., *Wisdom in Israel* (Nashville: Abingdon, 1972) 15-23. See also R. Murphy, "The Concept of Wisdom Literature," in *The Bible in Current Catholic Thought*, (ed. J. L. McKenzie; New York: Herder and Herder, 1962) 49-50; G. Fohrer, *Introduction to the Old Testament* (Nashville: Abingdon, 1968) 309; S. Blank, "Wisdom," *IDB* 4. 855-56; H.-J. Hermisson, *Studien zur israelitischen Spruchweisheit* (WMANT 28; Neukirchen: Neukirchener Verlag, 1968) *passim*; W. McKane. *Proverbs: A New Approach* (Philadelphia: Westminster, 1970) 8-9.

[3] See the review by Hermisson, *Spruchweisheit*, 117-18.

[4] Ibid., 115-33; S. Yeivin, "Social, Religious, and Cultural Trends in Jerusalem under the Davidic Dynasty," *VT* 3 (1953) 149-57; McKane, *Prophets and Wise Men* (*SBT* 44; Naperville, IL: Allenson, 1965) 36-47; E. W. Heaton, *The Hebrew Kingdoms* (London: Oxford, 1968) 165-96; J. G. Gammie, "Notes on Israelite Pedagogy in the Monarchic Period," unpublished paper presented for the Consultation on Wisdom, Annual Meeting of the Society of Biblical Literature; St. Louis, MO, Oct. 28-31, 1976.

[5] See McKane, *Prophets and Wise Men*, 15-23; see also Von Rad, *Wisdom in Israel*, 20-23.

[6] R. B. Y. Scott, "Solomon and the Beginnings of Wisdom in Israel," *Wisdom in Israel and in the Ancient Near East* (VTSup 3; eds. M. Noth and D. W. Thomas; Leiden: Brill, 1960) 262-79.

[7] Does it denote authorship, period of composition, or a style that flowered in a particular period that lived on for a time? See W. Baumgartner, *Israelitische und altorientlische Weisheit* (Tübingen: Mohr [Siebeck], 1933) 7; Scott, "Beginnings," 273.

[8] Translations cited here will be from R. O. Faulkner, E. F. Wente, Jr., W. K. Simpson, *The Literature of Ancient Egypt: An Anthology of Stories, Instructions, and Poetry* (New Haven: Yale, 1972), with the exception of Ani, which will be from J. Wilson's translation in *ANET*[2]. Further references will be found in these volumes.

A fuller discussion of the motif is found in W. L. Humphreys, "The Motif of the Wise Courtier in the Old Testament" (Ph.D. diss., Union Theological Seminary, 1970) 30-47; see also McKane,

*Proverbs*, pp. 51-67, 92-99, 102-10. While the motif is also found in the so-called "tomb biographies," in stories such as that dealing with Sinuhe, and in some letters, our attention will be confined to the Instructions.

⁹ There is a change in tone as one moves from the Instruction of Ptahhotep, with its assured gusto for life, to the more resigned and careful Instruction of Amenemope. See J. Wilson, *The Culture of Ancient Egypt* (Chicago: University of Chicago, 1951) 92. Yet, this is a change that occurs within an established frame of reference and is one of limited degree and not of kind. See H. Gese, *Lehre und Wirklichkeit in der alten Weisheit* (Tübingen: Mohr [Siebeck], 1958) 21.

¹⁰ J. Wilson, *Before Philosophy* (Baltimore: Penguin, 1949) 109. See also R. O. Faulkner, "Ptahhotpe [sic] and the Disputants," in *Ägyptologische Studien* 29, (ed. O. Firchow; Berlin: Akademie-Verlag, 1955) 81.

¹¹ H. Frankfort, *Ancient Egyptian Religion* (Harper Torchbooks; New York: Harper & Row, 1961) 62; Gese, *Lehre und Wirklichkeit*, p. 7; H. Brunner, "Der freie Wille Gottes in der ägyptischen Weisheit," *Les sagesses du Proche-Orient ancien* (Paris: Presses Universitaires de France, 1963) 103; A. Volten, "Der Begriff der Maat in den ägyptischen Weisheitstexten," Ibid., 72-102.

¹² See generally H. Frankfort, *Kingship and the Gods* (Chicago: University of Chicago, 1948); *idem., Ancient Egyptian Religion*, chs. 2-3; C. J. Gadd, *Ideas of Divine Rule in the Ancient Near East* (London: Oxford, 1948); C. Aldred, *The Egyptians* (New York: Praeger, 1961) 157-66.

¹³ Cited in Frankfort, *Ancient Egyptian Religion*, 42-43. See also the words of a 12th dynasty official to his children in *ANET* ², 431.

¹⁴ See, e.g., W. F. Albright, "Some Canaanite-Phoenician Sources of Hebrew Wisdom," VTSup 3 (1960) 13; W. O. E. Oesterley, *The Book of Proverbs with Introduction and Notes* (London: Methuen, 1929) xii-xxii; B. Gemser, *Sprüche Salomos* (HAT 16; Tübingen: Mohr, 1963) *passim*; H. Ringgren, *Sprüche*, (ATD 16/1; Göttingen: Vandenhoeck & Ruprecht, 1962) 10-11, 102; U. Skladny, *Die ältesten Spruchsammlungen in Israel* (Göttingen: Vandenhoeck & Ruprecht, 1962) 5-7, 80 nn. 1-4; R. B. Y. Scott, *Proverbs. Ecclesiastes* (AB 18; Garden City, NY: Doubleday, 1965) 17-26; A. Barucq, *Le livre des Proverbes* (Paris: Gabalda, 1964) 16.

¹⁵ Because of their form the sayings in Proverbs 10-15 have little in the way of address-clauses. However, the general situation seems to be that of the upper classes, including land owners and merchants. The possibility of oppression of the poor is noted in 11:1; 15:24-26.

¹⁶ Read *yappîl* for MT *yippōl*.

¹⁷ Von Rad, *Theology*, 431-32; "Die ältere Weisheit Israels," 64; Gese, *Lehre und Wirklichkeit*, 40.

¹⁸ Skladny, *Spruchsammlungen*, 7-13; H. H. Schmid, *Wesen und Geschichte der Weisheit* (Berlin: Töpelmann, 1966) 156-63.

¹⁹ Read the singular with LXX.

²⁰ Gemser (*Sprüche*, 54) suggests that this saying is either "ausserisraelitisch" or "vor prophetisch." See also H. Cazelles, Review of R. de Vaux, *Les Institutions de l'ancien testament, VT* 8 (1958) 324.

²¹ Vs. 26b has received much attention. *BHK*, Oesterley, Gemser, and *JB* suggest reading *yāšîb* ᶜālêhem ᵓônām (cf. Ps 94:23). G. R. Driver, "Problems in the Hebrew Text of Proverbs," *Bib* 32 (1951) 184, suggests this is an instrument of torture, but there is no evidence for this in the Near East, and his classical references are not compelling. Scott (*Proverbs*, 122) most reasonably suggests that the use is figurative: the reference is to a king driving his chariot over a fallen enemy.

²² Reading with LXX *ṣĕdāqâ* for *ḥesed*, which is already mentioned in the first line.

²³ H. Brunner, "Gerechtigkeit als Fundament des Thrones," *VT* 8 (1958) 428; see 426-28 generally.

²⁴ Gese, *Lehre und Wirklichkeit*, 36.

²⁵ Skladny, *Spruchsammlungen*, 29.

²⁶ The reference in the second line could be understood in relation to the Egyptian honorary title "king's friend." See Humphreys, "Motif," 20-22.

²⁷ Skladny, *Spruchsammlungen*, 25-46.

[28] Ibid., 46. See also Hermisson, *Studien*, 76; Murphy, "Concept of Wisdom Literature," 48-49. P. Skehan ("A Single Editor for the Whole Book of Proverbs," *Studies in Israelite Poetry and Wisdom* [CBQMS 1; Washington: Catholic Biblical Association, 1971] 15-26) suggests that the king-sayings in 16:10, 12-15 along with those in 14:28, 35 are the work of the final editor of the book, whose hand is seen in 14:26-16:15. That this block may reveal the presence of an editor is possible, but it need not be necessary that all of the material contained therein is from his hand. Prov 16:10, 12-15 and the Yahweh-sayings in ch. 16 could already have been present in this second of two collections, from which he sought to construct his larger collection of 375 sayings. His hand could account for the isolated king-saying in 14:35.

[29] A. Erman, "Das Weisheitsbuch des Amen-em-ope." *OLZ* 27 (1924) 241-52. See Scott, *Proverbs*, 20-21, 135-47 for the division into thirty chapters.

[30] Reading *šōnîm* with D. W. Thomas, "The Root *šnn* in Hebrew," *ZAW* 52 (1934) 236-37. Cf. Driver, "Problems," 189.

[31] See the reference in n. 23 for a discussion of this image.

[32] G. E. Bryce, "Another Wisdom 'Book' in Proverbs," *JBL* 9 (1972) 145-57.

[33] Skladny, *Spruchsammlungen*, 58.

[34] See n. 6.

[35] Contra B. W. Kovacs, "Is There a Class-Ethic in Proverbs?" *Essays in Old Testament Ethics* (eds. J. L. Crenshaw and J. T. Willis; New York: Ktav, 1974) 184-86. Cf. J. L. Crenshaw, "Introduction," *Studies in Ancient Israelite Wisdom* (New York: Ktav, 1976).

[36] It is striking that in the many studies of Israelite kingship, especially as it is compared with kingship elsewhere in the Near East, the material from Proverbs has not been utilized. It is especially surprising in the light of the prevailing hypothesis that the collections received their shape and were used in court schools in the training of future courtiers. See, e.g., M. Noth, "God, King, and Nation in the Old Testament," *The Laws in the Pentateuch and Other Studies* (Philadelphia: Fortress, 1967); S. Mowinckel, *He That Cometh* (New York: Abingdon, 1954), ch. 2; G. Widengren, *Sakrales Königtum im alten Testament und im Judentum* (Stuttgart: W. Kohlhammer, 1955); A. R. Johnson, *Sacral Kingship in Ancient Israel* (Cardiff: University of Wales, 1955); J. A. Soggin, *Das Königtum in Israel* (BZAW 104; Berlin: Töpelmann, 1972). The material reviewed in this essay supports the conclusions of Noth (p. 175), based on the royal psalms and historical traditions: "The fact that we appear to have deviations from conceptions of a divine king ideology, applied in the Old Testament to the Jerusalem monarchy, is strong evidence that this ideology itself was really not accepted on Israelite soil, and that it could not be accepted on the basis of Old Testament belief."

[37] W. L. Humphreys, "A Life-Style for Diaspora: A Study of the Tales of Esther and Daniel," *JBL* 92 (1973) 211-23.

[38] Gese, *Lehre und Wirklichkeit*, 33-40; von Rad, *Theology*, 427-41; Skladny, *Spruchsammlungen*, 71-75.

[39] Gese, *Lehre und Wirklichkeit*, 35-36; Skladny, *Spruchsammlungen*, 23-29.

[40] Von Rad, *Theology*, 438-41; Gese, *Lehre und Wirklichkeit*, 45-46.

[41] Humphreys, "Motif," 58-71.

[42] Gese, *Lehre und Wirklichkeit*, 45.

[43] While the statement (*Aussage*) can function didactically, the preponderance of this form in these collections over the admonition (*Mahnspruch*)—see, however, 25:6-10, 16, 21-23—suggests that they were not composed primarily as school materials, but perhaps as intellectual exercises or expressions of a style of life. See von Rad, *Theology*, 20-21; Kovacs, "Class-Ethic," 186-87.

[44] The possibility of commercial or merchant circles should not be overlooked. They were usually urban-based and would have a wide-ranging exposure to foreign materials as well as a tolerance for the latter. They would also come into contact in some cases with royalty, even if they cannot be narrowly defined as courtiers.

# QOHELETH THE IMMORALIST? (Qoh 7:16-17)

R. N. WHYBRAY

THE UNIVERSITY OF HULL, HULL, ENGLAND HU6 7RX

THE meaning of the admonition ʾal-tĕhî ṣaddîq harbēh (Qoh 7:16a), usually translated by "Do not be too righteous" or some equivalent phrase,[1] is a matter of crucial importance for the understanding of Qoheleth's teaching as a whole. The word ṣaddîq in biblical Hebrew is, in ethical contexts, an absolute term.[2] Qoheleth's apparent failure to commend righteous behavior whole-heartedly seems therefore to leave him open to the charge of teaching immorality. Many interpreters virtually admit his guilt, though not usually in so many words.[3] They speak of his doctrine of the golden mean.[4] Qoheleth, they say, was indeed advocating a middle path between virtue and vice, and for two reasons: (i) his experience had taught him that neither necessarily has any effect on men's fortunes in terms of divinely imposed reward or punishment; (ii) it had also taught him that extremes of any kind are in practice more likely to lead to disaster than is moderation.

Other interpreters have sought to understand the verse in some other way which would acquit Qoheleth from the charge of immorality. These interpretations are of many kinds, and cannot be discussed here in detail. Most commonly it is argued that by ʾal-tĕhî ṣaddîq harbēh Qoheleth does not mean "Do not be too righteous" but "Do not strive too hard to achieve righteousness"—that is, through an excessive concentration on legal observance or pious practices. Scholars have suggested two alternative reasons for the giving of such advice: (i) Such striving after perfection is not a virtue, but rather a sin: that of pride or blasphemy.[5] (ii) Such excessive behavior is not required by God, and is to be avoided: for on the one hand its goal is beyond man's capacity and so it can achieve nothing; and on the other hand it makes life joyless, leading to narrowness and bigotry. So, in one way or another, the striving after perfection produces misery.[6]

A rather different interpretation is put forward in this essay, namely that Qoheleth is not warning his readers either against an excess of righteousness nor against an excess of striving after it but against self-righteousness: against the state of mind which claims actually to have achieved righteousness or perfection.[7] Such a state of mind is often a consequence of an undue striving after perfection, but is nevertheless to be distinguished from it.

## A. Verse 16a and its immediate context

Vss. 16-17 comprise two tripartite poetical lines which appear to constitute a unit both of form and content:

| | | |
|---|---|---|
| 16a | אל־תהי צדיק הרבה | (3) |
| b | ואל־תתחכם יותר | (3) |
| c | למה תשומם | (2) |
| 17a | אל־תרשע הרבה | (2) |
| b | ואל־תהי סכל | (2) |
| c | למה תמות בלא עתך | (3) |

Their internal arrangement makes an almost symmetrical pattern of correspondences, parallels and contrasts. Each line consists of three parts, each of which begins with the same word: $^c$al, wĕ$^{\circ}$al, lāmmâ, . Each begins with a pair of negative admonitions or warnings joined by the copula, and within these there is again an almost complete parallelism: negative particle, verb or verbal clause, adverb (except in 17b where the adverb is lacking). The third clause of each line consists of an interrogative sentence introduced by lāmmâ and again followed by a verb or verbal clause. In each case the interrogative form conceals a positive assertion.

The parallel pairs 16ab, 17ab also correspond—at least ostensibly—in sense: they both refer respectively to righteousness/wickedness and wisdom/folly in an antithetic parallelism: the first appears to be a warning against "righteousness" and wisdom—or rather an excess of these qualities, the second against wickedness and folly. Three of these four clauses are qualified by harbēh or yôtēr, words functioning as adverbs with a superlative sense: "greatly, very." There is also a parallelism of sense in the two clauses 16c, 17c; they say what will happen if the advice is ignored.

A noteworthy feature of vs. 16a is that the auxiliary verb hāyâ ("to be") with an adjective ($^{\circ}$al-tĕhî ṣaddîq) is used instead of a simple verbal clause ($^{\circ}$al-tiṣdaq). The choice of this construction is especially noteworthy because both the parallel clause ($^{\circ}$al-tithakkam) and also the contrasting and corresponding clause in vs. 17a ($^{\circ}$al-tirša$^c$) use the simple verbal clause. The choice of the auxiliary construction in vs. 16a may be partly for stylistic reasons: it gives the clauses a neat chiastic form: auxiliary (16a), simple verbal clause (16b), simple verbal clause (17a), auxiliary (17b). Nevertheless it is unlikely that stylistic considerations would have overridden those of sense, and the possibility that there is some further significance in the choice of $^{\circ}$al-tĕhî ṣaddîq rather than $^{\circ}$al-tiṣdaq needs to be examined.

I

The use of the construction hāyâ + adjective (or noun) to express a continuous state of affairs or a permanent characteristic would of course have been unavoidable if no verb cognate with the adjective had existed. It would also have been a natural choice if the verb in question existed, but was not in common use. But when, as here, the auxiliary construction is used in preference to a cognate verb which is in common use the question arises whether it conveys some particular nuance which distinguishes it from the latter.

Such cases appear to be relatively rare; and usually there is some special reason for the choice of this construction. Among these reasons, which sometimes occur in combination, are the following: syntactical necessity or convenience; the desire to give special emphasis to a particular word; play on words; the existence of a technical or special meaning of the adjective or noun which cannot be conveyed by the verb; and the need to indicate the continuing existence of a state of affairs where the use of the verb might imply a single action. It would also appear—though in view of our limited knowledge of the range of biblical Hebrew this is difficult to assess—that in some cases, even though the verb in question occurs relatively frequently, the even greater frequency of the adjective has led to the choice of the latter rather than the former. Some examples may clarify the matter.

In Gen 3:1 (wĕhannāḥāš hāyâ ᶜārûm, "Now the serpent was wise(r)"), the adjective ᶜārûm may have been chosen for emphasis or because of the rarity of the verb ᶜāram, which occurs only four times in the qal; but the choice was more probably made for the sake of a play on the words ᶜārûm ("crafty") here and the plural adjective ᶜărûmmîm ("naked") in 2:25.

In Gen 34:25 bihĕyôtām kō²ăbîm, "while they were still sore," indicates a continuous state which the simple verb would not unambiguously convey.

In Gen 39:6 wayĕhî yôsēp yĕpēh-tō²ar wîpēh mar²eh, "And Joseph was handsome and good-looking," could hardly have been expressed by the rather rare verb yāpâ (which only occurs six times in the qal) because of the double qualification of Joseph's beauty. The repetition of the verb would have been clumsy.

In Exod 23:9 (gērîm hĕyîtem, "you were sojourners"), gēr is a technical term, and the verb gûr would therefore be inadequate to express the exact meaning intended.

In Deut 23:15 (Engl. 23:14) (wĕhāyâ mahănêykā qādôš, "and your camp shall be holy")[8] the adjective was probably chosen because the verb is rather rare in the qal and almost exclusively used[9] of things becoming "holy" as the result of contact with other holy things or persons.

In Josh 19:9 (kî-hāyâ ḥēleq bĕnê-yĕhûdâ rab mēhem, "for the portion received by the sons of Judah was too large for them") the choice of the adjective rab rather than the verb rābab may be due to the fact that the verb, though not entirely rare, is much less frequently used than the adjective, and also in order to emphasize that the meaning here is not "become (too) large" but "be (too) large."

In Job 1:1 wĕhāyâ hā²îš hahû² tām wĕyāšār, "and the man was perfect and upright," is more emphatic than would have been the use of the verbs tāmam and yāšar, which would necessarily have stood at the beginning of the sentence.

In Job 1:3 (wayĕhî hā²îš hahû² gādôl, "and the man was great") the adjective is used partly for the same reason as in Job 1:1 but mainly because the verb *gādal* normally means "grow up" rather than "be great."

In Ezek 18:5 there occurs the only example, apart from Qoh 7:16, of the use of *hāyâ* as an auxiliary verb followed by the adjective *ṣaddîq: wĕʾîš kî-yihyeh ṣaddîq wĕʿāśâh mišpāṭ ûṣĕdāqâ . . .*', "And if a man is righteous and does what is just and righteous. . . ." Here it would seem that Ezekiel has been influenced by the formula *ṣaddîq hûʾ*, "he is in the right," belonging to the priestly formula of judgment, and which he himself quotes at the end of this paragraph (vs. 9); and that he is, therefore, using *ṣaddîq* as a technical term. In fact he uses the verb *ṣādaq* in the qal only once, in the familiar phrase *ṣādaq min-*, "to be more righteous than. . . ." There may also be another reason for his choice of the adjective here. The remainder of this long and complex stentence—it ends only in verse 9—consists of a series of clauses which together define what Ezekiel means by *ṣaddîq*. These are all simple verbal clauses, beginning with *wĕʿāśâ*, "and does," which immediately follows *ṣaddîq*. The adjective is therefore most probably used here to distinguish the general designation of the category of person whose actions are then defined—that is, the *ṣaddîq*—from the defining clauses. If the verb *ṣādaq* had been used the sense would not have been clear.

Finally the use by Qoheleth himself elsewhere in his book of the construction *hāyâ +* adjective (or noun) must be considered. Apart from the two occurrences in 7:16-17 there are three such cases: 1:12; 2:19; 12:9.

In 1:12 (*ʾănî qōhelet hāyîtî melek ʿal-yiśrāʾēl bîrûšālāyim*, "I, Qoheleth, was king over Israel in Jerusalem"), the noun *melek* is clearly more appropriate than the verb *mālak*, even though "was king" is a possible translation of either expression. This is the formal opening of the "autobiographical" section of the book, the "Solomonic fiction." As has been pointed out by several commentators,[10] it is in the same tradition as that of the opening phrases of the type of composition known as the "royal instruction"; it is also reminiscent of the opening words of royal inscriptions.[11] The use of *melek* formally identifies the speaker, not only stating the fact that he ruled over Israel in Jerusalem, but also giving the title of the office which he held: that of *melek*, king.

In all the other instances in Ecclesiastes, including those currently under discussion (7:16, 17), the noun or adjective which accompanies the verb *hāyâ* is either *ḥākām*, "wise," or *sākāl*, "fool." In 2:19 (*ûmî yôdēaʿ hehākām yihyeh ʾô sākāl*, "And who knows whether he will be a wise man or a fool"), it would have been impossible to use verbs instead of adjectives, since in biblical (and also Mishnaic) Hebrew—as far as is known—there is no verb *sākal* in the qal meaning "to be a fool."[12] Qoheleth therefore had no alternative to the use of *hāyâ* with the adjective *sākāl*, and was consequently also bound to use the adjective *ḥākām* instead of the verb. In 7:17 also there was no verbal alternative to the adjective *sākāl*.

The remaining instance, 12:9, occurs in the passage generally attributed to one or more "epilogists," but it may be assumed that the style of the pupil is comparable with that of his teacher. Why did he write *hāyâ qōhelet ḥākām* instead of using the verb? It is unlikely that he had, in general, any reluctance to use the verb *ḥākam*, since Qoheleth himself uses it three times: in 2:15 (*lāmmâ ḥākamtî ʾănî*, "Why have I been wise?"; in 2:19, where both constructions are used: "Who knows whether he will be a wise man (*heḥākām yihyeh*) or a fool? Yet he will be master of all for which I toiled and exercised wisdom (*ḥākamtî*) under the sun," and in 7:23: *ʾāmartî ʾeḥkāmâ*, "I said, I will be wise." It would seem that in 12:9 the adjective *ḥākām* is used to denote a member of a certain category of intellectual persons, that of the "wise man," that is, the man who not only is wise in a general way but has acquired a reputation for being so. Whether or not this class of person can rightly be described in professional terms,[13] the use of *ḥākām* here falls into the same general category as *melek* in 1:12: it has a special, almost technical sense which the verb *ḥākam* is incapable of expressing.

The various examples given above suggest that in Qoh 7:16a also the choice of *ʾal-tĕhî ṣaddîq* rather than *ʾal-tiṣdaq* is not due to chance or to purely stylistic considerations, but has a deliberate purpose; and of the possible reasons for its choice the most plausible is that it was made in order to give some special meaning to the word *ṣaddîq* which could not be conveyed by the use of the verb. It is the contention of this essay that the phrase refers to the self-righteous man, the would-be *ṣaddîq*, the man who claims to be, or sees himself as, exceptionally righteous. This hypothesis will be tested in various ways with reference to the context in which it stands.

## II

The meaning of *ṣaddîq* elsewhere in Ecclesiastes must first be considered. As in other books of the OT, Qoheleth regularly uses the term in contrast to *rāšāʿ*, "wicked."[14] He has clearly taken over from the earlier wisdom literature the use of these terms in an ethical sense: they do not need to be defined more closely than the words "righteous" and "wicked" in English.[15] At the same time he recognizes that in the strict sense there is no *ṣaddîq* in existence (7:20). He does not distinguish between "righteous" and "perfect"; but uses the same word for both. There is no reason to suppose that in 7:16 he is using the term in any sense other than a general one: nothing is known of any closely defined group of people in his time known as the *ṣaddîqîm*. But if this is so, he must be using the term in an ironical sense: "Do not be a self-styled *ṣaddîq*."[16]

## III

We must further ask what is the meaning of *harbēh* here. This word is frequently translated in this verse by "too, over-, excessively," giving color to the view that Qoheleth is warning his readers against being "too righteous." But in fact neither in Ecclesiastes[17] nor elsewhere in the OT does *harbēh* have the sense of "too." Its meaning is always "much, many, great(ly), very" and the like: in other words, it has a superlative sense, but does not express any value-judgment such as is implied by "too great," "too much" etc. In Qoh 7:16 it is best taken as qualifying the whole of the preceding phrase. Qoheleth is not telling his readers that righteousness is a quality which can be, but should not be, overdone. Rather he uses the qualifying adverb *harbēh* to indicate that he recognizes a tendency in human nature towards self-righteousness: it is a common failing, and consequently his admonition ought not to be taken as a harsh general condemnation. He wishes to make it clear that his warning is directed not against his innate human tendency, but against the extreme cases: against the man who persistently and without qualification claims to be a *ṣaddîq*. His meaning is "Do not allow self-righteousness to become your dominating characteristic." It is therefore not correct to speak here of a golden mean applied to moral conduct, of an incitement to steer a moderate course between goodness and wickedness. What we have here is rather a gentle warning which takes account of human weakness.

IV

We next consider whether the parallel clause vs. 16b supports the above hypothesis. Vs. 16b does not use the construction of *hāyâ* with an adjective but simply the verb *hkm* in the hithpael. Does this construction correspond in meaning to *ʾal-těhî saddîq*?[18]

Clearly in using the hithpael of *hkm*, which occurs in only one other passage in the OT(*nithakkěmâ*, "Let us behave wisely, let us show our cleverness," Exod 1:10), Qoheleth did not intend simply to say "Do not be extremely wise." Of the meanings generally attributed to the hithpael[19] only three would yield any sense at all in Qoh 7:16: "to conduct oneself in a particular way" (as in Exod 1:10); "imagine/set oneself up to be" (as in *hiśtārēr*, "set oneself up to be a prince," Num 16:13); "pretend to be" (as in *hithāl*, "pretend to be ill," 2 Sam 13:5). In Qoh 7:16b the first of these would yield the meaning "Do not act with great wisdom," which can hardly be what is intended. Either of the last two senses—they in any case overlap—would make much better sense here and would fit well with the above interpretation of *ʾal-těhî saddîq* in vs. 16a. Having first warned his readers against setting themselves up to be, or pretending to be, absolutely righteous, Qoheleth now warns them against similar pretensions to wisdom.

If then the connotations of 16a and 16b are similar in that they both warn against certain human pretensions, why did not Qoheleth use the same grammatical constructions to express his meaning? It was the limitations of the Hebrew language which prevented him from doing this if his meaning was to be unambiguous. In vs. 16a the qal of *ṣdq* would not have carried the required meaning, and the hithpael might have been misunderstood as meaning "to justify oneself," as for example in Gen 44:16, *mah-niṣṭaddāq*, "How shall we justify ourselves?" Similarly the qal of *hkm* would have conveyed the meaning "Do not be very wise," which was not what Qoheleth wished to say, nor would the use of the adjective *hākām* have been clear, since the phrase might have been taken to mean "Moreover, do not become a ḥākām," that is, do not join the ranks of the learned men known as ḥākām, again a meaning which Qoheleth did not intend: indeed, he was himself known as a ḥākām (12:9), and he elsewhere indicates that he approves of such men, even though he also realizes the limitations of their knowledge and of its usefulness. In fact he had no choice of grammatical constructions if he wished to say unambiguously "Do not claim to be a ṣaddîq, and do not make great pretensions to wisdom." The use of the hithpael in vs. 16b therefore confirms the view expressed above about the meaning of vs. 16a.

## V

Consideration must now be given to vs. 17a, which is linked by a different kind of parallelism to vs. 16a. Here, as in vs. 16a, the word harbēh has been misunderstood by the commentators. ʾal-tiršaᶜ harbēh does not mean "Do not be too wicked" but "Do not be very wicked." The nuance is important. The admonition does not mean that a certain amount of wickedness is permissible, provided that one does not overdo it! As in vs. 16a, harbēh is a concession to human frailty. Vs. 17 as a whole is to be taken as a—perhaps somewhat ironical—counterbalance to vs. 16 rather than as parallel in meaning to it. Having warned his readers against pretensions to righteousness and wisdom, Qoheleth then adds a warning not to go to the other extreme and throw off all restraints and all striving towards these virtues, abandoning oneself to a life of crime or folly. But again he does not want to be too hard on his readers: he knows that one cannot entirely avoid either wickedness or folly (cf. vs. 20), and so he adds the word harbēh: what is to be avoided is the carrying of them to extremes. Once again there is no encouragement to immorality, but a recognition of human frailty.

## VI

It must further be asked whether additional light is shed on the meaning of the admonitions in vss. 16ab, 17ab by the questions which follow each pair: vss. 16c, 17c. In the first of these, lāmmâ tiššômēm, the meaning of tiššômēm is disputed. The phrase is most frequently translated "Why should you destroy yourself?," although some of the Versions have "be astonished." The context shows clearly that the phrase is intended to state the consequence of the two actions against which the reader has been warned. It is generally agreed that tiššômēm is an anomalous variant of titšômēm, the hithpoel of šmm, a verb which in its various parts appears in the OT in two senses, "be desolated, laid waste" and "be appalled, horrified" (usually at the fate of others). Although the hithpoel in its other occurrences[20] has the latter meaning, the Versions can hardly be right in giving it this meaning in Qoh 7:16. Both the immediate context and the parallel phrase in vs. 17c ("Why should you die before your time?") show that here it must have the former meaning: it must refer to some undesirable consequence which will befall the person who ignores the foregoing admonitions.

But the use of the verb elsewhere in the OT gives little indication of the precise nature of such a calamity in relation to an individual. In the great majority of cases—apart from those in which it means "be appalled"—it refers to the destruction of a land, or of its people, cities, crops, trees etc. by the action of a human enemy or an angry God. Very rarely is it applied to an individual or a group of individuals. However there are some examples of this: Tamar, who after her rape by Amnon, dwelt šōmēmâ (qal participle, meaning either "ruined" or "in isolation") in the house of Absalom (2 Sam 13:20), and the delicately nurtured Jerusalemites "perishing" (nāšammû, niphal) in the streets of the ruined city (Lam 4:5).

In their interpretations of this phrase in vs. 16c the translations and commentaries can be divided into two classes: the majority, which avoid a precise interpretation and restrict themselves to the general sense of "destruction": "Why should you destroy yourself?"— a meaning similar to that of ᵓōbēd in vs. 15—and those who attempt to define more closely what kind of "destruction" is intended. Among the latter, Power,[21] following the idea of desertion or isolation which may be the meaning of the verb in some passages, translates "ostracize thyself," and NEB, probably following the same line of thought, "make yourself a laughing-stock." Others suggest that the phrase refers to the joyless life which would be the consequence of the effort to be a ṣaddîq: "make your life horrible" (Scott);[22] "drive yourself too hard" (JB).

The meanings of šmm derived from the study of its other occurrences in the OT do not justify such precise interpretations, some of which appear not to be really independent but to have been chosen to fit particular interpretations of the word ṣaddîq earlier in the verse. Our knowledge of the verb is insufficient to justify any such precise interpretation. Nor, since, as has been indicated, vss. 16 and 17 are not parallel in thought but consecutive, does vs. 17c (lāmmâ tāmût bĕlōᵓ ᶜittekā) necessarily throw any light on it. It has been suggested[23] that the latter phrase indicates that Qoheleth retained in his beliefs a remnant of a doctrine of retribution: while in ordinary cases there appears to be no necessary connection between human behavior and human fortunes, a premature death is nevertheless to be expected in cases of exceptional wickedness or folly. Whether tiššômēm in vs. 16c testifies to a belief that self-righteousness and pretensions to wisdom, if pushed too far, will similarly be punished by divine intervention it is not possible to determine. Tiššômēm evidently refers to some expected calamity, but this could well be through a purely human cause: such pretensions rarely go unpunished by society.

We may note here Zimmerli's suggestion[24] that the use of the interrogative form ("Why should. . . ?") in vss. 16c, 17c is an indication that Qoheleth was uncertain whether disregard of his admonitions would or would not result in calamity, or was at least hesitant to affirm that they would. But this interpretation of the interrogative form cannot be accepted. The use in biblical Hebrew of interrogative forms to convey positive assertions is well known;[25] and among these *lāmmâ* followed by the imperfect is an established idiom: far from indicating doubt or hesitancy it is a particularly emphatic way of saying that if a particular course of action is not followed something undesirable will quite certainly occur. So in such passages as Gen 27:45; 47:19; Exod 32:12; 2 Sam 20:19; 2 Kgs 14:10; Pss 79:10; 115:2; Joel 2:17 the speaker has no doubt whatever about the outcome: e.g. in Gen 47:19 ("Why should we die before your eyes?") the starving Egyptians are in no doubt that they will die of hunger if they do not sell themselves and their land to Joseph; and in 2 Kgs 14:10 ("Why should you provoke trouble so that you fall?") Jehoash is warning Amaziah that if he attacks him he will certainly be defeated: to say that he *might perhaps* suffer defeat would entirely rob his speech of its force.

There is a further example of this idiom in Ecclesiastes itself: "Why should God be angry at your voice, and destroy the work of your hands?" (5:5 [Engl. 5:6]). In a previous verse (5:3 [Engl. 5:4]) Qoheleth has just made it clear that "God has no pleasure in fools," so it may be assumed that the construction *lāmmâ + imperfect* here also indicates certain and not merely possible destruction.

VII

It must further be asked whether the linking of the themes of righteousness (*ṣdq*) and wickedness (*ršᶜ*) with those of wisdom (*ḥkm*) and folly (*skl*) in verses 16 and 17 provides further elucidation of the meaning of vs. 16a. The evidence of the rest of the book suggests that for Qoheleth, as for earlier wisdom writers, these concepts are indeed very closely associated. In 9:1 ("The righteous and the wise and their deeds are in the hand of God") it is difficult to distinguish any difference of meaning between them. In the earlier wisdom books the connection between the two was principally the belief in retribution: since righteousness is the only kind of behavior which can lead to happiness and prosperity, its pursuit is clearly the mark of a wise man and its neglect or rejection the mark of a fool. Qoheleth has in general (e.g. in vs. 15) rejected the validity of this connection, though some passages suggest that he had reservations on the subject. Nevertheless wisdom remained for him a virtue, and one closely associated with God: it is his gift (2:26). It is therefore natural that he should associate the two qualities in 7:16 as he does in 9:1, making little or no distinction between them. Vs. 16ab (as also vs. 17ab) seems to be a poetical parallelism, in which the second clause echoes the first rather than making a material addition to it.

If this is so, vs. 16b does throw further light on the meaning of vs. 16a. *ʾal-tithakkam*, as has been argued above, means "do not claim wisdom for yourself." Now the person who claims or pretends to be wise is, according to traditional wisdom teaching, precisely the person who *lacks* both wisdom and righteousness.[26] *ʾal-tithakkam* is thus a warning against a form of folly, not in any sense against wisdom. This renders it the more probable that the parallel phrase ʾal-těhî ṣaddîq has the meaning which we have proposed for it. Qoheleth is not advising his readers against either righteousness as such or against an excess of it. The self-styled ṣaddîq is basically unrighteous just as the self-styled wise man is a fool.

We may conclude that in vss. 16-17 Qoheleth is neither recommending immorality nor teaching the golden mean. In vs. 16 he warns his readers against self-righteousness and against pretensions to wisdom especially when carried to extremes. In vs. 17 he attempts to guard himself against the possibility of being misunderstood by urging them not to run to the opposite extreme and abandon righteousness altogether, for wickedness and folly, when carried to extremes, are even more perilous: the man who follows such a course will without doubt die an early death at the hands of his contemporaries if not at the hand of God. Qoheleth nowhere advises his readers to steer a middle course between righteousness and wickedness.

## B. *The Wider Context*

It remains now to test this interpretation against the context in which vss. 16-17 stand. Since there is no general agreement among modern interpreters about the limits of this context as a literary unit or section of the book it will be best to examine this question by working forwards and backwards from vss. 16-17.

### I

Vs. 18 is a difficult verse. It is, however, generally recognized that in 18a ("It is good that you should take hold of this (bāzeh): and from this (mizzeh) do not withhold your hand"), "this" and "this" can only refer to the two pairs of admonitions in vss. 16 and 17. Vs. 18 is then the continuation of those verses, and the purpose of 18a is to give additional emphasis to their teaching. The main problem of the verse lies in its second half: kî-yěrēʾ ʾělōhîm yēṣēʾ ʾet-kullām. Here there is general agreement on two points: kî, "for," introduces a reason supporting the statement made in the first half of the verse, so in turn supporting vss. 16-17; and kullām refers to zeh . . . zeh and should be translated "both." It is also agreed that "he who fears God" describes the person who takes the advice given in those verses.

But what is meant by yēṣēʾ ʾet-kullām? The interpretations which have been offered of the meaning of the verb yāṣāʾ in this passage can be divided into two groups.[27]

1. "escape from, avoid."[28] According to this view the man who fears God is the man who avoids both extremes and steers a middle course between excessive righteousness (or wisdom) and excessive wickedness (or folly): the man who follows the "golden mean." But if this is so yāṣāʾ is the wrong verb to have used. Vs. 18a has turned the negative admonitions of vss. 16-17 into positives: "*It is good* that you *should* grasp the one and not withhold your hand from the other." We should then expect Qoheleth to say that the God-

fearer should *do* these things (using, e.g., the verb ʿāśâ), not that he should avoid them![29]

2. "do one's duty."[30] This interpretation has been most convincingly argued by Gordis.[31] Yāṣāʾ is used in this sense in the Mishnah, where it is an abbreviated form of the expression yṣʾ (m)ydy ḥwbh, "to be released from the power of an obligation (by fulfilling it)." This translation is supported by Vulg.'s *nihil negligit* and by Rashi. Gordis therefore translates yēṣēʾ ʾet-kullām by "will do his duty by both."[32] This positive interpretation of yāṣāʾ is the easier to accept in view of the similarity of Qoheleth's Hebrew in many respects to that of the Mishnah. A positive sense for it also makes much better sense in the context of vss. 16-18 than the negative "avoid."

The proponents of this meaning have not, however, appreciated its significance for the interpretation of vss. 16-18 as a whole. Except for those (e.g. Barton)[33] who regard vs. 18b as a gloss, they concur with the supporters of the negative interpretation of yāṣāʾ in that they also believe that Qoheleth is advocating the golden mean: whereas the other group of interpreters understands yāṣāʾ as meaning that the golden mean is to be achieved by avoiding the extremes of conduct, they understand it as meaning that it is to be achieved by carrying out Qoheleth's recommendations to avoid them. Their interpretation of yāṣāʾ has not in any way affected their interpretation of the passage as a whole.

But in fact the positive interpretation of yāṣāʾ permits a quite different interpretation of the passage, namely the interpretation which has been suggested in this essay, that Qoheleth is recommending not an excess of righteousness but of *self*-righteousness, not an excess of wisdom but of pretensions to wisdom (vs. 16), as well as warning against wickedness and folly (vs. 17). Once the idea of "avoiding" something has been shown not to be present in the passage it is possible to see that there is no question of "steering a course between extremes." Qoheleth's advice is positive: "Do not sin in either of these two ways."

This entirely moral conduct recommended in vss. 16-17 is then identified by Qoheleth with the fear of God. It is this identification which, in the opinion of the present writer, proves that the above exegesis is correct. The supporters of the golden mean theory are obliged, unless they regard vs. 18b as a gloss, to hold that Qoheleth's concept of the fear of God is entirely different from its meaning elsewhere in the OT: that for him it expresses the entirely immoral doctrine of the golden mean applied in the ethical sphere—the demoralization of righteousness. It may be, as some have argued,[34] that "the fear of God" has a somewhat different connotation in Qoheleth than it has elsewhere; but there is no reason, especially in view of 8:12-13, where the God-fearer is regarded as the opposite of the wicked man (rāšāʿ), to suppose such a total, extraordinary and indeed confusing reversal of its meaning. Such a view receives no support from the rest of the book. The evidence suggests that for Qoheleth the designation "he who fears God" is the highest accolade of moral virtue that can be bestowed.

## II

The connection of vss. 16-17 with vs. 15 is far more problematical. Vs. 15 ("In my vain life I have seen everything; there is a righteous man (ṣaddîq) who perishes in his righteousness, and there is a wicked man (rāšāᶜ) who prolongs his life in his evil-doing") is a clear statement that Qoheleth has learned from his observation of life that there is no necessary connection between human behavior and good or evil fortune. It is usually assumed that this verse is the beginning of the section in which vss. 16-17 occur, and that the function of those verses is to draw practical conclusions from Qoheleth's experience of life: if moral conduct does not affect one's fortunes, there is no point in being either very righteous or very wicked. But this assumption is improbable for two reasons. First, it makes sense only of the first pair of admonitions, not of the second: why should one not be wicked, if wickedness is at least as likely to bring good fortune as righteousness? Secondly, it makes nonsense of the two questions in vss. 16c, 17c. The paradox would be too harsh even for Qoheleth. It therefore seems improbable that vs. 15, in spite of the recurrence of ṣdq and ršᶜ both there and in vss. 16-17, was originally connected with those verses. Rather, its connection is with vs. 14. That verse states that God has prevented men from discerning what the future holds for them; in vs. 15 Qoheleth confirms this assertion from his own experience: he has been unable to discover any connection between men's conduct and their subsequent fortunes.

## III

It is not necessary in this essay to pursue further the question of the context of vss. 16-17. It is usually supposed that the section continues up to at least vs. 22. But a real sequence of thought after vs. 18 can only be found by a series of *tours de force*. The only verse among vss. 19-22 which has any direct relevance to vss. 16-18 is vs. 20: "Surely there is not a righteous man (ṣaddîq) on earth who does good and never sins." This statement is fully in accord with ᵓal-tĕhî ṣaddîq harbēh in v. 16a: it provides support for the warning against self-righteousness. If it occurred immediately before or after vs. 16 it would fit the context reasonably well. But in its present position, separated from vss. 16-18 by the quite unrelated vs. 19, it cannot be said to belong to the same context and should be treated as a separate saying.

Qoheleth, then, is no immoralist. His advice in 7:16a shows that, on the contrary, he is the enemy of false righteousness just as he is of false pretensions to wisdom.

---

[1] Cf. *RSV* "Do not be righteous overmuch"; *JB* "Do not be over-virtuous"; *NEB* "Do not be over-righteous."

[2] Its precise meaning (together with that of the nouns ṣedeq/ṣĕdāqâ) has been the subject of

much recent discussion. In the context of Qoh 7:16, however, "righteous" may be regarded as an adequate rendering.

3 However, D. B. Macdonald, (*The Hebrew Philosophical Genius* [Princeton: Princeton University, 1936; reprinted, New York: Russell and Russell, 1965] 86) goes as far as to say that according to Qoheleth "to live successfully in the world you must be amoral. . . . You must be prepared to be . . . moral or immoral . . . as . . . events require." Cf. also G. A. Barton, *Ecclesiastes* (ICC; Edinburgh: Clark, 1908) 143-44.

4 Almost every commentator speaks directly or indirectly of Qoheleth's doctrine of the golden mean, though this only implies immoral teaching on his part if vs. 16a has the meaning usually attributed to it.

5 So E. Plumptre, *Ecclesiastes* (Cambridge Bible for Schools and Colleges: Cambridge: Cambridge University, 1891) 167; H. W. Hertzberg, *Der Prediger* (KAT 17/4; Gütersloh: Mohn, 1963) 152-55; A. Strobel, *Das Buch Prediger (Kohelet)* (Die Welt der Bibel; Düsseldorf: Patmos-Verlag, 1967) 112-15; W. Zimmerli, *Das Buch des Predigers Salomo* (ATD 16; Göttingen: Vandenhoeck & Ruprecht, 1962) 209-10; E. Glasser, *Le procès du bonheur par Qohelet* (LD 61; Paris: Editions du Cerf, 1970) 116-17.

6 Note the translations of vs. 16c by *JB* ("Why drive yourself too hard?"), *NEB* ("Why make yourself a laughing-stock?") and R. B. Y. Scott ("Why make your life horrible?"), *Proverbs. Ecclesiastes* (AB 18; New York: Doubleday, 1965) 236; see also M. Jastrow, *A Gentle Cynic* (Philadelphia and London: Lippincott, 1919) 169-70.

7 This is also the view of G. R. Castellino, "Qohelet and his Wisdom," *CBQ* 30 (1968) 23-24. It is also perhaps suggested by G. Wildeboer (*Der Prediger* [Kurzer Hand-Commentar zum Alten Testament 17; ed. M. Marti; Freiburg i. B.: Mohr, 1898] 146) and by E. Podechard, (*L'Ecclésiaste* [EBib; Paris: Gabalda, 1912] 375-76).

8 On the apparently plural form *maḥăne(y)kā* see GKC (2d Engl. rev. ed.; Oxford: Clarendon, 1910) § 93*ss*.

9 Exod 29:21, 37; 30:29; Lev. 6:11, 20 (Engl. 6:18, 27); 17:2, 3 (Engl. 16:37, 38); Deut 22:9; Hag 2:12. The text in 1 Sam 21:6; Isa 65:5 is uncertain.

10 H. W. Hertzberg, *Der Prediger*, 82; W. Zimmerli, *Das Buch des Predigers Salomo*, 151; K. Galling, *Der Prediger* (HAT 1/18; 2d ed.; Tübingen, Mohr, 1969) 88.

11 R. B. Y. Scott, *Proverbs. Ecclesiastes*, 212-13.

12 Although other parts of the verb occur, these do not have the simple sense "to be a fool."

13 See R. N. Whybray, *The Intellectual Tradition in the Old Testament* (BZAW 135; Berlin: de Gruyter, 1974) 46-48.

14 3:17; 7:15; 8:14; 9:2.

15 Note the relationship between *ṣedeq* and *mišpāṭ* in 3:16; 5:7 (Engl. 5:8).

16 The remark of R. E. Murphy ("The Pensées of Coheleth," *CBQ* 17 [1955] 190) that there is an element of mockery in vss. 15-18 deserves to be borne in mind. See also his "A Form-Critical Consideration of Ecclesiastes VII," *SBL Seminar Papers* 1 (Cambridge, MA: Society of Biblical Literature, 1974) 77-85.

17 1:16; 2:7; 5:6; 11, 16, 19 (Engl. 5:7, 12, 17, 20); 6:11; 9:18; 11:8; 12:9, 12.

18 On this question see also Castellino, "Qohelet and his Wisdom."

19 GKC § 54*e*.

20 Isa 59:16; 63:5; Ps 143:4; Dan 8:27.

21 A. D. Power, *Ecclesiastes or The Preacher* (London: Longmans, 1952) 44, 95.

22 R. B. Y. Scott, *Proverbs. Ecclesiastes*, 236.

23 E.g. by Hertzberg (*Der Prediger*, 153-54) and Galling (*Der Prediger*, 107-08). See also Podechard, *L'Ecclésiaste*, 179; J. Pedersen, "Scepticisme israélite," *RHPR* 10 (1930) 359; and E. Glasser, *Le procès du bonheur par Qohelet*, 199-201.

24 Made by W. Zimmerli, *Das Buch des Predigers Salomo*, 210.

25 On the use of questions in the OT see R. N. Whybray, *The Heavenly Counsellor in Isaiah xl 13-14* (Society for Old Testament Study Monograph Series 1; Cambridge: Cambridge University, 1971) 19-26.

[26] Prov 3:7; 12:15; 26:12, 16; 28:11; cf. Isa 5:21. On this point see also Castellino, "Qohelet and his Wisdom," 24.

[27] There is no justification for emending yēṣēʾ to yôṣîʾ with Scott.

[28] G. Wildeboer (Der Prediger, 147), H. W. Hertzberg (Der Prediger, 137, 141, 154-55), A. Barucq (Ecclésiaste [VS 3; Paris: Beauchesne, 1968] 130), and W. Zimmerli (Das Buch des Predigers Salomo, 209-10). G. A. Barton (Ecclesiastes, 144) and A. D. Power (Ecclesiastes, 44, 96) take the sentence as a gloss.

[29] So also E. Podechard, L'Ecclésiaste, 378.

[30] This interpretation was already proposed by Grätz and Delitzsch and has been accepted by Barton (Ecclesiastes, 143-44). Podechard (L'Ecclésiaste, 377-78), O. S. Rankin ("The Book of Ecclesiastes: Introduction and Exegesis," IB 5 [New York and Nashville: Abingdon, 1956] 67), R. Kroeber (Der Prediger [Schriften und Quellen der Alten Welt 13; Berlin: Akademie-Verlag, 1963] 97, 119), Galling (Der Prediger, 107-08) and NEB.

[31] R. Gordis, Koheleth — The Man and his World (Texts and Studies of the Jewish Theological Seminary of America 19; 2d ed.; New York: Black, 1955) 267-68.

[32] Cf. Plumptre, "does his duty" (Ecclesiastes, 168), Barton, "shall be quit in regard to both" (Ecclesiastes, 143-44), Rankin, "will fulfill his duties in every case" (IB 5, 67), Kroeber and Galling, "tut beidem Genüge" (Der Prediger, 97; Der Prediger, 107), and NEB, "will succeed both ways."

[33] G. A. Barton, Ecclesiastes, 144.

[34] The interpretations of the phrase in Qoheleth in fact differ very widely: see, e.g., Hertzberg (Der Prediger, 154-55) and Kroeber (Der Prediger, 146), and also Pedersen, "Scepticisme israélite," 361; E. Würthwein, Die Weisheit Ägyptens und das Alte Testament (Schriften der Phillips-Universität Marburg 6; Marburg: Elwert Verlag, 1960) 14; reprinted in E. Würthwein, Wort und Existenz (Göttingen: Vandenhoeck & Ruprecht, 1970) 200; H. Gese, "Die Krisis der Weisheit bei Koheleth," Les Sagesses du Proche-Orient Ancien (Paris: Presses Universitaires de France, 1963) 150-51; W. Zimmerli, "Ort und Grenze der Weisheit im Rahmen der alttestamentliche Theologie," Les Sagesses du Proche-Orient Ancien, 135 (Engl. SJT 17 [1964] 158); E. Pfeiffer, "Die Gottesfurcht im Buche Kohelet," Gottes Wort und Gottes Land (Hertzberg Festschrift; ed. H. Graf Reventlow; Göttingen: Vandenhoeck & Ruprecht, 1965) 133-58.

# THE SHADOW OF DEATH IN QOHELETH

JAMES L. CRENSHAW

THE DIVINITY SCHOOL, VANDERBILT UNIVERSITY, NASHVILLE, TENNESSEE
37240

A STRIKING inconsistency in Job's attitude toward death prompted Samuel Terrien to write at length about "Fear and Fascination of Death" in *Job: Poet of Existence.*[1] In his view, Job went through three stages in his flirtation with death, while being tossed about between the fear and fascination of death. In 3:11-19 Job passed *from hatred of life to love of death*, as if in total agreement with Sophocles: "Not to be born is the most to be desired; but having seen the light, the next best thing is to go whence one came as soon as may be" (*Oedipus at Colonus*, 1225-28). A decisive change occurred in 6:8-13, where the earlier wish to escape gave way to *strong desire to remain faithful to a God of love.* At this stage Job went after death "not because he hated life, but because he feared, through the disintegration of his personality, the weakening of his will to trust."[2] In 7:1-21 Job no longer pursued death as solace or safeguard; instead, *fear of death replaced its fascination.*

This pilgrimage from a death wish that sprang from hatred of life, to a desire for death as a preventive of unfaithfulness to God, and ultimately to terror before death's power suffices to explain why at one moment Job calls for strangulation (Job 7:15), and complains of life's brevity at another (10:18-20). In Job's plaint about his brief stay on earth, Terrien found evidence that the suffering hero was slowly being reconciled to existence.[3]

Terrien's analysis of Job's fear and fascination of death throbs with existential pathos and theological profundity. The former reaches a high point in an observation about life's supreme irony: faith that does not know despair prevents one from forcing the riddle of self and existence; but despair kills faith, and, when carried to the extreme, may bring self-extermination.[4] Accordingly, death is taken with utmost seriousness — as worse than a hellish life, and the closing of a wound rather than the opening of a gate. The latter imagery connects with a theological observation that in unfaith "life is not worth living, for it is not the vestibule to heaven."[5] Job, who saw the futility of death, perceived the revelatory potential of creation. Still, in the presence of his friends, he faced nothingness, and even dared to suggest that in the scandal of Job's death, God would behold the void. In effect, Job "risked theological death in order to confront life in the raw."[6] As a reward, in Terrien's judgment, "God's lonely man is received into the society of God."[7]

In my study of Qoheleth I have encountered the same ambiguity about life

205

and death that Terrien found in Job.[8] On the one hand, Qoheleth writes that he hates life, and views death as something to be desired, particularly because it affords rest. On the other hand, he thinks the living have hope, albeit a qualified one. Consequently, he chases life with abandon. A study of this ambivalence in Qoheleth seems an appropriate tribute to one whose scholarship I have long admired and whose friendship I cherish.

### So I Hated Life

The starting point for a consideration of Qoheleth's attitude toward death must surely be his shocking conclusion to a series of experiments: "So I hated life because the work that is done under the sun is burdensome to me; for everything is empty and a chasing after wind" (2:17).[9] Having boasted that he had surpassed all royal predecessors in Jerusalem at acquiring wisdom (1:12-18), Qoheleth put that knowledge, painful as it was, to the test of experience (2:1-11). In each instance he raised a serious question about various answers to life's meaning. The cumulative negative verdicts forced him to ponder the value of wisdom. Noting that one fate strikes sage and fool, Qoheleth concluded that wisdom enjoys only relative advantage over folly. He reflected on approaching death, together with the resultant obliteration of all memory of his life, and pressed forward into radical denial of life's essential goodness.

Qoheleth's journey to this vantage point was a lonely one, while crowds thronged the road that led to wholesale endorsement of life as the highest good. On this well-trodden highway sages walked alongside prophets and priests, for all three believed that God usually rewarded virtue with long life, health and prosperity. The same theme punctuates their messages, whether spoken by a representative of priestly, prophetic, or sapiential thought.

> Lo, I have set before you today life and the good,
> death and the evil. . . . This day I call heaven and earth
> to witness against you. Life and death I have set
> before you, blessing and curse. Therefore, choose life
> so that you and your progeny can live.   (Deut 30:15, 19)

> For thus says the Lord to the house of Israel,
> "Seek me and live . . . Seek good, not evil,
> so that you may live . . . Hate evil, love good,
> and establish justice in the gate. Perhaps the Lord,
> God of hosts, will have compassion on the remnant of Joseph."   (Amos 5:4, 14a, 15)

> Long life is in her right hand, wealth and honor in her left . . .
> Come, eat my bread and drink the wine I have mixed.
> Leave folly, and live. Then walk in the
> path of understanding.   (Prov 3:16; 9:5-6)

With one voice those who traveled the main road identified life with the good, and looked upon death as an appropriate cipher for the evil. While an occasional prophet grew weary of life because of his special burden,[10] and others down on their luck glanced coquettishly at death,[11] the overwhelming majority seems to have equated life with the greatest good. Even those who dared to take their own life chose death because of an unbearable shame[12] or as an expression of supreme loyalty to a fallen king.[13]

At the same time that death connoted the evil that everyone sought to avoid, it also stood for the moment of transition from this world to Sheol, the land of the fathers. So long as that passage from one world into another came at the end of a long, full life, it caused no special anxiety. Just as Israelites harvested grain in season, God gathered his harvest and laid it safely away in a barn (Job 5:26). In such instances death hardly caused a wringing of the hands in despair. Furthermore, as long as corporate solidarity was the dominant mode of thinking, even an early death was amenable to belief in divine favor.[14]

For Qoheleth, too many examples of premature death canceled life's advantages. Admittedly, he can speak of death in nearly neutral terms: "A generation goes, and a generation comes; but the earth remains forever" (1:4); "a time to be born and a time to die, a time to plant and a time to pull up what was planted" (3:2). Still, we must ask whether such sayings have been affected by the stench of the tomb that H. Wheeler Robinson identified in Qoheleth.[15] Certainly the hyperbolic observation that "the woman whose heart is snares and nets and whose hands are fetters is more bitter than death" (7:26a) gives little, if any, support to a neutral understanding of death. For Qoheleth, death possesses a full measure of existential Angst.[16]

For that reason he pronounces the day of death better than the day of birth (7:1) and makes the startling declaration that it is "better to go to the house of mourning than to frequent the house of feasting, since it is the end of everyone, and the living should reflect upon it" (7:2). Pondering the moment of approaching death reminded Qoheleth of toil's futility, since its fruits will enrich his survivor, who may be a fool. Further reflection upon the injustice of hard-earned possessions falling into the hands of one who did not labor for them evoked feelings of despair.[17] Small wonder he concludes: "Sorrow is better than laughter, for in sadness of countenance a heart is glad; the heart of the wise is in a house of sorrow, and the heart of fools is in a house of gladness" (7:4).

Let it be noted that Qoheleth's despair arose in large measure from a powerful conviction that life ought to be embraced wholeheartedly. Hatred of life and a concomitant flirtation with death signal Qoheleth's fundamental opposition to injustice. Life devoid of equity, both human and divine, is hollow mockery. In such situations, death's lure can hardly be resisted.

## The Dead Find Rest

Death as rest from oppression functions as a powerful metaphor in Qoheleth's thought. Persuaded that comfort could not be found in the face of oppressors in whom power resides, he reasoned that the dead were more fortunate than the living since they are no longer subject to cruelty, and have come into a measure of rest. Better than the dead or the living, he conjectured, is the one who has never been, for (s)he has not beheld evil deeds (4:1-3). In this brief observation Qoheleth pauses twice to focus attention upon a lack of comfort for the tears of the oppressed, unless one should render the final word of verse one by *měnaqqēm* ("vindicator").[18] Similarly, he joins together chiastically all the oppressions that are done under the sun with the evil work that occurs under the sun (4:1, 3), and thus testifies to the impact of social injustice upon his thoughts about life and death.[19]

In yet another passage Qoheleth moved from an obvious injustice, this time of divine origin, to question the value of life as opposed to an aborted birth (6:1-6).[20] In this instance one who had acquired life's goods, consisting of wealth, possessions, and honor, lacked either the ability or the time to enjoy them, so that a stranger devoured them. This misfortune prompted Qoheleth to conjecture that a person who begat a hundred children and lived many years, but failed to enjoy the good and lacked a burial was less fortunate than the stillborn.

> For in vanity it [the stillborn] comes and in darkness it departs,
> and in darkness its name is covered;
> moreover, it has not seen the sun and has not known (anything);
> (yet) it has rest rather than he.   (6:4-5)

In these two texts (Qoh 4:1-3 and 6:1-6) Qoheleth seems to take a wholly positive view of death in certain circumstances. The first generalizes from an experience of common misery: since wickedness thrives on every hand, death — nay, non-existence — is better than life. Presumably, Qoheleth assumes that the innocent individual cannot throw off an oppressive yoke, and in the absence of hope, life becomes intolerable. The second text has a wholly different starting point. It recognizes that appearances often deceive, for in some instances persons who seem to be objects of divine favor bear a hidden burden. Long life does not always constitute a blessing. Sometimes a person may live to a ripe old age without having possessed the power to enjoy life at all.[21] Furthermore, an absence of proper burial[22] cancels any advantages of longevity. Consequently, no one can be assured of either, and lacking both, one becomes less fortunate than an aborted birth. At least a still-born child has no memory of unfulfilled desires while living in luxury's lap.

But Qoheleth knows that such judgments apply only to specific circumstances. Elsewhere he allows views to surface that qualify such an endorsement of death and non-existence. For example, in 7:16-17 he warns against extreme virtue and vice, and supports the counsel with two rhetorical questions: "Why should you destroy yourself?" (7:16); "Why should you die prematurely?" (7:17). Inasmuch as no one possesses power over the day of death (8:8),[23] or knowledge about the appropriate time of any significant event (3:11),[24] (s)he cannot embrace death with open arms.

Furthermore, the debilitating effects of approaching death—with its darkness (Qoh 12:2, 3b)—hardly recommend the days of death's darkness to anyone. Such is the powerful message of the final poetic allegory (12:1-8). In my view, Qoheleth suggests the correct perspective from which to interpret the somber description of death's encroachment upon one's waning years. He urges enjoyment tempered by a sobering remembrance that days of darkness will far outnumber the longest life under the sun (11:8).

Do such qualifications imply that Qoheleth did not really conceive of death as better than life? Was he led to extreme formulations that he sought to soften in further observations about death? On the surface, at least, it would seem so, for did not Qoheleth observe that a living dog has an advantage over a dead lion?

## The Living Have Hope

The context within which the supposedly positive view of life occurs bristles with polemic (8:16-9:6). Qoheleth determined to know wisdom and to perceive the expenditure of energy on earth, since sleep eludes the seeker both *by day* and by night. But God's work also escapes the eager searcher, though a sage may claim that he has actually found it. Qoheleth's boldness can hardly be missed: "But even if the wise man claims to know, he is not able to find out" (8:17b).

Still searching, Qoheleth reflected upon the fact that the righteous and wise, together with their deeds, reside in God's powerful hand, but no one knows whether God's disposition toward humans is love or hate.[25] One thing looms before them with absolute certainty: a single fate befalls righteous and unrighteous, clean and unclean, sacrificer and non-sacrificer, good and bad, swearer and the one who disdains oaths.[26] One fate puts an end to everything that is done under the sun; furthermore, human hearts are filled with evil and madness. Such is the evil Qoheleth spied out—a madness that death stills.[27]

Nevertheless, whoever is chosen among the living has hope, "for the living know that they will die, but the dead know nothing, and have no more reward, since their memory is forgotten" (9:5).[28] In addition, "their love, their hatred, their passion have already perished, and they no longer have a portion in anything that is accomplished on earth" (9:6).

To prove his point that the living have a modicum of hope, Qoheleth cites a familiar aphorism: "A living dog is better than a dead lion" (9:4b). Because of its amazing prowess as a hunter, the lion was early recognized as an apt metaphor for royalty (Gen 49:9, Hos 13:7). The lowly cur, restricted to a life of scavenging on the perimeters of human existence, functioned as a term of opprobrium. The epithet, "dog," was hurled in the faces of male prostitutes, who belonged, in the speaker's opinion, outside the domain of human beings (Deut 23:18-19). The term also became a means of self-abnegation,[29] particularly in the presence of nobility (1 Sam 24:14). One text even has a person shrink from a prophetic description of his role in a *coup d'état* with the words: "What is your servant, who is but a dog, that he should do this great thing?" (2 Kings 8:13, *RSV*).

Precisely what Qoheleth means by this aphorism remains uncertain.[30] One thing does present itself as a reasonable conclusion: knowledge that one must die seems to constitute no real advantage.[31] For that reason, Qoheleth's citation of a familiar saying hardly justifies a claim that he actually thought life was characterized by hope. Can one really say hope, which consists of knowledge that one must die, gives the living much advantage over the dead? At least those who have entered the land of darkness have sloughed off every vestige of passion and do not participate any longer in human madness.

It follows that Qoheleth's polemic against excessive claims to knowledge continues in the citation of a sapiential dictum.[32] The saying is quoted "tongue-in-cheek," and thus demands that one bestow upon it a certain ironical twist if (s)he wishes to recover Qoheleth's true intention. The hope that belongs to the living scarcely provides grounds for exultation.

The living would indeed have hope if they could depend upon God to grant life after death. Unfortunately, one returns just as (s)he came: naked (5:14). In his hand rests nothing of all that his toil accumulated, so what profit was it to have labored and spent many days burdened by life's heavy toll? (5:15-16). Man and beast share the same fate: both return to dust (3:18-20). But Qoheleth shrinks from the impact of this conclusion. Accordingly, he qualifies his scepticism by clothing it in the form of a rhetorical question: "Who knows whether man's breath ascends and animals' breath descends?" (3:21). Nevertheless, Qoheleth's "hideous caricature"[33] of the idea of God's testing his creatures (3:18) leaves little, if any, doubt about his own answer to the question. A God who tests mankind to show them that they are but beasts cannot be expected to separate the two in death. For at that very moment chance reigns.

> The race is not to the swift, nor the battle to the strong,
> nor bread to the wise, nor riches to the intelligent,
> nor favor to the men of skill; but time and chance[34]
> happen to them all.  (9:11, *RSV*)

The divine hunter's snare suddenly falls, and silence ensues.

Elsewhere Qoheleth distinguishes between dust, which returns to the earth, and breath, which returns to God who gave it (12:7). Surely here resides some foundation upon which to build an abiding hope. On the contrary, for Qoheleth goes on to sum up the meaning of the allegory on old age and death: "The emptiest emptiness, says Qoheleth, everything is empty" (12:8). One cannot imagine such a conclusion if the allusion to breath's return to God contained the slightest grounds for hope. In truth, divine support of life has vanished for Qoheleth.[35]

Now if death affords rest for the weary, and the living possess no *real* advantage over the dead, while in certain circumstances the stillborn or non-existent enjoys a superior status, suicide offers a compelling alternative to further living.[36] Its lure would seem irresistible for one who hates life and falls into despair's vice-like grip. The marvel is that Qoheleth shuns this easy resolution of his misery in favor of another powerful answer.

Go, eat your bread in joy, and drink your wine with a glad heart,
for God has already approved your behavior.
Let your clothing be white at all times,
and do not lack oil upon your head.

Enjoy life with the woman whom you love
all the days of your empty life
that he has given you under the sun —
all your empty days —
for there is no work, thought, knowledge, or wisdom
in Sheol, to which you are going.   (9:7-9a, 10b)[37]

The twofold repetition of "all the days of your empty life,"[38] together with the final sobering thought about human destiny, prove that Qoheleth has not forgotten the lessons forced upon him by death's ominous shadow. But neither has he allowed that threatening presence to rob him of fleeting pleasure, which he even dares to sanction by divine approval. One can only wonder about the source of this knowledge that God has granted approval before the act, particularly when the information comes from a person sceptical of similar claims.[39] Not only does Qoheleth deny that a sage actually discovers truth, but he also remarks in another place that the common fate that befalls sage and fool cancels any advantage of wisdom (2:13-14).[40] Despite the fact that a fool walks around in darkness, while a wise person possesses eyes, both stumble over the same obstacle: chance. As a result, Qoheleth questions his own aspirations to sagacity, and reflects upon the fact that he will die just like a fool (2:15-16). As a consequence, he hates life, because of the burdensome character of what is done under the sun. Nevertheless, he considers the sun's light sweet.[41] We have now returned to our initial observation about Qoheleth's hatred of life, and thus have come full circle. That circuitous route we have traversed has underscored a movement of thought similar to the one noted by Professor Terrien in Job. For Qoheleth it went from enthusiastic endorsement of life to flirtation with death as rest, from sheer pleasure over light's sweetness to hatred of life under certain circumstances. Truly, Qoheleth did not succumb to despair without a fight.

## Death in Proverbs and Sirach

In vain do we search canonical proverbs for this ambiguity towards death that characterizes Job and Qoheleth. Only one brief aphorism (14:13) approaches the spirit of Qoheleth's praise of mourning: "Even in laughter the heart is sad, and the end of joy is grief" (RSV).[42] Still, the author of this enigmatic text remains outside the tent within which Job and Qoheleth reside.

Death in Proverbs invariably wears the robe of bitterest foe. Men and women shun it with one accord, for nothing commends death to anyone. Those who please God escape Sheol and Abaddon's ravenous appetite, for God rewards them with riches and length of days.[43] Righteousness and the fear of the Lord prolong life; wickedness shortens it. Whereas a virtuous person may fall seven times and rise again each time, the lamp of a wicked person will be extinguished. The adulteress' feet go down to death, and the adulterer proceeds to die like an ox. No one who goes to a loose woman's house regains life, but those who visit Dame Wisdom obtain long life, riches and honor. Indeed, Wisdom is a tree of life, bestowing happiness upon those who pick her fruit. Similarly, the teaching of the wise is a fountain of life, enabling one to escape death's snares. The wicked, on the other hand, fall into a pit and all hope perishes. Such are the prevailing sentiments regarding death in the canonical proverbs.[44]

The situation is altogether different in Sirach. Here ambiguity occurs once again, although with slight variations. On the one hand, Ben Sira views death as God's instrument of punishment. Accordingly, this teacher frequently appeals to his students to reflect upon their death as a means of avoiding sin (7:36; 28:6).[45] Convinced that God has presented everyone with a choice between life and death, Ben Sira urges each person to choose wisely (15:16). Since death functions punitively, it follows that things go well for the godly one at death (1:13). Having entered the world as a result of woman's sin, death has become universal (25:24). Inasmuch as none can escape death's summons, Ben Sira manages to treat the subject half humorously. Thus he quotes an epitaph: "Remember my doom, for yours is like it: yesterday it was mine, and today it is yours" (38:22). Of course "all living beings become old like a garment, for the decree from of old is, 'You must surely die'" (14:17).

Although Ben Sira conceives of death as a punishment for sin, he also recognizes that some things are worse than death.

> Death is better than a miserable life,
> and eternal rest than chronic sickness. (30:17)
>
> My son, do not lead the life of a beggar;
> it is better to die than to beg. (40:28)
>
> Of three things my heart is afraid,
> and of a fourth I am frightened:
> The slander of a city, the gathering of a mob,
> and false accusation — all three are worse than death. (26:5) (*RSV*)

Such an understanding of reality led Ben Sira to welcome death in certain instances. He pleads for the shedding of tears in behalf of the dead who lack light, but he also encourages weeping for the fool who lacks intelligence. Actually, Ben Sira contends, one needs to weep less bitterly for the dead who have obtained rest, than for the fool, over whom mourning lasts for a lifetime (22:11).

In a single passage Ben Sira articulates the complexity of his view of death (41:1-4). Here he addresses death and laments its bitterness to one who lives at peace among his possessions, but he also concedes that death is entirely welcome to one who is in poverty, ill health, and advancing years. In a surprising conclusion, Ben Sira advises against fearing death since it is the Lord's decree for everyone, and asks: "How can you reject the good pleasure of the Most High?". Curiously, Ben Sira moves in this rhetorical question to an equation of death and divine intention, which hardly harmonizes with his belief that death results from sin.[46]

## Conclusion

To recapitulate, death for the authors of Proverbs functions in a wholly negative manner, while its ambiguity pervades the thinking of Job, Qoheleth, and Sirach. For Proverbs life signifies God's blessing, death, his curse. The universe is calculable, and God, trustworthy. He rewards virtue, and punishes vice. The sage secures his existence by observing nature and human behavior, as well as by appropriating inherited traditions. Man's ultimate limit, premature death, is controllable. Consequently, anyone who embraces death belongs to the company of evildoers. In Job a decisive change takes place. Because of a collapse in the principle of retribution, life itself assumes the form of a curse. No longer proof of divine favor, length of days merely prolongs human misery for one whose God has become a personal enemy. In such circumstances, death appears as a welcome friend, especially since it prevents loss of integrity that a weakened mind and body make likely. Qoheleth, too, refused to view life as God's gift for virtue. As a result, he shared Job's divided mind about death. Ben Sira attempted to salvage the view of Proverbs, although nuanced quite differently. For him death constituted punishment for sin, but it also hung over everyone's head as a divine decree. In addition, Ben Sira endorsed Job and Qoheleth's view that in certain instances death was preferable to life.[47] In the final resort, both Ben Sira and Qoheleth stopped short of Job's bold metaphor for death. Neither dared to use terms of endearment when addressing worms ("my mother and sister," Job 17:14b), although Ben Sira did remark that at death everyone comes into an inheritance of maggots and worms (10:11; cf. 19:3).[48] Truly, all three thinkers believed that "Quand on meurt, c'est pour longtemps."[49]

[1] Indianapolis and New York: Bobbs-Merrill, 1957, 40-65.

[2] *Job: Poet of Existence*, 55-56 (with tenses altered for stylistic reasons).

[3] Ibid., 61.

[4] Ibid., 41. Compare Ernest Becker's observation that "the irony of man's condition is that the deepest need is to be free of the anxiety of death and annihilation; but it is life itself which awakens it, and so we must shrink from being fully alive" (*The Denial of Death* [New York: Free, 1973] 66). Becker points out that we can "use anxiety as an eternal spring for growth into new dimensions of thought and trust" (p. 92).

[5] The dominant Old Testament view of death as final occurs in its stark form in 2 Sam 14:14 ("For we shall surely die, and like water that is spilled on the ground that cannot be gathered up . . ."). To this view may be compared the interesting exchange between Aqhat and Anat (*ANET*[3], 151).

[6] Terrien, *Job: Poet of Existence*, 18. Curiously, the Old Testament has provided two terms for the opposite of Job's risk, namely the evasion of life's full intensity (the Jonah syndrome) and tranquilizing oneself with trivia so as to live normal lives (Philistinism).

[7] Terrien, *Job: Poet of Existence*, 239. I do not intend to assess the validity of Terrien's analysis, but to use it as a clue for a similar study of Qoheleth. For further treatment, see Walter L. Michel, "Death in Job," *Dialog* 11 (1972) 183-89 and his Ph.D. dissertation entitled "The Ugaritic Texts and the Mythological Expressions in the Book of Job (including a New Translation of and Philological Notes on the Book of Job)," (University of Wisconsin, 1970).

[8] Fundamental differences between Job and Qoheleth grow out of their contrasting views of divine activity. For Job, death possessed the power to prevent his vindication and threatened a loss of trust in God, whereas Qoheleth needed no divine commendation, and completely lacks trust in a benevolent creator.

[9] Unless otherwise specified, translations are the author's. On *topoi* and themes in Qoheleth, see especially Oswald Loretz, *Qoheleth und der Alte Orient* (Freiburg: Herder, 1964) 196-212, 218-300.

[10] Elijah, Jeremiah, Jonah.

[11] Samson, Tobit, Joanna.

[12] Ahithophel.

[13] Saul's armorbearer.

[14] L. H. Silberman, "Death in the Hebrew Bible and Apocalyptic Literature," *Perspectives on Death* (ed. L. O. Mills; Nashville: Abingdon, 1969) 26.

[15] *Inspiration and Revelation in the Old Testament* (Oxford: Clarendon, 1946) 258. The fact that Qoheleth "reaches its climax in an eloquent but sombre picture of death" lends credibility to Robinson's observation. G. von Rad, *Wisdom in Israel* (Nashville and New York: Abingdon, 1972) 228, writes: "Behind the problem of the future, there lies for Koheleth the still more difficult question of death which casts its shadow over every meaningful interpretation of life. Whenever Koheleth speaks of fate (*miqreh*), death is always envisaged at the same time." But von Rad insists that Qoheleth's zest for life must not be confused with that which "as often settles in the shadow of despair" (p. 231).

[16] L. R. Bailey, "Death as a Theological Problem in the Old Testament," *Pastoral Psychology* 22 (1971) 20-32, emphasizes a more positive or neutral attitude toward death, suggesting that Israelites had a minimum of anxiety over death. He writes: "And this lack of sustained, systematic, thematic treatment suggests that death did not hold the terror for the Israelites that it does for us" (p. 22). Bailey concludes that in general the Old Testament view is death accepting as opposed to death denying or defying (p. 25). Qoheleth "diverges in this respect, as in others, from the true tradition of Israel" (R. Martin-Achard, *From Death to Life* [London: Oliver & Boyd, 1960] 7).

[17] George Barton, *The Book of Ecclesiastes* (ICC; Edinburgh: Clark, 1908) 82, writes: "The fact that death buries the wise and the foolish in the same oblivion, makes Qoheleth pronounce great wisdom vanity, in spite of the fact that he has just seen in wisdom the advantages of reality." Barton remarks that literary expression of Qoheleth's pessimism permitted him to continue to enjoy life (p. 93).

[18] The iteration of *měnaḥēm* functions rhetorically (Barton, *The Book of Ecclesiastes*, 114). On the sense of *měnaqqēm*, see G. E. Mendenhall, *The Tenth Generation* (Baltimore and London: The Johns Hopkins University, 1973) 69-104.

[19] Barton, *The Book of Ecclesiastes*, 114, comments that "the deep emotion which the tears of the oppressed excited in Qoheleth is evidence of his profound sympathies with the lower classes." R. Gordis makes a similar observation about 2:16 and 4:1, in which "the cynic's pose of studied indifference falls away and the impassioned spirit of Koheleth, the idealistic seeker of truth and justice, is revealed" (*Koheleth—The Man and His World* [New York: Schocken, 1951] 223). On this text, see also the remarks by Rudi Kroeber, *Der Prediger* (Schriften und Quellen der Alten Welt 13; Berlin: Akademie, 1963) 137.

[20] R. Gordis, *Koheleth — The Man and his World*, 257 observes: "There is a distinctly modern implication here of the essential loneliness of the individual personality." Gordis

recognizes the rhetorical power of 6:6, which begins with a protasis and ends with a question to which only a negative answer applies (pp. 259-60).

[21] The closer one comes to death, "cumulative quantitative weakness arrives at a qualitative difference" (Silberman, "Death in the Hebrew Bible and Apocalyptic Literature," 23). It follows that life in some circumstances is a form of death (cf. Lloyd Bailey's similar remarks about inauthentic existence as a form of death; "Death as a Theological Problem in the Old Testament," 29), and that one can even speak of "stages of dying" (H. W. Wolff, *Anthropology of the Old Testament* [Philadelphia: Fortress, 1974] 100-13).

[22] K. Galling, *Der Prediger* (HAT 18; Tübingen: Mohr [Siebeck], 1969) 104, concludes that the allusion to a proper burial implies that the numerous sons mentioned in 6:3 were impious.

[23] W. Zimmerli, "The Place and Limit of the Wisdom in the Framework of the Old Testament Theology," *SJT* 17 (1964) 156 *(Studies in Ancient Israelite Wisdom*, ed. J. L. Crenshaw [New York: Ktav, 1976] 324) writes that Qoheleth encountered the reality of the creator more clearly than any other Israelite sage. He adds: "In a manner hitherto unheard-of in the Old Testament, Ecclesiastes sees death as the power that takes away the power of the whole creation and even of man's Wisdom. The fact that every man's hour of death is incalculable gives full evidence of God's majesty and freedom."

[24] On Qoheleth's view that God has concealed vital knowledge from humans, see the author's essay entitled "The Eternal Gospel (Eccles. 3:11)," in *Essays in Old Testament Ethics* (eds. J. L. Crenshaw and J. T. Willis [New York: Ktav, 1974] 23-55). Von Rad, *Wisdom in Israel*, 234, remarks that "Koheleth . . . experiences the hiddenness of the future as one of the heaviest burdens of life."

[25] H. W. Hertzberg, *Der Prediger* (KAT 17: Gütersloh: Mohn, 1963) 176 writes that "nicht einmal über sein eigenes Ich ist er völlig Herr!" Qoheleth's denial that moral or religious virtues alter one's fixed fate strikes Hertzberg as a revolutionary idea in the Old Testament (p. 177).

[26] The final pair in this series of opposites reverses the order from positive to negative terms, perhaps to avoid closing on a negative note (Gordis, *Koheleth — The Man and his World*, 301). Qoheleth's exceptional stylistic powers dictate the use of *lamed* to govern the first three pairs and a coordinate construction of *kaph* for the last two pairs (Gordis, ibid.).

[27] "Die letzten Worte bilden absichtlich einem fragmentarischen Satz, der jah abbricht, wie das Leben" (Wildeboer). "The final words — and then off to the dead — form a consciously fragmentary sentence that breaks off like life itself." The translation of Wildeboer's striking observation is taken from Gordis, *Koheleth — The Man and his World*, 301.

[28] Hertzberg, *Der Prediger*, 178, perceives the sarcastic irony in 9:5. The living have practically nothing, and the dead have less than nothing. The verse has a particularly impressive use of paronomasia (*śākār : zikram*).

[29] George W. Coats, "Self-Abasement and Insult Formulas," *JBL* 89 (1970) 14-26.

[30] I have suggested elsewhere that this clever aphorism may have functioned as a defense for remarriage by a woman whose second husband came from a lower social class ("Riddle," IDBSup, 749).

[31] W. Zimmerli, *Man and His Hope in the Old Testament* (London: SCM, 1971) 21. Barton, *The Book of Ecclesiastes*, 160, misses the irony in Qoheleth's statement. He writes: "To have power to perceive that one must die is to be greater than the dead, who have no knowledge." Accordingly, "the dead are denied participation in the only world of which Qoheleth knows, this to his mind makes the pathos of death a tragedy."

[32] On Qoheleth's citation of popular wisdom, see above all Gordis, *Koheleth — the Man and his World, passim*, and H. P. Müller, "Wie Sprach Qohälät von Gott?," *VT* 18 (1968), 507-21.

[33] The language is taken from von Rad, *Wisdom in Israel*, 202, n. 10.

[34] Since the only other use of *pega*$^c$ (1 Kgs 5:18, MT) qualifies it with an adjective *ra*$^c$, the translation "chance" (*RSV, NEB*, Chicago Bible) seems more appropriate than "mischance" (*JB*), or "a time of calamity" (*NAB*) which ignores the *waw* and alters the syntax.

[35] Von Rad, *Wisdom in Israel*, 305 ("The fact of ultimate death first finds expression as a real intellectual problem in the teachings at the point where faith in Yahweh's support of life begins to

disappear"). Von Rad describes Qoheleth's quest as an attempt to answer the question of man's lot (salvation) without any confidence in life (p. 235).

[36] Outside Israel, pessimists openly endorse suicide ("A Dispute over Suicide," *ANET*[3], 405-07, "The Dialogue of Pessimism," *ANET*[3], 600-1). For some strange reason, Israel's skeptical tradition stops short of that radical decision. Was it because of a strong conviction that life belongs to Yahweh? A. F. Key, "The Concept of Death in Early Israelite Religion," *JBR* 32 (1964) 247, sums up Israel's attitude toward death as follows: "Thus, while death was accepted, it was accepted only passively. It was not something to be sought. It is only in the depths of despair that death is ever requested, and suicide is a very infrequent occurrence."

[37] M. Jastrow, *A Gentle Cynic* (Philadelphia and London: Lippincott, 1919) 137, observes that "Koheleth may talk about hating life . . . but he does not really think this," for the real Koheleth reveals himself in the opposite sentiment ("Light is sweet . . ." 11:7) and in his advice to eat, drink, and be merry. For advice similar to Qoheleth's, see Siduri's counsel to Gilgamesh (*ANET*[3], 90).

[38] With slight variation.

[39] Perhaps 2:24-26 throws light on this text. "Apart from God, who can enjoy anything?" implies that God approves whatever we do, or we would not be able to accomplish it.

[40] Contrast, however, 7:11-12.

[41] K. H. Miskotte, *When the Gods are Silent* (New York: Harper & Row, 1967) 450-60, emphasizes the importance and sweetness of light to Qoheleth.

[42] The translation is conjectural.

[43] The threat of death thus undergirds morality (Key, "The Concept of Death in Early Israelite Religion," 246).

[44] For these references, see Prov 2:16-19; 3:1-2, 16, 18; 5:5; 7:22-23; 10:2, 27; 11:7; 13:14; 24:16, 20; 27:20.

[45] On Ben Sira's use of a debate form, see my article entitled "The Problem of Theodicy in Sirach: On Human Bondage," *JBL* 94 (1975) 48-51.

[46] Possibly, Ben Sira means that the *time* of death is determined by God's good pleasure. The author of Wisdom of Solomon views death as God's means of preventing righteous persons from going astray, and measures life qualitatively rather than quantitatively (4:7-15).

[47] *In certain instances!* Still, this falls far short of the sentiment expressed at the conclusion of "The Dialogue of Pessimism": "Then what is good? To have my neck and yours broken and to be thrown into the river" (*ANET*[3], 601).

[48] While Job's remark contains bitter irony, Qoheleth's and Ben Sira's expression constitutes a parody on sacral language. God's gift to his people, her inheritance, is the privilege of being devoured by worms that dwell in the promised land. Stated differently, in Sheol "maggots and worms are the true sovereigns" (Wolff, *Anthropology of the Old Testament*, 103).

[49] This title of a popular French song is taken from Terrien, *Job: Poet of Existence*, 130.

# BEHEMOTH AND LEVIATHAN: ON THE DIDACTIC AND THEOLOGICAL SIGNIFICANCE OF JOB 40:15-41:26

JOHN G. GAMMIE

THE UNIVERSITY OF TULSA, TULSA, OKLAHOMA 74104

THE grand descriptions of *běhēmôt* (Job 40:15-24) and *liwyātān* (Job 40:25-41:26 [Engl. 41:1-34]) comprise the bulk of the second discourse of God in the Book of Job (40:6-41:26 [Engl. 41:34]). Contemporary scholars are divided as to whether these two creatures so elaborately described were understood by the Joban author or one of his followers as mythical monsters[1] or as the natural animals, the hippopotamus and the crocodile respectively.[2] No matter which view is taken, few contemporary scholars have seen in these two pericopes an attempt by the Joban author or a successor to speak directly to the major problems of the book: Job's suffering and his protestations.[3] The proponents of the "natural" interpretation see in Behemoth and Leviathan two magnificent creations of Yahweh which, like the natural phenomena and creatures described in chapters 38 and 39, accentuate the divine power. The proponents of the "mythical" interpretation see an advance in thought from chapters 38 and 39: Yahweh has not only created the wonders of nature but heavenly, mythic beings with which He alone is able to cope. Under both interpretations it is the divine power and majesty which is stressed and before which Job repents (Job 42:5-6). Job recants because he realizes in the course of the personal[4] self-manifestation of God that he cannot begin to fathom the ways of such an all powerful God. Under this prevailing view, however, God does not attempt to speak directly to Job's physical and spiritual agony. He pulls rank, so to speak, and because it is divine rank, it is enough to bring Job to confess his utter failure to comprehend the vastness of the divine omnipotence (Job 42:5). The prevailing contemporary interpretations thus see in the Book of Job the might and ordering power of God as the primary solution offered to the problem of suffering in the divine discourses (Job 38:1-42:6).

The present essay is written in basic agreement with the application of such an interpretation to the first discourse of God (Job 38:1-39:30); on the other hand, it will undertake to explore an alternative to the view that the descriptions of *běhēmôt* (Job 40:15-24) and *liwyātān* (Job 40:25-41:26 [Engl. 41:1-34]) are in the second discourse of God offered exclusively as further illustrations of the divine prowess and might. A display of God's creative power leads Job, at the conclusion of the first divine discourse, to silence (Job 40:1-5); but what is it in the second divine discourse which evokes from Job the profounder response of 42:1-6?

## The Second Discourse of God (Job 40:6–41:26 [Engl. 41:34])

The second discourse of God may be divided into three parts: (a) the introduction (Job 40:6-14); (b) the Behemoth pericope (Job 40:15-24) and (c) the Leviathan pericope (Job 40:25–41:26 [Engl. 41:1-34]).[5] Further strophic divisions within each section will be observed below. Each section in the second discourse of God, and particularly the last two, may now be examined to determine whether the theme of divine might is alone accentuated or whether it is not also accompanied by another dimension more directly relevant to Job's sufferings and protest.

### a. Introduction (Job 40:6-14)[6]

This section appears to be divided into two strophes: vss. 6-8 ("God's Charges Against Job") and vss. 9-14 ("God's Challenge to Job"). In vss. 6-8 the charge is levied that Job has found it necessary to place God in the wrong in order to justify himself (vs. 8). In vss. 9-14 God challenges Job to humble the haughty and to imprison them in the dust, upon the accomplishment of which even He, God, will bless Job. A major motif of this section is ʾap ("anger" or "wrath": vss. 8 and 11), not the divine wrath but the human wrath or anger of Job which would nullify God's justice (vs. 8) and which God challenges Job so to display now that he will "humble" all the proud and "tread upon the evil ones in their places" (vs. 12). A cursory glance at the introduction to the second divine discourse would seem to support the contention of most modern critics that the subject to be discussed in what follows is whether or not Job is possessed of the power to bring low "all the proud" (kōl-gēʾeh) and trample upon the wicked (vs. 12). Paradoxically, because his defense has placed God in the wrong (vs. 8), Job would now appear to be included in the category of the "wicked." Or, it may be in the light of vs. 12 that the reader should understand the "wicked" to be not human beings, but as Professor Terrien has suggested, those two symbols of the forces of evil, Behemoth and Leviathan.[7] As attractive as this suggestion is of Professor Terrien's, there is another perspective mentioned by him on Behemoth and Leviathan which we wish to probe more fully. In his book, *Job: Poet of Existence* he wrote, "These brutish creatures are not only caricatures in themselves, they are also caricatures of human endeavor."[8] Is it possible that the author of the pericopes on Behemoth and Leviathan is holding these two creatures up as mirrors through which Job may view his own existence of suffering and protest? In other words, were Behemoth and Leviathan intended by the author as caricatures of Job himself, images put forth not only to put him down, but also to instruct and console?

### b. *Behemoth (Job 40:15-24)*

The poem on Behemoth may be divided into two strophes of five verses each. The first deals with "The Strength of Behemoth and His Standing with God" (vss. 15-19); the second deals with "His Place in Nature and Capture" (vss. 20-24). A demonstrable feature of the poem is the way in which the author anticipates or leads into what is to follow in the next line by his choice of the last word in Hebrew in the preceding line. Thus the strength of Behemoth described in Job 40:16-18 is introduced by *yoʾkēl* ("he eats"), the last word in the opening vs. 15. Similarly, the last word in the opening vs. of the second strophe, *šām* ("there"), prepares the reader for the description of the habitat of Behemoth in vss. 21-23. Thus there is a parallel structure in both strophes. That which summarizes the first strophe is found in the first half of vs. 19: "he is the first fruits of the ways of God" and, in accordance with the principle observable elsewhere in the poem, the last half of the end of the first strophe anticipates the subject matter of the second strophe: "the One who made him brings near[9] His sword" (vs. 19b). The climax of the poem is found in the difficult vs. 24. The rendering of the first two Hebrew words is problematic[10] but the last portion of the vs. is plain: "in a snare He pierces his *ʾap* ("nose, anger").[11] The climax of the second strophe: that God has pierced the *ʾap* of Behemoth has already been anticipated by the climax of the first strophe, "the One who has made him brings near His sword." In view of the prominence given to *ʾap* ("[human] anger") in the introduction to the second discourse (Job 40:8, 11) it would be gratuitous to see no connection between it and the *ʾap* in the Behemoth pericope where *ʾap* is given considerable poetic stress, as we have seen. In the Behemoth pericope God demonstrates to Job how even though Behemoth possesses a place of preeminence with Him (Job 40:19a), He does bring His sword against him (Job 40:19b); that even though Behemoth has a high standing among his equals (Job 40:20), God in the end pierces even his "anger/nose," thus bringing him low (Job 40:12-13).

Nothing thus far dealt within the pericope would seem to preclude the mythic interpretation of Behemoth. If God pierces the wrath of even such a wondrous heavenly monster as Behemoth, will He not all the more do the same to the wrath of Job? The mythic interpretation thus suits a major feature of the Behemoth pericope but does not bear up well under further examination. We shall now press our search for clues as to the author's intention in the use of the Behemoth pericope by looking first for clues within the pericope and then by examining elsewhere the Joban treatment of animals in general and *běhēmôt* in particular.

1. *Behemoth as Mortal.* Three features in the opening verse (Job 40:15) suggest that the creature about to be described is an animal of the natural world: (i) the semantic force of the initial words of the verse, *hinnēh-nāʾ* ("Behold!") suggests that the creature could be seen;[12] (ii) he is one whom "I made with you," i.e., with Job; Job is mortal, therefore it is less strained to take it that Behemoth is also mortal; (iii) "he eats grass like cattle";

comparison is made to another animal of the world of nature; grass is, of course, a widely acknowledged symbol of mortality (cf. Isa 40:6-8). The next verse (Job 40:16) also commences with *hinnēh-nāʾ* as if to reiterate that the regenerative, sexual powers and organs(!)[13] to be described in this verse and the next were there for Job to behold. Job 40:18 also suggests a might in the limbs and a metalic quality in the bones (or "sides": LXX *pleurai*) of an animal which was there to see. The case is the same in the second strophe. The specific references to the hills and to the beasts of the field playing with him (vs. 20) bespeak an animal of the natural world.[14] Even more particularly, the detailed description of the habitat of this animal indicate a creature of the river banks where the cane grows and bushes provide shade from the sun (vss. 21-22).[15] With good reasons scholars have seen in this creature not a mythic monster but the mortal hippopotamus.[16] Instead of being one who is in opposition to God, as would be a symbol of evil, the Joban author reflects how the creature responds to oppression: "If the river wrongs him he does not flee in fear,/ he remains serene even if the waters reach up to his mouth (vs. 23)."[17] Here the poet seems to hold up Behemoth not as an opponent to God but as one who though subject to attack responds with trust.[18] Mighty as he is, upon examination, Behemoth appears to be for the Joban poet more a figure of mortal, and specifically human, rather than mythic proportions.

A similar conclusion suggests itself when the treatment of animals in general and of Behemoth in particular is examined elsewhere in the book. (1) Even the lions are subject to mortality if the breath of God's wrath blows upon them (Job 4:7-11). (2) Indeed, Job complains that even though he has sought to be righteous, God has hunted him as a lion and made him an object of attack (Job 10:13-17; cf. also Job 16:7-11; 19:6-12). (3) In contrast, in the first discourse of God one animal and bird after another[19] is held up as a creation of God which Job in his finitude could hardly expect to feed, to engender, to control, to match or instruct (Job 38:39-39:30). (4) One of the most interesting passages in the book on the subject of animals, however, is found in the first cycle of speeches, in a speech of Job (Job 12:7-8):

> But ask *bĕhēmôt* and he (or they) will teach you,
>     the birds of the air and they will declare to you
> or the shrubs of the earth and they will teach you,
>     and the fishes of the sea will tell you.

These verses occur in a strophe which more recently Terrien has convincingly demonstrated belong to a later hand.[20] It little affects our argument whether one follows Terrien in his judgment or not, for here *bĕhēmâ* ("cattle," "beasts") are not cited to illustrate their lack of sense (Job 18:3; cf. Job 39:13-17) nor are the *bahĕmôt* ("beasts") cited as examples of creatures whom the Almighty has taught less than men (Job 35:10-11), rather, here *bĕhēmôt* ("hippopotamus" or "beasts") is cited as one(s) who will instruct man.[21] Though the interpolation seems only to be confined to Job 12:7-12,[22] the entire chapter eloquently develops the theme of how the hand of God is responsible for Job's woe (Job 12:9), of how: "He pours out shame upon noble men and loosens the belt of the mighty" (Job 12:21).

We have thus seen that at least these four aspects relating to animals are brought out elsewhere in the book: (1) their mortality is determined by God; (2) Job asserts himself to be hunted as a lion; (3) they are God's magnificent creations; and (4) they are potential instruments of instruction for man. We have already observed how the poet of the Behemoth pericope has also stressed this animal's mortality and magnificence. We have also observed how at the climax of both strophes God (lit. "the One who made him") brings near His sword (Job 40:19b) and pierces his anger (Job 40:24b). Thus the second aspect of the use of animals elsewhere in the book, where Job is viewed as a hunted beast, appears also to be present in this pericope as well. It remains for us to inquire whether and to what extent the fourth is present in the pericope. That is to say, does Behemoth as described in these verses provide instruction for man's plight in general and Job's plight in particular?

2. *Behemoth as a Didactic Image for Job.* Two linguistic clues within the Behemoth pericope provide justification for pursuing the idea that the original poet intended the reader to see how the creature Behemoth instructed Job and therefore could instruct him. (i) In Job 40:15, the opening verse, we read: "Behold Behemoth whom I have made *with you (ʿimmāk)*." This word is not needed for the rest of the sentence to make sense; it seems to invite Job however to make a comparison between himself and the creature he is to describe. (ii) In Job 40:19a, the half-verse which we have seen summarizes the first strophe of the poem, it is said of Behemoth: "he is the first fruits of the ways of God." The meaning of this term is not clear from the context unless it is understood as a means of describing preeminence, excellence, prominence and even, in the light of vs. 20, superiority. There is, it would seem however, another dimension to this expression. In the concluding verses of chapter 26, after Job has cited the creative powers of God in the heavens and over the waters (Job 26:7-12) in words which anticipate the similar heavenly works of God described so magnificently in the first discourse of God (Job 38:4-37), he says:

> With His strength he stilled the waters
>> by His skill he smote Rahab.
> The heavens He has swept with his breath,
>> His hand has pierced the fleeing serpent.
> Should these be the remotest of His ways (*qěṣôt děrākāyw*)[23]
>> what a whispering utterance have we heard of Him.
> And the thundering of His might, who can comprehend?   (Job 26:12-14)

To the "last" or "remotest" or "end" of his ways belong the Almighty's heavenly creations, his subduing the waters (described with obvious mythic overtones). Behemoth, however, is the *rēʾšît* ("first," "first fruits") "of the ways of God." That is to say, in contrast to the remotest of God's ways, Behemoth belongs to one of the ways of God which is closer to man's ability to comprehend. The heavens are object lessons of God's glory furthest removed from man's feeble powers to understand; but Behemoth is the closest to him, the prime object lesson to which Job is invited by God to direct his attention. Even if there may be differences among interpreters with respect to details, some such explanation of the phrase $rē'šît darkê-'ēl$ ("first fruits of the ways of God") seems justified in the light of a comparison with the sister phrase $qĕṣôt dĕrākāyw$ ("remotest of his ways") in Job 26:14.[24]

Linguistic clues within the Behemoth pericope itself as well as clues found elsewhere in the Book of Job thus support the notion that animals can provide instruction for man. Under this interpretation of the poem the various parts fall into place and the following specific instruction seems to be proferred:

(i) The Almighty's chief problem with this beast in whom He is proud is not to slay him but to pierce his anger, i.e., temper his temperament; (Job 40:19b, 24).

(ii) Thus Job's intimation that it was the Almighty who was seeking him out (Job 10:13-17; 16:7-11) was correct, but not the sole object lesson of the divine instruction;

(iii) for, Behemoth when oppressed, neither fled in fear nor abandoned trust (Job 40:23).

(iv) Just as the Almighty had brought darkness on Job (Job 30:26; cf. 12:22-25), Behemoth was made to dwell as his natural habitat in the river's shades (Job 40:21-22); Job could therefore take heart that even there in his dark valleys there was a protective covering and covert.

(v) Even though he had been smitten and his family struck down, regenerative powers (Job 40:16-17) and a measure of physical strength (Job 40:18) remained to him on the basis of which he could begin his life and family again.

Thus understood Behemoth serves not only as a didactic but also as a consoling image, which speaks explicitly to Job's sufferings and loss. It now remains for us to determine whether or not the Joban poet or his successors seem also to have intended the Leviathan pericope for a similar purpose.

### c. *Leviathan (Job 40:25–41:26 [Engl. 41:1-34])*

The Leviathan pericope in the second discourse of God may be divided into eight strophes of four lines each for the first six strophes, and of five lines each for the last two.[25] The first two strophes deal with "The Taming of Leviathan" (Job 40:25-28, 29-32 [Engl. 41:1-4, 5-8]); the third strophe is transitional and may not be as easily characterized inasmuch as it touches on a variety of topics (Job 41:1-4 [Engl. 41:9-12]); the fourth through the sixth strophes contain "God's Boasting of Leviathan's Strength and his Mighty Defenses" (Job 41:5-8, 9-12, 13-16 [Engl. 41:13-16, 17-20, 21-24]); the last two strophes deal with "Leviathan's Proud Withstanding of Oppression" (Job 41:17-21, 22-26 [Engl. 41:25-29, 30-34]). In contrast to the Behemoth pericope, this poem contains a number of rhetorical questions.[26] Something of the same pattern of stress and anticipation observed in the Behemoth pericope, however, also obtains here. That is: (i) final words are often key words, signaling subject matter to be discussed in what follows, and (ii) final lines in strophes often anticipate subject matter of following strophes. As an illustration of (i) we may note especially: the last word in Job 41:25 (Engl. 41:1), lĕšōnô ("his tongue") not only leads into the next two verses, it also alerts the reader to what will constitute a major subject of the poem, namely, what comes forth from the mouth of Leviathan (Job 40:27; 41:5, 10-13 [Engl. 41:3, 13, 18-21]). As an illustration of (ii) we may note: the third (transitional) strophe concludes with a boasting of the strength of the armor of Leviathan (Job 41:4 [Engl. 41:12]), a subject which is to be discussed in the following three strophes (Job 41:5-16 [Engl. 41:13-24]). It is not the ˀap of Leviathan to which the poet directs our attention, although it is mentioned in Job 40:26 (Engl. 41:2), it is rather to his tongue and what comes forth from his mouth (Job 41:11, 13 [Engl. 41:19, 21]; cf. 40:27 [Engl. 41:3]). As with Behemoth, Leviathan is a creature *par excellence:*

> He has no equal upon the dust,
>> he was created[27] without fear.
> He surveys everything which is exalted,
>> he is the king of all majestic wild beasts.[28]   (Job 41:25-26 [Engl. 41:33-34])

With these two lines the grand Leviathan pericope comes to an end.

Further similarities and differences between the two pericopes will be alluded to below. From this brief description of some of the strophic and poetic features of the poem we may now turn to consider the extent to which the interpreter should regard this kingly beast as possessed of mythic and/or other dimensions.

1. *Leviathan as a Mythic Animal?* The Hebrew word *liwyātān* ("serpent," "Leviathan [sea monster]," "crocodile") occurs but six times in the Hebrew Bible. Twice in Job (Job 3:8; 40:25), twice in the book of Psalms (Pss 74:14; 104:26) and twice in the Isaiah apocalypse (Isa 27:1 [bis]). In view of the passages in Ps 74:12-14 where God's victory over the many-headed sea-monster (Heb. *tannin*[*îm*], Ps 74:13), "Leviathan," is described, and in view of the anticipation of God's punishment over the same in Isa 27:1, it is certain that Leviathan in Job 40:25-41:26 [Engl. 41:1-34) has mythic dimensions, i.e., that the Joban author intended some mythological overtones to be present by his very choice of the word *liwyātān*. The rich ancient Near Eastern mythology of the slain watery serpent[29] and allusions to this myth elsewhere in Job (Job 7:12; 9:13-14; 26:12-13; 27:22; cf. 3:8)[30] makes this conclusion even more certain. Further, specific features used to describe Leviathan within the poem may best be understood as accentuating this dimension, e.g.: (i) "terror is about his teeth" (Job 41:6b [Engl. 41:14b]); (ii) "From his mouth comes daggers,/the fiery sparks fly out" (Job 41:11 [Engl. 41:19]); (iii) "From his nostrils smoke comes forth,/like a kettle blown and glowing" (Job 41:12

[Engl. 41:20]); (iv) "He makes [it] boil like a pot,/he works the sea like a mixing jar" (Job 41:23 [Engl. 41:31]); (v) "Behind him he illumines a path,/he makes one think the deep [*tĕhôm*] is hoary" (Job 41:24 [Engl. 41:32]). Despite these undoubted mythological overtones, there are a number of features in the poem, however, which will not so easily yield to a purely mythological interpretation. To these we may now turn.

Many points of correspondence between the crocodile and the Leviathan described in Job 40:25–41:26 (Engl. 41:1-34) have been observed: (i) an ingenious method of catching and dragging the crocodile with a hook was known in, and described from, antiquity by Herodotus (*Histories*, 2. 68-70);[31] this hunting method suggests a correspondence because it is used for Leviathan in Job 40:25-26 (Engl. 41:1-2). (ii) The crocodile which inhabits the Nile River is possessed of powerful jaws (cf. Job 40:26 [Engl. 41:2]) and teeth (cf. Job 41:6 [Engl. 41:14]);[32] (iii) the hide of Leviathan, which consists of closely interlocked "shields" (*māginnîm*: Job 41:7 [Engl. 41:15]; cf. Job 41:7-9, 18-21 [Engl. 41:15-17, 26-29]), corresponds remarkably well with the crocodile hide;[33] (iv) the description of his belly as comparable to "shards of pottery" (*hadudê hāres:* Job 41:22a [Engl. 41:30a]) is also apt;[34] (v) as is the description (by the river bank) of the mud clay (*tît*) which he smites as with a threshing sledge (Job 41:22b [Engl. 41:30b]).[35]

The issue which emerges from a consideration of points of comparison between the crocodile and Leviathan of Job 40:25–41:26 (Engl. 41:1-34) is not which identification is correct: "Is Leviathan a crocodile?" or, "Is Leviathan a mythic being?" but rather "What was in the poet's mind when he (or they) included this long passage at the conclusion of the second divine discourse to Job?" Was the poet *focusing* on a "mythological" Leviathan, or on the crocodile, or on something else? To what extent can a purely or even heavily weighted "mythological" interpretation withstand scrutiny if some of the so-called mythological aspects are seen in a slightly different light? Is there evidence that in the figure of Leviathan the author is speaking to the central issues of the book of Job: his suffering and protests? To these questions we may now turn.

2. *Leviathan as a Didactic Image for Job.* Four intractable facts make it difficult to dismiss lightly the line of interpretation toward which we are tending in this essay: (i) In his first lament, Job 3:1-26, Job likens himself at birth to Leviathan: "Let those who curse the day curse it,/those midwives who laid bare[36] Leviathan" (Job 3:8).[37] (ii) The penultimate verse of the poem stresses that this Leviathan has no equal *on the dust* (*ᶜal ᶜāpār*, Job 41:25a [Engl. 41:33a]). In view of the prominence given to Job's position on the dust elsewhere in the book (Job 2:8; 30:19; 42:6) this feature cannot be easily dismissed. (iii) In the final verse of the poem the one described is said to be *melek ᶜal-kōl-bĕnê-šāhaṣ* ("king of all majestic wild beasts").[38] The term *šāhaṣ* is used elsewhere in the book in parallelism with *šāhal* ("[young] lion," Job 28:8); the latter term does not have a mythological overtone when used elsewhere in Job (cf. Job 4:10; 10:16). Thus the seeming mythological focus of

the poem may not be as great as some interpreters have held.[39] (iv) Job throughout the book is portrayed as one of regal proportions, and this is so not only in the Prologue and Epilogue but in the poetic sections as well (Job 3–31):[40] he speaks of kings (Job 3:14; 12:18) and princes (Job 29:9-10), he likens his life before his calamity as unto that of a king ("I dwelt like a king [*melek*] midst troops," Job 29:25); indeed toward the end of his impassioned final defense he likens himself once again to a prince (*nāgîd*, Job 31:37). These considerations take beyond the realm of fanciful, scholarly speculation the notion that the Leviathan in the Leviathan pericope was intended, in part at least, as a figure of Job. The text itself bears indications that such is one of the dimensions of interpretation the original poet intended.

If such is the case, what "lesson" did he intend? The poem focuses, as we have seen in the brief sketch above at the outset of section c., upon the "tongue" of Leviathan and that which comes forth from his mouth (Job 40:27; 41:5, 10-13 [Engl. 41:3, 13, 18-21]), upon his "Mighty Defenses" (3 strophes: Job 41:5-8, 9-12, 13-16 [Engl. 41:13-16, 17-20, 21-24]), and in the final two strophes upon "Leviathan's Proud Withstanding of Oppression" (Job 41:17-21, 22-26 [Engl. 41:25-29, 30-34]). We do not deny the presence of other themes—especially in the first two strophes. It seems apparent, however, that the poet may clearly have had a didactic intention of holding up to Job a caricature of his verbal defenses and yet an affirmation of his very protests. On the face of it, it looks as if the monster of Job 41:10-13 [Engl. 41:18-21) is a flame-throwing dragon; upon closer look, however, it is entirely plausible that we have instead the employment of poetic hyperbole to act as a mirror, as it were, wherein Job could gather perspective on his own fulminations. Further, it seems to me, if this line of interpretation is correct, that neither the protests nor the fulminations are without merit in the sight of God. Both the following lines for example are not merely caricatures: (i) "His sputterings (lit. "sneezings") let light shine" (Job 41:10a [Engl. 41:18a]) and (ii) "Behind him he illumines a path, / he makes one think the deep is hoary" (Job 41:24 [Engl. 41:32]). In the former there is affirmation of the insight in the "sputterings" (*ʿetîsotāyw*); in the latter there may be a *double entendre* that: (a) the thrashings of Leviathan on the water have made a white wake behind him and (b) that Leviathan (Job) has brought forth some of the wisdom of hoary old age in his thrashings.[41] Along the same line, even the defensive shields of Leviathan joined one to the other (Job 41:7-9 [Engl. 41:15-17]) may be seen as caricatures of Job's speeches. In any event, the proud beast proved himself to be invincible;[42] the defenses with which he was provided by the Almighty (Job 41:7-9 [Engl. 41:15-17]) proved sufficient against all assaults: arrows, slings, swords and cudgel (Job 41:18-21 [Engl. 41:26-29]). In these passages may not the poet again have been intending to instruct the assaulted and beaten down hero of the poem that though assaulted (cf. Job 6:4; 16:13-14; 19:11-12, etc.) he not only could, indeed he had emerged without peer on the dust, as a victorious king?[43]

## Summary

Understood in the light of our findings in sections b. and c. above, the divine affirmation of Job and of the correctness of Job's speech is not confined to the Epilogue (Job 42:7) but belongs to the Behemoth pericope (Job 40:19a) and especially to the climax of the second discourse of God (Job 41:10a, 24, 26 [Engl. 41:18a, 32, 34]). Understood in the same light, the second discourse of God deals specifically with the central issues of the book: sufferings and protest. Further, our analyses led us to conclude that neither the Behemoth nor the Leviathan pericope provides an answer to the question of theodicy beyond this: (i) wisdom comes to light in the very midst of man's protestations, and (ii) even though God may seem to be in attack upon man, He Himself has provided man with the sexual strength to start again (Job 40:16-18) and with the defenses with which he may victoriously resist all attack (Job 40:18-19; 41:7-9, 18-21 [Engl. 41:15-17, 26-29]).

In a word, we have argued above that the second discourse of God must be viewed as a passage replete with an irony of divine comfort and affirmation: seeming to portray exemplars of the divine defeat of proudful man (Job 40:12-14), it portrays instead the divine pride in human triumph over oppression (Job 40:19a; 41:26 [Engl. 41: 34]); seeming to portray Job's inability to conquer such marvelously wrought beasts as Behemoth and Leviathan, the beasts themselves celebrate instead Job's triumph.[44]

---

[1] See M. Pope, *Job* (AB 15; Garden City, NY: Doubleday, 1965) 265-87; S. Terrien, *Job* (CAT 13; Neuchâtel: Delauchaux et Niestlé, 1963) 258-67; N. H. Tur-Sinai (H. Torczyner), *The Book of Job: A New Commentary* (Jerusalem: Kiryath Sepher, 1957) 556-57; A. Weiser, *Das Buch Hiob* (ATD 13; 5th ed.; Göttingen: Vandenhoeck & Ruprecht, 1968) 255-61; E. Ruprecht, "Das Nilpferd im Hiobbuch," *VT* 21 (1971) 209-31.

[2] See N. H. Snaith, *The Book of Job* (SBT 2/11; London: SCM, 1968); R. Gordis, *The Book of God and Man: A Study of Job* (Chicago: University of Chicago, 1965); G. Fohrer, *Das Buch Hiob* (KAT 16; Gütersloh: Mohn, 1964) 521-31; E. J. Kissane, *The Book of Job* (Dublin: Browne and Nolan, 1939) 280-92; E. Dhorme, *A Commentary on the Book of Job* (Engl.; Leiden: Brill, 1967) 618-25; S. R. Driver and G. B. Gray, *The Book of Job* (ICC; Edinburgh: Clark, 1921) 351-71.

[3] Thus Kissane says: "Neither [speech of God] is a direct answer to the problem discussed by Job and his three friends; in fact, the problem of the suffering of the just is not mentioned at all" (E. J. Kissane, *The Book of Job*, 261). Robert Gordis puts it: "Most readers have been struck by the fact that these chapters [Job 38-41] make no reference whatsoever to the theme of man's suffering, with which the rest of Job is concerned" R. Gordis, *The Book of God and Man*, 121).

Professor Terrien is one of a few exceptions; although he adheres to the "mythic" view, for him Behemoth and Leviathan symbolize the "forces of evil" and are thus directly related to the subject matter of the book as a whole; see, e.g., *JB* and S. Terrien, *Job* (CAT 13) 246, 261-67; *Job: Poet of Existence* (New York and Indianapolis: Bobbs-Merrill, 1957) 237-38; "The Book of Job: Introduction and Exegesis," *IB* 3 (Nashville and New York: Abingdon, 1954) 1186-90.

[4] For a recent emphasis on the personal nature of the divine manifestation, see R. Laurin, "The Theological Structure of Job," *ZAW* 84 (1972) 86-89.

[5] Although a 3 + 3 meter dominates in the first section, the first and last verse are 2 + 2 (Job 40:6, 14); although a 2 + 2 meter dominates in the second section, the first and penultimate verse

appear to be 3 + 3 (Job 40:15, 23); in the last section the meter is more mixed with 2 + 2 dominating in 41:1-10 (Engl. 41:9-18) and at the conclusion (Job 41:22-26 [Engl. 41:30-34]). For brief but helpful discussions on the poetry (and the strophic structure) of Job, see esp. E. J. Kissane, *The Book of Job* liii-lviii, and S. Terrien, *Job* (CAT 13) 31-34. W. J. Urbrock has recently conducted some interesting and exegetically important research on formulaic patterns (esp. word pairs and paired-substitutes) in the book of Job; see "Oral Antecedents to Job: A Survey of Formulas and Formulaic Systems," *Semeia* 5 (1975) 111-37.

⁶ For the purposes of this essay attention will be focused on the discourse as a unit and upon its role in the entire book of Job as it stands. A number of interesting form-critical matters will not be discussed in the course of this essay, e.g., the relationship of Job 40:8 to the only prose vss. in the poetic section (Job 32:1-5), the repetitions in Job 40:6-7, cf. Job 38:1, 3, etc. For a highly influential form-critical analysis of Job see B. Duhm, *Das Buch Hiob* (Tübingen: Mohr [Siebeck], 1897) v-xx.

⁷ S. Terrien, *Job* (CAT 13) 246, 261-67.

⁸ S. Terrien, *Job: Poet of Existence*, 237.

⁹ The imperfect here and in the rest of the verses of the poem are used to indicate habitual, customary or "re-iterated" actions and thus may properly be rendered in translation as a present tense. On the meaning of the Imperfect see S. R. Driver, *A Treatise on the Use of the Tenses in Hebrew* (3d ed.; Oxford: Clarendon, 1892) 27-49 and T. O. Lambdin, *Introduction to Biblical Hebrew* (New York: Scribners, 1971) 100. Driver, in the aforementioned work, renders the verb *yaggēš* as a jussive "let him bring nigh [his sword]" (pp. 217-18). This rendering accords with the introduction to the Behemoth pericope (where Job is challenged to humble the haughty: Job 40:11-12) but not with the pericope itself—for God is clearly identified as the maker of Behemoth in Job 40:15.

¹⁰ We suggest that the addition of words to the Hebrew text, as is common, is unnecessary. In the light of the recently discovered Targum on Job found in Qumran, Cave 11 and esp. van der Ploeg's and van der Woude's discussion of this vs., we suggest the rendering "when his eyelids are blinked, in a snare He pierces his nose/anger." See J. P. M. van der Ploeg and A. S. van der Woude, *Le Targum de Job de la Grotte XI de Qumrân* (Leiden: Brill, 1971) 80-81; they suggest that the Aramaic ᶜ*ynwhy* may be translated either as "his eyes" or as "his eyelids." The MT must, of course, be emended slightly for our rendering, reading: *kĕᶜênāyw* rather than *bĕᶜênāyw*. For a still unsurpassed treatment on the text of Job see G. Beer, *Der Text des Buches Hiob* (Marburg: Elwert, 1897).

¹¹ To read "his anger" or "his nose" the MT must be emended from ᵓ*āp* to ᵓ*appô*. The dual meaning of this word cannot readily be translated into English.

¹² See BDB (Oxford: Clarendon, 1907; reprinted with corrections, 1966) for the meaning of *hinnēh* as "pointing to persons or things" (p. 243). For a most useful recent discussion of *hinnēh* and *hinnēh-nāᵓ* which challenges the correctness of the usual rendering of *hinnēh* as "behold!" but stresses nonetheless its function "as a predicator of existence" and how "it emphasizes the immediacy, the here-and-now-ness, of the situation," see T. O. Lambdin, *Introduction to Biblical Hebrew*, 168-71.

¹³ The sexual allusions are obvious, as has been recognized by many interpreters: Albertus Magnus, St. Thomas Aquinas, etc. For quotations see M. Pope, *Job*, 271-72. See also S. Terrien, *Job* (CAT 13) 262: "La description insiste sur la puissance du monstre, en particuler sur sa vigueur sexuelle." These verses may be translated:

> Behold the strength in his loins,
> > the generative power in the hardness of his belly.
> He makes his extremity stiff like a cedar,
> > his mighty sinews are interlaced.

Unless otherwise indicated the translations used in this essay are mine.

¹⁴ The LXX provides, we believe, a clue for a reconstruction of the MT of this verse which has not to our knowledge been suggested elsewhere. The LXX *epelthōn* ("when he has come")

suggests that MT *bûl* should rather be read *bôʾ* ("he comes") and that the entire MT should be rendered, "When he comes the hills exalt him and all the beasts of the field play [with him] there."

[15] These vss. may be rendered:

> Under the thorny bushes he reclines
> in a marshy covert of cane.
> The thorny bushes cover his shadow,
> the evening currents flow around him.

[16] For bibliographic details on the identification of *běhēmōt* with the Egyptian *p-eḥe-moût* in the past 300 years, see E. Ruprecht, "Das Nilpferd im Hiobbuch," *VT* (1971) 217-19. For a discussion of the role of this animal in Egyptian mythology, see T. Save-Söderbergh, *On Egyptian Representation of Hippopotamus Hunting as a Religious Motive*. (Horae Soederblomianae 3; Uppsala: Gleerup, 1953). The Egyptians were evidently struck by the sexual prowess of this animal also; see pp. 17-19 of the aforementioned work.

Most scholars explain the plural as a plural of majesty; so Dhorme (*Job*, 619), Kissane (Job 286), etc.; that is, he is the beast *par excellence* (cf. Job 40:19a).

[17] In the rendering of the second part of this verse we follow Terrien (*Job* [CAT 13], 262-63). The MT has *yārdēn* in this vs. which Terrien renders as *onde* ("wave" or "waters"). The word may also simply be translated as "Jordan" (i.e., the river Jordan). F. S. Bodenheimer avers that the hippopotamus became extinct in Palestine before the eighteenth century (F. S. Bodenheimer, *Animal and Man in Bible Lands* [Collection de travaux de l'académie internationale d'histoire des science 10; Leiden: Bill, 1960] 129-30). On the other hand, scholars such as P. Humbert argue in favor of an observation of the hippopotamus (and the crocodile: Job 40:25-41:26 [Engl. Job 41:1-34]) in Egypt itself; see P. Humbert, *Recherches sur les sources égyptienne de la littérature sapientale d'Israël* (Mémoires de l' Université de Neuchâtel 7; Neuchâtel: P. Attinger, 1929) 98-99.

[18] Cf. in Job 40:23b the Hebrew *yěbṭāḥ* (lit. "he trusts").

[19] These are the lion and raven (Job 38:39-41), the mountain goat (Job 39:1-4); the wild ass (Job 39:5-8); the ostrich (Job 39:13-18); the war horse (Job 39:19-25); the falcon and the eagle (Job 39:26-30). Many authors have commented on the irony in these passages. We catch the flavor of it in the two verses:

> Art thou the one who givest the falcon skill
> (when) he spreads his wings to the south wind?
> Is it at thy command that the eagle flies
> and makes his nest on high?   (Job 39:26-27).

[20] S. Terrien, *Job* (CAT 13) 111-12; the interpolated strophe consists of vss. 7-12. A major reason for this judgment is the use of the name for God, Yahweh (vs. 9) which is otherwise absent altogether from the poetic sections. F. Horst (*Hiob* [BKAT 16/1; Neukirchen-Vluyn: Neukirchener Verlag, 1968] 184, 190-91) considers only vss. 7-10 to be interpolated. Duhm considered vss. 4-6 as well as vss. 7-10 to be "from a younger hand," (*Das Buch Hiob*, xix-xx). See also n. 22 below.

[21] The only other place where *běhēmōt* (with precisely this pointing) occurs elsewhere in Book of Job is in Job 40:15.

[22] G. Fohrer, however, sees Job 12:13-25 also as being a later interpolation (*Das Buch Hiob*, 240). Whether Terrien or Fohrer is correct, the relationship of the entire chapter to the conclusion of the book merits particular attention.

[23] Reading with the *qěrēʾ*, Targum, Syriac and Vulgate; MT *kětíb* is sg., *darkô* ("his way").

[24] The word *derek* occurs some thirty-two times in the Book of Job, but only six times with reference to God. Two of the passages have already been mentioned (Job 40:19a and 26:14). In two passages the term seems to be used to connote the pattern(s) of morally upright conduct which God has laid down for man: Job 23:11 and 34:27. In Job 36:23 it is used to connote the (moral) activities of God; in Job 28:23 it is only God who knows the "way" to wisdom. Our

understanding of *rēʾšît darkê-ʾēl* as prime object lesson from which Job can derive instruction for his conduct is thus in concert with the use of *derek* in Job 23:11 and 34:27 esp. and to a slightly lesser extent with Job 28:23.

For a further discussion on *derek* and related concepts in Egypt and Mesopotamia as well as in the OT see the article, *"derek"* by J. Bergmann, A. Haldar, H. Ringgren and K. Koch in *TWAT* 2/3 (Stuttgart: W. Kohlhammer, 1974) 289-311. Koch comments on the scarcity of references to the divine *derek* in the wisdom literature; there are only two such references in the Book of Proverbs (Prov 10:29 and 8:22). In the former, the way of God is a stronghold for the man of integrity (a verse which would lend support to the line of interpretation we have taken here); in the latter the expression *rēʾšît darkô* ("first [fruits] of his way") is applied to "wisdom"and clearly has a temporal connotation. As we have seen the priority in time of Behemoth does not appear to be the meaning of *rēʾšît darkê-ʾēl* in Job 40:19a.

25 Other analyses are as follows: E. Kissane (*Job*, lx, 290-92) see in this poem a regular alternation of a five line strophe with a six line strophe. S. Terrien (*Job* [CAT 13] 263-67) prefers five line strophes (Job 40:25-29; 41:4-8, 10-14, 22-26) with one strophe of six lines Job 40:30-32; 41:1-3) and one of seven lines (Job 41:15-21). P. Skehan in a provocative study of the strophic structure of Job sees the divine discourses of 38:2-41:26 as deliberate poetic counterparts of Job 29-31 (Job 29-30 is a "kind of diptych of Job's past and present condition"; "the speech of the Lord in 38-39 is a diptych of the Lord's creative marvels"; Job 40:7-41:26 is viewed as a kind of response, to overshadow "the magnificence of ch. 31"); see P. Skehan, "Job's Final Plea "Job 29-31) and The Lord's Reply (Job 38-41)," *Studies in Israelite Poetry and Wisdom* (CBQMS 1; Washington, D.C.: Catholic Biblical Association, 1971) 114-23 [Reprint from *Bib* 45 [1964] 51-61]). Fr. Skehan follows the strophic divisions of Kissane for Job 40:25-41:26.

26 These are concentrated in the first four strophes. The interrogative *hē* occurs five times (Job 40:26, 27, 28, 29 and 31) and the interrogative pronoun *mî* ("who?") five times (Job 41:2b, 3, 5a, 5b, 6). The MT of Job 40:15-24 contains no questions at all as the text stands.

27 Reading *heʿāśûy* instead of *heʿāśû*.

28 The final word in the MT is *šāḥaṣ*. W. H. Holladay, *A Concise Hebrew and Aramaic Lexicon of the Old Testament* (Grand Rapids, Michigan: Erdmans, 1971) suggests the translation of *šāḥaṣ* here and in Job 28:8 as " 'proud beasts'(with mythological overtones)" p. 366. The extent to which we believe Holladay's parenthetical comment to be correct will be discussed in section c.1 and 2 below.

29 See, e.g., the well known Creation Epic from Mesopotamia wherein Marduk slays *tiamat* (*ANET* [2d ed.; Princeton, NJ: Princeton University, 1955] 60-72) or the dramatic tales of the storm god Baʿal's conquest of "Prince Sea,"(*ANET* [2d ed.] 129-42 and esp. 129-31, 136-37; G. R. Driver, *Canaanite Myths and Legends* [Old Testament Studies 3; Edinburgh: Clark, 1956] 78-121 and esp. 78-89, 102-05).

30 As we shall see below in section c.2., however, Job 3:8 does not necessarily draw as much force from the mythological backdrop of Leviathan as is commonly believed.

31 *Herodoti Historiae* (2 vols.; 3d ed.; ed. C. Hude; Oxford: Clarendon, 1975) 1:2.68-70. (Engl., *Herodotus/ The Histories* [tr. A. de Sélincourt; Middlesex: Penguin, 1972] 155-57). It is of interest to note that immediately following his description of the crocodile (2.68-70), Herodotus describes the hippopotamus (2.71). For an informative and helpful commentary on these passages in Herodotus, see the recent work by Alan B. Lloyd, *Herodotus, Book II: Commentary 1-98* (Etudes préliminaires aux religious orientales dans l' Empire romain 43; Leiden: Brill, 1976) 305-14.

32 S. Driver comments: "The teeth of the crocodile, 'in the upper jaw usually 36, in the lower 20, long and pointed, are the more formidable to look at, as there are no lips to cover them'," S. Driver and G. Gray, *Job* (ICC) 365. The quotation is taken from A. Dillmann's commentary.

33 "The creature's scales are called fig. 'shields'; each scale of the crocodile is a hard, horny, rectangular plate; they extend in rows along the animal's back, forming a strong protective covering. . . ." S. Driver and G. Gray, *Job* (ICC) 366.

34 ". . . the scales of the belly, which, though less hard than those on the back, are still sharp,

particularly those under the tail, so that, when the animal has been lying in the mud by the river-bank, they leave an impression upon it as if a sharp threshing-drag had been there," (ibid., 369).

[35] See the previous note. The crocodile may have inhabited Palestine in antiquity (cf. the anc. town 'Crocodilonopolis' some four miles north of Caesarea); see also F. S. Bodenheimer, *Animal and Man in Bible Lands*, 129-30. In ancient Egypt the crocodile was worshipped as the god Sobek, esp. in the Faiyûm area where the crocodile was captured but not killed; see *inter alia* A. Lloyd, *Herodotus, Book II*, 308-09.

[36] Reading *ᶜorrê* instead of *ᶜorēr*.

[37] In addition to the fact that *liwyātān* occurs only in Job 3:8 and 41:25, the use of similar phrases in ch. 3 and Job 40:25–41:26 supports the contention that the author of the latter was not disregarding Job's identification of himself with Leviathan in Job 3:8, e.g., *ᶜapᶜpê šāḥar* occurs only in Job 3:9 and in 41:10; piel of *gdm* occurs in Job 3:10 and 41:3 and only once elsewhere (Job 30:27; cf. also the expression *daltê biṭnî* (Job 3:10) and *daltê pānāyw* (Job 41:6); nowhere else in Job is the construct of *delet* used except in these two passages; the dual of the noun is found twice elsewhere in Job 38:8, 10. Contrary to widespread opinion, there is nothing in Job 3:8, in my judgment, which makes a mythological interpretation mandatory. The linguistic evidence suggests rather that we should in part understand the meaning of *liwyātān* in Job 3:8 in the light of Job 40:25–41:26.

[38] 11QtgJob, col. 37, line 2, reads *mlk ᶜl kl rhs* ("king over all reptiles"); see J. P. M. van der Ploeg and A. S. van der Woude, *Le Targum de Job*, 84. A later targum reads *mlyk ᶜl kl bny kwwry* (lit., "king over all the sons of the fish"); see P. de Lagarde (ed.), *Hagiographa chaldaice* (Leipzig: Teubner, 1873) 117. For the rendering "fish," see M. Jastrow, *A Dictionary of the Targumim, the Talmud babli and Yerushalmi* (2 vols.; New York: Putnam, 1895) 1. 616.

[39] Mythological development of both Behemoth and Leviathan certainly did take place within the apocalyptic literature of Judaism (cf. 1 Enoch 60:7-10, 24); it is all the more striking therefore that the mythological interpretation does not seem to have been applied to either creature in the targumim.

Helpful articles on the character and significance of the Targum of Job have been written by J. Fitzmyer ("Some Observations on the Targum of Job from Qumran Cave 11,") *CBQ* 36/4 [Patrick W. Skehan Festschrift; 1974] 503-24 and J. Gray ("The Massoretic Text of Job, the Light of the Qumran Targum (11 Qtarg Job)," *ZAW* 86 (1974) 331-50. In addition to the *editio princeps*, students of 11 Qtg Job will also wish to consult M. Sokoloff's fine commentary (with a useful glossary), *The Targum to Job From Qumran Cave XI* (Jerusalem: Ahva, 1974).

For a useful summary of rabbinic interpretation of Job in the years following 11QtgJob, see I. Wiernikowski, *Das Buch Hiob nach der Auffassung des Talmud und Midrasch. I* (Inaugural Dissertation: Breslau: Fleischmann, 1902).

[40] In the seldom cited appendix to the book of Job found in the LXX, Job is explicitly identified with the Jobab of Gen 36:31-5. The former passage is repeated (not quite verbatim), so that here Job is viewed not only as a son of Abraham, through Esau, but also specifically as one of those who was a "king" (*melek*; LXX *basileus*) in Edom; cf. also 1 Chron 1:43-44.

[41] The correctness of this observation is in part borne out by an ironical remark of Job in Job 12:12, "Among the elderly is wisdom, and length of days is understanding." For further discussion (and allusions) on the association of wisdom and white hair, see in this volume A. Caquot, "Israelite Perceptions of Wisdom and Strength in the Light of the Ras Shamra Texts," section I (near the end) and n. 7.

[42] So goes the judgment of S. Terrien (*Job* [CAT 13] 266), Kissane (*The Book of Job*, 289), et al.

[43] Of the commentators and critics of Job reviewed by the present writer John Calvin in particular endeavored to apply directly what was said about Behemoth and Leviathan to the plight of man (*Sermons de M. Iean Calvin de livre de Iob* [Geneva: M. Berjon, 1611 cf. esp. Sermons 155 and 156, pp. 797-808). Calvin warned against attempting to press the comparison between man and Leviathan in every part (p. 807). He urged, however, that this beast was possessed of such faith as to laugh at lance, sword, and spear (Job 41:18-21) in order to show "that

if we are armed with the virtue of our God we are well defended (en bonne seurté) and have no need either to be anxious or afraid" (p. 807).

44 The Book of Job can hardly be interpreted aright without regard to the author's widespread use of irony and double meanings. By irony we mean here: (i) a literary device whereby the real intent of the writer is opposite from or oblique to the surface meaning of the words and speeches and (ii) a reversal or unexpected turn of events wherein the final outcome of the action or discussion is the opposite from or oblique to that which was originally anticipated either by the characters portrayed or by the reader or both. For further discussion see esp. the works of S. Terrien on Job, R. Gordis (*The Book of God and Man*, ch. 14), E. M. Good (*Irony in the Old Testament* [Philadelphia: Westminster, 1965]), and J. A. Power, "A Study of Irony in the Book of Job" (Ph.D. diss., University of Toronto, 1961). Terrien speaks in very moving terms of the "irony of love" and the "irony of faith" (*Job* [CAT 13] 267-71 and esp. *Job: Poet of Existence*, 218-49.) The present essay in a sense seeks to call attention to the author's employment of both the "irony of love" (God in his compassion comes to Job to bring comfort) and "the irony of faith" (through reenforcing his conviction that God in the end is not his attacker but his companion).

The author wishes to express his gratitude to The University of Tulsa for their moral and financial support throughout this entire project and to the National Endowment for the Humanities for a fellowship at the University of Pennsylvania, which afforded greater leisure for research and editorial duties.

V

# ON THE THEOLOGICAL PERCEPTIONS
# OF THE BOOK OF SIRACH

# THE VISION OF MAN IN SIRACH 16:24-*17:14*

LUIS ALONSO SCHÖKEL, S.J.

PONTIFICAL BIBLICAL INSTITUTE, 00187 ROME

Translated by Clevy Strout, Tulsa, Oklahoma 74104

*To Professor Terrien:*

We first met, without knowing one another, among the anonymous mass of readers and spectators of a great drama, the Book of Job.

Next we came closer, still unaware of each other, as critics and analyzers of that fascinating book.

Having finished our task in the service of new readers, we were able to recognize each other in our enthusiasm.

That common love and service are the reasons for my presenting this modest essay with sincere gratitude.[1]

IN three strophes Jesus Ben Sira offers us a deep reflection on man—or upon the position of man in creation, if we read those three strophes as the literary unit 16:24-17:14.

It is necessary to read it as a unit because the author articulates his teaching in a series of significant correspondences and oppositions. I mean, in more modern terms, that those relations are not exclusively of a semiotic order, as a play of forms; they are also semantic, with significant references.

The author considers the two traditional planes: heaven and earth. On earth he distinguishes living beings in general and man. Thus, he creates two asymmetric groups, with a certain internal tension. Man shares with living beings one quality; he shares with the celestial beings a series of conditions or situations; he stands out in his uniqueness against the backdrop of all creation.

As all living things on the earth are to die, so must man, because he is of the earth. As the celestial beings have a dominion, a function, a mandate, and companions, so does man have dominion, function, law, and companions. Let us reduce the preceding to a diagram:

| HEAVEN | EARTH |
|---|---|
| Stars | Living Things/Man |
| (1) *ouk exelipon* | *apostrophe, apestrepsen* |
| (2) *eis geneas* | *hēmeras arithmou* |
| (3) *archas* | *exousian, phobon, katakyreuein* |
| (4) *erga autou* | *ergon autou* |

|  | erga autōn | ergon autou |
|---|---|---|
| (5) | hrēmatos | nomon, krimata, eipen, eneteilato |
| (6) | ouk apeithēsousin | prosechete apo |
| (7) | ton plēsion autou | peri tou plēsion |

(1) While the living, including man, are to die, the stars do not tire, do not fade away, and do not fail. (2) Whereas man has assigned to him a limited time—a generation if he does not waste it, stars last for generations. (4) Stars have one task; man must be occupied with the tasks of another—although he has his own work. (5) A word of God controls the stars; a law or mandate, man. (6) The stars obey without fail, and man also? (7) The stars form a well-ordered group; man belongs to a community. And, at the end of the list of correspondences, there begins what is proper and exclusive to man, prerogatives which the other animals do not have, nor do the stars of heaven.

If in Sirach 43 creation is the protagonist, here everything moves to exalt the position of man. There is on earth something more important than the stars of heaven, as Psalm 8, so close to our text, already had made clear. As God "looked upon earth" (eis ten gēn epeblepsen, Sir 16:29a), so does the author concern himself with man.

### First Strophe (Sir 16:26-17:4)

Ben Sira gathers and develops three aspects about the creation of man: his mortal condition, his dominion over the earth, his being an image of God—in that order, which is not the traditional one. Many readers probably expect the following order: image of God, dominion over earth, sin-death. Does the change matter?

In the way we read the verses, the mortal condition of man is inherent in his terrestrial or earthly nature, it is not the effect of sin. Man is created mortal directly, as the other living things of the earth. This consequence is confirmed by the fact that moral knowledge and law come afterwards.

Is it that Ben Sira inverts the order in order to make a connection, without a break, with 16:30: "He has covered the face of the earth with the life of all creatures; and their return is unto it"? Such a connection was not needed, when we have seen the network of relations from a distance. That this is a purely formal matter is not borne out by the categorical affirmation of the author: Man is not only mortal, but his life lasts a numerable, and, in comparison to the stars, a limitable period (remember Psalm 72:5 and parallels).

Then, does Ben Sira change the doctrine of Genesis 2-3, according to which death penetrates as a consequence of sin? There is no need to advance further; it may be that Ben Sira is interpreting Genesis more rigorously than a later tradition, attested in the Wisdom of Solomon 2:23-24 and Romans 5:12-14.

In effect, according to Gen 3:3, God promulgates a law with a penalty clause (to use the terminology of Gerstenberger), that is to say, a prohibition "under penalty of death." Now then, a penalty of death is threatened to a mortal creature. Biological death is anticipated violently, and it is made to be felt as punishment; the Wisdom of Solomon says in another case, 18: 19: "in order that they not perish without knowing the reason of their misfortune." It happens in the tale of Genesis that, after the sin, God commutes the penalty of death to perpetual exile, the same thing that will happen to Cain. Thus, instead of eating delightful fruit without effort, he shall have to work and sweat in order to eat the grain of the earth. In Gen 3:19 the punishment is formulated with the correspondence of the *lex talionis* "for having eaten . . . you shall eat. . . ." The return to dust is not pronounced as part of the punishment, but as the extreme limit of its duration: forced labor for life. Certainly, Adam is reminded emphatically of his mortal condition. Death, a biological reality, takes on the function of punishment and exerts its dominion. Yet Adam will be able to fulfill all the time of his existence, he will not be put to death before his time nor will he die violently; nor will Cain.

Ben Sira joins precisely with these concepts and he places them at the beginning of his reflection about man: he is mortal and has a life of limited duration. The first is a consequence of his earthly condition, the limit is assigned by God, according to the doctrine of Gen 6:3.

There is another way of reading Genesis 2-3; but that does not mean that Ben Sira has changed the traditional doctrine. On the contrary, it seems that he has held faithfully to it and he is a historic witness of great importance.

The author reiterates his thought in two other passages, one of a somber tone, another resigned. In 40:1-11 he describes somberly the human condition, "great fatigue, heavy yoke," and he concludes: "What comes from the earth returns to the earth, what comes from heaven returns to heaven" (cf. Ps 104:29). Then, is there a difference between the good and the bad?—Yes: "This happens to all flesh, from men to animals, and seven times more to sinners" (Sir 40:8). In 41:3-4 he invites one to resignation:

> Do not fear your sentence of death,
>> remember those who preceded you and will follow you;
> It is the destiny that God assigns everything living,
>> And, are you going to refuse the law of the Most High?

We move into the mental world of Psalm 90, comprised of grief, melancholy and resignation; one verb sounds similar, *epistrepsate*—and the plants occupy a similar position by way of comparison.

With the beginning of the strophe understood in this manner, what follows appears in paradoxical relief: man is mortal by earthly condition, and nevertheless, God gives him power, impresses on him his own image, and makes him master. The resonances of Psalm 8 are echoed here, although there are no verbal correspondences:

| Psalm 8 | Sir 17 |
|---|---|
| *estephanōsas* | *enedysen* |
| *doxa kai timē* | *ischyn* |
| *katestēsas epi* | *edōken exousian* |

| | |
|---|---|
| *hypetaxas panta* | *katakyrieuein* |
| *probata, ktēnē* | *pasēs sarkos* |
| *peteina* | *theriōn kai peteinōn* |

Judging by the Greek text alone, one would say that the author has put forth an effort to avoid superficial repetitions, preserving the identical underlying structure. Throughout Psalm 8 there sounds a reference not dissimilar to Gen 1:28; on the other hand, the fear of the animals proceeds from Gen 9:2.

To be the image of God is the culminating prerogative of this series (Sir 17:1-4). The distributions of the thematic parallelisms seem to underline it. The synonomies proceed thus: 1b=2a / 2b=3a / 4a=4b. Two lines are taken out, in which God acts directly, and which in Gen 1:24 are placed together:

> 1a   *ektisen ek gēs*
> 3b   *kat'eikona autou epoiēsen*

The irregularity confirms the desire to place later the third quality of man, by placing it in the climatic position. Man's strength is like a garment (*enedysen*), but the new look, as if he were a living statue, is the image.[2]

To sum it up, an earthly and mortal creature, dressed in power almost divine, a living image of God, is the one who casts his dominion over all animals. This is the vision of the first strophe, and now we have the stars of the heavens excelled.

### Second Strophe (Sir 17:6-10)

The poet approaches to describe with more detail his anonymous and universal personnage. Man possesses a series of organs and faculties, several qualities and definite functions.

He can talk, see and hear, understand and evaluate. Whether or not we read "mouth" as an original reading (as is attested by the Syriac), speaking comes before seeing and understanding. I see no special reason for such an order, therefore, I focus on the author's selection: two sense organs are mentioned which (in vs. 6) are framed by the organs which have the faculties of speaking (an external activity) and of thinking (an internal acitivity). We may put this into a diagram:

|  |  | eyes |  |  |  |
|---|---|---|---|---|---|
| vs. 6 | tongue |  | heart | } | for understanding |
|  |  | ears |  |  |  |

But note also:

|  | eyes |  |  |
|---|---|---|---|
| vs. 8 |  | } | for evaluating[3] |
|  | heart |  |  |

According to the traditional doctrine, the ability to evaluate or estimate was in the eyes; also here the objects to be evaluated are shown or put before one (*hypedeixen*, vs. 7).

The functions or tasks correspond to the faculties. The heart or mind is to pay attention, says vs. 8 in the correction proposed by Smend;[4] the eyes are to see the deeds of God, the mouth is to praise His Name or glory—telling or describing it in detail (*diēgōntai*). Does this imply a listening with one's ears?

It is the destiny of man to praise God by the contemplation of his works—a destiny which excels that of the stars. These are works of God which have no knowledge of nor do they sing his glory. (Ben Sira does not pick up the suggestion of Psalm 19). Man can look at them and understand them and rise consciously to the Creator. This corresponds also to the vision of Psalm 8 and other similar ones, and it is a doctrine which Ben Sira repeats and practices in other passages, such as 39:14, 15, 35 and—to cite two sentences from a magnificent hymn—43:30. To see God as artisan of works and protagonist of actions is indeed to act as image and likeness, closing through an inference a circle of comprehension, namely: if man is created in the image of God, God resembles man (inference), and it is therefore possible to understand (circle of comprehension) and say something about God. Only man can do this.

The capacity to evaluate and therefore to choose is enunciated in Sir 17:7—an important verse, clear in itself, but doubtful in its connections. Let us begin with what is clear.

Here indeed the author sets himself apart from Gen 2-3 in order to be inspired by the last part of Deuteronomy, especially Deut 30:15, 19:

| Deuteronomy | Sirach |
|---|---|
| *dedōka pro prosōpou* | *hypedeixen* |
| *to agathon / to kakon* | *kai agatha kai kaka* |

The distinction between the good and the evil is something which God shows (*hypedeixen*) just as he does his works. From that it does not follow that there is a strict revelation, as we ourselves usually understand it, since also the stars are a work which God shows (works and actions are *erga*; Hebrew *maʿăśîm*); indeed they do proceed from the divine initiative, as does all creation. God creates man with all his concrete characteristics. Now, if the showing of works leads to praise, it seems that the showing of the good and the evil ought to lead to conscious choosing. This may seem so to us yet the author does not explicitly say it just now.[5] Does he reserve it for the third strophe?

Now let us pass to the doubtful connections. If we join in sense 7a and 7b "he filled them with intelligence and wisdom and taught them good and evil," it turns out that through intelligence (*epistēmē syneseōs*) God disposes man to discern what he presents to him. In such a case we are dealing with a capacity inherent in man as an intelligent being: everyone can understand and discern what God presents to all. Thus a psychological conscience flows into an ethical conscience.

If in preserving the Greek text, we join 7b to 8a, "he showed them good and evil and began to observe their heart," it turns out to be an intelligible reading and also one which would find support in other texts. For example, in Deut 8:2, God submits the people to a test to see what they have in their hearts, in order to examine their attitudes and decisions. Difficulties arise, however. The Greek expression *ethēken ton ophthalmon autou epi* would correspond to a Hebrew *śîm ʿēnāyw ʿal*, which would mean in this context to look after one for good or for evil (Jer 39:12; 40:4 and Jer 24:6, Amos 9:4); it would not mean here to watch over. Besides, under this reading vs. 8a would not join with the following. Considering the difficulty of the text, therefore, I prefer the solution of reading a period at 7b and beginning a sentence at 8a.

In the second strophe we meet conscious man, capable of seeing and transcending his own vision, capable of seeing marvels and of responding with his praise. Is praising a responsible answer? Psalm 8 sets praise over and against the rebellion of some (Ps 8:3b [Engl. 8:2b]). Ben Sira would like for the praise to burst forth naturally, as the perfume of a flower (39:14). With all the tradition he would consider it assumed that to praise God is good and due (Ps 92:2, 33:1); accordingly the master inculcates it in his students (39:14-16, 32-35). The language of this strophe draws upon the specific traditions of Israel, namely, Deuteronomy.

At the outset of this strophe some manuscripts add an interesting gloss: "he received the use of five works of the Lord, as a sixth gift he granted them intelligence and as a seventh, language which interprets the works of God" (Sir 17:5). The five works are the five senses. With surprise we read an ancient author speaking of the hermeneutic function of language; it sounds strangely modern. This does not distort the teaching of Ben Sira, since by praising, man interprets nature as creation, and the prodigies as works of God.

In any event, speech and praise close the strophe in a kind of mental *inclusio*.

### Third Strophe (Sir 17:11-14)

We now enter into a fully Israelitic theme, so much so that some have wanted to isolate these verses as a separate unit. The present strophe presents three notable links with the two preceding: the theme of life (16:30) is specified in connection with the law (17:11b); the eyes and ears (17:6) are enabled to see and hear (17:13); and to the intelligence of vs. 7 is added another dimension related to the law (17:11a).

The relation between wisdom/intelligence and law is expressly attested in 45:5: *nomon zoēs kai epistēmēs*. It is a well-established doctrine in the book that the law is the new wisdom, especially in the culminating chapter of the first part of the book (24:23). We do not know if the Hebrew repeated the same word in 7a and 11a such as we read in the Greek text wherein man receives a general "knowledge" (*epistēmē*) at the beginning and a special "knowledge" (*epistēmē*) afterwards by means of the law.

This is a "law of life," because it assures or guarantees the life of the one who fulfills it. It is a favored doctrine in Deuteronomy. (Although the formula "law of life" is not read there, it would be *tôrat ḥayîm*.) Combining this notion of the law with the saying in vs. 2a, we understand that man can frustrate or spoil the time which God grants to him for life. In other words, to break the law will necessarily involve a retribution which affects the life of the guilty.

Ben Sira however, prefers a positive formulation. His thought is tranquilly traditional; it does not count on a life after death.

His positive vision of the law is reinforced in the verb *eklērodotēsen* (probably *hinḥîl wĕhôrîš*). The law, as the promised land, is a gift; it is a "heritage" or an "inheritance." One generation possesses it and transmits it to the following. In 24:23 we read: *nomon . . . klēronomian synagōgais Iakōb* ("the law . . . an inheritance for the congregations of Jacob").

In vs. 12 covenant and precepts form a parallelism (*diathēkēn* and *krimata* = *bĕrît* and *mišpaṭîm*) in accord with tradition. The covenant is qualified as eternal: the adjective usually is used when one deals with the Davidic covenant (2 Sam 23:5), or the Aaronic (Sir 45:15), or more frequently with the new (Isa 61:8; Jer 32:40; Ezek 16:60 and 37:26). Isa 55:3 links the new with the Davidic; Gen 9:16 refers to that of Noah; and there is a late text, which has a universal horizon: "they broke the perpetual covenant" (Isa 24:5). Ben Sira does not enter into such distinctions: if his human horizon is universal, such as we shall see, the universality has to be of value in time: the covenant granted by God shall last throughout history, transcending the generations. Thus it can be an inheritance, and can be compared to the eternal dominion of the stars (16:27). The verb used, *estēsen* (Hebr. *heqîm berît*) is of the Priestly tradition.

The second verse in this strophe (17:12), interests us also—especially *hypedeixen* which in Greek is an echo of 7b: the one who "has shown" the good and the evil for the moral discernment also "has shown" the precepts for authentically orienting man. In the order in which the present pericope is arranged, it turns out: there is good and there is evil, and to these there corresponds mandate and prohibition, a positive and a negative command. In contrast, in the order in which Deut 30 is arranged, it turns out: the law has been given; to observe it is good, to break it is evil.

In the full context of the covenant it is easy to hear now the resonances of Exodus 19: the manifestation of glory and the voice of the Lord. Thus was the law promulgated and the covenant was sealed on Sinai.

The final verse tries to synthesize the content of the law in a parallelism. Are the two parts synonymous or complementary? As the second part refers expressly to the neighbor—duties of the second table of the Decalogue—, it is very probable that also the first is specialized, by virtue of linguistic polarization. That is, the author expresses man's duties toward God in the form of a prohibition. What is it against which man must guard? The word used in Greek, *adikou*, does not offer a sufficient clue for going back to the original, which, indeed, could have been less ambiguous. The root *kdb* of the Syriac would take us to a *kzb* in Hebrew, which may refer to idolatry (Amos 2:4) or disloyalty to the covenant (Isa 57:11; Ps 89:36).

In this strophe, toward the end of the unit on which we are commenting, the author pronounces twice (vs. 13a, 13b) the term "glory." In the final verse the author introduces God speaking. The glory of God, not only his works, has been manifested to the eyes and ears of men—as if alluding to or correcting the phrase of Deut 29:3: "The Lord has not given you until today intelligence to understand nor eyes to see nor ears to hear." Until they come to see and listen to the glory of God, the eyes and ears of man have not fulfilled completely their function. So the tongue also has to mature in the praise of the Lord.

Man is a creature who relates personally with his peers and also with God in a conscious, responsible, and lasting manner.

### The Exordium (Sir 16:24-25)

Working back now from the end we may understand better a datum of the exordium, such as it is read in the Greek text: the repetition of the word *epistēmē* in 24a and in 25b as the last word in both instances. (We cannot find consistency in the way the Greek translates terms for wisdom). That word which twice appears in the exordium is repeated strikingly in the second and third strophes (17:7a, 11a). The wise man with his discourse wishes to communicate to his disciples a piece of knowledge, an understanding, which God has granted to man in two successive moments: first as the capacity to comprehend, exceeding the purely sensory perceptions, and, afterwards, as an instruction in the law so as to set one's conduct in order.

In this handling of the words we also discover how wisdom or discernment which these teachers cultivate is to be found between human reason and man's openness to revelation. The wise man is conscious of that position which he occupies and wants to make his disciples conscious that there is no opposition between reason and faith; there is rather a mutual correspondence. The wise man can appeal equally to the experience of the intelligent man and to the sacred writings.

Of this method Jesus Ben Sira is a model: with assurance his discourse recommends, *ton logon mou*, not to supplant the word of God, but to lead to it.

### The Synthesis

The exordium, considered at the end of this exegesis, will aid us in stating a question central to the pericope: Is it talking about man in general or of Israel?; or does the discourse on man-in-general pass over to focus upon the people of the covenant? Up until the present the gigantic and irresistible scissors of the critic have not cut this passage into pieces. We can still read it as a literary unit.[6] For it is still accepted that a Ben Sira has consciously composed this piece as a literary unit.

In order to answer the questions presented, a comparison with different passages of the book will serve. It is of great use to have read and reread and studied the entire work of the author. Although the coherence discovered and felt as the result of familiar handling may be difficult to document, I shall try to comply with the two forces at work within me: through relying on my long dedication to this book, I shall expound my feelings, and I shall also try to document them.

In sum, I think that Ben Sira is talking from the beginning to the end about *man in general.*
  — Never is a name mentioned nor is a concrete person alluded to—in contrast to Sir 45:1-5, which supplies several elements to the present pericope.
  — The two pieces which frame the unit studied, deal with a universally human theme: God sees (16:17-23); God gives retribution (17:15-23).
  — The step from the singular to the plural already has happened in verse 2, showing that *anthrōpos* is understood in a universal or collective sense.

He speaks of man in general *from the point of view of Israel.* The historic experience of Israel, as manifested in its canonical writings, is like a hilltop or a vantage point for understanding the common human condition. This can be explained in two ways: (a) in Israel something granted at the beginning of humanity is realized again. By means of Israel we can understand or perceive for ourselves what that human beginning was; by the mediation of Israel all persons will be able to understand themselves in their nature, which is defined by its origin—as in Latin *natura* comes from *natus.* (b) A profound tendency and exigency of mankind comes to be realized in Israel by a divine gift and election—not as a monopoly, but in order that Israel may share it with others. If the Greeks of that time had something to offer to other peoples, a wise Jew has something more important to offer. This is the great wisdom of which they speak in Deut 4:6-8 and Baruch 4:1.

The author considers it *wisdom of Israel for all.* Although his immediate disciples had been Jews, the author mentally opens the windows of his school so that those on the outside may hear. His grandchild and translator understood it correctly:

> We have received many gifts from the law and the prophets and those who followed them, because of whom Israel merits the praise of the wise and learned. And it is the duty of those who read the scriptures not only to understand, but to become capable of aiding those on the outside by spoken word and written word . . .

"Those on the outside" are non-Israelites among whom he lives, and with whom the Jewish diaspora live. It was a time of great intellectual curiosity, not only when the grandchild wrote, towards the end of the second century, but already when the author was writing, about 180 B.C.

All mankind has a point of common origin. As the Yahwist had already seen, the historical experience of Israel provided the basis for her projections about that common origin. Thus the elect people becomes a model for understanding man, and as a model from which man may learn.

Traditional wisdom has been marked from the beginning by that universalism: its product was free for export and import, its themes and preoccupations were shared without boundaries. Jesus Ben Sira grows in that tradition and leads it to a new stage. We have spoken of a vantage point that serves as an observatory for looking around and embracing far-off reaches of land. We can add that that high point has gathered a light from Heaven which now it can irradiate roundabout to all mankind: "I shall make my teaching shine as the dawn so that I may illumine the distances" (24:32). Here we have expressed and shared, in part, the grand idea for universal peace about which another inspired poet has also dreamt (Isa 2:2-4; Mic 4:1-4).


## BIBLIOGRAPHICAL NOTE

For the study of Ecclesiasticus or Ben Sira the work of Rudolf Smend continues to be fundamental, specifically:

> R. Smend, *Die Weisheit des Jesus Sirach erklärt*. Berlin: Reimer, 1906; and *Griechish-syrisch-hebräisher Index zur Weisheit des Jesus Sirach*. Berlin: Reimer, 1907.

Smend has masterfully dealt with the problems of textual criticism, he has opened the way to strophic analysis and has given us a most useful index, starting with the Greek.

The index can be completed today with that prepared by Rickenbacher with the collaboration of Barthélemy, starting with the Hebrew:

> D. Barthélemy and O. Rickenbacher, *Konkordanz zum hebräischen Sirach*. With a Syriac-Hebrew Index. Göttingen: Vandenhoeck & Ruprecht, 1973.

Of this index I have made use no less than of that compiled by Smend; however, in texts not preserved in Hebrew, as is ours, it is indispensable to begin with Smend.

In some points of textual criticism the revision made by Prato is valuable, besides his book offers a rich bibliography of fifteen pages and an abundance of parallels. The book is rich in diverse material and because of that his various analytical indices are especially useful.

> G. L. Prato, *Il problema della teodicea in Ben Sira*. AnBib 65; Rome: Pontifical Biblical Institute, 1975.

In problems of composition the study of Haspecker is an important advance over Smend—especially in those pericopes which deal with the "fear of God." Ours (Sir 16:24—17:14) has fallen into the net, by virtue of the reading *phobos* instead of *ophthalmos* in some manuscripts. Haspecker has taught us to contemplate larger units in order to discover relationships within them. To our passage he dedicates pages 148-55.

> Josef Haspecker, *Gottesfurcht bei Jesus Sirach*. AnBib 30; Rome: Pontifical Biblical Institute, 1967.

Haspecker would have been capable of giving us partial syntheses of the composition of the book and perhaps a total synthesis; but he died without being able to carry out that work.

Coming to our pericope in particular, in addition to the respective contributions of Prato and Haspecker, we relied on some commentaries and two articles. I started work on this pericope in my concise commentary to Ecclesiasticus, published in the series The Sacred Books:

> Luis Alonso Schökel, *Proverbios y Ecclesiástico*. Los Libros Sagrados 14; Madrid: Ediciones Cristiandad, 1968.

In this work, treatment is given of the composition, the development, many significant correspondences within the text, and some parallels outside of the text. (See esp. the commentary on ch. 24). Other commentaries are duly registered in the bibliography of Prato.

Of the two articles, one is brief, and unpretentious with a pastoral tone, albeit by an expert.

> H. Duesberg, "La dignité de l'homme (Sir 16, 24-17, 14)" *Bible et vie Chrétienne* 82 (1968) 15-21.

Truly important is the article of

> J. DeFraine, "Het loglied op de menselijke waardigheid in Eccli 17, 1-14." *Bijdragen 11* (1950) 10-23.

The article is rich in parallels. The author underlines that which is most pertinent: he insists on the universal character of the covenant and of revelation; he affirms the collective or universal sense which man has in the pericope; he develops, with parallels, the equation between wisdom and word of God. I feel myself the continuator of this work. I have taken more care with respect to matters of composition and literary relations, and have elaborated upon various theological points. It did not seem to me appropriate to multiply minute citations from his writing.

One can also see J. Marböck, "Gesetz und Weisheit. Zum Verständnis des Gesetzes bei Jesus ben Sira," *BZ* 20 (1976) 3-6 and J. Hadot, *Penchant mauvais et volonté libre dans la sagesse de Ben Sira*. Brussels: Presses Universitaires de Bruxelles, 1969, 105-20.

Other studies on specialized points, such as the image (J. Jervell), life (E. Schmitt), lying (M. A. Klopfenstein), literary forms (W. Baumgartner), the beyond (V. Hamp) and others, can be found in the bibliographies of Haspecker and Prato.

The particular work which I almost overlooked when I referred above to the critic's scissors was the doctoral dissertation of W. Fuss, "Tradition and Komposition in Buch Jesus Sirach," about which there is information in two columns of *TLZ* 88 (1973) 948-49.

Finally for the relations with Hellenism, one must go today to the documented study of Th. Middendorp, *Die Stellung Jesu Ben Sirach zwischen Judentum und Hellenismus*, Leiden: Brill, 1973.

---

[1] The commentary to which Professor Alonso Schökel alludes is *Job* (Los Libros Sagrados 16; Traducción de Luis Alonso Schökel y José Luz Ojeda, con la colaboración de José Mendoza de la Mora y revisión de José Maria Valverde. Comentario de Luis Alonso Schökel; Madrid: Ediciones Cristiandad, 1971). [Ed.]

[2] The Letter of Jeremiah insists on dressing luxuriously the images of the gods, vss. 10-12, 57-58, 71.

[3] Note also on the eyes (vs. 13), on the tongue (vs. 10) and on the ears (vs. 13).

[4] R. Smend, *Die Weisheit des Jesus Sirach erklärt* (Berlin: Reimer, 1906) 157.

[5] The process by which man chooses is different in Sir 15:14-17.

[6] I correct myself: there has been an attempt without consequences. See the bibliography at the end of this essay.

# WISDOM AND RELIGION IN SIRACH

EDMOND JACOB

FACULTÉ DE THÉOLOGIE PROTESTANTE, UNIVERSITÉ DE STRASBOURG,
67084 STRASBOURG, FRANCE

Translated by Martin Schwarz, The University of Tulsa, Tulsa, Oklahoma 74104

*To Professor Samuel Terrien:*

Among the collaborators of this volume, I am most probably the one who has
known you for the longest period—close to half a century. Together we studied in
Paris under the unforgettable Adolphe Lods. Together we were introduced to
Oriental studies by René Dussaud and Edouard Dhorme. Together we were the
first to lay eyes on the first texts of Ras Shamra with Charles Virolleaud. When I
returned from a stay at l'École biblique in Jerusalem you followed me there. Then
our paths diverged, but they always remained parallel. At times they converged,
particularly at the occasion of the ecumenical translation of the Bible to which you
brought your collaboration to the delight of many French friends.

Now that you and I are among the elders, and have assumed the place of our
masters, we must repeat, with gratitude and hopefulness, the prayer of the
Psalmist: "Instruct us how to use our days well, that we may enter into the heart of
wisdom" (Ps 90:12).

ONE may speak today of a renewal of studies concerning Ben Sira.
Several reasons account for this fact: the presence of Hebrew fragments
in Qumran, but above all the discovery in Masada of a scroll of seven columns
(chs. 39–43) of this author—unfortunately very mutilated—which brought
him to the forefront of current interest. The problem of the text was entirely
reopened, and while we are awaiting more precise conclusions about that
point, we can already state: that the Masada manuscript, which Yadin dates
from the first century B.C., is the oldest of all the manuscripts; that the
manuscripts of the Geniza of Cairo, whose manuscript B comes closest to the
text of Masada, represent an original Hebrew version, and not a return to the
Syriac text; that they contain numerous errors of copyists and glossarists but
that they go back to a relatively ancient period. We must add another
discovery, this one from Qumran: the scroll of the Psalms of cave 11 which
contains, among others, the acrostic psalm of chapter 51 in Sirach under its
probably primitive form, which Ben Sira integrated into his work after
bringing to it important modifications.

These discoveries have brought greater emphasis to the place of our text in
Jewish tradition, and lead us to ask the question about its historical and

theological ties. The result is a portrait of Sirach which rehabilitates the man who had too often been considered as an imitator and petty bourgeois without depth. Among the monographs of these last few years, one must mention those by J. Haspecker,[1] J. Hadot,[2] J. Marböck,[3] Th. Middendorp,[4] O. Rickenbacher,[5] and Luigi Prato.[6] One must add—because these are almost monographs—the chapter of M. Hengel in his important book *Judentum und Hellenismus*,[7] and the chapter of von Rad about Sirach in his stimulating work on *Wisdom in Israel*.[8] The list would be considerably longer if we mentioned the many articles which have appeared in journals. Most of these writings deal with the attitude of Ben Sira toward Hellenism. Even though no consensus has been reached on all the points, the specialists divorce themselves from the judgment of R. Smend: "He hates with all his heart Hellenism and the Greeks, as well as the small pagan neighboring nations, and yearns for the day of God's reckoning with them . . . in fact, no Greek influence is discernible in his works."[9] Among the moderns, the only one who remained fairly close to Smend's view is Tcherikover: "Ben Sira fought against the spirit of Greek civilization all his life, for he understood the danger threatening Judaism from Hellenism: free inquiry which was not afraid to ask questions about nature and morality, or to answer them by the power of the human mind alone. Greek wisdom, unassociated with the fear of God, aroused the fear of Ben Sira, who saw in it a contradiction to the spirit of Judaism, and warned his pupils from treading this path."[10] Such a Manichaean stand must be nuanced. During Ben Sira's lifetime Hellenism in Palestine was no longer a foreign reality which had to be stemmed. Since at least the third century B.C., the Greek language, and with it a large part of the Greek spirit, had found its way into the country. One could no more ignore it than the air which he breathed daily. This situation found its counterpart in the fact that many pagans opened themselves to Jewish culture. It is the historical background, for example, which one can remember from the legends told in the Letter of Aristeas. Judaism had undergone a transformation, but was this transformation not going to change into alienation; and that which one considered as progress from many points of view, was it not going to become an infidelity? Was wisdom going to become an ally of religion, or develop outside and against it? All of these questions faced Sirach; he wondered about them, and made them the object of his teaching.

I

We know the individual fairly well, even if his real name is somewhat of a problem. According to the textual evidence of Sir 50:27, his name was either Jesus or Simon, and we don't know exactly whether Sirach was his father or grandfather, or even a more distant ancestor. The important thing is that his name was reported, since this is unique in Jewish sapiential literature, which was often presented anonymously, or more frequently still under the pseudonym of Solomon. Should this break with tradition be considered an adoption of a Greek custom? The question must be asked. Similarly with regard to the "Eulogy of the Ancestors," from chapter 44 on, we are reminded of a genre which is close to *De Viris illustribus* of classical antiquity. He enjoys speaking about himself, and though his "I" is not hidden, it never becomes overbearing. On the other hand, the author evokes sympathy by the balance of his thought and ethics, and by his refusal to compromise about the essentials. He shows himself as a *ḥākām* and a *sōpēr* (38:24; 50:27), his book is a source of intelligence and knowledge, *paideia syneseōs kai epistēmas* (50:27). He began this pursuit of wisdom very early (51:13); and it seems probable that he never undertook one of those manual trades about which, following certain Egyptian texts, he speaks with condescension (38:24-34). Wisdom has shaped him to such an extent, that he becomes an incarnation, or at least a reflection, of it. Thus, in 24:30, after having Wisdom speak, he continues: "As for me, I was like a canal leading from a river . . ."[11] He leaves the wisdom which he has acquired to future generations, and he is aware of being the inheritor of a long tradition of sages, whose kinship with the prophets he seems to accept (24:33). He is the last of the line, a gleaner after the grape gathering (33:16), but the Lord's blessing allowed him to make up for lost time (vs. 17). Interpreting certain affirmations of a general sort as autobiographical, some have viewed him as the husband of a shrew, (sin and death were brought into the world by a woman, 25:24), or the father of contentious children (30:7-9) and of flighty daughters (42:9-12), or as a physician—even though his "Praise of Medicine" in ch. 38 is far from a personal testimony. What is more serious is to wonder if this wise man was a school teacher. The origin and the nature of the school in Israel remain a problem. The existence of schools directed by sages for the benefit of future civil servants of the Kingdom is generally accepted, but experts remain cautious as to the methods of the instruction. R. N. Whybray, in his recent work *The Intellectual Tradition in the Old Testament*,[12] reviews the problem and concludes: "The evidence for the existence of schools with professional teachers is not conclusive; it remains no more than a possibility."[13] It would be difficult to be more cautious. M. Hengel[14] also looks into this problem. According to him the schools had opposite aims. Some oriented their teaching so that the maximum of Hellenistic culture would be absorbed. Others wished to preserve as best they could the ancestral Jewish heritage through a well oriented catechism. Sirach would fall into the latter category, but with a wide open door for the first. In our view a positive argument in favor of the theory that he was a school master is that in the same chapter he uses the term *bêt midrāš* (51:23), which appears here for the first time in the Bible, and the term *yĕšîwâ*, which literally means the teacher's seat, although that school might originally have resembled a synagogue more than a school. Middendorp is more affirmative, since according to him Ben Sira was not only a school master, but his book was a school text, or better, a book used by the teacher for the orientation of his instruction.[15] He strengthens this affirmation by recalling the numerous repetitions, and the advice of all sorts, of which a great part addresses itself to young people. In a footnote Middendorp[16] mentions a Greek papyrus from Egypt, which according to its editors, Guéraud and Jouguet,[17] dates from the last quarter of the third century B.C., and which begins with the teaching of the alphabet, turns into a poetical anthology, and after a detour through mathematics, returns to a narrative tale whose humoristic tone aims at making the listeners laugh. The morals, nature and history, which make up the content of this papyrus, recur in Ben Sira, whose encyclopedic nature cannot be denied, even though this aspect was characteristic of all the sapiential writings, whatever their function or literary genre.

In order to show that Ben Sira's encyclopedic knowledge was more Greek than Oriental, a list of the Greek authors which were more or less quoted has been drawn up. In the first place comes Theognis, then Sophocles, Xenophon, Euripides, Hesiod and Homer.[18] From the latter, Ben Sira is said to have borrowed the statement of the Iliad: "It is with the races of men as with the leaves of the trees: some, detached by the wind, cover the earth, while others, reproduced by the greening forests are reborn in the spring."[19] Sirach 14:18 puts it as follows: "In the thick foliage of a growing tree one crop of leaves falls and another grows instead; so the generations of flesh and blood pass with the death of one and the birth of another." The image is the same, but can one conclude, from the use of such a common image, that one author borrowed from another? It is wise to remain doubtful. Still according to Middendorp,[20] Ben Sira must have had access to a Greek anthology since he says about the sage, hence also about himself, that "he studies the wisdom of all the men of old" (Sir 39:1).[21]

If Ben Sira did use Greek sources, these were certainly not the only ones; the most striking parallels in Sirach are found after the canonical Book of Proverbs, in the Aramaean sapiential piece *Aḥiqar*. We shall only point out two of them.[22] Compare: "Do not enter into judgment with a man on the day of his power, and do not resist the river when it comes flooding" (*Aḥiqar* 3:83) with "Do not attempt to oppose the flowing of a river"[23] (Sir 4:26); and "He who shines through his clothes also shines through his language, and he who appears lowly through his clothes appears likewise through his language" (*Aḥiqar* 2:39) may be compared with: "You can tell a man by his looks and recognize good sense at first sight. A man's clothes, and the way he laughs, and his gait, reveal his character" (Sir 19:29-30). This somewhat parodoxical image has no biblical parallel and in this instance one can speak with greater probability of a borrowing. This is far from impossible, since the entire sapiential literature is engulfed by a current which moves multiple elements and which are often found far from their original source.

Ben Sira's wisdom comes to him not only from his books, but also from his travels. But as was the case with the schools, the travels could be two-edged swords. If there are trips for those who wish to learn, there are also trips for businessmen whose sole aim is to make money. Ben Sira does not at all hold the same opinion as the author of the Letter of Aristeas who thinks that the contact with sages, albeit in a closed environment, is preferable to trips: "You can see the effect of traveling and exchanging views, since by dealing with perverse individuals, they live with sages and people with common sense, they acquire in lieu of their ignorance, a straight line of conduct" (*Ep. Arist.* 130). Ben Sira, on the other hand, accepts the risks of traveling: "A man who has travelled has learned much and a man of wide experience knows whereof he speaks. The one who has not been put to the test knows little, but the one who has travelled is full of resources. I have seen many things in the course of my travels, and understand more than I can tell. I have often been in mortal danger but I was spared thanks to my experience" (Sir 34:9-12).[24] In fact, the last words are simply "thanks to that" and we do not know whether "that" refers to the aforementioned skill or to God, who will be mentioned in the following verses. This might be a deliberate ambiguity of the double meaning in which the sages of the Talmud excel. In any case, travels are advised, and this positive point of view will be taken up again by Philo: "There are some who sail for their business, because of their desire for wealth or a diplomatic mission, or in order to visit a foreign region for the love of learning, all are moved by a power which drives them away, the first for love of wealth, the second to serve the city in difficult and grave circumstances, the last to seek what they ignored beforehand, and it will afford their soul both satisfaction and a sense of purpose" (*De Abr.* 65). The same Philo sees Abraham the traveller as the type of the sage, and also as the soul in search of God. The commentary of the apocryphal Genesis of Qumran also stresses the travels of Abraham, but less in order to draw a lesson from them than to justify his rights to the possession of the country. It is not impossible that Ben Sira took part in some political mission, comparable to the one of John, father of Eupolemos, who was sent to Rome as an ambassador to negotiate an alliance treaty (2 Mac 4:11) or like Philo himself who undertook a mission with Caligula. Middendorp thinks that Ben Sira based his views on descriptions and images and never crossed the borders of Palestine, but others think that in order to have been in danger of death (34:12) he must have ventured onto the open sea.[25]

## II

The person of Ben Sira cannot be understood solely from his personal experience; it is also illuminated by general circumstances of history. His era must be dated. His book is indeed the only one in the Bible which we can date with a minimal margin of error, around the first quarter of the second century B.C. between 200 and 175, probably between 190 and 180. Reading the Book of Sirach, one enters into the complex milieu of pre-Maccabean history, into the different classes of a society which was in the throes of painful religious and national conflict. Ben Sira lived before the great crisis. It was a relatively calm period, but one which was about to deteriorate. The Seleucids who succeeded the Ptolemies continued to practice a rather liberal policy toward the Jewish people, one which showed respect for the Jewish particularity, especially so since the Jews had contributed to the ascension of the Seleucids by helping them to rout the Egyptian garrison which had established itself in the citadel of Jerusalem. The charter granted by Antiochus III, mentioned by Josephus in the Book of Antiquities (*Ant.* 12. 3, 3-4 § 129-53),[26] and whose authenticity is confirmed by epigraphic documents,[27] included the following main points:

(a) the king would contribute, partly in cash and partly in kind, to the expenses necessitated by the sacrifices;

(b) all materials used for the completion of the construction of the Temple would be exempted from taxes, whatever their origin;

(c) the people must live according to the laws of their ancestors. (They had religious freedom, but this freedom was controlled);

(d) the Senate, the *gerousia*, to which Ben Sira might have belonged, the priests, scribes of the Temple, and sacred singers would be exempt from poll tax, crown tax, and tax on salt;

(e) there would be a three year tax exemption for those who lived in the city, and those who settled in it again before the end of the year; and

(f) after this period, there would follow exemption from a third of the taxes and emancipation of the inhabitants who had been reduced to slavery.

These measures however did not prevent internal dissensions in Judaism from becoming more and more pronounced. On the one hand there was the conflict between the sacral families of the Tobiads and the Oniads; on the other there was the antagonism between the Jews and the Samaritans. The priesthood itself, under Jason and Menelaus, allowed for progressive accommodation with foreign customs instead of preserving ethnic and religious purity. Matters were further aggravated by the necessity of the Seleucid sovereigns to tax the province more and more after the loss to the Romans in Magnesia in 190 B.C. In the end the combined internal dissensions and external demands for tribute forced the Seleucid power structure to curtail the freedoms which had been generously granted. It is probable that Ben Sira felt the effect of these events and, as a result, at times modified his attitude, and became harder. Chapter 36 of his book clashes with the others and some would see in it a subsequent addition. It is indeed a prayer of the most nationalistic tone, which asks for: the intervention of God's wrath against foreign nations; the ruination of enemy leaders who say "I am the only one"; the reestablishment of the glory of Jerusalem; and, the gathering of all of Jacob's tribes. It is possible that rather than being an addition, it is a borrowing by Ben Sira from the liturgical tradition, which did not escape his encyclopedic knowledge, and that he rallied to it in a late period of his life. It is probably also the situation of the degradation of the priesthood which explains the large place occupied by the eulogy of the great priest Simon II, who had died in 195 B.C. and whom Ben Sira glorifies in order to contrast him with his unworthy successors. Aside from this, there is no historical allusion, but the ones which we have just pointed out are sufficiently important to help us throw some light on the historical surroundings in which he lived.

## III

The scribe in Ben Sira must have been familiar with the literary tradition of his people, all the more so since the largest portion had received canonical investiture. Among the works which are chronologically and thematically close to Sirach, Qoheleth often makes similar reflections, but they represent two different temperaments. Faced with reality, Qoheleth is critical: "There is nothing new under the sun" (Qoh 1:9c). Ben Sira, on the contrary has a positive and receptive attitude towards reality, and above all towards creation, all the stronger since he connects it to the tradition of the covenant, which allows him to speak of God in terms which do not make him a distant God. The Book of Tobit is entirely devoted to duties of piety and the observance of the law, which occupy a far from negligible, but certainly not the only place in the Book of Sirach. Baruch speaks in 3:9–4:4 of personified wisdom, in terms which could have been borrowed from Ben Sira, but he is unable to establish a harmonious union between the wisdom in creation and in law. It would be more fruitful, we think, to attempt to link Ben Sira with writings which manifestly came after him, but which denote a like thought, and possibly a like origin.

The *Testaments of the XII Patriarchs*, where the ritual element is eclipsed by moral exhortation and the call for piety of heart, and from which all anti-Hellenistic polemic is absent, call for a comparison with the Book of Sirach. The text attributed to the anonymous Samaritan found between 200 B.C. and the revolt of the Maccabees, hence shortly after Sirach, the works of Aristobulus and Eupolemos, which date from after the revolt, confront Judaism with Hellenism much more than Sirach does. These works sought to show the ancient origin of Judaism and thus its priority over Greek philosophy. They purported to demonstrate that the best in Greek philosophy was due to the Israelite sources which inspired it. With Sirach we are far from this apologetics which knew some success by bringing Greeks over to Judaism, but which in the long run, by its lack of respect for historical reality, could not be taken seriously. One may conclude that the thought of Sirach follows an original track; the construction which he erects is without parallel; he is equidistant from a hasty apologetics and an orthodoxy which is content to affirm without ever proving.

## IV

The first and the last word of his message is wisdom. This must be pointed out particularly in opposition to Haspecker's thesis, according to which the central message of Ben Sira is the fear of God. Certainly the fear of God occupies an important place in his book; it is always, as in the Proverbs, the beginning of wisdom (Sir 1:14); but Ben Sira does not take the fear of God as a starting point in order to reach wisdom. It is by starting with wisdom that he manages to see in the fear of God one aspect and one expression of this wisdom. We must recognize that Ben Sira is the first to elaborate a true theology of wisdom in Israel.[28] He undoubtedly had predecessors, in particular the author of Proverbs 8 and that of Job 28; but both speak of a theological wisdom close to God, and neither points out the consequences of this wisdom. They probably deem it too contaminated by mythology, so that they stop short by linking wisdom to the fear of God in its double aspect as respect before the divine mystery and as an ethical attitude. The framework of the Book of Sirach is made up of sapiential pericopes which shore it up in the beginning (1:1-10), in the middle (ch. 24), and at the end (51:13-30). The other sapiential pericopes also occupy a strategic position. They make up the transition between two large unities with different contents, as if to stress that in reflection as well as in action the great and only source of inspiration is wisdom.

The first great sapiential pericope is a hymn which immediately gives the essential characteristics of wisdom (1:1-10):

(a) all wisdom comes from God;

(b) it has been in existence from all eternity;

(c) it is a gift bestowed unto creation and given to men; and,

(d) Israel is not mentioned, but is perhaps implied at the end of vs. 10, since those who love it are the members of the people loved by God.

The second pericope (Sirach 24), which ends the first part of the book, is also a hymn, which because of its form and chronological nearness can be linked with the aretalogies of Isis,[29] even though the feminine Wisdom as a *paredros* of God could have found its inspiration from other models, particularly Mesopotamian ones. We find in it that:

(a) Wisdom has a divine origin. It is glorified as much in the divine Assembly as in the midst of its people, in heaven and on earth; between the celestial world and the people of Israel, there is a correlation. This theme will be developed in apocalyptic literature.

(b) Wisdom is a Word. The mist (*homichlē*)[30] which is mentioned in vs. 3 is reminiscent of a myth; but it is only used for comparison, because for Ben Sira that which comes out of God's mouth can be nothing but the Word of creation.

(c) The Wisdom-Word is the active principle in creation and history. This is in line with the Old Testament (Pss 33:4, 9; 104:7; 147:15; Isa 48:13; 50:2, etc.).

(d) The Word is rendered concrete and incarnate in the Torah; the word "torah" has in the Book of Sirach a large meaning and designates both history and the narration of history.

(e) Israel is the place where Wisdom resides, and the place from which it will move into time.[31]

The third sapiential pericope (Sir 51.13-30) is a hymn whose primitive form was found in Qumran, where it is the sapiential adaptation of a love song. Though they are strongly attenuated, erotic traits can still be noticed in

Ben Sira's text. The relationship between man and wisdom is a love relationship. Wisdom takes on the form of a nurse maid for the youngest ones, and of a friend for the adults. We must therefore ask ourselves if the theme of the union of man and Wisdom is not the continuation of the prophetic theme of the marriage between Yahweh and the people, transposed onto an individual plane. The use of the term "knowledge" could have facilitated this transposition, which was only to be temporary, and a work like the Song of Songs gives once again its full value to the prophetic image, while it also perhaps gives its due to the sapiential aspect.

The other sapiential pericopes (4:11-19; 14:20-15:10; 6:18-37) are hortatory, and insist less on the nature of wisdom than upon the privilege of possessing it.

Let us attempt now to characterize the theology of wisdom in Ben Sira with the help of the elements which we have just illuminated.

(1) Wisdom manifests itself first in creation. Thanks to it, creation is one. But it is a unity in duality. Ben Sira affirms several times that there are two aspects in everything that exists: "Opposite evil there is good, opposite death there is life; likewise, opposite the pious man is the sinner, and opposite light, darkness. Consider all the works of the Almighty, they are two by two, one opposite the other (33:14-15). All things come in two's, one opposite the other; there is nothing imperfect" (42:24). The same idea is found in the Testament of Asher, especially in chapter 5. This duality, which is in no way a dualism, is a sign of harmony, order and beauty, a harmony which Ben Sira designates by the word "glory." The term "glory" is one of the key words of our author, he uses the word *doxa* 53 times, and the verb *doxazein* 31 times. It is in the final chapters that the use is most frequent. At a time when the interventions of God in history seem absent, when the voice of the prophet is still, Ben Sira insists on "glory," the permanent element whose full weight creation stresses, and from which no human being can consequently escape. But this theme of glory had also been linked with the history of Israel, in which God manifests his glory, particularly in the priesthood and in the liturgical tradition.[32]

(2) History is far from lacking in Sirach. The word "torah" is not taken in a legalistic sense. It designates the Pentateuch and perhaps even the totality of the biblical books (Sir 24:23). To have introduced history into the sapiential speculation is the great novelty of Sirach. His enumeration of the great ancestors (Sirach 44–49) is an original presentation of the history of Israel as it was taught in the schools of wisdom. This history of Israel is presented against the background of universal history. It is probable that in his introduction to the "Praise of the Fathers" he also thought about the great men of pagan antiquity. And even if one discards this assumption, one must recognize that he spoke about the ancestors of his people in such a fashion that other nations could easily apply this list to themselves. "Men who were dominant in their kingdom, renowned through their universal visionary power, inventors of melodic songs and poetic narratives" (Sir 44:3, 5) were not necessarily

Israelites. Moreover the mention in Sirach 49:14-16 of Enoch, Noah and Adam, denotes a universalist vision, which joins the theology of glory.

The election of Israel, the covenant, the law, do not push wisdom into the background in order to take its place. Von Rad is perfectly correct to say that Ben Sira wishes to legitimize and interpret Torah, and thus history, with wisdom as its starting point.[33] Ben Sira thus joins a tradition which had been started by Deuteronomy. In the introductory discourses of Deuteronomy it is said with reference to Torah, "This will be your wisdom (ḥokmâ) and intelligence (bînâ) in the eyes of the nations"; these nations will say, "It can only be a wise and intelligent people, this great nation; since what nation is sufficiently great so that the gods be as close to it, as is Yahweh our God" (Deut 4:6-7). The law is therefore a wisdom which, as is generally the case with all wisdom, is close to man and which he can and must accomplish (cf. Deut 30:14). Deuteronomy already attempted to introduce wisdom into Torah, lifting it out of a narrow frame in order to give it wide open air. By "torahfying" and historifying wisdom, Sirach gives it a place where it can find its rest, that is to say, where it can incarnate itself. However one must recognize that neither during the time of Deuteronomy nor that of Ben Sira, could this ideal become a fact. But in no way can Ben Sira be made responsible for the evolution toward literalism or legalism. The fact that Ben Sira was above all a theologian of wisdom is again seen in the manner in which he explicitly links the covenant to the creation. After having spoken of man's creation in the image of God, of man who must find his purpose in power, knowledge, and praise, he continues:

> Moreover he granted them knowledge;
>    he gratified them with the law of life.
> He concluded with them an eternal covenant;
>    he showed them his judgments.
> Their eyes have seen the magnificance of his glory;
>    their ears have heard the glory of his voice.
> He said to them, "Keep away from all injustice";
>    he gave each of them commands concerning his fellowman.   (Sir 17:11-14)[34]

It would be impossible to affirm with greater certainty the universalist vocation of the election of Israel.

(3) Wisdom is finally manifested in the fear of God. But Ben Sira is not content in repeating this current notion, he brings fresh values to it. L. Derousseaux writes the following with regard to the fear of God in Ben Sira:

> The extreme abundance of the expression "fearing God" already shows that we are far from the classical themes of wisdom and its expressions. "Fearing the Lord" is not that which adopts a certain moral behavior, but that which implies a personal relationship of trust and love with the Lord. Even if the idea of retribution is present, it is never an automatic retribution but a salvation which is granted by the compassionate and merciful Lord.[35]

Haspecker, by showing that trust and humility are the two principal aspects of the fear of God, correctly insists on the inner attitude made of trust and humility.³⁶ But trust and humility are more in the line of the prophets, particularly Isaiah, than of traditional wisdom. Trust and humility are best expressed in prayer. Ben Sira often speaks of prayer (Sir 1:28; 2:7-11; 17:25, etc.) and the text of prayer which we have from him has tones of interiorization and spiritual asceticism which we will find, for example, in the *Hôdāyôt* of Qumran (Sir 23:1-6).

If prayer is a matter of inner piety, praise stresses the public expression of piety. In the description of the cult celebrated by the high priest, the accent is on praise (50:16-24), the true center of the cult, as in the work of the Chronicler, with which the entire people most associate itself: "And now bless Yahweh, God of Israel, who accomplishes miracles on earth" (Sir 50:22 [Hebr.]). But—and here we see the face of the sage and the humanist—man is also an object of fear and praise, precisely because he is the image of God on earth (17:1-10). The liturgy of the temple is the place of convergence of creation, history, and the fear of God. This convergence lends to the liturgy a cosmic dimension; and the latter is expressed through the term "glory." The temple of Jerusalem is the place where wisdom is anchored, but from there it turns into a river which is a kind of new paradise (Sir 24:10-22).

Concentration and expansion are in Ben Sira, as in the prophets, the means to achieve the universality implied by the election. Does this universality have an eschatological dimension? If one can speak of eschatology in our author, it is more hidden than apparent, expressed less by words than by a general orientation. In an important study A. Caquot has shown himself to be very negative on the question of messianism in Sirach.³⁷ He sets aside Davidic messianism—which is indeed absent—but he also casts doubt on an Adamic eschatology which might be found in Sirach 49:16. We wonder however if this last feature, as well as the importance given to Elijah (Sir 48:10) and the importance of praise and glory,³⁸ are not the expression of some eschatology.³⁹

Ben Sira was entirely a theologian of wisdom, but precisely because he was "theo-logian," wisdom never takes the place of God in his work. He affirms several times that there are things which cannot be known and which we are forbidden to seek (Sir 3:23). The works of the Lord are admirable, but hidden from human beings (Sir 11:4). "He is the Great One, he surpasses all his works" (Sir 43:28). It is in the light of this last verse that one must read the surprising verse which comes immediately before: "He is the All (*hû³ hakōl*)." Some wondered if this was not a Stoic interpolation or if Ben Sira was not in the last analysis a Stoic himself. It is a bit rash to draw such conclusions. Ben Sira means that God, the God of Israel, has created everything (cf. Sir 36:1; 39:21; 43:33; 45:23), and thereby he is in the pure Israelite and prophetic tradition: "It is I, Yahweh, who makes everything, I have spread out the heavens, who was helping me?" (Isa 45:7). But this God, whose transcendence Ben Sira never fails to stress, is present, not to say immanent, in the world through his wisdom, whose glory shines everywhere.

In conclusion, we will say that Ben Sira is the witness of a traditional

Judaism which, according to its specific vocation, has a mission for the world and the nations. He is not one of those who, as was the case later with the rabbis, wished to build a hedge around the Torah, because the Torah, as he conceives of it, would immediately break this hedge. The fact that Ezra is not mentioned in the "Praise of the Fathers" (Sirach 44–49) has often been pointed out, and it is likely that even though the wisdom of God was in the hands of Ezra (Ezra 7:25) Ben Sira did not see in his work the wished-for orientation of Judaism. Living during the eve of one of the strongest identity-crises known by Judaism, the sage that he is knows that one cannot go back into history, and in this he is the inheritor of the prophets and not of the sectarians oriented toward the past. Firmly convinced of the unity of Israel—strongly compromised by the bad Samaritans, against whom he shows a temporary feeling of anger (Sir 50:25)—he does not wish to create a party. Therefore we shall not enter into the game of those who see him either as a Sadducee or a pre-Sadducee, a proto-Pharisee or the first of the Qumranians. By virtue of his faith in the unity of Israel, he works to avoid the break between the metropolis and the diaspora. With as much intelligence as generosity, he wishes to build bridges between the various families of Judaism, and between Judaism and the Hellenic world, looking for what could constitute a common ground, without thereby effecting a repudiation. By acting in this manner, he also builds a bridge between wisdom and religion, which only become fruitful when they have been linked. The march of events did not allow the realization of his program, but his grandson speculated that in entirely new circumstances the voice of his grandather still deserved to be heard, as a testimonial to wisdom and truth (Sir 4:28), worthy of being included, if not in the canon, then in the least marginal margin of the inspired books (Prol. 10-20).

---

[1] J. Haspecker, *Gottesfurcht bei Jesus Sirach: Ihre religiöse Struktur und ihre literarische und doktrinäre Bedeutung* (AnBib 30; Rome: Pontificial Biblical Institute, 1967).

[2] J. Hadot. *Penchant mauvais et volonté libre dans la sagesse de Ben Sira* (Brussels: Presses universitaires de Bruxelles, 1969).

[3] J. Marböck, *Weisheit im Wandel* (BBB 37; Bonn: Hanstein, 1971).

[4] Th. Middendorp, *Die Stellung Jesu Ben Siras zwischen Judentum und Hellenismus* (Leiden: Brill, 1973).

[5] O. Rickenbacher, *Weisheitsperikopen bei Ben Sira* (Orbis biblicus et orientalis; Göttingen: Vandenhoeck & Ruprecht, 1973).

[6] L. Prato, *Il problema della teodicea in Ben Sira* (AnBib 65; Rome: Pontifical Biblical Institute, 1975).

[7] M. Hengel, *Judentum und Hellenismus: Studien zu ihrer Begegnung unter besonderer Berücksichtigung Palästinas bis zur Mitte des 2. Jahrhunderts vor Christi* (WUNT 10; 2d ed.; Tübingen: Mohr [Siebeck], 1973) 241-75; Engl. *Judaism and Hellenism* (2 vols.; London, SCM, 1974) 1. 131-53.

[8] G. von Rad, *Weisheit in Israel* (Neukirchen-Vluyn: Neukirchener Verlag, 1970) 309-36; Engl., *Wisdom in Israel* (Nashville and New York: Abingdon, 1972) 240-62.

[9] R. Smend, *Die Weisheit des Jesus Sirach erklärt* (Berlin: Reimer, 1906) xxiv.

[10] V. A. Tcherikover, *Hellenistic Civilization and the Jews* (Philadelphia: Jewish Publication Society of America, 1961) 144.

[11] This translation and others are from the *NEB* unless otherwise noted.

[12] R. N. Whybray, *The Intellectual Tradition in the Old Testament* (BZAW 135; Berlin: de Gruyter, 1974) 33-45.

[13] Ibid., 43.

[14] M. Hengel, *Judentum und Hellenismus*, 143-52; Engl., *Judaism and Hellenism*, 1. 78-83.

[15] Th. Middendorp, *Die Stellung Jesu Ben Siras*, 32-34.

[16] Ibid., 32.

[17] O. Guéraud and P. Jouguet, "Un livre d'écolier du III^e siècle avant J.C. (*Publications de la Société Royale Egyptienne de Papyrologie. Textes et documents 2*; Cairo: L'Institut français d'archéologie orientale, 1938).

[18] For a fuller discussion see Th. Middendorp, *Die Stellung Jesu Ben Siras*, 7-31.

[19] Homer, *Iliad* 6. 146-48; cf. 21.464. The translation is by M. Schwarz.

[20] Th. Middendorp, *Die Stellung Jesu Ben Siras*, 25.

[21] This translation accords with the rendering of Professor Jacob. [Tr.]

[22] F. N. Nau (*Histoire et Sagesse d'Ahikar l'Assyrien* [Paris: Letouzey et Ané, 1909] 60-63) lists about twenty more or less convincing parallels which show that in any event we are situated in a neighboring climate.

[23] The translation accords with the rendering of Professor Jacob. [Tr.]

[24] The translation is adopted from *NEB*. [Tr.]

[25] Th. Middendorp, *Die Stellung Jesu Ben Siras*, 170.

[26] Fl. Josephus, *Jewish Antiquities* (LCL; 9 vols.; eds. R. Marcus et. al.; London: Heinemann, 1943), 7. 64-79.

[27] In an exhaustive study on the Seleucid charter of Jerusalem, E. Bickermann (*Revue des études Juives* 99 [1935] 4-35) underlines that Antiochus III had the same attitude toward Jerusalem as he did toward other conquered cities and that, following the example of Artaxerxes, Alexander and the Lagids, he took into account the particular sociological structure of the holy city. Bickermann concluded without reservation that the document reported by Josephus was authentic. He reached this conclusion on the basis of an internal analysis of two epigraphic records. One was found at Sardis (*Sardis: Greek and Latin Inscriptions* [eds. W. H. Buckler and D. M. Robinson; Leiden: Brill, 1932] vol. 7, pt. 1); and relates to a city the name of which is lost but which procured sizeable exemptions from duty in view of the damage it had endured. The other found at Broussa dates about 190 B.C. and deals with a royal city of Pergamum. The inscription guarantees the usage of the city's own laws and of traditional government. The last mentioned was published and analyzed by M. Holleaux, "Inscription trouvée à Brousse," *Bulletin de correspondance hellénique* 48 (1924) 1-57. On the decree of Antiochus III see also the brief notice of A. Alt, "Zum Antiochus III Erlass für Jerusalem," *ZAW* 47 (1939) 283-85.

[28] G. von Rad expresses a similar sentiment; see *Wisdom in Israel*, 240-51.

[29] M. Hengel, *Judentum und Hellenismus*, 287 (*Judaism and Hellenism*, 1. 158-59) thinks that Sirach was familiar with the aretalogies of Isis through a wisdom hymn. H. Conzelmann ("Die Mutter der Weisheit," *Zeit und Geschichte* [Dankesgabe an R. Bultmann; ed. E. Dinkler; Tübingen: Mohr, 1964] 225-34) emphasizes more strongly the analogy with the aretalogies.

[30] The word *homichlē*: "mist, cloud, fog," is also in Sir 43:22 where the Hebrew text has ^c*ānān*. Chapter 24 is absent from the Hebrew versions. In Sir 43:22 it was found next to the "dew" as a vivifying element. Ben Sira probably thinks about the ^ɔ*ēd* of Gen 2:6 and the *rûah* of Gen 1:2. The Aramaean versions translates ^ɔ*ēd* by ^c*ānān*; the Targum Jerushalmi I paraphrases Gen 2:6 as follows: "But a cloud of glory descended from the throne of glory; it was filled with the water of the ocean, then it ascended from the earth and caused rain to fall and it watered the surface of the soil." Thereby he intends to combine the two traditions of Genesis and to give a relatively scientific explanation of creation. This image taken from nature allows him to show that wisdom is both in the heavens and on earth, that it is revealed and yet accessible to reason.

[31] One of the most recent studies about Sirach 24 is the one of M. Gilbert ("L'éloge de la

Sagesse [Siracide 24]," *Revue théologique de Louvain* 5 [1974] 326-48) which sees the movement of concentration and expansion of Wisdom as the overall structure of the chapter. This author also thinks that one cannot speak of anti-Hellenism in Ben Sira, since he allows for the double acceptance of Torah by Wisdom and of Wisdom by Torah.

[32] The positive attitude of Ben Sira toward the liturgy is not universally shared. J. G. Snaith ("Ben Sira's supposed love of liturgy" *VT* 25 [1975] 167-74) thinks that he attaches greater importance to social justice and to moral law than to ritual. If his attitude toward the cult places him in the line of prophetic preaching, e.g. 34:18-35:15, it is nonetheless true that during his time the cult was about the only means for Israel to affirm its identity.

[33] See G. von Rad, *Wisdom in Israel*, 245-47.

[34] This translation accords with the rendering of Professor Jacob. [Tr.] For a further explication of these vss. and the pericope of which they form the conclusion, see the preceding essay in this volume by Professor Alonso Schökel. [Ed.]

[35] L. Derousseaux, *La Crainte de Dieu dans l'Ancien Testament* (LD 63; Paris: Editions du Cerf, 1970) 349.

[36] J. Haspecker, *Gottesfurcht bei Jesus Sirach*, 205-342.

[37] A. Caquot, "Ben Sira et le messianisme," *Sem* 16 (1966) 43-68.

[38] On the importance of praise and glory in Ben Sira, see the preceding paragraph and our comments above in point number (1) of our summary of his theology of wisdom.

[39] Cf. our study on "L'Histoire d'Israël vue par Ben Sira" in *Mélanges bibliques rédigés en l'honneur de André Robert* (Travaux l'Institut Catholique de Paris 4; Paris: Bloud & Gay, 1958) 288-94.

# VI
# ON THE RELATIONSHIP OF
# ISRAELITE WISDOM TO
# APOCALYPTIC

# OBSERVATIONS ON QUANTITATIVE AND QUALITATIVE TIME IN WISDOM AND APOCALYPTIC

SIMON J. DE VRIES

METHODIST THEOLOGICAL SCHOOL IN OHIO, DELAWARE, OHIO 43015

To a revered teacher and cherished friend, Samuel Terrien:
ʾîš nābôn wĕḥākām . . . ʾîš ʾăšer rûaḥ ʾĕlōhîm bô (Gen 41:33, 38-39).

T HE aim of this essay is to call attention to the point at which
wisdom and apocalyptic[1] are generically related to each other. Many of
their elements of apparent resemblance are, upon close inspection, incidental
or superficial, yet they do share an essential ideological kinship in their
conception of time and history. Our thesis is that this kinship is so truly central
as to define the essence of their affinity for each other, while explaining their
relative isolation within the mainstream of Israel's religious literature, which
is that which embodies the tradition of an immanent, divine-human
interaction in the process of the national life, as witnessed in sacred
historiography, deuteronomic parenesis, and prophetism.[2]

## I

There has been little recognition of a common bond between wisdom and
apocalyptic except on the part of those scholars who have found it important
to dissociate apocalyptic from prophecy. Even the casual reader recognizes
that wisdom is practical and utilitarian, being designed for making the best of
things as they are, while apocalyptic is radically other-worldly, visionary, and
escapist, despairing of things as they are—or as they seem to be—and
yearning for a world to come. What common bond can there actually be
between things so opposite? Nevertheless, we intend to show that, despite
apocalyptic's drastic futurism, the two do share a common approach to the
phenomenon of time.

Evidence that the Jewish apocalypticists felt themselves to belong within
the wisdom tradition is the fact that they drew upon various of its most
characteristic elements. We observe for instance the cosmological curiosity of
Ethiopic Enoch, producing a veritable catalogue of wisdom phenomena (1
Enoch 21-36); also its intricate astronomical speculations (chs. 72-82). Surely
this book belongs within the stream of what Norman Whybray has called "the
intellectual tradition,"[3] as do books like Daniel and 4 Ezra. One could point

furthermore to the recurring appearance of wisdom admonitions within the Testaments of the Twelve Patriarchs (as at T. Levi 13, T. Jud. 18, T. Naph. 8, etc.), where their function is more than mere embellishment.

In his recent article on Daniel, John G. Gammie defines apocalyptic form-critically as a composite literary genre, characteristically containing one or more of a variety of subgenres, among which are parenesis, blessing, hymn, nature wisdom, story, fable, allegory, riddle, and parable.[4] Although Gammie does not stress this, these subgenres are found also in the wisdom writings or are drawn from the wisdom tradition. This reminds us that wisdom is itself a complex phenomenon, coming to expression in a number of similar genres and subgenres. It must be more than coincidence that apocalyptic and wisdom share the formal characteristic of structural complexity and the material characteristic of encompassing comparable subelements.

We are thus entirely ready to admit that Gerhard von Rad is justified in stressing the strong affinity of apocalyptic with wisdom.[5] But he is surely wrong in deriving apocalyptic directly from wisdom. His argument begs the question of precisely what apocalyptic is, for the apocalyptic books in which he identifies a potent wisdom influence—particularly 1 Enoch and Daniel—represent apocalyptic in a fully developed form.[6] Von Rad has simply trimmed his definition of apocalyptic to exclude those earlier biblical writings that the majority of scholars identify as apocalyptical in nature but which happen to lack the recognizable forms and motifs of wisdom. We are thinking of such passages as Isaiah 24–27, Isaiah 56–66, Ezekiel 38–39, Ezekiel 40–48, Joel 3–4, and Zechariah 9–14. Von Rad rightly recognizes that these passages are prophetic in their essential affinities and their historical derivation—yet they clearly display some of the peculiar elements that make the apocalyptic literature distinctive and separate it sharply from classical prophetism.

Some recent discussions of this problem, stressing the importance of preparing the ground by offering careful definitions, succumb nevertheless to the tendency to define apocalyptic on the basis of its fully developed forms.[7] It would seem to be sound method to probe for the point at which the something new and recognizably different that we may properly call apocalyptic first began to emerge. We would expect emergent forms to be relatively simple in form and conception—not complex and sophisticated like Daniel or 1 Enoch.

It is precisely that ideological element which has led von Rad to stress the radical discontinuity between apocalyptic and prophecy, connecting it instead to wisdom—viz., a sharply different conception of time and history—that in fact provides the essential clue to the historical point at which we may first observe apocalypticism taking form. We find that the crucial moment came many years prior to the second century, b.c., when 1 Enoch and Daniel were written. Primitive apocalyptic is a product of the sixth century, appearing in the so-called Gog apocalypse of Ezekiel 38–39. Leaving aside a baroque mass of later embellishments upon this text, we follow Walther Zimmerli in identifying an original oracle cast in classic prophetic style but directed against a mythical enemy. Jerusalem is at the time of actual speaking a waste, and the land of Judah is a desolation, yet Yahweh commands this mythical "Gog" to prepare himself with his allies for an attack on Jerusalem in the distant future:

> Be ready and keep ready, you and all the hosts that are assembled about you, and be a guard for them. After many days (*miyyāmîm rabbîm*) you will be mustered; in the latter years (*bĕʾaḥărît haššānîm*) you will go against the land that is restored from war, the land where people were gathered from many nations upon the mountains of Israel, which has been a continual waste; its people were brought out from the nations and now dwell securely, all of them. (38:7-8)

Here is an unprecedented level of objectifying the future, completely bypassing the crisis of the present condition of deportation and exile. Time has been radically quantified and categorized; apocalyptic is beginning to form in the place of traditional prophetic eschatology. Zimmerli appropriately queries:

> Within the framework of Ezekiel's proclamation, which elsewhere very specifically refers to the proximate future, is it conceivable that the same prophet in this specific instance is looking toward a remote future, involving a second step in the divine action beyond that which is to be immediately expected . . .? Here without question something brand new appears. A first step on the way to apocalyptic, endeavoring to establish a sequence of coming experiences, has taken place.[8]

We must disagree with Zimmerli in identifying this manner of speaking as merely "a first step on the way to apocalyptic"—(von Rad would not have disagreed with that way of putting it). What we have here is apocalyptic itself—embryonic no doubt, yet unmistakably alive and irreversibly different from anything that had previously been seen. Prior to this, Israel's prophets had prognosticated the future deliverance on two factors: (1) their knowledge of the past and the present; (2) their conception of Yahweh's character and purpose. But now we see something truly new: within a single, unredacted context, the forecast of the coming restoration is no longer the climax of the prediction, but has become a premise upon which a distant, fresh peril—the condition for an ultimate deliverance—is posited. Redactors were reshaping materials in this way, but here the original writer does it himself.[9] We may answer Zimmerli's query as he did: no, it could hardly have been the Ezekiel that we know who would have written thus. Yet enough of that prophet's literary style and historical outlook remain at the original compositional level to guarantee that whoever did write Ezek 38:7-8 was someone from Ezekiel's immediate school.[10]

Thus sometime late in the exilic period apocalypticism made its first appearance within the religious literature of ancient Israel. The exile produced also the core of Ezekiel's temple vision. In the early postexilic period apocalypticism becomes an identifiable influence in the night-vision(s) of Zechariah,[11] in expansions to the books of Isaiah, Obadiah, Malachi, Joel, and Zechariah, and in additions to the exilic apocalyptic passages themselves.[12] The fact that emergent apocalyptic employs prophetic forms such as the vision and the judgment oracle, elaborates prophetic themes such as the holy war, and attaches itself like a placenta to the organism of the prophetic literature is proof that prophecy is its true mother. Who the father may have been remains as the question before us.

## II

What von Rad has done in clarifying the crucial differences among the various Scriptural witnesses on the subject of time and history will remain as one of his greatest contributions to biblical theology. He has devoted special sections of his *Old Testament Theology* to the contrasting prophetic and apocalyptic views.[13] An analysis of wisdom's view, somewhat slighted there, receives more than ample treatment in his last major work, *Wisdom in Israel*.[14] We should mention also his labors on Deuteronomy, featuring that book's frequent references to the present day (*hayyôm*) as a moment of crucial decision; also his study of the Deuteronomist's understanding of history.[15] These studies are all indispensable and invite supplementation and expansion, rather than correction.

A book by the writer of the present essay, *Yesterday, Today and Tomorrow: Time and History in the Old Testament*,[16] helps bring von Rad's analysis to greater clarity by providing a minute discussion of Israel's prime time-word, *yôm*, "day," especially as this is used in the frequently occurring formulae, *bayyôm hahû* and *hayyôm*. Though von Rad recognized the crucial importance of *hayyôm* in his treatment of Deuteronomy, he had no opportunity to enter as fully as we have done into its analysis. A number of our conclusions have direct relevance for the subject matter under discussion here.

One important thing to understand is that the word *yôm* has definite priority over other time-words such as *ʿēt*, both lexicographically and literarily. That is, *yôm* is a pure time-word even when used inexactly or metaphorically, whereas *ʿēt* (usually translated "time") refers first of all to a situation and only by extension to the specific time-element that may be part of a given situation.[17] Our English word "time" is an appropriate rendering of Hebrew *ʿēt* because it combines as *ʿēt* does the temporal and the situational aspects. When we survey the combinations with *yôm*, we find very many of them within the historiographic and prophetic corpora but very few of them in wisdom or apocalyptic. When we look for combinations with *ʿēt*, on the other hand, we find fewer of them in the former and more of them in the latter. *Yôm* is sharp and specific, *ʿēt* is generalizing and vague; and the movement away from *yôm* to *ʿēt* parallels the development within Hebraic literature away from historiography and prophecy onward toward wisdom and apocalyptic—two literary types that tend to generalize human experience and catalogue cosmic reality.

Returning to this essay's title, "Quantitative and Qualitative Time in Wisdom and Apocalyptic," we would advise the reader that we apply the distinction implied here in our own special way. We do not intend to make value judgments or take sides with the one approach to time at the expense of the other, nor do we follow Boman, Marsh, and Cullmann in equating the concept of qualitative time with what is called "filled time" or "the right time" (*kairos*).[18] Our use of "quantitative" and "qualitative" is directly dependent upon our own detailed analysis of the *yôm*-formulae. On p. 343 of *Yesterday, Today and Tomorrow* one may find the following statement about the quantitative and the qualitative approaches to time:

> The first sees time as a succession of essentially commensurate entities—a given number of days or months or years. These temporal entities are susceptible to being spanned by the same measuring-staff, hence can be tabulated mathematically. This is time as a *quantum*, comparable to space (and, as Einstein showed, simply another dimension of it). The other approach sees time as a succession of essentially unique, incommensurate experiences. The day is an apprehensional unity, primitively conceived according to the event that gives it character.

Our empirical basis for this distinction has been a closely argued demonstration that formulae like *hayyôm* and *bayyôm hahûᵓ* perform a quantifying function when they correlate one particular day (seen as a minimal duration) to others within a series, but a far more frequent qualifying function when they identify one day's essential character upon the basis of the historical event that is unique to it.

To understand our intended distinction, one need not depart from the etymology of the term "qualitative" (Lat. *qualis*, "of what sort"—interrogative or relative pronoun) or from the etymology of "quantitative" (Lat. *quantum*, "how much"). When a unique or unparalleled event occurs, there is by definition nothing whatever to which it can be compared, hence the event in question becomes revelatory of "the other"—even of "the wholly other." But constantly the human mind strives to offset the dread of confronting something entirely unique[19] by reducing it to categories of intellectual understanding, either by way of measurement or by way of comparison. One method known to the ancient Hebrews was to align one day of divine revelation with another, so that each became a new "day of Yahweh."[20] While maintaining the transcendental element unreduced, this mode of conceptuality would have brought a measure of assurance to such persons as were able to trust that the God known from the past would remain true to his revealed nature in the events of a future day.

But the mind of religious man seeks more drastic means for reducing the experience of "the other" in time. Quantifying measurement enters into use as an abstractive process by which one "time" is correlated with others purely on the basis of the passage of moving objects (the sun, moon, stars, timepieces, and the like) within a regular orbit or recurring routine. So also the qualifying approach that reduces temporal experience to analogies. Identifying a particular day for its special characteristics, the analytical mind makes intellectual and then linguistic comparisons with other days perceived to be somehow like it. Ultimately, all of life and history may be regularized and brought under the control of man. The fact is that each unique historical experience, bordering on absoluteness and incontingency, nevertheless remains contingent and thus vulnerable to the leveling process involved in identification and categorization. Separating and labeling reality is the essence of God's creative work as described in Genesis 1, but this represents equally as much the organizing and controlling process that is followed by the human mind.

This is essentially what wisdom does. As may be seen in its various manifestations throughout the ancient Near East, its constant aim is to manage reality by reducing its vast array of variegated phenomena to a complex set of rules. Sometimes it turns these rules against itself, as in Job and Qoheleth, but it remains instinctively optimistic that comprehensive understanding can lead to harmony and happiness. Searching for analogies amid distinctions, it strives to put all things into their proper framework and relate each item of experience to all other phenomena.

It is in this connection that one can appreciate another discovery that has emerged from our research on the *yôm*-formulae: both cultic and gnomic (= wisdom) discourse speak characteristically not about the existentially experienced, historical present but about an ideal present that constantly recurs within a particular pattern of conceptuality. On p. 45 of *Yesterday, Today and Tomorrow*, following a discussion of the variety of ways in which historical time may be qualified, we have the following statement respecting this special kind of time-language:

> The gnomic present, using a form of *yôm* or of *ʿēt*, is the present of various kinds of gnomic discourse: exhortations, proverbs, aphorisms. It is the present to which the wisdom sayings pertain, hence it is repeated and repeatable as long as the sayings are true. The cultic present is very similar: it is the ongoing present to which every sort of ritual and cult legislation pertains. These two kinds of present are, together, ideologically opposite to the historical present. The essential difference is that the historical present is always unique — an experience unto itself — whereas the gnomic and cultic present is everything but unique. If the historical present is disjunctive, even irruptive, the gnomic/cultic present is repetitive, cyclical, and institutional.

We must pause to say something about the cultic present. Within the cult an ideal, constantly recurring present must be seen as an abstraction from a mythical (or in Israel, quasi-mythical) prototype in the past. Numerous examples could be given,[21] but none would be more impressive than the legislation for an historicized Passover–Mazzoth festival in Exod 13:3-10. There Moses commands the people to remember *hayyôm hazzeh* ("this day" as nominal object) for its historical significance, but then immediately modifies this as a prohibition against the eating of leavened bread (vs. 3). Next follows a prediction (with the participle and perfect-consecutives) of the historical "going out" from Egypt and "entering into" Canaan that are to take place on *this day* (vss. 4-5). This is followed in turn by a stipulation of the festival's seven-day duration (vss. 6-7) and by admonitions to teach and memorialize Yahweh's deed (vss. 8-9). The passage ends in a solemn command (vs. 10) ensuring the observance of the festival in unvaried order (*lĕmôʿădāh*, "at its appointed time") and in perpetuity (*miyyāmîm yāmîmâ*, "year after year").

The historically unique is here abstracted no less effectively than in the Priestly historian's schematic chronologizing[22] and in his unparalleled modification of the expression, *bĕʿeṣem hayyôm hazzeh* ("on this very same day") to refer to chronologically past events, such as the flood (Gen 7:11, 13), the giving of circumcision (Gen 17:23, 26), and the departure from Egypt (Exod 12:41), in effect objectifying them as contemporary realities.[23]

Within the wisdom tradition, on the other hand, an ideal, recurring present appears as an abstraction from cumulative human experience— leading in the most extreme instance to Qoheleth's cynical conclusion that "there is nothing new under the sun." In wisdom no less than in the cult, the interpreter is not personally or directly involved—unless, like Qoheleth, he insists on taking it all personally. Each human experience is viewed as exemplary in a positive or in a negative way, setting a standard for interpreting all applicable situations.

Strikingly, the biblical wisdom texts seem to emphasize the distressing side of temporal experience. Borrowing from the language of historiography, to which the description of individual and collective disasters immediately belongs, wisdom sayings scattered through the Bible speak of a "day of anger" (Job 20:28), a "day of wrath" (Job 21:30, Prov 11:4), a "day of distress" (Job 21:30), a "day of battle and warfare" (Job 38:23), and a "day of slaughter" (Jer 12:3). Especially common are combinations of *yôm*—especially in the plural—and *ʿēt* with the genitival qualifiers, *rāʿâ*, "evil," and *ṣārâ*, "distress."[24]

The common tendency to move from the unique to the universal, shared by cultic and by wisdom language, exemplifies an intellectual process of objectification showing significant similarities in both traditions, and if we carry our analysis a bit further we shall perceive an additional bond linking these two with apocalyptic. It may be said that on the one hand myth— perpetuated in ritual—and on the other hand wisdom, aim at reducing experiential reality to ultimate principles. Myth raises up prototypes within the primitive order of creation, while wisdom searches for a rational pattern within experienced reality.

Israel was distinctive in its cultural environment in historicizing its myth, but its ritual preserved the timelessness of myth. Israel was distinctive, too, in personalizing the image of the creative principle standing behind experiential reality. But how does apocalyptic come in? We can surely perceive that under the impact of national disruption in its late history, Israel was led by its seers to transform what are essentially mythic images into the various patterns of apocalyptical dualism[25] and futurism that come to greater and greater prominence in the postexilic literature. It was thereby transporting the principle of ultimate meaning from a remote past or an idealized present to a future that interpenetrates the historical present, extending itself quantitatively beyond history as well.[26]

Peter von der Osten-Sacken has argued that the Hebraic doctrine of creation is the ideological link between apocalyptic and wisdom;[27] but, while it can be shown that Yahwistic creationism is clearly presupposed in both literary traditions, it cannot be proven that it was this doctrine specifically that transformed prophecy into apocalyptic. A more essential bond tying apocalyptic to wisdom—and to the cult[28]—is its timelessness, the most pervasive manifestation of their common tendency toward reducing all of reality to a simple, universal principle.

Thus apocalyptic is not eschatological in the normative biblical conception. Applying an objectifying process of reduction to qualitative time, it produces a transhistorical dualism within the order of historical existence; applying a quantifying process of periodization, it produces a posthistorical futurism. Either way, it aims to identify ultimate meaning above or beyond history, freezing it into a state of absolute and final perfection.[29]

If eschatology is teleology, apocalyptic is not eschatological.[30] In fact, it is radically ateleological with respect to mankind's actual, experienced existence, which is within history. It concedes that God has an "eschatological" purpose, but man clearly does not. It is only Israel's heilsgeschichtlich literature that sees this kind of progress and purpose in history. It alone is willing to trust to the intuitive apperception of transcendental uniqueness within historical encounter, inviting and anticipating its repetition. The combination of a covenantal-electional personalism with this openness to experiential participation produced an assurance that a benign presence is superintending history, guaranteeing its salvific purpose.

III

Discussions of the concept of time as it appears in the wisdom literature inevitably center on Qoheleth's catalogue of counterbalancing "times" in 3:1-8,[31] and we must comment on it, too. But first let it be pointed out that Qoheleth's resignation to determinism, though strongly influenced by Hellenistic scepticism,[32] has its ultimate roots in the dominant time-concept of the pagan Near East,[33] in which each "time" had a pre-ordained character which could be forecast by a special class of functionaries having the secret of manipulating its omens.[34] Qoheleth is far beyond the purely mythological conception of decreeing the times that appears in the Babylonian New Year ritual, but he goes far beyond the Hebraic creation doctrine as well. Counteracting eastern mythology, as this comes to expression in *Enuma eliš* V, the Priestly writer of Genesis 1 had identified Israel's God as the creator of the heavenly bodies designed to regulate quantified time. We note that, with all his capacity for objectifying time, this very writer studiously avoided saying that God himself decreed the times, but only that he placed what he had created into a framework of time ("day one," "second day," etc.) to guarantee its historical existence.

To Jesus ben Sira, the author of Ecclesiasticus, this Hebraic doctrine came to mean that each created thing exists within a temporal pattern that is positively congenial to its salutory existence. Thus we read in 39:33-34 (cf. vss. 16-21):

> The works of the Lord are all good,
>   and he will supply every need in its hour ($h\bar{o}rq$; Heb. $^c\bar{e}t$);
> and no one can say, "This is worse than that,"
>   for all things will prove good in their season ($kair\bar{q}$; Heb. $^c\bar{e}t$).

Constantly, Sirach recommends such behavior as is appropriate to the particular time, for it is the very essence of the wisdom impulse to correlate human actions with corresponding qualities of time. Yet, he warns that one should not become so totally absorbed in the prevailing conditions of a particular time as to forget that the situation may quickly change. As he says in Sir 18:26, "From morning to evening conditions change, and all things move swiftly before the Lord." For Sirach, anxious to preserve divine sovereignty in human life, an awareness of change and temporality produces an attentive prudentialism in which, while God remains ever in charge of the course of human events, man feels himself obliged to respond appropriately, purposefully, and diligently, seeking an action that best suits the time.[35] This accords authentically with the classical Hebraic concept of history.

For Qoheleth such an awareness only produces resignation. He acknowledges that there may indeed be a beneficent design in the way the creator has arranged his universe, assigning to each activity its proper time, but since man is unable to penetrate the curtain of divine inscrutability in order to trace the chain of cause and effect from beginning to end (Qoh 3:11), man can secure no "profit" for his toil and must content himself with such a modicum of happiness as God may allow him in the passing moment (Qoh 3:9; cf. 5:15, 17).[36]

It is the notion that time is a trap (Qoh 9:11-12), not an opportunity, that colors the interpretation of Qoheleth's catalogue in 3:1-8. One is interested to see that, although the Hebrew Bible employs a great variety of genitival qualifier with $y\hat{o}m$, "day,"[37] Qoheleth avoids most of them along with the $y\hat{o}m$-formulae that we have studied. Individual days have now lost much of their significance, and Qoheleth is interested only in a pattern of opposing "times" or situations. We observe two things in particular: (1) that comparative trivialities such as rending and sewing garments (perhaps also the enigmatic casting and gathering of stones)[38] are included among the more weighty matters, as though to encompass the totality of reality; also (2) that except at the end of vs. 8 infinitival phrases (almost always with $l\check{e}$) substitute for nouns in the construct chains that define the individual "times." This is striking, because elsewhere in the Hebrew Bible the infinitival construction with *lĕ*, in reference to the word *ᶜēt*, expresses purpose—specifically, that of performing something not as yet occurring.[39] In other words, Qoheleth is listing categories, not just of customary and habitual activities, but of teleologically directed actions—and by balancing the one against the other he seems deliberately to underscore a radical negation of purpose.

Recalling what has previously been said about wisdom's tendency to reduce qualitative time to manageable categories, we see that Qoheleth has gone beyond traditional Israelite wisdom to an absolute denial of the eschatological aspect of time. There can be little question but that this provoked the radical counter-reaction, first of Sirach's mediating doctrine of wisdom—leading ultimately to torah-orthodoxy—and second of full-blown apocalyptic, seen early on in the second century in 1 Enoch and Daniel, and later in Qumran Essenism. It is now clear, however, that wisdom was not the matrix of apocalyptic, as von Rad said, but represented only one manifestation of a widely shared mentality exerting influence on the late prophetic tradition so as to cause it to produce these new forms. Encompassing the entirety of "the intellectual tradition," apocalyptic's ancestry included also the priesthood and the cult. Paul D. Hanson is mistaken, therefore, in his vigorous effort to prove that early apocalyptic was directed against the priestly establishment.[40] The influence of the "Zadokite" priesthood is directly apparent in such emergent forms as Ezekiel's temple vision and the night-vision(s) of Zechariah, and it persists to a later period in the theology and protocol of Qumran.[41] Objectification is manifest here as dualism, if not as futurism, though increasingly the two aspects appear together.

Like wisdom, apocalyptic ranges far and wide in search of an ultimate principle. Let us not be deceived by its seemingly encyclopedic curiosity. It is not really interested in everything. It brings much in array that all may, if possible, be reduced to one final, simple answer. The ultimate failure of this effort is to be seen in the bitter despair of 4 Ezra. Qoheleth despairs because he gives up on history. The writer of 4 Ezra despairs because he continues, in spite of everything, to take history in earnest without knowing what to do with it.

Apocalyptic departs from wisdom, we see, in abandoning empirical observation for esoteric speculation. Yet it does remain, in the final analysis, an intellectual pursuit in which mankind seeks to control its existence. A man is *ḥākām* if he is able to devise rules for harmonious social life; but he may also be *ḥākām* if, like Joseph, he knows the times. Among Israel's "wise men" there were always those who could discern the times (*ḥăkāmîm yōdĕᶜê hāᶜittîm*, Esth 1:13), who, turning many to righteousness, "[shone] like the brightness of the firmament" (Dan 12:3).[42]

¹ Because the apocalyptic literature originated at the end of the OT period, NT scholars have, until recently, been more interested in it than OT scholars. The former have been unable to ignore it because of apocalyptic imagery in the background of the NT. Counteracting the tendency of the Bultmann school to sluff it off as irrelevant to the apostolic kerygma, Klaus Koch (following the lead of Ernst Käsemann) has placed it in the foreground, identifying it as an irreducible element in the early Christian message. For the literature on apocalyptic see Koch's book, *Ratlos vor der Apokalyptik* (Gütersloh: Mohn, 1970; Engl. *The Rediscovery of Apocalyptic* [SBT 2/22; London: SCM, 1972]).

² It has been Wellhausen's theory of evolutionistic development that has influenced OT scholarship in its handling of wisdom and apocalyptic. These have been seen, at best, as non-essential appendages to the prophetic books and, at worst, as abnormalities and aberrations, expressions of a relativizing narrowness and without permanent value within the mainstream of biblical theology.

³ R. N. Whybray, *The Intellectual Tradition in the Old Testament* (BZAW, 135; Berlin: Töpelmann, 1974), discusses Daniel on pp. 101-04 but omits the apocryphal literature. His analysis of the root *ḥkm* leads to the conclusion that the title *ḥākām* was not reserved for professional teachers and court councilors.

⁴ "The Classification, Stages of Growth, and Changing Intentions in the Book of Daniel," *JBL* 95 (1976) 192-94.

⁵ *Old Testament Theology* (2 vols.; New York: Harper & Row, 1965) 2. 301-08.

⁶ M. Hengel (*Judentum und Hellenismus* [Tübingen: Mohr, 1969], 199-381) follows von Rad in characterizing the movement coming to expression in these books, which constitute "der erste Höhepunkt jüdischer Apokalyptik," as being directly under the influence of Qoheleth and the "Hellenistic reform."

⁷ E.g., Gammie (*JBL* 95 [1976] 192-94) follows Koch in basing his own definition of apocalyptic as a genre on six late books, Daniel, 1 Enoch, 2 Baruch, 2 Esdras, the Apocalypse of Abraham and Revelation. In the present essay "apocalyptic" may refer to a genre or to the ideology, while "apocalypticism" identifies the tendency toward the ideology or the direct influence of it.

⁸ *Ezechiel* (BKAT 13/2; Neukirchen-Vluyn: Neukirchener Verlag, 1969), 945.

⁹ For numerous illustrative examples of the former, see S. J. De Vries, *Yesterday, Today and Tomorrow, Time and History in the Old Testament* (Grand Rapids and London: Eerdmans and SPCK, 1975), 297-310.

¹⁰ Several of the individual expansions to the original core (Zimmerli: 38:10-13, 14-16, 17, 18-23; 39:6-8, 9-10, 11-16, 21-29) are unmistakably postexilic. It is tempting to read the epexegetical query of 38:17 ("Are you he of whom I spoke in former days . . .?") as a direct reference to Alexander, which thus marks the end of an extended period of editorial expansion.

¹¹ H. Gese ("Anfang und Ende der Apokalyptik," *ZTK* 70 [1973] 20-49), recognizing that 1:8-2:17 and 4:1-6:8 comprise one single, composite vision, identifies this as the earliest clear example of the schematic complexity that characterizes what he would call authentic apocalyptic.

¹² We would sketch briefly the main stages through which apocalyptic(ism) probably passed prior to the rise of Christianity. Insights derived especially from Hengel, *Judentum und Hellenismus*, and O. Plöger, *Theokratie und Eschatologie* (WMANT 2; Neukirchen-Vluyn: Neukirchener Verlag, 1959) may be organized as follows:

(1) *Restorationism.* Situation: imminent end of the exile. Presupposed is P's model of a purely sacral Israel. Ezekiel 38-39 and expansions to Obadiah develop the holy-war theme. Ezekiel 40-48 (successively expanded) and Zechariah 1-6 furnish models for the ideal congregation. Trito-Isaiah, Malachi, Joel 1-2 express a prophetically oriented disillusionment and envision Yahweh's imminent return to purge worship. Time-speculation is not yet a prominent feature, despite the Gog apocalypse.

(2) *Theocratic dualism.* A new development under the auspices of the eschatological wing of the theocratic party (cf. Plöger, *Theokratie und Eschatologie*, 134-36), who are the editorial redactors of the prophetic collection. The time is the early Hellenistic era, since the development

presupposes Ezra's reform, the work of the Chronicler, and the Samaritan schism, which cut off deviant groups from "Israel." Alexander's conquest has definitively removed further hope for a national restoration or an historical solution to foreign oppression. Persian dominance is reflected in the growth of dualism. Here we assign the additions to Ezekiel 38–39, Joel 3-4, Isaiah 24–27, and Zechariah 9–14. Gone is prophetism's ethical call (Zech 13:4), for the antithesis is now between ideal Israel and the reprobate gentiles. Time-speculation is prominent but its ideology is not periodizing or highly schematic.

(3) *Hasidism.* Against the background of the Seleucid policy of assimilation, strengthened by disillusionment with priestly venality, full-blown or "normative" apocalyptic arises, as in Jubilees, 1 Enoch, Testaments of the Twelve Patriarchs, and early Daniel; Epiphanian persecution produces the latest stages of Daniel. Here are featured a sharpened particularism and dualism, cosmic speculation, and the radical periodization of time. The speculative aspects of priestly ideology are seen in efforts at calendrical reform (Jubilees, 1 Enoch).

(4) *Essenism.* Reflecting disillusionment with Hasmonean rule and Sadducean domination in the temple, a new apocalypticism appears in a demand for a totally separated Israel, with a "Zadokite" aristocracy, which opposes the apostate leadership within Judaism. An early phrase (CD, 1QH, 1QS) emphasizes separation, asceticism, and torah rigorism, based on an absolute dualism expressed in the doctrine of two opposing spirits. A later phase refocuses on the foreign enemy, activistically merging the eschaton with the present age (1QM).

[13] G. von Rad, *Old Testament Theology*, 2. 112-25 and 301-08. Cf. also the extensive discussion in D. S. Russell, *The Method and Message of Jewish Apocalyptic* (Philadelphia: Westminster, 1964) 205-34, 263-84.

[14] (Nashville and New York: Abingdon, 1972) 138-43, 233-34, 263-83.

[15] *Old Testament Theology* (1962) 1. 334-47; also pp. 205-21 in *The Problem of the Hexateuch and Other Essays* (New York: McGraw-Hill, 1966), and *Deuteronomy* (OTL; Philadelphia: Westminster, 1966), *passim*.

[16] See n. 9.

[17] Cf. *ibid.*, pp. 41-42. The etymology of $^c\bar{e}t$ is in dispute, but what matters is its semantic range and contextual specification. One may note, e.g., that in Lev 15:25 the plural of *yôm* identifies a precise period of time, while $^c\bar{e}t$ is both temporal and situational ($^c et$-*niddātāh* compared with *yĕmê niddātāh*). John R. Wilch (*Time and Event* [Leiden: Brill, 1969], *passim*) recognizes the primarily non-temporal bearing of $^c\bar{e}t$, but offers "occasion" as its closest equivalent in English; however, "occasion" fails to suit most passages, because it refers to particular instances or occurrences. "Situation," designating a "relative position or combination of circumstances at a given moment" (Webster) is better. The situational bearing is especially evident in the use of transitional *wĕ$^c$attâ*; cf. E. Jenni in *TZ* 28 (1972) 1-12, but now also the Arad letters, which regularly use *w$^c$t* to introduce the business in hand (cf. M. Weippert, "Zum Präskript der hebräischen Briefe von Arad," *VT* 25 [1975] 202-12). So also $^c$*attâ*, frequent in the OT but demanding a purely temporal translation only in Gen 29:34; Num 24:17; Deut 12:9; Josh 5:14; 14:11; Judg 8:6, 15; 13:12; Isa 43:19; 48:7; 49:19; Jer 4:12; 27:16; Ezek 7:3, 8; 26:18; 39:25; Hos 8:8, 10; Mic 7:4; Hag 2:3; Ps 20:7; Job 4:5; and 2 Chr 35:3.

[18] Relevant literature is cited in J. Barr, *Biblical Words for Time* (Naperville: Allenson, 1962). Important contributions of Barr's study are: (1) its critique of Orelli's etymologizing interpretations; (2) its critique of a tendentious interpretation of *kairos* as "suitable occasion," which ignores the numerous instances in which it is synonymous with, or functions as *chronos* (= durative, quantitative time); and (3) its demonstration of the role of chronological time in the OT.

[19] Cf. R. Otto, *The Idea of the Holy* (London: Oxford University, 1923). Man confronts the temporally unique in his ever-changing encounters with nature and with his fellow-men, but especially at such points where "eternity" breaks in upon him. Amid all of life's monotonous sameness, nothing can be really the same when it occurs again, and nothing is entirely the same afterward.

[20] See De Vries, *Yesterday, Today and Tomorrow*, 340-42.

[21] Cf. *ibid.*, 46-47, 346-50.

[22] P schematizes patriarchal history to support his model of an ideal holy congregation, then

Jubilees rigidifies this scheme within his elaborate framework of weeks, thus establishing a cultic pattern that is intended as normative for the eschatological age, which is in fact that of his own encounter with hellenizing apostasy (early second century B.C.); see G. S. Davenport, *The Eschatology of the Book of Jubilees* (Leiden: Brill, 1971).

²³ Cf. De Vries, *Yesterday, Today and Tomorrow*, 141-42.

²⁴ Wisdom's time-language strongly emphasizes the gloomy side of life (cf. *ibid.*, pp. 45-46), hence it prepares the way for Qoheleth's pessimism.

²⁵ Cf. J. G. Gammie, "Spatial and Ethical Dualism in Jewish Wisdom and Apocalyptic Literature," *JBL* 93 (1974) 356-85.

²⁶ One goes astray in overemphasizing apocalyptic's futurism, for equally important is its dualism. Only in understanding this can one apprehend a reason in the vacillation between images of the coming ideal within time (transhistory) and images of the ideal beyond time (posthistory).

²⁷ *Die Apokalyptik in ihrem Verhältnis zu Prophetie und Weisheit* (Munich: Kaiser, 1969). The writer bases his conclusion on a comparison of Daniel 2, 7, 8-12 with Second Isaiah and the wisdom writings, passing by much relevant material within postexilic prophecy.

²⁸ Egyptian myth offers the most striking example of cultically oriented timelessness. Cf. De Vries, *Yesterday, Today and Tomorrow*, 344; also, S. Morenz, *Egyptian Religion* (Ithaca: Cornell University, 1973) 75-80.

²⁹ This is especially apparent in Zechariah 14, where "the last great day of Yahweh has been crammed with everybody's dream and stretched into an era of endless bliss" (De Vries, *Yesterday, Today and Tomorrow*, 308); cf. the statement on pp. 325, 329 on the significance of *hyh* as a main verb within eschatological passages introduced by (*wĕhāyâ*) *bayyôm hahû²* (Isa 4:2, 7:23; 17:9; 19:16, 18f., 23f.; 28:5; Jer 25:33; 39:16; 48:41; 49:22; Ezek 39:11; Zech 12:8; 13:1; 14:6, 9, 13, 20f.).

³⁰ Von Rad (*Old Testament Theology*, 2. 114-18) is right in brushing aside the objection of Mowinckel and Russell against applying the term "eschatological" to classical prophetism, since the term is not generally restricted to its precise etymological derivation. Our point is that apocalyptic is futuristic but not *genuinely* teleological because *man's* struggle has no purpose. See below.

³¹ See especially, K. Galling, "Das Rätsel der Zeit im Urteil Kohelets (Koh 3:1-15)," *ZTK* 58 (1961) 1-15; also, H. Gese, "Die Krisis der Weisheit bei Kohelet," *Les Sagesses du Proche-Orient Ancien* (Paris: Presses Universitaire de France, 1963) 139-51.

³² Cf. Hengel, *Judentum und Hellenismus*, 210-37, and a valuable special study by R. Braun, *Kohelet und die frühhellenistische Popularphilosophie* (BZAW 130; Berlin: Töpelmann, 1973).

³³ Cf. O. Loretz, *Qohelet und der alte Orient* (Freiburg: Herder, 1964) 247-60.

³⁴ See, De Vries, *Yesterday, Today and Tomorrow*, 344; cf. W. W. Hallo (with W. K. Simpson), *The Ancient Near East, a History* (New York: Harcourt Brace Jovanovich, 1971) 158-63.

³⁵ Cf. von Rad's insightful comparison of Sirach and Qoheleth in *Wisdom in Israel*, 263-66.

³⁶ On *yitrôn* and *ḥēleq*, see J. G. Williams, "What Does it Profit a Man? The Wisdom of Qoheleth," *Judaism* 20 (ed. R. Gordis; New York: American Jewish Congress, 179-93) = pp. 375-89 in *Studies in Ancient Israelite Wisdom*; J. Crenshaw, ed.; New York: Ktav, 1976.

³⁷ Cf. De Vries, *Yesterday, Today and Tomorrow*, 42-50.

³⁸ This reference is given a dubious sexual connotation in traditional Jewish interpretation; cf. R. Gordis, *Koheleth—The Man and His World* (New York: Bloch, 1968). According to Galling ("Das Rätzel der Zeit"; cf. *Die Fünf Megilloth*; HAT 18; Tübingen: Mohr [Siebeck], 1940, p. 94) the reference is to "dice," but this is far from certain.

³⁹ Thus ᶜēt lidrôš ²et-YHWH, Hos 10:12; ᶜet-bêt YHWH lĕhibbānôt, Hag 1:2; ᶜet . . . lāšebet bĕbāttêkem, Hag 1:4; ᶜēt lĕhenĕnâ, Ps 102:14; ᶜēt laᶜăśôt laYHWH, Ps 119:126.

⁴⁰ *The Dawn of Apocalyptic* (Philadelphia: Fortress, 1975). Hanson relies heavily on sociological principles in dividing between the "Zadokite" priests as the "haves" and the apocalypticists as the "have nots," denying that Ezekiel and the night-vision(s) are in fact apocalyptic. An invalid syllogism leads Hanson to his *a priori* exclusion of such materials. His argument is, in essence, that (1) early apocalypticism (seen especially in Third Isaiah and Deutero-Zechariah) is radically anti-establishment—meaning anti-priestly and anti-cultic; (2) the visions

of temple restoration in Ezekiel and Zechariah strongly affirm the cult and the privileged status of the Zadokite priesthood; (3) therefore, these materials cannot be apocalyptic in spite of their expanded visionary structures (*contra* Gese). Hanson barely mentions Ezekiel 38-39 and does less than justice to the important analysis of Otto Plöger (see n. 12), which identifies prominent elements of dynamic tension within the heterogeneous movement associated with the priestly program of the restoration period. The appeal of Hanson's argument lies in the unquestionable fact that the estranged and the desperate instinctively do turn to apocalyptic as a vehicle for expressing their aspirations. Its weakness lies in the failure to recognize that priests could be disillusioned too. We must allow for a disparity between priestly ideology, which may include eschatological elements (cf. P), and reductionistic tendencies within all institutions, including the cult.

[41] Cf. Russell, "The Apocalypticist and the Priest," *Method and Message of Jewish Apocalyptic*, 173-75; also, R. G. Hamerton-Kelly, "The Temple and the Origins of Jewish Apocalyptic," *VT* 20 (1970) 1-15, where an overly rigid dichotomy is posited between the respective temple images of P and Ezekiel.

[42] Cf. von Rad, *Wisdom in Israel*, 263-83.

# WISDOM AT QUMRAN

W. LOWNDES LIPSCOMB

WOODHAVEN, NEW YORK 11421

WITH

JAMES A. SANDERS

SCHOOL OF THEOLOGY AT CLAREMONT, CLAREMONT, CALIFORNIA 91711

I N his discussion of the wisdom elements of 11QPs[a], Professor James A. Sanders noted that "no work has been done . . . on Wisdom thinking generally in Qumrân literature."[1] In spite of the appearance of wisdom terminology and concepts and of actual wisdom texts among the Qumran finds, the response to Sanders' call has been limited. To date, only one dissertation[2] and a small number of articles have dealt either directly or obliquely with the subject of wisdom at Qumran. It is the purpose of this essay to summarize and evaluate the contributions that have been made to the study of wisdom in the Qumran texts and to comment upon the possibilities for further research in this field.

## I. Documents of Sectarian Authorship[3]

It has been noted that many of the terms for "wisdom" and "insight" common in the biblical wisdom literature are found in the sectarian compositions. The terms *hkmh, śkl, d^ct, d^ch, yd^c, bynh, ^crmh, mhšbh,* and *twšyh* occur frequently in wisdom texts and in the Qumran scrolls.[4] The sectaries viewed such wisdom or insight as a possession of God (1QS 3:15; CD 2:3-4; 1QH 1:7, 14; et. al.) and also as their own possession through divine revelation (CD 2:12-13; 1QH 1:21; 11:9-10; et. al.).[5] Communication of this divinely revealed knowledge through teaching is an important activity in the community. The founder of the sect, the *mwrh, hsdq,* has received his wisdom from God (1QpHab 7:4) and has communicated the divinely revealed truths to the sectarians (1QH 2:9-10; cf. 1QpHab 2:1-3). The term *mśkyl* frequently refers to a teaching functionary in the community who teaches the doctrines of the sect to its members (1QS 3:13-15; 9:12-20). The terms *lmd* (piel), *hwdy^c, hbyn,* and *hśkyl* in the scrolls commonly refer both to God's revelation of wisdom to the sect and to teaching within the community. Thus the motifs of wisdom and instruction are important in the Qumran literature.[6]

Although numerous passages among the sectarian compositions employ wisdom terminology in reflecting a concern for knowledge and teaching, the content of these passages is not sapiential. The object of wisdom at Qumran was the revealed mysteries of God's predestined plan of salvation, knowledge of sectarian doctrine, for example, as it is elaborated in 1QS 3:13–4:26. The search for knowledge gained through consistent personal experience of the divine world order found in wisdom texts does not appear in the Essene documents. Nor may these passages be designated sapiential on the basis of form. The focal thought of the Essene community was apocalyptic, not sapiential, and the sapiential terminology employed at Qumran provides only the external garb which clothes the central concern of the sect about God's predestined plan and the imminent eschaton.[7]

It has also been observed that the ethical dualism of the Qumran scrolls, particularly as it is exhibited in 1QS 3:13-4:26, has its roots in the ethical dualism of biblical and postbiblical wisdom literature. Otzen[8] and Gammie[9] note that the division of mankind into two diametrically opposed groups in the scrolls (1QM 1:5-6: the people of God and the Kittim; 1QS 3:13-4:26: the sons of truth and the sons of error) and a concern for their reward and punishment may be traced back to the antitheses between the righteous and wicked, good and sinner, wise and scoffer in Proverbs 10-15.[10] Winter has demonstrated parallels between the dualistic teaching of two ways in Ben Sira 33(36):7-15; 42:24 and that in 1QS.[11] Otzen also finds in the terminology, individual expressions, and form of the descriptive lists of vices and virtues in Proverbs (esp. 1-9) the best OT parallels to the dualistic catalogues in 1QS 4:2-14.[12]

Although we may look to the wisdom literature for an explanation of the origins of ethical dualism at Qumran, we cannot explain the cosmic and psychological aspects of Qumran dualism on the basis of wisdom influence.[13] Nor is ethical dualism found only in the wisdom books of the OT.[14] Finally, the dichotomy between the righteous and the wicked in wisdom literature is gleaned from humanity's own experience of the divine world order. Knowledge of it is available to every person, and its content is pragmatic, teaching how to succeed in life. In contrast, the ethical dualism at Qumran is divinely predestined truth revealed by God only to the true Israel.

In summary, there are no true wisdom texts among the scrolls of undisputed Essene authorship. While the Essene documents contain vocabulary, a concern for knowledge and instruction, and an ethical dualism found in the wisdom literature, these wisdom elements are superimposed upon the esoteric sectarian doctrine of an apocalyptic community which considered itself alone to be the true Israel.[15] It is only when we turn to texts found at Qumran but which may not have been composed there that we may speak of wisdom texts.

## II. Documents of Unknown Authorship

Included among the Qumran texts of unknown authorship are actual wisdom compositions. Three wisdom psalms[16] are included in 11QPs[a]; and

4Q184 ("The Wiles of the Wicked Woman") is a wisdom poem modelled on the "wicked woman" passages in Proverbs.

## A. 11QPs<sup>a</sup>

In the Psalms scroll of Qumran cave eleven, columns 18; 21:11-22:1; and 26:9-15 contain wisdom psalms. In addition, column 27:2-11 is of interest because it depicts David as a wise man.

*Col. 18.* 11QPs[a] 18 provides us with the Hebrew *Vorlage*[17] of Ps 154:3-19 (= Syr. Ps. II). Although Delcor argues that the psalm contains references to the Qumran community and is Essene in origin,[18] Sanders is surely correct in affirming that there is nothing in the psalm which may be classified as of exclusively Essene origin.[19]

Sanders' discussions of the text have adequately underlined the wisdom content of the psalm.[20] Wisdom is personified as a woman; her voice, song (lines 10-11), word (line 13), and gates (lines 5-6) are referred to. Wisdom is given to man to aid him in proclaiming the glory of God (lines 4-5). Of the three groups named in the psalm, it is the righteous who know wisdom (lines 10-12) while the wicked and insolent do not know her (line 15), and the senseless must be taught God's might with the help of wisdom (lines 2-4). The terms which characterize the three groups and the verbs which refer to instruction are common in the wisdom literature.[21]

*Col. 21:11-17; 22:1.* 11QPs[a] 21:11-17; 22:1 has received the most attention of all the psalms in the 11Q Psalms scroll because it preserves the original Hebrew text[22] of the first portion of the acrostic poem which concludes Ben Sira (51:13-30). The authorship of the poem has been a major object of debate. While Sanders has denied that Ben Sira wrote the poem[23] and Dupont-Sommer believes it was composed at Qumran,[24] Lehmann,[25] Skehan,[26] and Rabinowitz[27] favor Siracide authorship. Most scholars agree, therefore, that it was not of Essene or Qumran origin.

Sanders has adequately presented the wisdom elements of the poem in his discussions of the text.[28] The poem tells the story of a young man who sought wisdom and who dedicated himself to her as he matured. The passions which developed with his maturation were devoted to the pursuit of wisdom. Wisdom is personified as a woman who had been the nurse and teacher of the young man, and now will become his mistress. In describing the young man's pursuit of wisdom, the poet employs *mots à double entente* which reflect both the erotic and pious connotations of the young man's desire.[29] This use of sexual imagery is common in the wisdom literature. The canticle may be placed alongside Wis 8:2-21 and Sir 15:1-8 as a hymn of praise to wisdom in which wisdom is the desired bride of youth, and may also be compared to the discussions of wisdom in Proverbs 8 and 9 which contrast her allurements with those of the loose woman. The remainder of the poem, which was undoubtedly contained in the original scroll, consisted of an exhortation by the wisdom teacher that his students should follow his example and direct their passions toward the pursuit of wisdom.[30]

*Col. 26:9-15.* 11QPs[a] 26:9-15 contains the first seven lines of a hitherto unknown sapiential composition.[31] It is a hymn to the creator which acknowledges the role of wisdom in creation; God established the dawn by the knowledge ($d^c t$) of his mind, established the world by his wisdom (*ḥkmh*), and stretched out the heavens by his understanding (*tbwnh*). No conclusions can be drawn from the language or content of the hymn regarding its authorship.

By way of parenthesis it may be noted that column 27:2-11 presents the figure David as a wise composer of psalms. He is called wise (*ḥkm*, line 2), literate (*swpr*, line 2), discerning (*nbwn*, line 3), and perfect (*tmym*, line 3), and is said to have been given a discerning and enlightened spirit (*rwḥ nbwnh w³wrh*, line 4).[32]

## B. 4Q184 ("The Wiles of the Wicked Woman")[33]

Scholarly discussion of 4Q184 has been guided by two presuppositions. It has been commonly assumed that the text was composed at Qumran, and that the wicked woman described in the text is an allegorical representation of an opponent of the Qumran sect. This opponent has been identified as Rome,[34] a rival sect,[35] all official Judaean authorities,[36] and Simon the Maccabee.[37] Among those who assume Qumran authorship, only Dupont-Sommer, Strugnell, and Worrell deny the allegorical interpretation. Dupont-Sommer sees in the text a reflection of the misogynist attitude of the sect,[38] while Strugnell and Worrell believe the wicked woman is folly personified.[39]

The judgment of Jacob Licht is more sober. Licht notes that there are no clear signs that the text is sectarian or that it contains an allegorical meaning. We may conclude only that the text, largely biblical in style and vocabulary, embodies an adaptation of the "wicked woman" passages in Proverbs and denounces the harlot, loose woman, or adulteress.[40] It is parallel in content, vocabulary, and to a lesser extent, in form, with the passages warning against various types of "wicked women" in Prov 2:16-19; 5:3-6, 20; 6:24-26; 7:5-27; 9:13-18, and as such may be designated a sapiential composition.

## III. Conclusion

In conclusion, the study of wisdom at Qumran suggests a division between texts of Qumran authorship and texts of unknown authorship.[41]

(i) While the Essene texts contain wisdom vocabulary and expressions, a concern for knowledge and instruction, and an ethical dualism characteristic of the wisdom literature, these elements are external to and superimposed upon the basically apocalyptic fabric of Qumran thought. While the Essenes understood themselves to possess wisdom and cast that wisdom into a dualistic framework, the content of wisdom at Qumran is a sectarian apocalyptic vision of truth.

(ii) It is only among the texts of unknown authorship that we encounter wisdom compositions. These compositions contribute to our understanding of Jewish wisdom in Hellenistic-Roman times, but say nothing definitive about wisdom thinking at Qumran.

Further precision in defining "wisdom influence" at Qumran is limited by two factors. First, the state of the discussion of wisdom influence upon literature outside the wisdom corpus is in disarray; no consistent method has been developed to determine the nature and extent of "wisdom influence."[42] Secondly, the relationship between wisdom and apocalyptic has not been adequately clarified. In our study we have sought to show that the presence in the Qumran texts of sapiential vocabulary and motifs alone cannot constitute proof we are dealing either with true wisdom texts or with an integration of wisdom and apocalyptic ideas. Thus we have sought to address only one aspect of the relationship between wisdom and apocalyptic. Until these methodological issues receive further treatment, little more can be said about "wisdom influence" upon the sectarian texts.

[1] J. A. Sanders, "Two Non-Canonical Psalms in 11QPs[a]," *ZAW* 76 (1964) 65; *The Psalms Scroll of Qumran Cave 11* (DJD 4; Oxford: Clarendon, 1965) 69. B. Otzen ("Old Testament Wisdom Literature and Dualistic Thinking in Late Judaism," *Congress Volume, Edinburgh, 1974* [VTSup 28; 1975] 146-57) has taken up Sanders' call, and suggests the investigation be extended to pseudepigraphic literature as well.

[2] J. E. Worrell, "Concepts of Wisdom in the Dead Sea Scrolls," Ph.D. diss., Claremont Graduate School, 1968, 430 pp. The dissertation is divided into two parts. In part one, Worrell summarizes his understanding of the origins of wisdom and its development in Israel. Part two, which deals with wisdom in the Qumran scrolls, contains six chapters. Chapter one treats wisdom in the Qumran community. Worrell attempts to define Qumran as a "wisdom community" based on the comments of Philo and Josephus about the wisdom of the Essenes, the use of ʿ*sh* and *swd* in the scrolls to designate both the community *council* and its *counselling* function, and the importance of instruction and the possession of revealed knowledge among the Essenes. Chapter two contains a discussion of wisdom in the Qumran vocabulary. After taking note of the relative infrequency of *ḥkmh* in the scrolls, Worrell presents a study of vocabulary and "motifs" which characterize both the scrolls and the wisdom literature. In chapter three, Worrell discusses wisdom passages in the scrolls in which wisdom terms and motifs are concentrated. Chapter four deals with wisdom in the dualism of Qumran. The doctrine of the two spirits, light/darkness dualism, and the wisdom of the sect in opposition to the folly of its opponents receive special attention. In chapter five, Worrell discusses figures to whom the Qumran texts attribute great wisdom, viz. David (11QPs[a] 27), the "enigmatic subject" of 4QMess ar, the "man of God's refining" (1QS 4:20ff.), the "wonderful counsellor" (1QH 3:1-18), and the Teacher of Righteousness. In chapter six, Worrell concludes that in the period of the existence of the Qumran community, the vernacular of the sages became widespread; that "terms and forms which had their original *Sitze im Leben* among the teaching sages became the property of an era," although they were reemployed for specific ends by a multiformity of persuasions (p. 386). The appropriation of wisdom concepts at Qumran shows that "their categories for self-understanding came through the 'sapiential milieu'" (p. 393).

While it is outside the scope of the present essay to comment upon Worrell's dissertation in detail, two criticisms of a more general nature must be made. First, Worrell gives no attention to method in determining wisdom influence. It is fundamental to establish method before analyzing texts. Secondly, Worrell's failure to establish method creates lack of organization, unclarity of expression, and imprecision in discussing texts which present significant problems for the reader and detract from the force of Worrell's arguments throughout the dissertation.

[3] 1QS, 1QH, and CD have received the most extensive consideration in the study of wisdom in the texts of Qumran authorship, but they are by no means the only sectarian compositions exhibiting wisdom. Although at least parts of CD are not Qumranic, the document is Essene and is therefore included among texts of sectarian authorship; cf. J. Murphy-O'Connor, "The Essenes and Their History," *RB* 81 (1974) 215-44.

[4] H. Ringgren, *The Faith of Qumran* (Philadelphia: Fortress, 1963) 115, and Worrell, "Concepts of Wisdom," 186-212.

[5] B. Sharvit ("The Virtue of Wisdom in the Image of the Righteous Man in 1QS," *Beth Mikra* 19 [1974] 526-30 [in Hebrew]) notes that the outstanding characteristic of the righteous man or ideal sectarian in 1 QS 4:2-14 is wisdom. This emphasis is a product of neither Greek nor gnostic influence, but is to be read in the light of biblical wisdom (Prov) and postbiblical texts (Enoch, Jubilees, T. Levi, Wisdom, and Ben Sira) which characterize the righteous man as one who possesses wisdom.

[6] Worrell discusses the importance of instruction at Qumran ("Concepts of Wisdom," 154-68) and the functions of the Teacher of Righteousness (pp. 163-68) and the *mśkyl* (pp. 150-53). He characterizes 1QS and CD as teaching manuals (p. 122).

[7] Worrell (ibid., 237-79) discusses the following passages as "wisdom passages" in the Qumran scrolls: 1QS 2:2-4; 3:13–4:26; 9:12-21; 11:10b-11; CD 2:2-13; 2:14ff.; 1QH 1; 2:9; 2:17-19; 11:15b-17, 23f., 31f.; 10:1-12; 11:3-14, 27b-28; 12:11ff.; 13. Most of these passages were selected because of the frequency in them of wisdom vocabulary pertaining to the wisdom or insight of the sect. Caution must also be exercised in labeling those passages which comment on the role of wisdom in creation as wisdom passages. In 1QH 1 and 1QS 3:13–4:26, God's wisdom participates in creation, but what is created is the predestined dualistic world order. Again the terminology of wisdom is superimposed upon an apocalyptic system of thought. A third group among these passages contrasts the finitude of man with the incomprehensibility of God. This theme is not an exclusively wisdom theme.

We do not wish to imply that wisdom and apocalyptic are mutually exclusive systems of thought; on the contrary, it is clear that wisdom was one of many factors which contributed to the origin and development of apocalyptic thought. The fact that wisdom ideas play no integral role in the apocalyptic thought of the Dead Sea Scrolls suggests, however, that the scrolls do not provide an exemplary or fruitful locus in which to pursue the discussion of the wisdom origins of apocalyptic.

[8] Otzen, "Old Testament Wisdom," VTSup 28 (1975) 146-57.

[9] J. G. Gammie, "Spatial and Ethical Dualism in Jewish Wisdom and Apocalyptic Literature," *JBL* 93 (1974) 356-85.

[10] Gammie (ibid., 372-75) points to the same contrast in OT wisdom psalms, Ecclesiastes, Wisdom 1–5, 16–19, and also in 1QH 1:5-9; 14:23-25; 15:14-20. See also the discussion of dualism in Worrell ("Concepts of Wisdom," 280-357).

[11] P. Winter, "Ben Sira and the Teaching of 'Two Ways,'" *VT* 5 (1955) 315-18. Winter notes several differences between the two texts, but finds enough similarities to presume a connection between them. Parallels between Ben Sira and the Qumran texts are also pointed out by Manfred R. Lehmann, "Ben Sira and the Qumran Literature," *RQ* 3 (1961) 103-16, but no attention is given to wisdom.

[12] Otzen ("Old Testament Wisdom," VTSup 28 [1975], 152-53) refers to the catalogues of virtues in Prov 1:2-6; 2:6-10; 8:12-20 and of vices in Prov 2:12-29; 6:16-19. The righteous and wicked are compared to light and darkness in Prov 4:18-19, and their reward and punishment is discussed in Prov 2:21-22, et al. In addition to this ethical dualism, Gammie (*JBL* 93 [1974] 362-66) also finds a spatial dualism between heaven and earth and the mundane and supra-mundane common to the wisdom and Qumran literature. While Gammie's examples show there existed concepts of heaven and earth which are occasionally juxtaposed, they are isolated reflections of belief in a three-tiered universe and are not set forth as a dualistic paradigm indicating a spatial dualistic *Weltanschauung* in late wisdom and apocalyptic.

[13] H. G. May ("Cosmological Reference in the Qumran Doctrine of the Two Spirits and in OT

Imagery," *JBL* 82 [1963] 1-14) sees a cosmic and psychological dualism in 1QS 3:13–4:26; cf. P. Wernberg-Møller ("A Reconsideration of the Two Spirits in the Rule of the Community (1Q Serek III, 13–IV, 26)," *RQ* 3 [1961-62] 413-41) and M. Treves ("The Two Spirits in the Rule of the Community," *RQ* 3 [1961-62] 449-52) who see only a psychological dualism; and J. Licht ("An Analysis of the Treatise of the Two Spirits in DSD," *Scripta Hierosolymitana* 4 [1958] 88-100) who views the dualism in 1QS as anthropological (ethical) and cosmic, but not psychological. While Otzen (VTSup 28 [1975] 147) feels the psychological and cosmic aspects of Qumran dualism do not originate in the wisdom literature, Gammie (*JBL* 93 [1974] 381) understands the psychological and cosmic dualism at Qumran to be an internalization and extension of an ethical dualism.

¹⁴ A. R. C. Leaney (*The Rule of Qumran and Its Meaning* [Philadelphia: Westminster, 1966] 47) cites passages from the law and prophets which embody an "embryonic form of dualism." Thus in Deut 30:15-20, the ways of life and good, death and evil are set before Israel; those who follow the former receive reward and those who follow the latter are punished (cf. Jer 21:8). Contrasts between the righteous and wicked and their reward and punishment are common throughout the OT. The concept of ethical dualism, however, is most clearly articulated in Prov.

¹⁵ In this connection, it must be noted that G. von Rad (*Old Testament Theology* [2 vols.; New York: Harper & Row, 1962-65] 2. 301-08 and *Wisdom in Israel* [Nashville and New York: Abingdon, 1972] 263-83) has argued that the origins of apocalyptic thought may be seen in the wisdom literature, and both Otzen (VTSup 28 [1975] 146, 148, 155-56) and Worrell ("Concepts of Wisdom," 77-79, 351-57) draw upon his arguments. Von Rad's discussion of the relationship between wisdom and apocalyptic is much too general to assist our search for wisdom influence in the scrolls. Furthermore, P. von der Osten-Sacken, "Die Apokalyptik in ihrem Verhältnis zu Prophetie und Weisheit," *Theologische Existenz Heute* 157 (1965), and K. Koch, *Ratlos vor der Apokalyptik* (Gütersloh: Mohn, 1970), have presented cogent challenges to von Rad's theory.

¹⁶ On the classification of wisdom psalms, see esp. R. E. Murphy, "A Consideration of the Classification of 'Wisdom Psalms,'" *Congress Volume, Bonn 1962* (VTSup 9 1963) 156-67.

¹⁷ Sanders, "Two Non-Canonical Psalms," 57; DJD 4. 66; *The Dead Sea Psalms Scroll* (Ithaca, N.Y.: Cornell University, 1967) 106. The Hebrew text is given in all three publications.

¹⁸ M. Delcor, "Zum Psalter von Qumran," *BZ* 10 (1966) 15-29. Delcor (p. 25) sees the terms *tmymym, ṣdyqym, ḥsydym,* and *ṭwbym* to be designations of the Qumran community. The gathering of an assembly (*yḥd*, line 1), eating and drinking together (line 11), contemplation of the law (line 12), and God's acceptance of praise in the same manner as a cultic offering (lines 7-8) are reminiscent of Qumran practices and beliefs. Delcor follows the suggestion of Sanders, "Two Non-Canonical Psalms," 67, that the psalm may have originated from an early period in the Essene movement when the group was still seeking its identity.

¹⁹ Sanders, DJD 4. 69; *Dead Sea Psalms Scroll,* 109. Although in his first publication of this psalm (see n. 18) Sanders suggested a proto-Essenian or Hasidic origin, he nevertheless saw nothing of necessity Qumranic in the psalm and argued that it was considered Davidic at Qumran and would not have been included in the Qumran psalter had its authorship been known. D. Lührmann ("Ein Weisheitspsalm aus Qumran (11QPsᵃ XVIII)," *ZAW* 80 [1968] 87-98) also argues against Qumranic authorship. He finds nothing in the psalm which may be considered exclusively Qumranic (p. 88), and argues on form-critical grounds that this psalm is different from the avowedly Essene psalms of 1QH (p. 90-91). Lührmann argues unconvincingly that the Essenes cannot have written the psalm because it is a wisdom composition in form and content. He points to parallels with Ben Sira and suggests that 11QPsᵃ 18 may be somewhat earlier than or contemporaneous with Ben Sira (p. 97).

²⁰ Sanders, "Two Non-Canonical Psalms," 61-67; DJD 4. 64-69; *Dead Sea Psalms Scroll* (106-08). Lührmann (*ZAW* 80 [1968] 90-97) and Worrell ("Concepts of Wisdom," 271-75) also discuss the wisdom elements of the psalm.

²¹ Wisdom terms are used to describe the righteous (*ṣdyqym, yšrym, ᵓmwnym, ṭwbym, tmymym, ḥsydym*), the wicked (*ršᶜym, zrym*), and the senseless (*pwtᵓym*). The verbs of instruction are *lhwdyᶜ, lspr,* and *lhśkyl.*

²² Sanders, DJD 4. 79, 83.

[23] Sanders, DJD 4. 79: "If Jesus, son of Sira, of Jerusalem had penned the canticle it would hardly be found in 11QPs[a], which claims Davidic authorship." S. Talmon, "The Psalms Scroll from Qumran," *Tarbiz* 37 (1968) 103 [in Hebrew], denies that all the psalms in the scroll were considered Davidic.

[24] A. Dupont-Sommer ("Hébreu et Araméen," *Annuaire du Collège de France* 67 [1967] 368) argues that the poem is filled with Essene doctrines and that it was first composed at Qumran as a Davidic psalm, was integrated into a collection of Davidic psalms, and was later attached to Ben Sira, which received its final shape at Qumran.

[25] M. R. Lehmann, "The Dead Sea Scrolls and Ben Sira," *Tarbiz* 39 (1970) 232-47 [in Hebrew], finds loose quotations of Ben Sira throughout 11QPs[a], and claims that the entire scroll, including the Ben Sira 51 canticle, is dependent upon Ben Sira.

[26] P. W. Skehan ("The Acrostic Poem in Sirach 51:13-30," *HTR* 64 [1971] 387-400) implies on the basis of parallels he adduces between the canticle and the rest of Ben Sira that Ben Sira was the author of the canticle. Sanders maintains that such parallels show only the reason why the canticle became attached to Ben Sira (*Dead Sea Psalms Scroll*, 112-13).

[27] I. Rabinowitz ("The Qumran Hebrew Original of Ben Sira's Concluding Acrostic on Wisdom," *HUCA* 42 [1971] 173) states only that there is no reason to think Ben Sira was not the author of the poem.

[28] The ensuing summary follows Sanders, DJD 4. 81-82, 84; *Dead Sea Psalms Scroll*, 114-17.

[29] *rgl* (line 13) = "foot, phallus"; *yd*[c] (line 13) = "to know, have intercourse,"; *lqh* (line 14) = "persuasion, seductive speech"; *hwd* (line 15) = "glory, virility"; *yd* (line 17) = "hand, phallus." Although M. Delcor ("Le Texte Hébreu du Cantique de Siracide LI, 13 et ss. et les anciennes Versions," *Textus* 6 [1968] 27-47) confirms the existence of double meaning in the text, others have rejected the suggestion. Rabinowitz maintains that the pursuit of wisdom is described in this text without recourse to erotically ambiguous language, and Skehan, "Acrostic Poem," makes no comment regarding erotic language in the poem. For Sanders' response to the textual studies of Rabinowitz and Skehan, see J. A. Sanders, "The Qumran Psalms Scroll (11QPs[a]) Reviewed," *On Language, Culture, and Religion: In Honor of Eugene A. Nida* (eds. M. Black and W. A. Smalley; Paris: Mouton, 1974) 88-95.

[30] Sanders, *Dead Sea Psalms Scroll*, 117. For a reconstruction of the Hebrew text based on the versions and informed by the first eleven verses preserved in 11QPs[a], see Skehan, "Acrostic Poem," and J. A. Sanders, "The Sirach 51 Acrostic," *Hommages à André Dupont-Sommer* (Paris: Librairie Adrien Maissonneuve, 1971) 429-38.

[31] So Sanders, DJD 4. 83; *Dead Sea Psalms Scroll*, 129. See the useful discussion of the hymn in P. W. Skehan, "A Liturgical Complex in 11QPs[a]," *CBQ* 35 (1973) 202-05, and "*Jubilees* and the Qumran Psalter," *CBQ* 37 (1975) 343-47.

[32] As Sanders, DJD 4. 92-93 and *Dead Sea Psalms Scroll*, 134-35 notes, some of the terms and expressions used in attributing wisdom to David are drawn from 2 Sam 14:20; 1 Sam 16:12b-23; 2 Sam 23:4. The first line of the column contains a portion of 2 Sam 23:7. Worrell ("Concepts of Wisdom," 277-79, 359-64) discusses the wisdom elements of the text.

[33] The text was published by J. M. Allegro, "'The Wiles of the Wicked Woman.' A Sapiential Work from Qumran's Fourth Cave," *PEQ* 96 (1964) 53-54; *Qumran Cave 4* (DJD 5; Oxford: Clarendon, 1968) 82. For corrections of faulty readings, see J. Strugnell, "Notes en Marge du Volume V des *Discoveries in the Judaean Desert of Jordan*," *RQ* 7 (1970) 263-68.

[34] Allegro, "Wiles," 53, suggests only that the wicked woman is used figuratively "for some other object of the writer's polemic" which may be, as in the Book of Revelation, Rome.

[35] J. Carmignac ("Poeme Allégorique Sur la Secte Rivale," *RQ* 5 [1965] 361-74) finds the meter and poetic style similar to that of 1QH and claims that the phraseology of Qumran has influenced the document. According to Carmignac, those led astray by the harlot are clearly the people of Qumran, yet the sectarians were not susceptible to being taken in by such women. Therefore the object of the polemic cannot be the prostitute, but a rival sect whose interpretation of the law was a danger for the rigorists of Qumran. The traits of the prostitute coincide with the traits of the sect's enemies given in 1QH, CD, and the Pesharim.

[36] A. M. Gazov-Ginsberg ("Double Meaning in a Qumran Work ('The Wiles of the Wicked

Woman')," *RQ* 6 [1967] 279-85) finds several words in the text endowed with a double meaning, referring on the one hand to the prostitute and on the other hand to the political authorities in Palestine and perhaps also to the Pharisees.

37 H. Burgmann ("'The Wicked Woman:' Der Makkabäer Simon," *RQ* 8 [1974] 323-59) points to parallels between the description of the wicked woman in 4Q184, the "man of mockery" and "preacher of lies" in CD and 1QpHab, and Simon the Maccabee in 1 Mac, Josephus, and Pss. Sol. The wicked woman is an allegorical representation of Simon, and her followers represent a rival sect led by Simon.

A variation of the allegorical interpretation is found in S. B. Hoenig, "Another Satirical Qumran Fragment," *JQR* 55 (1965) 256-59. Hoenig claims the document was "penned by an aroused Karaitic sectarian, fomenting against the prevailing rabbinic teachings" (p. 259).

38 A. Dupont-Sommer ("Hébreu et Araméen," *Annuaire du College de France* 65 [1965] 353) does not find in the text a denunciation of the prostitute, but rather a warning against the malice and seductions of woman in general.

39 J. Strugnell ("Notes en Marge," 266) and Worrell ("Concepts of Wisdom," 328-48) point to the personification of folly in Prov and refer to the complementary personification of wisdom in 11QPsᵃ 18 and 21. Against Strugnell and Worrell, it must be noted that folly is personified only in Prov 9:13-18 (*ksylwt*), where she is contrasted with personified wisdom in 9:1-6. However, 4Q184 is no more closely related to Prov 9:13-18 on linguistic or structural grounds than to other passages in Prov (2:16-19; 5:3-6, 20; 6:24-26; 7:5-27) which describe the harlot, adulteress, loose woman, or foreign woman and do not personify folly. These suggestions help us to understand how the text may have been read at Qumran, but are not helpful in understanding the original intent of the composition.

40 J. Licht, "The Wiles of the Wicked Woman," *The Bible and the History of Israel* (ed. B. Oppenheimer; Tel Aviv: Tel Aviv University Faculty of Humanities, 1972) 289-96 [in Hebrew].

41 This distinction may be eradicated with the publication of further Qumran texts.

42 Compare, for example, the diverse methods employed by H. W. Wolff, *Amos the Prophet* (Philadelphia: Fortress, 1973); S. Terrien, "Amos and Wisdom," *Israel's Prophetic Heritage* (eds. B. W. Anderson and W. Harrelson; New York: Harper & Bros., 1962) 108-15; G. von Rad, "The Joseph Narrative and Ancient Wisdom," *The Problem of the Hexateuch and Other Essays* (New York: McGraw-Hill, 1966) 292-300; R. N. Whybray, *The Succession Narrative* (Naperville, IL: Allenson, 1968), passim. J. L. Crenshaw, "Method in Determining Wisdom Influence upon 'Historical' Literature," *JBL* 88 (1969) 129-42, rightly criticizes the status of current discussion of the topic, but also fails to establish clear criteria for determining wisdom influence.

# INDEX OF BIBLICAL PASSAGES
# AND ANCIENT AUTHORITIES

*Ugaritic Texts*

25-33, 101 n. 16, 214 n. 7, 230
  n. 41, 247
51:IV41;    V65;    126:IV3;
  ᶜ*nt*:V38—33 n. 11
52—33 n. 12

*Ugaritic Texts* (cont.)

67:V18-21—33 n. 19
67:VI23-24—33 n. 18
126:V26-30—33 n. 13
RS 24.266—33 n. 18

*Vulgate*—109-112, 228 n. 23
Xenophon—250

# INDEX OF AUTHORS

302

# INDEX OF SUBJECTS

309

Righteousness, 191, 195; as foundation of throne, 182, 186; pretension to, 197; prolongs life, 211-212; false, in Qoheleth, 202; quality of, 195; relation to *mišpāṭ*, 195 & n. 15; of the many, accomplished by the righteous one, 128-135; and wisdom, 199. *See also* Maat, Self-Righteousness

Ritual battle, and Psalm 73, 166

Royal establishment, Jeremiah and, 88-89, 91

*ruaḥ* (wind), 67-68

Rulers of the house of Israel, 78

Sacred and profane, 40

Sacrifice, 132

*ṣaddîq* (righteous), 191-202

Sages. *See* Wise

*šāḥaṣ* (proud beasts), 224, 229 n. 28

Samaritans, in Sirach, 258; text of the Anonymous Samaritan, 253

Sampson, 214 n. 11

Sanctuaries of God, in Ps. 73, 165-169

Sardis, 259 n. 27

Scepticism, 1, 122-123; in Qoheleth, 210

Schools, ancient Near Eastern, 167, 177; court school, 37; Judaean, 177; in Israel, 167, 249; uncertain nature of, 41. *See also* Education, Egypt

Sea, confined by Yahweh's word, 52-53, 57 n. 34; metaphorical importance of, 50; Yahweh's power against, 50

*ṣĕdāqâ* (righteousness), 96-98

Self-control, 181, 184

Self-Righteousness, in Qoheleth, 191, 195, 196

Seleucids, policy toward Jews, 252. *See also* Antiochus III

*šemeš* (sun), 65-67

Servant of Yahweh, 121-135; death of, 132-133; work of, 133-135; knowledge of God, 134-135

Sexual powers, of Behemoth, 220, 226, 227 n. 13; of the hippopotamus, 228 n. 16

Sihon, 141-142

Silence, as discretion, 181

Simon II, eulogized by Sirach, 252

Sinuhe, 188 n. 8

*šîr* (song), 141, 158 n. 79

Sirach, Book of, 235-245, 247-258; and creation, 43; and death, 212; and Deuteronomy, 255-256; God, 43, 257; and Hellenism, 248; and history, 251-253; historical background, 255; and humankind, 235-244; instruction, 249-250; and knowledge, 250, 252; literary affinities, 253-254; and nationalism, 252; and

Qoheleth, 272; at Qumran, 279-280, 282 n. 11; and Samaritans, 258; textual criticism, 244; theology of wisdom, 255-258; and time, 271; and Torah, 39; and travel, 250-251; universalism, 255-256

*šmm*, 197-198

Sobek, 230 n. 35

Solomon, skill of 47, 56 n. 20; wisdom of, 37

Speech, divine, 182; and the wise courtier, 181-184

Stars, in Sirach, 235-236, 241

Style, 59-73. *See also* Life-Style

Suffering, 52; in the Book of Job, 54, 217, 222, 226 & n. 3; of the servant of Yahweh, 131-134

Suicide, 210; in ancient Near East, 216 n. 36; and despair, 205; and shame, 206

Tamar, 198

Targum, of Job (Qumran), 224 n. 39

Teleology, negation of, in Qoheleth, 271-272

Temple, liturgy, 256; and origins of apocalyptic, 272

Theodicy, 52, 57 n. 28; in wisdom schools, 167

Theology, biblical in relation to dogmatic, 11; and creation, 6, 9-10, 36-39, 43-55; of the cross, 55, 99; of Davidic-royal history, 86-89; of glory, 99, 255-256; of Mosaic-covenantal history, 86-89; of the place and destiny of man, 235-244; of the presence of God, 8-12; of the servant in Second Isaiah, 122-135; of wisdom, 256-258; of womanhood, 10. *See also* Creation, Death, Faith, Genesis, Man, Order, Purpose, Righteousness, Time, Wisdom and Yahweh.

Time, in apocalyptic and wisdom, 263, 265; beauty in, 48; as created, 49; cultic present differentiated from historical present, 268; Gr. *kairos*, 267; in contrast with *chronos*, 267 & n. 18; in Qoheleth, 271-272; quantitative and qualitative, 267; in Sirach, 271; timelessness in wisdom and apocalyptic, 270

Tobiads, 252

Tobit, 214 n. 11; Book of, affinities to Sirach, 253

Tongue, in Job, 222-223, 225

Torah, 127; identified with wisdom, 38-39

Trespass offering, 131-133

Trust, 54; and suffering, 52

Uqaritic, 28 & nn. 11-15, 18, 19; 162 & nn. 17, 21; 167 & n. 77. *See also* Ras Shamra; Poetry, Canaanite

Understanding (Gr. *epistemē*), in Sirach, 242

Universalism, and covenant, 54-55; and nationalism, 127, 130-131; of traditional wisdom, 243

Vengeance, 60

Virtue, and reward in Job, 213

Vizier, author of "Instruction for Kagemni," 179; of Thutmose III, 180

Vows, in laments, 168

Wicked, 46, 52, 53; in Qoheleth, 192, 199-200; in Psalm 73, 164, 165, 167

Wickedness, and despair, 208

Wise, wiseman (Hebr. ḥākām), 194, 195, 249, 273 n. 3; characteristics of, 272; class of, 40-41; David as, in Qumran Psalms Scroll, 280; as discerner of the times, 272; Ecclesiastes and Ben Sira as, 241; as hearer, 179; ranks of, 196; as silent man, 179, 180, 181, 186

Wise courtier, 180, 181, 183-184, 186, 187-188; education of, 161, 184, 186 & n. 36, 187; Egyptian, 178-181, 183-184, 186; as family man, 178; loyalties of, 186; in Proverbs, 187

Wisdom (Heb. ḥokmâ), 47, 56 n. 18; admonitions in *Testaments of the XII Patriarchs*, 264; and age, 27, 225; aim of, 268; and Amos, 7, 82-83, 121; anthropocentric character of, 48; and apocalyptic, 263-272, 278 & n. 15; as attribute of God, 38; and the Book of Jonah, 149-150; comparative study of, 4-5, 7; court background of, 42 n. 12; and creation, 39, 43-55; and cult, 54, 167, 269; and culture, 44; Dame Wisdom, 212; definition of, 25-26, 56 n. 18, 85-86; divine, 123-124; and ethical dualism, 278; folk, 37; and folly, 206; in gnosticism, 38; as hypostasis, 38-39; hypotheses pertaining to, 35; and Jeremiah, 53; and life, 212; love of, 254; and *maat*, 41 n. 4; mentality of, 39-40, 56 n. 18; and Micah, 77-83; and nature, 44; origins of, 37-38, 254; as a *paredros* of God, 254; personified, 38-

39, 44, 253-255; as a postexilic phenomenon, 41; practical, 263; pretension to, 196, 197, 198, 199, 202; and prophets, 85-86, 89, 90-91, 121-122; in Psalm, 73, 161-170; in Psalm 104, 47; in Qoheleth, 59-73, 191-202, 205-213; at Qumran, 277-281; and religion, in Sirach, 247-258; and riches, 93-95, 97-98; and righteousness, 199; royal, 37, 185; and strength, 25-31; style, 59-73, 90-93; in Sirach, 250-251, 253-258; teachers, 85-86; text, "Wiles of the Wicked Woman," from Qumran, 280; and theodicy, 52; and Torah, 38-39; value of, 205; as vanity, in Qoheleth, 214 n. 17; vocabulary of, 40, 56 n. 18, 57 n. 33, 124, 128, 174 n. 80; universalism in, 243; and woe sayings, 81-82; as Word, 254; Yahwism and, 42 n. 21

Woe, 81-83; woe pronouncements, 140-141

Women, in Proverbs, 179-181; *See also* Humankind

World, created by Yahweh, 46; conditions of, 47; as intelligible, 48, 52, 55 n. 10; wisdom's attempt to orient to, 54; *See also* Creation, Earth, Order

Yahweh, as bestower of knowledge, 46; counsel of, 124-126; as creator, 4-5, 9-10, 36, 43-55; as eternal, 50; as king, 50-51, 57 n. 27, 182; freedom of, 186-187; judgment of, 112-118; knowledge of, 95-96; presence of, 8-12; power of, 50-51, 53-54; sayings about, 182, 183, 185, 186; sovereignty of, 86, 88-89, 98; speeches of, in Job, 43, 52, 217-226; struggle with chaos, 49-54; turning to suffering, 54; as wise and strong, 29-31; word of, confining sea to limits, 52; wrath of, 112-116

Yahwist, 243

*Yāṣaʾ* (do one's duty), 200-201

*yôm* (day), 266-267

Zedekiah, reign of, 116-117